Traders of Our Time

Traders of Our Time

Navigating the Market's Impossible Landscape

Bogdan Stoichescu
& Alexander Haywood

First published in 2025 by
Axia Trading Biblioteca
an imprint of Axia Editions Limited.
4 Endsleigh Street
London
WC1H 0DS
(www.axiaeditions.com)

Copyright © Axia Futures Limited and Axia Markets Pro Limited, 2025

ISBN 9781068661501
eBook ISBN 9781068661518

Bogdan Stoichescu and Alexander Haywood assert the moral right to be identified as the authors of this work.

The authors and publisher hereby express their sincere gratitude to Axia Futures (www.axiafutures.com) and Axia Markets Pro (www.axiamarketspro.com) for their invaluable support and contributions to the production of this work.

All rights reserved. No part of this publication may be reproduced, stored in a retrieval system or transmitted in any form or by any means, electronic, mechanical, photocopying, recording or otherwise, without prior written permission of the authors.

While every effort has been made to trace the owners of copyright material reproduced herein, the authors would like to apologise for any omissions and will be pleased to incorporate missing acknowledgements in any future editions.

All photographs and illustrations in this book © Axia Futures Limited, unless otherwise stated:

M.C. Escher's Drawing Hands © 2024 The M.C. Escher Company – The Netherlands. All rights reserved. (www.mcescher.com)

Author photo for Bogdan Stoichescu (cover) by Rosalind Furlong © 2022
Author photo for Alex Haywood (cover) by Antonis Engrafou © 2024

Designed and typeset by Tom Cabot/Ketchup
Cover design by Valeria Slahova
Project management by Whitefox (www.wearewhitefox.com)
Printed and bound by CPI Group (UK) Ltd, Croydon CR0 4YY

CONTENTS

How to Read This Book 9

Beyond the Disclaimer 11

Preface: Thinking Upstream 13

Introduction: The Trader Is Dead. Long Live the Trader! . . 25

Chapter One: The Trading Desks 35

Chapter Two: The Razor 58

Chapter Three: The Collector 100

Chapter Four: The Adventurer 123

Chapter Five: The Warrior: Part I 149

Chapter Six: The Warrior: Part II 200

Chapter Seven: The Student 228

Chapter Eight: The Godfather 268

Chapter Nine: The Engineer: Part I 310

Chapter Ten: The Engineer Part II 338

Chapter Eleven: The Hero 373

Chapter Twelve: The Voyager 403

Chapter Thirteen: The Sphinx 419

Epilogue 459

Acknowledgements 467

Bibliography 469

Index 473

"Such a globe reflection collects almost one's whole surroundings in one disk-shaped image. The whole room, four walls, the floor and the ceiling, everything, albeit distorted, is compressed into that small circle. Your own head, or more exactly, the point between your eyes, is in the absolute centre. No matter how you turn or twist yourself, you can't get out of that central point. You are immovably the focus, the unshakable core, of your world."

———M.C. Escher
On Hand with Reflecting Sphere
(Self-Portrait in Spherical Mirror)

HOW TO READ THIS BOOK

With a pen or pencil, of course! Get one right now. Write in the damn margins. *Do it!* Go bananas. Rip and tear, copy it down—contemplate, think, challenge, question—play devil's advocate. Break down and rebuild everything you read, think and feel. Make notes on what resonates with you, what is useful or what reveals itself to you. Then it becomes your book, a companion.

Squiggle some lines, leave questions in the margins and converse with the book. An unmarked book that never felt the grace of ink or graphite is a sad bundle of paper, a potential future never explored or taken. Then, a few years from now, when you re-read your book, you will see how far you have come and how much further you must go.

And read with your feet—move, walk, get some air, take your notes with you; pause, sit under a tree and read. Write down more questions, and then continue in contemplation.

But never read this book while you are meant to be trading the markets! That entire space must be preserved for deep observation to permit decisive action. This is your balancing act as a trader, to learn to navigate the frustrating antagonism of action and reflection, of the strange contradictions between the demands of learning and those of performing.

So, when you do read... do it slowly. It's far better to read a single chapter deeply... digest... ruminate... over months... than to skim the entire thing, to only tick a box and say—I've read a hundred books this year!

Because somewhere in your notes, in your conversation, in your questions will come a breakthrough, a reflection, a re-assessment.

In these very margins, you will *become*.

BEYOND THE DISCLAIMER

This is not a playground. Livelihoods are at stake. Do not confuse the dark humour and stories typically found in high-pressure, high-risk jobs, such as brain surgeons, fighter pilots and firefighters, as a sign of something trivial or easy. Their mastery only makes it seem so. Every grin and joke is the product of ten days of stress and chaos. Because when the rare sun shines and the rainbows come out, we do celebrate. Good God, man!—*have fun*. When the few budding flowers spring among all that turmoil, it is cause for celebration. A time to appreciate and laugh and cry about those stories. But be professional when the clouds gather and the storms begin again. This is what you are getting paid for.

There are those within our industry and those outside it who attempt to relegate trading as "just a game." This frivolousness is a coping mechanism for some or serves as a tag-line exposition on the absurdity of the modern life—of modern finance. Or it is said as a rallying cry, the drumbeat for those who venture into our domain with a strange idea to prove one's *guts*, of conflating bravery with financial recklessness. To replay life as the class clown, consequences be damned in the face of being *serious!*

This is a professional domain, taken as intensely as athletes at the peak of "their game." You are out for fun, but they are out for blood.

Your entertainment is their livelihood. Do not seek the same at the expense of yours.

Trading account wipe-out is easy and extremely likely. By its nature, it will happen exactly when you do not expect it. The barriers to entry to trading activity are the lowest they have ever been, for better or worse. But this is a double-edged sword, and just because you can enter does not mean you should. Most traders have a lifespan shorter than a start-up, with the same existential risks involved: all the commitment and all the costs that eventually materialise into nothing… *dematerialisation* of one's entire life effort is the market's standard operating procedure.

If you are cavalier with money and short on skill, you should at least be prudent with the finite days you have left on Earth. The opportunity cost of another life lived is greater than all else.

Tourists do not survive. Hobbyists do not survive. Part-timers do not survive. There is no amateur league in trading, no middle ground. You either ascend to the stars or burn up along the way. Give yourself a chance and be professional. Get real; get serious. Pray for hard times first so you learn how to survive until the good times come. Because the reverse can be fatal. It is all or nothing from here on out.

Good trading to you all,
                      and may you go all the way.

PREFACE

THINKING UPSTREAM

We are writing the book we wish to have read, still wish to read and will continue to read. Like those who start a business to scratch their own itch, we have vigorously done just that over the past three years. One book ... *to capture it all.*

We conducted hundreds of hours of interviews, of writing and reflection, and more writing and re-writing, asking ourselves: what is this thing in our hands? It's *alive!* Like the path of trading itself, would we have come this far if we had accurately anticipated how long it would take? *Nine months... tops.*

But in doing so, we captured ten traders between 2021 and 2023 in what seemed to be their prime, only for them to reach even greater heights.

And what will become of *you* reading this right now? A trader in *2123*? We do not know. Godspeed, as they say. Yet, what we do know is that a trader from 1923, Jessie Livermore, is still read, loved and cited a hundred years after the publication of Edwin Lefèvre's *Reminiscences of a Stock Operator*.

But why so?

Because as traders, we are practitioners first, and Lefèvre's book endures as it is still useful after so much has changed, because it does not tell you *what* to do. The specifics, the details, are as long gone as the pit trading days and the boy plunger. And our current trading world, in the way we know it, will be gone by 2123. *Reminiscences* is powerful because it is rooted in story.

And did you know that story is a powerful piece of technology? As Angus Fletcher writes in *Wonderworks*, that story, literature with its narrative and rhetorical effects, elicits actual neurological stimulus; it provokes change (Fletcher, 2021b: 24–26).

And if that change is permanent, in behaviour or perception, then you really have learnt something. From a *book*, no less! We seek the newest and best technology to improve ourselves as traders, yet one of the most powerful and potent was here all along, filtered through the ravages of millennia to still work as simply words strung together in a very special way. Because, if done right, those words will transmute to the reader… *truth*. And so, a whole universe, in such a small container of a book, reveals itself—"an entire world," as Andrey Tarkovsky wrote, "reflected as in a drop of water."

Therefore, we will not base our book on the fallacy of the latest indicator, software, formulas or technology—there are plenty of *those* materials. Instead, we will stake our claim on something much older, wiser and more enduring. Like Lefèvre, we choose the *power of story* as the vessel to preserve the experiences of these ten traders.

That is why our book is a showcase, to be treated as a companion lugged under your arm, ready for your questions. It will feel strange, different perhaps, as there are many themes and theses that vie for the 'central message'—unlike the one-message, bullet, modern 'business book,' akin to a blog post expanded to three hundred pages, that we have been trained to read… and then to forget. Thereby, nothing has been learnt, no change elicited.

Rather, a river of multiple themes, ideas, concepts and threads courses through this book, streaming on top of the stories of a trader's life and career. Many of the chapters can contradict each other. There will be friction, as in life. Yet, this is a feature and not a bug.

Some threads across chapters are tied up, and others are left to sit there for the reader, the trader and the practitioner to tie up how they see fit. If you spot a contradiction, you have been paying attention—now the real work starts: why is there one? So, the central message is what will be most relevant to you at this moment in time. Check in again a few years from now—this will be a whole new book.

So, be wary of the too-neat, the definitive, simple, digestible book. Because you do not know what was reduced, cut and thrown away to get there; in that very refuse could have been your treasure. We include 'Learner Impressions' for each chapter, but the bullet points, the highlights and the notes are for *you* to make, not us. This is why we were so particular about engagement and questioning in the "How to Read This Book" section just before this Preface.

And that is how you make the great *greater*. To the tiny demographic of elite performing traders, you know that trading methods, details or specifics will be of no use to you in the way they might be to beginners. Instead of writing down a specific idea or method to serve one person, a story serves all. It holds a mirror that uniquely addresses a trader's problem and, as a by-product, life itself. There is an endless Rolodex of truth within a story, and your reflections help you find the one you need and seemingly, beautifully, always at the right time.

It holds a mirror to life itself? Yes! You wish to mantle the understanding of life on something so mercurial, so modern and artificial as trading and the financial markets? *Yes!* Because one can understand the vast by looking at the small. Reveal infinity by encapsulating the finite. You cannot *see* life but only feel its aftershocks, see its shadows or hear its echoes. And that is what a book is—an attempt to bottle infinity, an attempt at timelessness by capturing a fleeting moment in time, as per Tarkovsky.

A book is also a time capsule. Inside, we leave shards of ourselves as authors, glinting with the memories of the traders captured in their time—in *our* time. Because no one steps foot into the same river twice.

And so, we transmute to you, reader, what we experienced on our own little rock. Simply what we captured in a bottle as we filled it by the river. A tangible place to find the intangible truths. As others draw from sport, art and business, this is our cross-section of lived experience: the human story. We transmute these niche stories to you because it is the world we grew up in. Because our domain is an aspiration for many, but reality for a few, and therefore a vessel for high tragedy: drama, life, *truth*.

Each chapter will resonate differently depending on where a trader is in their career. Some chapters overlap, but each trader approaches the markets in different ways; by definition, success is predicated on uniqueness, of emergence away from the masses. It is as if we shine a light on the markets—an impossible shape—and so ten unique shadows are cast onto the floor as they take the shape of each trader. We begin with the fundamentals—*The Razor*—and layer up highly applied details with *The Warrior* and *The Engineer*, but then return to the very basics, a revisit of the market's very nature with *The Sphinx*. You are welcome to read it à la carte, but we very much urge the reader to read it in order. Many extra things will reveal themselves in a way we would never have imagined ourselves.

So, reader, this *ain't* going to be the trading book you are used to. But know that this book is written *for the practitioner* first. All of us, the traders in this book—its authors—are born from the trader's rib, at the very desks. And so, our ideal reader is one who has been run roughshod through the market and is now *really* ready to develop, but also the trader in their fifteenth year who must now reinvent and relearn. Because one day you will find yourself the latter.

So, we are not here for strategy specifics but instead to aid you in devising your own. That is the whole point! Indeed, we examine specific trades in their relevant context to understand the higher-level meta-learning principles. We even supply QR codes to direct you to supplementary material to support all of it.

But you will not find a detailed breakdown of indicators or other transient details since they age like milk. Instead, we focus on processes, frameworks and the principles of thinking—learning how to learn. To focus on what really matters. That is to *think upstream*.

HOUSEKEEPING

And what of these strange aliases? Simply, we wanted to provide the option for all the traders covered here to remain anonymous. Some wish to wear their mask tightly, while others take it off immediately. We are specific on profit and loss (P&L) numbers where appropriate; some traders consented to the use of exact amounts, some wanted to remain vaguer. We have corroborated their performances through third parties. Where relevant and based on how much the trader wished to share, we also provide details of trading strategies and specifics. But as we stressed earlier, this is not the point of the book. We are here for something far more precious and endurable.

Note that each of these traders covered in this book trades *futures* contracts, as a product, through various global exchanges like the Chicago Mercantile Exchange or the Eurex Exchange. If we refer to markets like Gold or WTI Crude Oil, we are specifically referring to their futures contracts. In fact, we will capitalise the name of each market to make this distinction clear. Therefore, we do not quote foreign currency market moves as *pips* or measure bonds in *basis points*; rather, we equivalise it all in "ticks," as is the real-life vernacular at a proprietary trading firm that deals in futures.

And know that the 'trading world' is as varied and different as the business world. Saying "I am a trader" is as informative as saying "I am an entrepreneur." The traders captured in this book all trade through, or at, Axia Markets Pro, formerly FCT Europe. There are no clients or outside investors—hence 'proprietary'—and each trader risks their own funds or the firm's. Nor are they restricted to an asset class, and are as free to buy Yen futures as they are selling U.S. Thirty-Year Treasury futures as they are buying Natural Gas futures. We do not trade stocks but futures contracts on various equity indices. We are not market makers, not brokers, not investors, not a fund, nor a bank, nor high-frequency traders, nor quantitative traders. We are just individual, *human*, point-and-click market operators who trade on futures exchanges through various markets that are broadly categorised as equities, commodities, fixed income and currencies.

Speaking of humans, we want to acknowledge that all the traders profiled in this book are men, which is not to imply that women cannot successfully trade. Indeed, there are and have been successful female traders in the history of our industry, extending well before the electronic age, as there will be in the future—likely far more numerous than ever before. One side-effect of these aliases is your ability to turn these traders into characters as if on stage at the theatre, interchangeable with any other human—or you. *That's the point! The Hero* can be us; it *will* be you. The power of the story breaks such boundaries.

Nevertheless, that is a limitation of this book. These traders are the products of the past few decades, which, for many reasons, have been overwhelmingly male-dominated. Further, as readers will see with *The Collector*, the last decade has seen the demise of a large portion of *human* traders. The absolute number of traders of every demographic was suddenly and aggressively culled. So, the small slice that was *not* male was reduced at the same time. That is why it is harder than ever to not only find *human* traders compared to any other time in financial history, but also female ones.

Yet, let us look ahead. As we will explain later, part of this book is about recreating the human trader. And while market electronisation and the "age of the machine" have exerted a profound impact, there is another secular wave on the horizon. Connectivity around the world and lower barriers to entry—not to mention *awareness*—of our domain will enable entire populations of all demographics to access the markets from which talent can be recruited. Other industries have benefited from these trends already, but we are standing at the foot of this change within proprietary trading. And that future looks better than ever, as it is very much in our interest to recruit as much of this talent as possible. Of *human* talent.

CAUTION AHEAD!

Make sure to never conflate trading and investing. If you have come for the latter, be *extremely* wary of what you are seeking to do. Trading and investing are comparable to what professional sports are to a job, as exercise is for health. Professional sport, and all its remuneration, glories and more, is actually disastrous for your health. Just ask Andre Agassi's spine. You do not prescribe professional sport to anyone as a way of exercise. But prudent, responsible, realistic investing is as necessary for your financial health as moderate exercise is for everyone. Yet, trading is an extreme sport, survived by the very few. It is not 'exercise' for those who have some spare cash to 'invest'. It is never to be prescribed and only to be taken up by those who understand they are embarking upon a *professional* career path—or rather, a new mode of living, in the way sport swallows an athlete in its totality—of sacrificing *all* modes of living. Because the costs are great, and we are not speaking of the financial ones.

That is why we will not dwell on comparing returns as a relative percentage or in terms of percentages at all. To compare the returns on investing and trading strategies is to match apples to oranges, or a horse-drawn carriage to a rocket fresh off the prototype assembly line. When a trader transforms a £50,000 account into eight figures over five years, it makes percentages absolutely meaningless, especially when compared to the prudent, conservative, long-term, no-leverage investors. We do not want to be assessed or judged by investors, *or as investors*, nor do we wish to do the same to them.

It also renders *expectations* absolutely meaningless. That also includes risk, return, what risk was taken to get there and what it implies for future returns. By their nature, each trader in this book takes advantage of volatility distortions with pinpoint-accurate leverage and loads the boat with that leverage at a specific moment in time. That means their trades and their careers are "fat-tailed." A cluster of trades will provide overwhelming, near-impossible-to-conceptualise returns on their accounts. So, by their nature, the returns and expectations cannot be predicted or measured—and it is fallacious to compare. There is no point in crunching and examining either Sharpe ratios, Sortino ratios or whatever other ratios.

And the talk of these ratios would sound absolutely foreign across *our* trading desks. Rather, the traders think in "lots"; they *clip* in chunks of hundreds of lots, entered with a few mouse clicks. They 'size' their trades accordingly—a single lot for the novice trader who was just let out into this dangerous world, all the way to a thousand lots—and above—for some of the traders. The risk taken to grow accounts and how it is conceptualised *changes* over time—perhaps a specific amount, in hard cash, that can be risked in a single day, to prioritise consistency and "build days." Over time, this changes to various means and methods relevant to that trader, their strategies, their objectives and their place in their career. The amount of "daily risk" is now conceptualised differently. Instead, risk becomes a three-dimensional consideration in the face of the opportunity as probabilities change, time progresses and the reward shifts. Yet, all of them are consistent, steady traders; none violate the basic tenets of risk—make more than you lose, never get blown out in one go and be wary of sweeping risks under the rug.

These traders do not forget that their returns are not portfolio metrics to be shown in investor presentations, but are often the sole or greatest source of income. They have complete and utter skin in the game. They do not kid themselves.

And consider the rate of engagement. Each trader has roughly two hundred and fifty market engagement periods in a year, many far higher than this. That is how frequently they are tested; rocks are thrown at their sustainability and consistency. And sometimes, far more often than you would think, an entire asteroid threatens all. But each time, they learn and are strengthened. How often is your participation in the markets stressed in such a way? Once more, apples and oranges.

That brings us to the question of morality, of seeming opportunism. But in doing so, we risk entering a hall of mirrors. You will read about the profitable trading of events that have had a great impact across the world, with terrible consequences for many, such as assassination, war and the pandemic. And this contrast of fortunes is not lost on us, as it is not lost on the traders navigating these events within the markets. Many have families; many have a great deal more to lose in their lives than just money, trading accounts or financial glory. *If it can happen to them, it can happen to me.* We do not cheer on the end of other people's worlds. And yet, some events that you read about have impacted them in the 'real world' more directly than you would think. But they traded it all the same.

If it is a question of the fashionable term *optics*, then, unlike the pundits suggest, it is never clear-cut. What is more opportunistic, shorting an equity market in March 2020 as the world reacts to Covid-19, or buying and holding the same equity market at a fantastic discount after the dust has settled?

How about *buying* bonds during a potential war escalation, as a U.S. airstrike killed Iranian General Soleimani in January 2020, as opposed to *selling* equity? It is the same trade! One just looks better than the other. "Shorting" gets a bad reputation for various reasons, mainly *optics*. It is easy to politicise or deflect blame. But when you go long on a market, you just give business to a participant who went short! You need to buy from someone who would sell it to you. The ability to go long or short is a critical, utterly fundamental part of a market system and its health. *Market "sellers" are bad?* What happens when you exit your long position?

Or how about the 'morality' of the "stay-at-home" shareholders that greatly benefited from a surge in their respective stock prices as various pandemic measures came into effect? Or the media companies cashing in on so much chaos in the world in the past few years? And so on, and so forth. A hall of mirrors.

But we do stress that we do not trade *other people's money*. We are not intertwined in the institutional financial system that so very often gets into trouble on behalf of others. There is no moral hazard here of the financial alchemy type that led to the 2007–2009 Great Financial Crisis. Because if we blow up, we affect no one but ourselves. And unlike the stack of institutional dominos that tipped over and precipitated real-world events of 2007–2015, nor do we cause any sort of nefarious real-world events to *then* profit from, like a few movie villains here and there. We bite each bullet that comes our way, downside and all.

THE TEXTBOOK COMPLEX

Ah, some say, what about *survivorship bias?* We simply acknowledge it as an unavoidable force, and that is all we can do. Because the ones who fail—the vast majority—will lament about it louder than the ones who succeed. They tell you that if *they* cannot do it, *you* cannot do it. And then they write an entire textbook about it. Or create a whole industry around it. Or tweet about it. Yet, we should learn from all sources.

But what of the efficient market hypothesis (EMH)? We respond to the EMH as we do to the accusation of survivorship bias. Note that we deal with empirical observations of actual market performers that defy all those who tell them their existence is impossible. And if you so ardently stick to the EMH cudgel to bludgeon any alternatives, then there are plenty of other things for you to get stuck into. But we imagine you are here for the trading, and no EMH, accusations of survivor bias or talkers and planners on the internet will dissuade you.

Indeed, what you are attempting—trading as a long and sustainable career—is extremely difficult. And for all that is good in this world, *do not* fall for the social media inspiration game, the scammers and the promises that guarantee you'll find easy money or salvation through trading, a cure for all your troubles. Professional extreme sport is not light exercise to manage your frail body back to health. If you believe this, please make your way immediately to "The Warrior: Part I" and read the first ten pages. Or "The Hero," Because that is what it takes—that is the minimum price of what the markets will take from you as a 'successful' trader.

If you are living on social media, or in a movie-fuelled fantasy, there are also other things for you to get stuck into. This is one of the many reasons we're writing. We want to be transparent in our desire to bring fresh blood to our industry but also to provide a sober reassessment to those who dearly need it.

Nevertheless, you have to *go for it*, to see what happens because there are so many things that can talk you out of it. Especially the planners and plotters who tell you it cannot be done, when *you* could have been the one to do it. As some domains in the social sciences refuse to acknowledge, the world does not move forward on the rational but on acts of vision in the face of the odds.

INTRODUCTION

THE TRADER IS DEAD. LONG LIVE THE TRADER!

"So how is your firm preparing for the future?" the panel host asked Alex Haywood. And all the heads turned to him, their smirks politely holstered, the stage lights blinding—*ambush!*

But this was anticipated. Before he took the stage, Haywood realised that the "wide-ranging" industry event he had been invited to was entirely composed of high-frequency trading firms, systematic trading funds, quants and the various companies catering to them. In other words, all conversations and people were concerned about the *machine* future. Of course! What other future was there?

Dance, monkey, dance! On-stage was a primate who solely represented the discretionary, human point-and-click trader. So, this was a group hunt! It was 2015, and what can better remind us of our triumphant rise above all the other animals than cramming their inanimate bodies in a display case? *And ain't they kinda cute? Look at them—so worked up, clicking on their little mouse, shouting and waving their arms.* Quaint.

And what a year it was! By 2015, volatility was a thing of the past, not to be experienced but prised from formulas. This was a total industry collapse of the human point-and-click trader. Entire proprietary firms, some once 150-strong, were reduced by more than two-thirds in a blink. *The game was up!* There was no investment in new blood, and the old guard was no longer making any money. Market exchanges no longer supported new discretionary proprietary traders through incentive programmes and instead focused on the emerging high-frequency trading business.

And that business was good. In a zero-interest-rate policy and highly accommodative world, many asset classes grind up. The world becomes more one-dimensional—"if x, do y" scenarios. Like a controlled scientific experiment, many of the variables were isolated and seemingly snuffed out. In a complex web of many variables, a dynamic world is where the human trader thrives. But if only a handful of variables become relevant, especially if it becomes central bank policy, then much edge and profit is to be had among the server racks of speed and automation until they later start to eat each other, too—but that is another story.

Haywood noticed that the demise of humans was attributed to the rise of the machine instead of the environment itself. Such spoke the zeitgeist, and thus, the audience repeated it at this industry event. It was only logical that it would be so. It was a given that machines would permanently replace human traders. They spoke of opportunities disappearing, Haywood recalled, as opposed to *changing*. Yet change is natural for any domain, is it not?

"So .. your future?" the taxidermist prodded.

"Well, I don't have the skill in programming…" Haywood began. *Oh! It was too much! Too much!*

"…But what we do have is the ability to understand how we develop, learn, and evolve. To look at ourselves. We are still investing in the *human*." Because everyone else wrote the latter off. And what better time, then, to take the risk on the human, on those who survived and then thrived in a skill and talent bear market?

But soon, the fates spoke too as events at Firm Y burned down the house and all of their traders and their accounts to go with it. This included nearly every trader in this book, and Haywood too, who was coaching traders at Firm Y. More on this later.

For all the calamity, perhaps this was a purging, a violent catharsis, from the old guard's cynical, defeatist, isolated mentality. "The standard of the space was that *everyone* stopped communicating," Haywood says. "They were scared to share 'edge,' siloed in their pods—the very isolation of the mind."

An opportunity, then, to recreate from the ashes, to break free from the past and create the future. "That is what we wanted to change with AXIA. My belief now, and at the time, is to recreate the human trader," Haywood continues. "What are the new systems of best practice, learning and collaboration? The latter is an art in itself—how you connect people at the *right* time with the right discussion. To begin first as a group and then broker relationships between individuals. To take an upcoming trader who never knew *The Warrior*, for example, and to communicate with him. All of sudden, he could digest *The Warrior*'s best practices and then build on his. You get a fantastic compounding effect. The very act of simply sharing recorded trades on YouTube was enough to reinvigorate so many we knew in the industry—'You can do *that* with *this* amount of size?'—you just need to garner belief, to know and see what is possible when others think it is impossible. To reinvigorate the spirit of the human potential."

Haywood says the critical tool for survival since 2016 has been adopting a high-performance mentality. Learning and adopting practices from different domains was an approach and mind-set that seldom existed for the majority of traders in the preceding years:

reading widely, thinking differently and being receptive from all angles. Recreation must always ingest the new, the different and the disparate, because what comes out are diamonds.

So that is where we now meet, reader, in this quest seven to eight years later! This book has also captured us, as authors, in a moment in time as it captures you—a chance meeting at the crossroads of our lives.

For myself—*Bogdan speaking*—I will write in the first person for perhaps the only time! I took on this book project for highly pragmatic reasons: to gain access to the tremendous traders at the firm, with Haywood to support. Of course, one can and should have the same kind of access on a highly collaborative trading floor. But this book project was to be as comprehensive and expansive as it was a product of intense focus, labour and love.

So, this is part of my contribution as one prong of our dual-pronged approach as authors and interviewers. As a struggling, relatively 'new' trader, although many years into my career, I questioned these high-performing traders to tease out what is useful for the learner, the *practitioner* and the new trader struggling to become a professional. Through that journeyman's eye, I then identified core principles in an effort to understand how that trader evolved to reach such a level, because the meandering act of a trader's emergence is often more revealing than the current product. And all of that benefits my trading! If it helps me, it will likely help many of our readers and traders. To write for oneself is to write for all.

But now, Haywood and I will meld back into one entity…

"Yes!" Haywood continues. He has wanted to write a book for so long—a marker of where we have come from and where we are about to go. It is a manifesto, among many other things, of what happened when we doubled down on the human trader since 2015, when the game was seemingly finished. Yet, the human has flourished.

He is the other prong, then, in this dual approach of bringing a top-down perspective, that is, a combination of his own trading experience and working closely with other traders, with all the stories and lessons that emerge from over twenty years in the industry. "If we can dissect these ten traders in this book, and their very best practices, then our *own traders* who will come in the future can take those principles and practices and build upon them, in their own unique way," Haywood continues.

And what a sounding board he is! "That's a learning principle *there*. That is a best practice over *here*"—so he continues as we interview as a pair. "*Here's* a learning system so strong that if all junior traders adopt it and build their own identity on top of it, they will compound productively." Compare that to the new trader who tries to solve it all by themselves and will take a lifetime to develop. Every great trader has gone through a *lineage* whereby they have learnt from those who have come before and have benchmarked against them. So, this book presents the new benchmarks, born from extremely difficult market environments, adapted from the mistakes of others, and recreated for our times. Then you can use it to evolve and *emerge*.

Because here is an interesting payoff that not every book enjoys. If these pages greatly help the next seven- or eight-figure trader to emerge from among our desks—even just one—then all that has been invested in making this book possible has been made back many, many times.

And if *you* emerge—even if not at our firm, but within our discretionary proprietary trading industry—then you prove and show that the human will keep on thriving, a trader *evolved*. That very thesis, a defiant act of vision, all those years ago!

But we do not aim to live in the shadow of the machine. They are just other participants. In fact, discretionary traders should learn and adapt what they can from every domain. And we are doing that right now, with the flourishing of large language models, to understand how to best improve ourselves as discretionary traders *first*. To not supplant one another but synthesise the best of each.

The rise of the machine and the human demise was the obvious surface-level effect of a deep change in the environment, a product of *that* time. That 'new,' difficult, low-volatility environment raised the bar and decimated all but the exceptional. This was not the end of the human, but the demise of the average. Because the latter never survives change. The best just get better. The game, then, is the same as ever—only more so.

The trader is dead. Long live the trader!

WHY THINK META?

Remember the following as we venture forth: the simpler the rules that govern a system, an environment or even a game, the more complex the behaviour that emerges. And that has *deep implications* for approaching your trading.

Consider that there are only a few rules that govern the markets. We do not mean this didactically, nor are we referring to regulatory rules. What we mean is to understand the fundamental mechanism between how each participant engages with the other, the rules of engagement. These are the rules carved into stone, as unchangeable as the number of squares permitted on a chess board in a standard game. Alter that, and you are fundamentally playing a different game.

And the rules of the game are not only few, but simple too. They are just the decisions to buy and sell, go long or short. That is it. Yes, there are nuances, like the difference between "hitting the bid" and setting a limit order on the offer to wait to be filled short, a difference of intention or urgency. But essentially, every market participant—from server racks engaged in high-frequency trading to the venerated halls of value investors—is either a buyer or a seller at a moment in time. The method of engaging the market cannot be made simpler or changed.

Then suddenly, out of these simple rules of engagement, a complex environment develops. That is, *complex*, like a rainforest, and not *complicated*, like a racing car. It becomes a self-reinforcing, chaotic, fat-tailed environment of perpetual novelty in the throes of "adaptive behaviour" between participants. And in the action between these participants something new comes off the top; new behaviours and properties emerge. Why?*

Because in this simple two-rule game, the activity between its participants has given the game the ability to "look at itself" and change its own behaviour! Something *extra* has just emerged. More than you could have predicted just by looking at each individual participant. Consider an alternative game with a highly structured, rigid and long list of prescribed hard rules and permitted actions. The amount of *emergent* gameplay, novel strategies and techniques that could change over time suddenly becomes more limited. There is only so much you can do in a very limited, small box; the dimensions of the game have been clipped.

But in a 'simple' game of few rules, the box is virtually limitless. And change will come because it is not only about how you play the game, but how you can look at yourself, then the game itself, then others, then how you can *think* about how to think of playing the game. Creativity, then, becomes a prerequisite for even surviving in a simple game of few rules. To stay ahead of change.

---

* In this section, we are much indebted to John H. Holland on "self-reinforcing, chaotic ... perpetual novelty ... adaptive behaviour" (Holland, 2014: 1–10); Melanie Mitchell on emergence and systems that are "complex, like a rainforest" (Mitchell, 2011: 1–13); and Douglas R. Hofstadter for their materials and work surrounding complexity, emergence, and interrelated subjects. See 'Chapter Thirteen: The Sphinx' for all the resources we reference on these topics.

So, emergence occurs in said environment because of *how* you play this seemingly simple game. And *how* you play is more important because each market participant that buys and sells bases their actions on what other participants are doing and might do in the future. Those very same participants are thinking of the same thing *and* changing their behaviour in turn too.

This is what it means to understand the *meta-game*—the game behind the game, the background "hidden" processes behind the obvious, flashy, dramatic processes and action that happens right in front of you, that is, to understand how strategies, best practices and processes evolve over time as the game evolves too. This also happens in reverse.

And then to understand how to evolve your understanding of the game and improve your performance. To look behind the meta-game, too, the meta-meta-game! From two simple rules, there is now tremendous depth to this environment, our bountiful cruel markets.

And so, the life of a trader is that of contradiction, and performance necessitates the navigation of a complex, impossibly shaped landscape! A paradoxical, self-referencing shape where the future drives the present and the present drives the future. We act on what we expect future prices to be, and that drives today's trading. Yet today's trading is what actually creates those very same expected prices! *Which came first?* Persistent change and novel behaviour emerge from this small kernel of operation. Contradiction is at the very heart of the markets. That is how they are made.

It is also why contradictions between traders are a *feature* of this complex environment. Counter-intuitive thinking is the hallmark of operating in complexity. This often demands creativity, explicitly demanding to go your own way, doing something unique, therefore different, perhaps antagonistic to many others. As a trader, you are defined by the trades you *do not* take, and thereby also which type of trader you are not. So, of course, these traders will contradict each other. They must!

A trader is a navigator of a strange world whose *only* constant is, indeed, change. Details are transient, but a highly refined process to harness the most up-to-date details demanded by the market is where the professional thrives. This book looks not at the markets, but behind them—at traders themselves and their processes. *And behind those once more!*

And if markets are an expression of perpetual conflict, how can their traders be any different? There are contrasts in beliefs, styles, methods and mentalities between them. Perhaps even within themselves, they seemingly contradict in theory and action! Yet they are still very successful, lonesome navigators of this impossible landscape, where one finds a reason to go long and another short, a place where disparate participants engage with each other. Hence a market is made. And a trader becomes. Their imperfections we leave intact for your learning.

And so, a storm will form after the winds of this book collide with the experiences, ideas and concepts that swirl in your head. It will be messy. Endure it. After the storm passes you will walk the shoreline and reassemble the pieces of what works for you—as a *practitioner* first. Lay the pieces together and make them yours—make the result beautiful. Between these lacquered fissures is how you *emerge*: unique, created by the messy. But remember to smash it again from time to time. Then rebuild once more. Survival necessitates it because opportunities never disappear, only change. That is how you stay ahead! Reset, reorient, rebuild.

Because to be human is to recreate, to *emerge* from the ashes.

The trader is dead. Long live the trader!

CHAPTER ONE

THE TRADING DESKS

Among several London townhouses, each with its own colouring and design, sits a particularly *peculiar* floor at 4 Endsleigh Street. Situated within is a cadre of successful traders whose behaviours, activities, idiosyncrasies and energies are detailed within this book, a study of their experiences. Boisterous, loud and completely alien to a nine-to-five temperament, these market navigators confuse and shock the polite society of normal office workers.

Yet, the office is a misnomer. Trading is too embodied, too physical to be relegated to a mere office—a stadium fits better. The open-plan floor is instead a staging ground, a holding pen, for the gladiatorial battles that inhabit it. Consider *The Hero*'s poetic conclusion (Chapter 11): "If you come in here and tell me that trading is sitting in an elegant office wearing a nice suit, and you just click and pull money out of the markets, well, that's bollocks. It's not how it works."

These traders embody the counter-intuitive, of ingenuity and stark doggedness. Or perhaps they are simply mad, that is to say, a-useful-genius-mad, not Emperor-Caligula's-senatorial-horse-mad. Certainly, the space is enigmatic. The trading floor itself and the physical positions of the traders on it are as important as the people who inhabit the space. Before we study the traders, we must start with the floor, which is as important as a ship is to pirates.

There is no walking onto the first floor. Rather, you do as the Romans do, and barge in. The act confers a sense of urgency to the God(s) watching above: punish me for my many sins—but not sloth! As you barge in, then, you notice that tall townhouse ceiling, the windows flanking your left and right and the white walls splashed with murals depicting sportsmen and the much-loved Mario Draghi. A reminder of the physicality, the *sport* of trading. Then, there are the desks.

Each year, these desks experience a thousand triumphs, defeats, comedy and tragedy. Perhaps the essence of the professional trader is to ensure their career story continues as comedy rather than the other ancient Greek favourite, which is far more numerous in this industry. The desks are wide and deep and are surprisingly accommodating, like a bridge should be to an earthquake, as they endure a flurry of foot-stomping, a hail of fist-slamming, cursing, yelling and sarcasm. Upon these desks sit rows of eight and up to sixteen computer screens. At the side of the monitors are two mice connected to two separate computers: one for trade execution and the other for everything else. These computers are connected to battery back-ups that take over in case of power failure. Dedicated ethernet lines lead from the PCs to the in-house server room and connect to the futures market exchanges around the world.

Like truckers whose cabins reflect their temperaments and interests, so it is for the traders, who often sit at their desks as if in their second homes, residing there for ten to twelve hours a day, sometimes in for the long haul if the situation demands it. Some traders covet oddities like a poker-chip-themed chair cushion. The family men treasure reminders of home. Others stack books and harbour neatly arranged trinkets. Some have nothing at all. There is something holy about the desk. You can do almost anything on a trading floor except meddle with another trader's desk space. That is sacrilege.

Then there is the smell, and its transformation is a keeper of passing time as reliable as the tides. Cold air, caffeine and optimism greet the morning as early as six o'clock. By midday, half of London's takeaways arrive through the door. But lunch is eaten at one's desk, of course; God(s) punish such indolent luxuries as going on a lunch break. The air becomes a spice bazaar; the Greek loukaniko filters through the air to meet the harissa chicken, the potatoes lined with buttermilk and squash. The gorging of cheesy pizzas, in turn, overrides the near-odourless poké bowls and sushi. The bins fill up, plates stacked high, chicken bones atop. By afternoon, the locker-room smell sets in. The stale air of food waste combines with the frequent emotional turbulence, shouting, pleading and praying—*bargaining!*—matched by the occasional solemnity of silence. This is love at first sniff, the waft generated by red-blooded risk-takers, the smell of skin in the game. And it is fresh, with a distinct lack of bullshit.

Then on a very special day, you barge in but feel 'it' in the air. Your figure lights up, and your extremities tingle and become restless. There is a current that passes through each trader, electrifying the room, the culmination of a collective energy into which you just burst in to. This is the anticipation before a big event, the feeling of witnessing history in the making, as if standing before a great monument or a wonder of nature. It is awe of the cosmic kind. It is intoxicating; you live for it—they live for it! Yet, instead of feeling insignificantly finite in the cosmos, it feels as if these events now revolve around you and the traders, but as participants, not mere spectators. Ones ready to dive into the volatile market whirlpool with only a jerry-rigged plan and a knife wedged between their teeth. Mad.

But then—*good God man, the sounds!*—dings, pings and bleeping alarms ricochet around the room as the flurry of news headlines hit, all coded to a specific auditory signal. And then the voices! A disembodied robotic speech reads out important headlines while various "squawk" services—humans—who hold watch over general developments brave their microphones to announce the news to hundreds of global traders. But... hopefully... do so calmly. Blurt anything out, and the traders will dive back to their desks as if the greatest calamity. "Why you shouting?" the traders yell at the voice in the ceiling; nothing justifies the shouting, lest the market hears it. And all of this cues a real crescendo effect—prices moving, headlines dropping—*dingding!*—traders roar, the monotone baritone ceiling voice recites the litany of surprise headlines—*bleepbleep!*—prices explode off the screens—more stomping; more risk. *Pingping!* "ECB sources..." The hours feel like seconds; then—silence. The final reverberation of the stadium.

Then you realise that you are not among people who dress to impress clients, to put on airs, because they have no clients; the only real civilising force upon these traders are the markets themselves. These are your spit-and-sawdust traders, one might say—*and what sawdust!* Mountains of it produced after carving the nautical power of this pirate ship. And this metaphor is apt as these traders burn with fierce individualist streaks, many of whom dropped out of any strait-laced corporate life or never entertained one at all. They are not traders of grand financial institutions and pedigree, of massive pension funds, hedge funds, and not your academically bound quant variety, nor are they loaded with moral hazard—they eat what they kill, their accounts have been grown from zero or negative; the trades are theirs, and only theirs. A million dollars is a rounding error for an institution, but these traders haul it in and keep nearly all of it, or as much as one can after the taxman takes his cut. There are no mandates, committees or assets under management; there is no hierarchy or separation between an execution trader, analyst and manager. These traders execute, analyse, think, react, risk and manage it all: individual free-footed pirates on a common cause upon a very different kind of ship. There are some fine institutional people in glass skyscrapers whose smarts are, or perhaps were, propped up by the 'Fed put' and a decade of quantitative easing, who have not likely heard of these good old traders who form what we loosely term as proprietary trading firms. If the institutions are the navy, then you are now among pirates.

Other institutions may look down on our traders with disdain, *those archaic, point-and-click traders—punters!* So says he who bets on horses, from aristocrats at the Royal Enclosure to the apparently ignorant plebian gambler at the muddy sidelines. The prop trader is the everyman trader who is in the finance industry not through connections or hoop-jumping, and is not comforted by a salary and bonus—there are none—but rather endures the snakes and ladders of the brutally meritocratic financial markets—open to all, prejudiced against all, yet survived only by a select few.

And few they are. It does not take long for the new entrants, the new grads, the new traders sitting on your left and right to lose their novice status very quickly, not through performance but through the sheer act of survival. Those that came after are long gone, and that makes this grad special already. Though tomorrow this grad may abruptly leave this immaterial, impossible plane too. *Feeling older yet?* Thus it always has been in our trading world, and always will be. If capitalism is "creative destruction," then welcome to the meat grinder. The veil between normality and abject chaos is but an egg membrane. This is financial ultra-violence, risk management as an exercise in pain management.

Consider, then, the gravitas cast by those who *thrive* in these little prop firms. Because they are, pound for pound, the most complete, direct, enduring and finest speculators you are ever likely to find. All the risk, all the reward; pure, unbridled, naked exposure to the market. And in the nude, they are in want of nothing else.

Now, having learnt the ways of this trading floor, you still barge in, and as you turn to your right, you spot the desks of *The Godfather, The Warrior, The Sphinx* and Alex Haywood. You have cruised over to the mostly Mediterranean side of the room—the global macro-news traders, who specialise in fast-moving market narratives and possess the fiery Greek blood as a temperament to match their quick fingers, faster thinking and gregarious risk-taking. On the end of this assembly of desks resides the runner—fresh-faced, eager—and sits right in the middle of the maelstrom, tasked to deal with odd jobs in the worst of the volatility. But, as a delight to the powers that be, all new runners arrive jinxed, yet we'll leave it to *The Warrior* to explain one day. The de-jinxing is a special process.

As you venture to the left side of the room, the climate changes and the cooler Northern European part of the floor houses *The Engineer, The Hero* and *The Student*. Their methods reflect their temperament too. They are strategic, puzzle-piece-solving aficionados, the relatively quieter and meditative traders who deal with the 'market profile' and overt frameworks of operation.* They are the "technical" traders—for the serious lack of a better word, and there is a dire need for a new one. Nonetheless, the collective, yet occasional, roar and cries of pain from *The Hero* and *The Student* pack a good punch if the markets are especially capricious. And right in the middle of it all sits *The Collector*, an amalgamation of these temperaments and approaches that has created something wholly new!

A trading floor also reflects the specific edge and the approach of the traders that inhabit it. The trading floor in Wrocław, Poland, is the product of one man, *The Razor*, who painstakingly designed it over four years, fusing his craftsman focus into the custom-made wooden

---

* *Please note: "Market Profile®" is a registered trademark of the Chicago Board of Trade (CBOT), as is "CBOT Market Profile®".*

THE TRADING DESKS

desks alongside the precision engineering involved within the soundproofed server room adjacent to the floor. This is perhaps the closest to a pirate's polite society; the building and office reflect it.

Here, the traders believe the Gods look the other way and that going out for lunch is survivable. The smooth wooden desks sport uniform eight to ten monitors and "silent-click" mice with exactly replicated and neatly labelled computers. The wall art and peculiar abstract paintings, the lights and the furniture are all handpicked by *The Razor*. The smell: that of a luxury department store at all times.

But these traders do not burst through the glass doors! And they forgo the long, trucker-like shifts pulled in the London office. That is because their trading strategies are different. Some of the Londoners wait upon news headlines, which have their own whims. For others, to perform their methodical, market profile puzzle-piece assembly requires long periods of observation. For the Wrocław floor, their precise trades occur in specific market conditions. There is a time to be vigilant and a time to stand down, enabling a relatively freer and clearer routine. It does not make it easier, but the burdens are different, shouldered better by some individuals—a topic we explore with *The Razor* and many other traders in the book.

Finally, there is *The Adventurer*, who forgoes an office entirely, the exception within this group, and who trades as frequently in hotel rooms as he does at home. But not the beach—no one seriously trades on the beach.

Whichever trader's desk you whisk past in London, Wrocław or, by the time of this book's publication, Limassol, there is one particular item that is visible on computer monitors and remains in clear view of the traders, which speaks to its importance. It is what these traders are all bound by, as much as they stare at it, for it is their mechanism for operating in markets and sustaining their performance and careers. It is a long and narrow grid-like column known as the "price ladder."

ORDER FLOW

The price ladder, or the "depth of market," visualises the beating heart of the futures market (see Figure 1.1). A row of consecutive numbers sits vertically in ascending order, their values different per futures market yet ascending in minimum price increments—a *tick*.

Side by side, this middle column features the bid and the offer, or the *ask*, as it is to our American friends. The bids are another column of numbers that descend towards the bottom of the screen. The offers

	Market Price	(Ask/Offers)
	165.27	173
	165.26	123
	165.25	124
	165.24	115
	165.23	104
	165.22	99
	165.21	89
	165.20	101
	165.19	74
	165.18	22
119	165.17	
96	165.16	
102	165.15	
96	165.14	
175	165.13	
115	165.12	
133	165.11	
135	165.10	
150	165.09	
160	165.08	
(Bids)	Market Price	

Figure 1.1: A price ladder of the Bund (FGBL) on the Eurex Exchange.

ascend towards the top as if hanging from the ceiling. The bid and offer never cross paths at the same price; there is always a minimum tick difference during regular trading.

The values of the bid and offer change per market depending on various conditions. The New York Mercantile Exchange's West Texas Intermediate Crude Oil contract has bids and offers that are usually in the low double or single digits. The Eurex Exchange's two-year German sovereign bond futures, the Schatz, featured thousands of bids and offers sitting at each price during the Eurozone's negative-interest-rate era of the 2010s.

This is a visual shorthand for the immediate "liquidity" of the market. The larger the numbers, the more liquid the market. Or so it goes, since, as every participant eventually discovers, the depth, the liquidity or the market's "normal" behaviour is only there until you really need it. Because when it really hits the fan, you will watch those numbers evaporate to nothing, the bid and offer parting like the Red Sea. Volatility and (il)liquidity have a fascinating, intricate, looped relationship. *Which came first?*

Yet this is only part of the story; the real action occurs by "hitting the bid" or "lifting the offer," and for a brief moment in time, this activity consumes the liquidity at that specific price.

To lift is to buy; lift a single lot into a thousand lots sitting at the offer, and the world shrugs in indifference. Buy a hundred lots into an offer as thin as ten, then you move the market higher, trading the next consecutive price, the next one and the next, eating all the liquidity until you have your fill—ensuring a sharp and violent reaction. In reality, that would be a disaster for the buyer, and they are usually much smarter than this. Unless, of course, they are forced to do this… but these special moments are for you to figure out.

Nevertheless, watching the price ladder in real time reveals the activity of thousands of participants jostling to trade in and out of the market, all buying and selling for different purposes. Yet, eating this liquidity is one half of executing in the market; the other is adding to the liquidity to queue with your own bids or offers as you wait for someone to fill *you* at a desired price.

Until the mid- to late 1990s, this activity was physical. The trading pits like in London, Chicago and Singapore were full of traders sporting bright-coloured jackets in tight spaces, executing orders through hand signals, then relayed through others, shouted into the phone and transmitted to the outside world. The pit traders generated visible bouts of spontaneous action, frantic crescendos following dreary periods. At other times, the market activity diffuses into slow yet powerful one-way action or sharp run-you-off-the-road counter-reactions that all create flow—a tempo, a beat of the heart. The personality, mood, fear and excitement is termed as *order flow*.

The electronisation of this process has created the price ladder; panicked order flow is now a rupture of numbers sliding down the screen rather than the frenzied cries of pit traders signalling to one another. However, the cries are still there—only they are directed to a computer screen instead of another brightly coloured jacket across the pit. The order flow, the action on the price ladder, is still emotive and demands an ability to read the story behind the numbers, a powerful skill with a vast ceiling. And every trader in this book is a master of understanding flow.

Watch a single price ladder, and you appreciate a story, but to watch multiple ladders is to behold a saga. The convergence of multiple asset classes and participants creates an interlinked market-wide flow, each taking a cue from the other. Buying activity in equity futures tugs on bond futures to trade lower, a seesaw of action termed as "risk-on" flow. At other times, the opposite happens, and a savvy order flow navigator must be a keen observer of keeping track of market relationships over time as they change.

Sporadic lifting of Gold and Yen futures ripple into various bond futures, allowing them to follow suit, unnerving the equity markets as fast as they get hit: classic "risk-off" flow. Other times, stubborn selling activity in the two-year government bond futures outpaces the relatively lagging thirty-year. This flow, known as 'bear flattening' of the yield curve, is now a frequent occurrence in 2022 as the markets price in central bank rate hikes—an attempt to grapple with inflation, which has roared out of its generational slumber. All of this happens some of the time, but not all of the time. Knowing *when* is another aspect of the skill. Such are the waters navigated by the traders in this book.

Order flow experienced through the price ladders leaves a strong residue of activity that indicates potential participant intent or reveals those who are committed to their positions. They come in all shapes and sizes: a cluster of lowly one-lot traders to the large institutional, fund and commercial participants of different mandates and purposes. In fact, the majority trades not for pure profit as we do, but to hedge, that is, to insure against potential future events. The traders in this book piece these clues together.

Larger participants who weave their oversized orders into the market often create anomalies; they temporarily redirect the order flow like water streaming around the feet of those crossing a river. Understanding their tactics and adapting to them creates a game-theory-like decision-making process. But then they adapt to you, to the market—they have learnt *your* art of war; they have understood their Napoleon. So, you must adapt too, and the cycle continues. The traders in this book understand these opportunities. All of this is possible because of the price ladder. It starts and ends with it.

THE ENDURING

There is one very special room at the heart of 4 Endsleigh Street: central operations. The Risk Room. And that is where Mario Kyriacou is now sweating bullets. Hundred-thousand-dollar bullets. "C'mon! What's that!—What's that!" Forgetting about all the others squashed in that small room.

"When are these lows in the five-year going to break? Everyone is piling in!" It is the night of the Federal Open Market Committee (FOMC) press conference, and Kyriacou sits tortured in his chair. He does not directly have *a* position on. He has *everyone's* position on. He stress-eats and pulls out some peanuts from a can. "You want some?" Like the sports club manager who bounces up and down at the side of the pitch, the man is possessed, because *everything* is exposed to the market. And that is in the talent, the people, the traders, a special group who are trusted with the fireworks but are proven to only singe eyebrows at the worst of times, or perhaps lose just a finger or two. Especially as tonight, Chairman Powell's words schism the long-end bonds from the short-end across the yield curve, sending interest rate products and bond futures creaking lower. "But why won't it break!?"

There is one aspect of the job, Kyriacou says, that his "risk manager" title obscures, which is the repertories of roles it contains and the moving and shaking it requires. Haywood and Kyriacou both confer how even the proprietary firm risk manager had to evolve from a faceless and placid spreadsheet back-office role as the traders evolved too. Now the risk manager has to be a coach-mentor-fatherly-motherly-brotherly-Rolodex to dynamically manage a trader at the right time, push them, pull them away—give them the size if the time is right, and if the work has been done. And this is one of the most potent and hidden 'edge' behind all the traders in this book. That is, for the firm as a whole to grow the trader at the right time, it is not a formula but a deeply qualitative judgement call. As certain military leaders have said—*more or less!*—strategy is for amateurs, but logistics are for professionals. And Kyriacou knows every nook and cranny of getting you that pallet of artillery shells and all the way down to the cardboard boxes with your fresh socks and pants.

But Kyriacou does not get out of his classic role! That is—*In Case of Emergency, Break Glass*—the ceiling begins to rumble due to the traders above, the market flow thrashes them around; you hear the traders yelling, banging their feet as waves of buying upturn those short in the U.S. Five-Year Treasury futures. "But why won't it break?!" And then you feel the mountain of computer screens making the room smaller, the air of some impending doom, and Kyriacou is telegraphing messages on a phone call or two, the ceiling still getting pounded from above, as if the plaster is about to crumble. Tonight, he is no less than Atlas holding up the very heavens of all the traders at the firm. And now the traders send frantic messages from the gunports above, but their screams say it all. "But why won't it break?!" The triage starts. "*The Warrior*… he's down some, but that's normal, he's accumulating… *The Godfather* played it smart and is buying the thirty-year, but let's see… Ok, *The Hero* recovered; his computer froze, but we got him out…" Kyriacou's finger slides down rows and rows of traders, some green and others red: *12,403; 104,403; 234,130; –30,501; –120,124; 76,540; –5,403…* "eh, could be better"—even from just reading the numbers, watching the markets and intimately knowing the traders, he feels the situation out. "They nearly had us!" But those damn Treasury futures finally released, and the traders all worked their positions, some building on it, others scaling in—they weathered the storm; their profits start to swell. The ceiling now ceases shaking; the risk room becomes a normal office again. But these were just the first shots of the night, first blood. More is yet to come… but that was… a relatively calm evening! The peanuts, however, are all gone.

DUSK

The end then, the evening, is merely half-time. The trading floor exists in a strange temporal and removed space, as it is always half-time; evenings are half-time, the weekend, the month and the year. Bloodied and bruised—*Well, old boy, it's only half-time!*—and so the evenings are like a temporary slump on the boxing ring corner stool as you spit blood into the bucket and your cuts are prodded with cotton swabs. Tomorrow, we go again.

So too evenings are done differently on the first floor of Endsleigh Street. Some have their feet up, tilted back on their chairs, yet with an eye on the markets. A few digest the day's events, sedated in a food-like coma. Some type up their journals to debrief the day or message a person sitting four metres away. Because, of course, God(s) hear idle chat—but the instant message is silent. You think to leave, yet know that no one barges *out* of the first floor—only in. An abrupt exit in a state of sorry, tears or fury is permissible, but to barge out… relatively calmly… without compulsion… guarantees *it* happens. The big trade that happens as you leave the room. *Sod's law!* And slipping out is your only hope. Others never say their goodbyes. To slip out also ensures no one can ask you about your day. Endure a bad one, and you would not want to talk about it. Tolerate a good one, and you would not want to jinx it, another hedge of sorts—least those above punish some degree of optimism. Our own Pascal's wager, if you please. Yet today, you take one for the team and leave first. Remind them later to throw you a bone as you conjure the trade of the year by your exit.

Speaking of teams, the trading floors are designed by "thinking in teams"; its organisation, its training and design factors are all organised around this principle. The floor is an amalgamation, pockets of traders who are often the few survivors of their generation, of their peer groups or graduate programmes, and they have often grown, learnt and endured together. They bring a lineage of culture and knowledge that has been transmuted over decades, like the physicality of pit trading. The evolution of the market and the economic environment drives the generational nature of how the trader perceives markets as a product of the times. The slow, methodical technical traders found their start within the doldrums of market volatility in the mid-2010s. The news-trader origins are frequently found in the days of the European sovereign debt crisis, as it began in 2009, or the Great Financial Crisis of 2007–2009 that preceded it. Spread traders, those who trade the relative value or difference across the yield curve, likely grew up as traders at the turn of the millennium, when there had been functional and dynamic curve movement. Or they just traded any spread, really, anything between two or more prices.

Over time, these small surviving tribes have amalgamated onto the AXIA floor, whereby it has come into its own, fortifying it with a unique identity. Such is the case of all trading floors as they eventually add to it with a cadre of home-grown traders infused with this lineage, only to later pass it down themselves. From tribe to kingdom, this becomes the true measure of the value of a trading floor or community—the relationship, efficiency and communication that goes on between the individual parts, in effect, is a network.

And it can also be assessed by real-time communication! Eyes in the right place at the right time can make all the difference for the team. The quick-fire communication between *The Warrior, The Godfather, The Sphinx* and *The Collector* is as diagnostic for the health of the team as it is to spread the burden of attention. Like the sailors standing in an old galleon's crow's nest, the quiet of the Wrocław trading floor is interspersed by a trader drawing attention to distinct order flow anomalies that blipped onto the price ladders. So, too, the very presence of other traders confers distinct advantages. In particular, the feelings on a trading floor, its mood and atmosphere provide important information to colour the story behind the price ladder and the markets.

Moreover, the realisation of what is possible when the trader on your left is trading a hundred or a thousand lots has been career-changing for many who would not have believed it otherwise possible. Ideas and practices, both good and bad, follow with its people; the contact that occurs with new traders and the floor allows for bad practices to melt away and create better ones. The durable ideas and practices are re-adapted, each trader doing so in their own way. The act of creation, then—the rejoining of the parts in novel ways—and the efficiency and rate at which this occurs is ultimately the peak utility of a trading floor or community and should be assessed as such. That is, how well a trading floor stays ahead of the market's evolving meta-game is strongly linked to its fortunes. Or, in some cases, even creating a new meta-game.

But it does not stop there! A floor's fortunes are also strongly linked to its *future* talent—not only its current—no matter how great they are. Time will catch up, and if you realise you are in a demographic crisis then it is likely already too late. Hence—*the training room*. Descend the flights of stairs in the Endsleigh Street office, and that is where you find a certain Richard Bailey, training those both in-house and remote, supplemented by those like Eric Jousse, who fulfil key mentorship roles. Here, all that is learnt from the trading floors above goes straight into training the next generation of traders. And this is a unique edge for this flagship career programme. It is inexorably linked to a performing, dynamic trading floor, because the training must always evolve too—*it has to!*—as it too is based off the freshest, yet ever changing meta-game.

Bailey himself was already a senior and burgeoning trader at Firm Y before *The Warrior, The Engineer* and *The Hero* ever set foot on its floors. He navigated both the macro-dominated heydays of the Great Financial Crisis, and later adopted the market profile and put it to good use in the following years. Therefore, his wide repertoire is perfectly positioned to train new talent, placing him within one of Axia Futures' most important roles.

DAWN

These traders certainly are survivors! Shipwrecked, as many of the traders in this book passed through the gates of an older but now-defunct trading firm, referred to as Firm Y in their stories. Defunct as it had transpired that management *mismanaged*—to put it lightly, *pilfered!*—all of their trading accounts. Overnight, they were left with nothing; some lost entire seven-figure trading accounts. But all traders now lost the means to ever trade again. Nothing except skills, spit and *No Plan B*.

But then entered Kyriacou and Roger Carlsson. The saviour ship on the horizon, passing by our stranded survivors, came in the form of FCT Europe, a company with its heritage rooted in the 1980s trading pits around the world—well-capitalised, serious, iron-clad credibility. These traders will not be burnt again! As it happened, Kyriacou was winding down proprietary trading operations; Carlsson wanted to move on. "Now you're getting me back in again?" *Just when I thought I was out...*

Yet immense loss tugs even greater opportunity behind it—as true for trading as it was for the frantic blur that was to become summer 2016, a display of pure synchronicity and of immense trust between strangers. *The Warrior* and Haywood only just met Kyriacou—perhaps they could do something together, start something new? But within a month, a promising but tentative, nebulous idea became the *only* plan as Firm Y melted down. There was an immense chain of trust and responsibilities; the traders rendered their faith onto *The Warrior* and Haywood, themselves onto Kyriacou, himself onto Carlsson! And standing before a new and tiny team of traders was the June Brexit Referendum result. Mere weeks away! Crunch time to re-set up a new office, paperwork, approvals, KYCs, phone calls, rent some office space, fund the traders: *Go! Go! Go!*

It all coalesced into the week leading up to *that* Brexit night, with the traders still fighting around in the markets, treading water and fiddling with their monitors and desks. *Did we make the right decision?*

But it is now the eve of the Referendum! The traders are all crammed inside a cupboard trading floor. Messy; cables, screens, keyboards everywhere.

Bookmakers are offering odds on roughly a ninety-per-cent chance on *Vote: Remain*. And financial markets have traded and then closed in a way to imply calm expectations of the same. Such has been the conclusion of its participants, and so they are all positioned this way.

It is now 10 p.m. in London and the voting polls shut. Preliminary indications place Remain ahead; even Leave campaigners start to concede. But the results keep coming in—

THE TRADING DESKS

Surprise! Vote: Leave.
Cable! It's going and going!—
1.45–1.40–1.35–1.30!

Reality suddenly and totally comes calling. GBPUSD, the colloquially named Cable—ruptures. It depreciates ten per cent in a matter of hours. Still open, American equity futures are sharply sold off and their bond futures aggressively bid higher in kind as "risk-off" flow hits the markets.

Yet European markets are closed. They need to catch up, to re-price, and they will be screaming. Such will be the scene of the Eurex Exchange 7 a.m. open.

Now *this* is our kind of trading. Seizing such an overwhelming, opportune moment in time where risking it all is just too safe. The rest is mere detail.

Because this is a moment where the markets have got it wrong—very wrong. The market reaction is going to be general risk-off—selling equities and buying bonds—as the calm certainty of last night has just met an uncertain, Brexit-confirmed future. Your models and derived rules *ain't* going to save you now. Because we are trading an instance that just broke all your rules.

So this is the play: simply the "open trade." The markets, a variety of them, are going to "gap" against the many who positioned for Remain on the 7 a.m. open. They need to get out, or rush to hedge—forced to act. There will be many market orders and few to fulfil them, with desperation to trade before everyone else. This illiquidity within a narrow window of time in which to act is grounds for financial violence of the highest order.

A gap forms due to the pre-market auction, or "netting"—participants place their bids and offers, and their aggregate subsequently determines the opening price of that market. Often this can be far from the previous day's closing price, and so a gap is formed. This is not 'regular' trading as no orders are executed inside that gap. And pressure on various participants will double again as a market can gap *beyond* their 'stop.' These are automated orders that trigger an exit at any 'best' price. Or rather, *any* price they can get.

So all their stops will trigger the first moment the markets open. Shorts cover; longs liquidate. In many cases, their actual exit will be well beyond what price they *would* have liked to exit. And in this fast scramble, a split-second dash to chase *best* possible prices creates opportunity. This is jet fuel for a one-way trip—isolation of an instance where the markets can only do *one* thing before anything else.

And this opportune instance is what our little team of traders are going for. But the "open trade" demands perfect execution, because once the stops are cleared, the market can turn in but a flash: career-ending. Yet they will still bet a career-defining moment where perfection is but a minimum; it is their fervent duty to maximise such opportunity that these wily markets have delivered unto them. But it is also lost on no one what failure is likely to mean here. Because it will be the proving grounds for the traders, Haywood's thesis and defence of the *human*, and Kyriacou's entrepreneurial spirit, the risk to start up again. It is the only time *The Warrior*, a dauntless risk-taker, would describe anything as a "scary, scary moment."

It is 7 a.m.; the netting begins.

And Kyriacou is shocked.

"They all have max size on," he messages Haywood.

"—Yes."

Kyriacou has cleared many traders over the years, but not like this. These strange and salvaged traders are now risking many multiples more on a generational moment on a comparatively esoteric pre-open trade where *God knows what*'s going to happen after the netting completes.

But do not be mistaken! These traders did not get here by betting on *any* odds, but only on the best odds stacked even better through their skills. And these odds are now obscenely opportune in their favour. They have seen it before, done it before, *believe* in it—grounds ripe for maximum conviction—so they risk the same in kind.

The netting continues. The traders have already placed their own orders within it.

Upon market open they will have maximum, full-size long positions in the Bund futures, the German ten-year sovereign bond. And full-size short positions in the Eurostoxx 50 Futures, a European equity index.

But—

Bund keeps going! 200—250—300 ticks higher on the netting! The traders keep dragging their orders higher and higher.

"Bund has gone nuts; stupidly high—do we bail? Do—"

"No. Stops *have* to be taken out on the open—one hundred per cent—the shorts still have to cover."

The bigger the gap, the bigger the stops.

Many other participants are in this netting too, all dragging orders higher and higher in response to others doing the same, creating a self-reinforcing vortex.

It's nearly time.

The traders fall silent. They know that by the end of this morning they will either come back as traders or they will not come back at all.

The netting ceases—

Market open!—

The Bund gap is now over 450 ticks wide! *Gigantic.* It blips higher but then melts, collapses—then it *white-boxes!* A volatility halt! This trading suspension kicks in when it all gets too out-of-hand; to cool off—allow some 'orderly' trading to come back. The Bund effectively just collapsed straight into another netting phase, and no orders can be executed until this phase finishes.

So you can't get in, and you can't get *out*. You are stuck with whatever position you have on just before the halt. The white-box will let you out when it wants to, your losses be damned.

The Bund keeps netting lower and lower; goes and goes and goes; it is absolutely manic as it liquifies an entire point lower, a hundred ticks. And this happens in mere seconds.

Christ! The entire team is long! They're trapped! Who—

But there they are, sitting beside the charnel house. Singed, battered, frayed, but alive. They grabbed what they could as the Bund pinged over fifty ticks higher and *got out* before it reversed.

This was a raid. Such had always been the plan of the "open trade"—get filled on the opening price and exit at a higher price nearly simultaneously as the market jumps higher.

And their efforts were mirrored in the Eurostoxx. It gapped lower following its own netting, and instantly sliced lower again as it took out other people's stops like a stack of dominos. The Stoxx trade proved the more lucrative out of the two.

If the little trading team blinked and took little risk, the reward might have been too small to resuscitate their careers. But, too stubborn, if they overstayed their welcome and asked for too much, their entire accounts would have been caught and obliterated in *that* white-box. It all happened to be just right—from that morning's trade execution, all the way back to the improbable timing of *The Warrior* and Kyriacou first meeting for a beer or two on a terrace in Cyprus.

Their old world had fallen; burnt, sacked... gone... but its few survivors now made landfall. They started anew. And this little team became Axia Futures, one *all-in* bet on a single morning. The day demanded nothing less, and they answered in kind.

So, eight years later, in a new city of their own, all of those in this book are seven-to-eight-figure traders. Throughout the writing of this book, they all climbed the leagues and added to their achievements. Eight-figure trading years, multi-seven-figure trading days, the survival of account destruction to account resurrection. All of them sharp in their consistency—a few with no down-days for long stretches of time, most traders with few down-months a year, and down-years nearly non-existent. Their career equity curves snake upwards across peaks and troughs as if gliding along the silhouette of ever-growing mountains.

But they have only just started climbing, as they are emerging… *becoming*.

And these are their stories,

        their journeys of *our* time.

SUPPORTING MATERIALS

Explore recordings of price ladders in action.

axiafutures.com/
toot-desks

CHAPTER TWO

THE RAZOR

Sunday, 15 March 2020
Wrocław, Poland

There was once a trade over a decade in the making. The entire trading careers of others have come and gone in that time, yet our protagonist, our trader in this story, has been waiting for *it*. He first observed this trade during the Great Financial Crisis, and it was to only reveal itself a few times in the many years that followed, never at full potential.

Then! A pandemic swept the world, lockdowns ensued, a great unknown, and then a full, yet belated, panic.

So, on a Sunday in March, before the futures market opened, the Federal Reserve launched a massive emergency intervention in response to the global implications and reactions to Covid-19.

The S&P 500 futures contract opened for trading. The market shot higher yet ricocheted and collapsed below. The order flow, nervous, then manic, traded on thin participation. Everyone wanted out, but no one wanted to take their place.

Our trader watched. *Could it be?*

The bid and offer spread widened, volumes thinned and the S&P flow screeched and flailed as it collapsed through prices on its way down, but then—a floor.

Silence. The S&P was held at a single price. Twitching, then frozen, the bid caged artificially. Within fifteen minutes of the opening, the Chicago Mercantile Exchange halted trading on the S&P contract, as it collapsed by five per cent.

The doors to the store were now shut, yet hordes of people plastered the windows outside, all desperate to trade, *to get out! To hedge! To do something!* The queue on the market's offer grew, with thousands of contracts piling on top. You could buy from the crowd, but you sure as hell couldn't sell, because we were now *limit-down*.

The trade!

Anticipating the queue, our trader was already in the front ranks. He managed to trade six hundred lots seconds before the crowd caught up and swarmed behind him. *Good*, he thought, he would need them later because all conditions were now met... *after twelve years*. He was now positioned short.

Yet, not without an insidious twist, a delightful morsel to the powers that be, the 'limit-down' trade could only work upon the full reopening of the contract in America on Monday, now fifteen hours away!

Our trader now found himself on a very special ride: trapped at his desk, as if on a long flight around the world that required absolute focus and alertness should he have to buy back his short position, to exit a temporal window as wide as fractions of a second.

And it could occur at *any* time—miss a single click of the mouse, or would his eyes momentarily dart away and back to his screens, then losses in the millions were possible. But what awaited on the other side was more than financial reward. It was his career's magnum opus, his masterpiece.

These acts of mastery conclude when a trader has to fight for their very conception, to struggle for it—to fight for expression against anything that might devour it. One great act of defiance. Magisterial careers, then, are born from continual resistance. Hesitation cannot be accommodated.

The phone started ringing.

Alex Haywood picked up the phone. He made it on the last flight out to Poland just before the border shut in response to the pandemic.

The brokers were on the other end. Margins were going up all around the world. That was the cash set aside to allow a trader to finance existing positions. The extraordinary market volatility induced by the pandemic created a vicious cycle of illiquidity and forced market participants to shore up more cash to keep their positions. Otherwise, they would get liquidated—trade *kaput*.

But now the brokers were demanding an additional seven million dollars as margin just to keep our trader in his position.

More hurried phone calls passed. Mario Kyriacou was on the line—officially the risk manager—yet he was once again reprising the role of Atlas, holding up the worlds of dozens of traders as they frantically dived into history-making events.

"Alex, he has to reduce his position…" Kyriacou begins.

"Everyone is running scared with this volatility, the brokers, the exchanges, *everybody*. No one knows what is going to happen, they are all panicking."

Exasperated, Haywood battled it out on the phone. "We both know how long he's been waiting for this trade. He has planned it with me—with you! There is *no way* he'll back out!"

"Listen, they are demanding the margin," Kyriacou shot back. "They don't want it tomorrow; they want it *now*. They are threatening to liquidate him, and I'm the only one preventing that from happening."

He was right. Kyriacou needed to back and support his traders yet also to manage the critical and fragile relationship with brokers, clearing houses and exchanges. He had to find solutions before others would find them for him. The sacrifice of one trader would mean the sacrifice of all. *Intolerable!* He would find a way.

In Poland, hours passed by. Our trader braved his position. As dawn slowly approached, he had not slept, paused or moved from his seat. Millions of dollars were on the line, not to mention the trade of a lifetime.

Meanwhile, Haywood juggled the politics. He needed to remain calm beside our trader while cycling through phone calls in the deserted hallway outside. Expectations had to be managed.

Softly, Haywood approached our trader. "Look, you know margins are going up around the world. I need you to prepare yourself. You might have to close the trade; you might even get auto-liquidated."

Our trader's eyes remained peeled to the screen. He sat there… *just sat there…*

"Alex, I've been waiting for this trade my whole life. If I can't take this trade, I'm going to quit!"

The phone rang again for the final time.

◆ ◆ ◆

"Reticent…" *aha…* "Guarded"… *m-hm…* "Shy, private"… *yeah.* Haywood explained in the taxi as it drove towards Wrocław city centre. It seemed that time was kind to the city following the upheaval of the late 1980s; the grass in public spaces was *trimmed!* The old socialist apartment blocks were neatly maintained, not dilapidated—even *modern!* As far as Eastern Europe was concerned, this part of Poland did not make it out too bad.

"He is very special, an old and good friend. I just hope he will be forthcoming," Haywood continued. He is enigmatic, like a hermit beholden to secrets, mythological among the desks of Endsleigh Street—*Did you hear he never loses? That—did you see that?*—the trainee points to the flickering, unreadable price ladder—*He trades that!* Everyone knows stories, his stories, and the hundred alleged ways he trades. The mind conjures wonderful things to fill in the blanks.

The taxi stopped at the OVO building, an office complex with a spaceship form and slices of white that decry modern minimalism. How very international. Walking through serpentine corridors and past other offices, we finally arrived.

And then—glass doors and walls on a trading floor! The London office experience would like to suggest wood as the appropriate material to survive the ruckus. But glass suggests a polite society in the space age—genteel. And beautiful it was so, all desks uniform, custom, with furnishings, lighting, carpet, art pieces and the smells to complete.

Yet, Saturday meant an empty office, except for a lone, shoe-less figure vacuuming a far-flung corner. There were cleaners employed, it was said, but as the lone man told us, they don't catch *all* the dust specks. As he emerged from across the room, the man carried himself with a soft-spoken grace, the air of a nineteenth-century gentleman surgeon or scholar, but then—a wide grin, his restrained stance broke into laughter, back-slapping and inside jokes as he and Haywood greeted each other as if long-lost friends. So, this trader, worth millions, still returned to the office on weekends to re-clean such a pristine space? Because everything must be perfect, *perfect*, he said, for himself and the traders for the week ahead. This office is also his baby!

Everything is of equal importance, from the carpets to trade execution; it all adds up. Perfection, by definition, is not negotiable.

What followed was an intense nine-hour interview session. That was the first day. He was neither reticent, nor guarded, nor a hermit. In fact, he'd enjoyed something of *la dolce vita* in the restaurants and bars of Wrocław all these years, as well as travelling the world to make up for what he sacrificed to get here. He is a maximalist in fun and a maximalist at work, with no trouble shifting from one to the other.

And our trader was radiant, warm and hospitable, full of astute observations on both trading and life. But we shall focus on one thing, performance, and in the mind of our trader, that meant *only* one thing: unyielding, unbreakable consistency.

Consistency serves not as a default talking point but practiced with ruthlessly sharp application. Since his debut in 2007, our trader has only experienced nine individual scattered months of losses. That is *years* between some of these down-months. Espresso in one hand and computer mouse in the other, our trader revealed to us his immaculate spreadsheets of returns and other data.

And an endless green tee stretched across the screen! *What's that?* We pointed to a solitary red blot. "That month unfortunately turned negative when my account was charged for exchange data fees and software costs. But those are as important as fuel costs are to a racing car, so nothing to complain about," our trader said, "they are part of the job." An eight-figure trader who is still factoring in fixed costs and round trips into his P&L! Most traders would be thankful to have losses so minute. And the upside—many months of over-six-figure profit, becoming routine years ago, mere clockwork.

We chose to begin with this trader in particular, as he embodies the most pure, precise, crystalline, fundamental principles of what makes *a* trader. To start, as it were, with the ingredients, the vegetables, the meats, the water—the most fundamental of all. Throw in immovable patience, relentless focus, obsessive meticulousness, and professionalism, then cut them with the sharp knife of consistency, and you have the makings of an eight-figure trader.

How do you encapsulate this? In 2017, our trader spent a cumulative total of *four minutes* in the markets—exposed to risk, in active positions—throughout the year. In those two hundred and forty seconds, he extracted seven figures in profit. A knife—a razor, if you will, sharpened on leather with no slack.

Stories about *The Razor* exist among other trading desks as his approach is highly distinctive, even eccentric to some, a niche of niches. He emphasises extreme risk aversion, yet it is better understood as an aversion to outcomes of high variance. His sublime skill is to understand how he can position himself in limited, virtually binary trades, where the market should never trade against him. If it does, it is telling you something—and at times, often at worst, to exit the position at the same price as entry, termed as a "scratch trade."

His trades resolve within mere fractions of a second, practically instantaneous. But trades like these "have to fit you like a suit," *The Razor* says, as he restates how personal and crafted the trades must be to ensure such consistency. This sartorial advice leads to extreme selectivity and, therefore, low trade frequency, as only the finest and highest-quality trades are considered, permitting a very high success rate.

But when these low-frequency trades do surface, *The Razor* is not meek. He trades immense contract sizes—hundreds and hundreds of "lots"—in markets with double digits on the bid and offer. An aggressiveness with a calculated and cold precision *brutality*, as if waging guerrilla warfare on top of a pinhead, conducted, as Haywood says, with the silent swagger that comes from possessing the largest testicular fortitude found across the desks. A fortitude of unshakable conviction. *Not risk-averse, but variance-averse!*

THE RAZOR

NO PLAN B

Our trader grew up in Italy of very modest means. Raised only by his mother, their strong relationship was frequently mentioned as he discussed his early life. He breezed through school, yet he found ways to satisfy his strong competitive desires. Sport followed at a high level for his age group, notwithstanding long stints in video game arcades of the '80s where other children resorted to pulling the machine's power supply to end their incessant waiting for our future trader to finally fail and give up his turn, which he seldom did. *Mio Dio—il rasoio!*

Like all good traders, this one was born with a stubborn streak. And so, his schoolteacher's insistent advice to avoid engineering at university merely emboldened him. *Of course I can!* Yet, love for the profession did not last, and our future trader was left aimless after disillusionment of a career with no meritocracy and insurmountable office politics. His mother, however, had sacrificed much to provide financial assistance for his studies, and so he soldiered on.

In a near-consistent theme for all traders who endure long enough, the first lone forays or brushes with the market end in disaster; a pound of flesh is to be extracted sooner or later. *The Razor*'s fate was sealed in the internet bubble of the 1990s. Newfound connectivity, technology and accessibility attracted many new retail traders, like himself, for the first time, not unlike the recent great run-up in cryptocurrencies in the late 2010s.

Then, one day in 2003, our university student saw that the price of Parmalat shares, a dairy company that was a household name in Italy, had dramatically decreased. "Just a bad day for them!—I guess."

Early the next day, he noticed that the Parmalat shares were about to open again with a double-digit loss—nearly half-price in just a couple of days! So, our nascent, enterprising trader decided to buy them, only for the exchange to later suspend trading altogether. But Parmalat never reopened, and he thereby lost his entire position, which was also his entire account, funded completely by his mother's life savings.

In time, he made his peace, helped by his characteristic ability to rise from the lows and find a way through. Loss is like rejection, and nothing, it seems, creates a stronger drive. And so, like any tentative, nascent trader, he was emboldened once again. *Of course, I can!* But now, at least a direction, a spark. To many, the initial loss is the originator of a lifelong infatuation; all efforts were now redirected to become a professional trader.

At the age of twenty-four, our trader embarked on this journey but he would not land on a trading floor for another *eight* years. Frustration abounded with the lack of career opportunities in Italy and the commitment to see through his university studies and balance a demanding financial situation.

Our trader worked part-time, sometimes at a biscuit factory, to save enough funds to look abroad for career opportunities. And those factory bosses still called him for years after to come back, he says, as he was so precise and thorough in his work. Then finally—*something!*—as he was accepted onto a trader training programme. But this proprietary trading firm was located abroad, in England.

Whatever the recruiters made out through the language barrier, it was enough. Perhaps his fixation shone through, but his training programme had to be deferred for another year, as he had to work full-time to squirrel away enough savings to last twelve months. By April 2007, he was finally on a trading floor; eight years in the making—at the age of thirty-two—this was his *only* chance.

"There was no Plan B," our trader recounted. With only so many savings and living in a small, dreary town in England, he understood that this was *it*. The end of the line; it was harder to *start* another career in his early thirties. *The opportunity cost!* One last throw, and he would bank it on this very moment. Yet, this prop firm had a reputation for ruthless trader management. People were fired on a whim, and those who were not profitable quickly would soon find their immediate future very bleak.

So, our trader had been walking the tightrope since the very beginning. What was it all for, to come all this way and disappoint now? The days ate at his life savings; the trading floor pressures ate at his liver. Yet, other traders who were certifiably determined, our trader says, still blew it. He observed how so many glorified the upside—swung for the fences—and could not help themselves to protect, save, stop, to control the downside. Somehow, the need to gloriously make it now overrode the need to survive, to run before walking. His strong propensity for risk aversion, then, was fortunate as consistency was paramount for survival. The need to square away sequential, small, yet profitable days was key.

After three months, *The Razor* left the simulation environment for live trading, where the rope really shortened. Yet, he experienced only three days of losses in the first ninety days of trading. Instead, our trader was only concerned about his downside and remains so to this day; caution seared into his brain to ensure continued existence—eventually, he made this his very own niche, a moat. And he was thereby destined to become AXIA's most uncannily consistent trader in the company of remarkably steady traders.

His strategy, attitude and risk profile are born from the need to prioritise survival. His entire financial lifeline originated from his trading account. A large or total loss would mean career loss, and that meant wasting years and savings for a chance to make this work. The opportunity cost would override any other factor. Now, it has manifested in its ultimate form—the sacrificing of additional upside to ensure extreme consistency. It has stuck with him and thereby forged a unique trader, safety above all else.

HONING THE BLADE

The Razor does the fundamentals extremely well, a master of first principles. Therefore, he can prime us to understand the importance of lucidly *composing* a trade. It can be said that each trader's edge in this book emerged once they consciously understood how to do just that, even if they may not label this process as such. Hone the basics here—get it right—and it will take care of so much more. That is how you leverage your limited time wisely, to think and act *upstream*.

Consider that a trade's composition is individualised and, therefore, it is the *subjective* application and execution of strategy upon an *objective* recurring pattern of market phenomena.

Regard any pattern of market phenomena—a knee-jerk reaction, then retracement, then a slow trend after a key central banker's comments drop over the newswires. Or a cluster of vulnerable lows in a stubborn market that is finally traded through and causes aggressive liquidation. Or recurrent order flow activity created by the appearance of large orders in the market. All these patterns have a specific *sequence of events*—a beginning, middle and end, like a movie. The linear development through time of these patterns is objective; one cannot 'argue' that a move did not happen when it certainly did. If you observe and analyse these sequences, the trader can identify specific points they could have traded pertaining to their edge—the subjective, skilled application of strategy.

So, *The Razor*'s conception of what formulates a trade is as simple as it is robust. It is a process of *observation*, to then spot a *pattern*, which

THE RAZOR

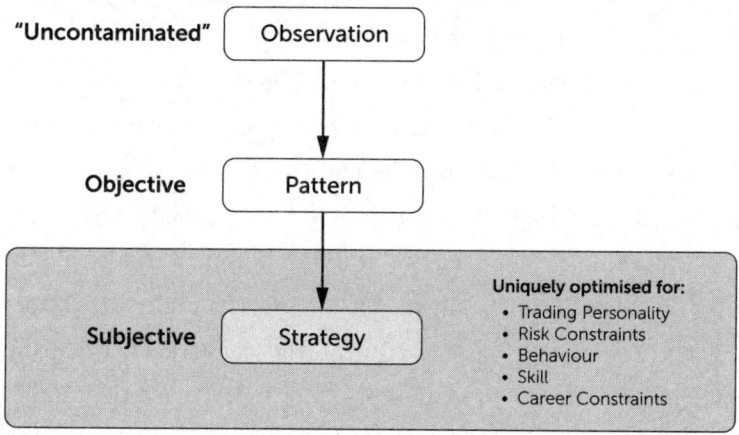

Figure 2.1: A summary of *The Razor*'s framework.

is then monetised through the execution of a *strategy*. We have summarised this above in Figure 2.1.

Yet, many new traders confuse a pattern with a strategy, often arguing with each other over the 'interpretation' of a pattern. In fact, they are confusing the subjectivity of a trading strategy over an objective market pattern.

The confusion, then, produces the misunderstanding that a popular, known pattern must be traded the same way—as if the pattern dictates the strategy and its execution, to say there is only *one* way to trade it! For example, take the garden variety, good old "breakout" pattern. Where the current market price violently extends out of a range of prices in which it had spent time consolidating. The price ladder lights up, and there is a flurry of activity—the order flow abruptly changes from meandering sleepwalking to roaring out of the door. This pattern, too, has a beginning, middle and end, yet it is as if most assume that only the middle is tradeable when the end sequence of the pattern could be the most optimal deployment of *their* strategy—of greater safety and probability of success.

The closest we can describe one of *The Razor*'s key strategies is executing within the strong order flow during a breakout, of going with the market. He did not fully embrace the adage "the trend is your friend" during the Parmalat episode, but he took that lesson and made it the core of his operations. It is his motto, and nearly all of his trades are taken in this context. But he operates under the smallest rock left completely unturned by nearly all market participants, trading it in a way few think possible.

So, *The Razor* throws out most recurrent patterns that do not allow for *his* optimum strategy that confers safety, and heaps of it. An acceptable pattern that resolves the same way, our trader says, means it does so "eighty per cent of the time, or more. When I enter the trade, it is more likely it goes one tick in my favour than one tick against me."

And how he finds these patterns is through pure, unfiltered *observation*. And that is critically important! One of the few persistent commonalities of all the successful traders in this book is their strong powers of observation, and their belief, their confidence in their observations.

"I really believe that you must watch the price ladders for hours each day, for months," *The Razor* said. "You will have this moment where you just feel it, where you understand what is happening. It is rather difficult to explain, you need to feel the emotions that are behind the numbers that are constantly changing."

The Razor was determined to re-emphasise the point of observation, but specifically to preserve the purity of it. "It is crucial in this process to not be *contaminated*. If you want to achieve greatness, you need to watch the market and see what it tells you. What picture does it want to paint? Because if you follow others, you will never be the first one. You can still make it in trading but never achieve greatness.

This is because you do not fully *feel* the strategy that you are implementing. If you never do anything differently, you will never go further than the people before you who are implementing the same strategy."

To achieve greatness through differentiation—*start with unique observations*—is not dissimilar to the argument of Peter Thiel and Blake Masters, with which they begin *Zero to One: Notes on Startups, or How to Build the Future* (2014: 1):

> Every moment in business happens only once. The next Bill Gates will not build an operating system ... if you are copying these guys you aren't learning from them ... Doing what we already know how to do takes the world from *1 to n*, adding more of something familiar. But every time we create something new, we go from *0 to 1*. The act of creation is singular, as is the moment of creation, and the result is something fresh and strange.

The Razor is certainly the product of a "*0 to 1*" moment. In an industry where differentiation, not replication, ensures longevity as a trader, it is one of the most important factors.

"Sometimes I feel like I want to immediately show some traders a few possible strategies when they join the office," *The Razor* continued. "But I discovered that they need to follow their own path. Otherwise, it is very difficult for them to change it, as they would just sit down and trade that strategy everywhere, but it simply does not work like that. They will not develop their own way, even if they are better in other ways than the path I put them on," he stressed.

"And it is not only detrimental, but I would also have to share the limited cake with more people. Yet I could still describe my basket of four or five trades, which I think are quite risk-averse. I figured out these trades by myself, nobody told me to do them. And they are quite personal as they are expressly optimised for me, so I try not to go too deep as there are endless ways to execute them."

Consider, then, the archetypical contaminated novice trader in Figure 2.2, which we have encountered many times with intakes of new traders among the AXIA desks and the wider community. Specifically, these traders come onto the desks after a couple of years with no progress and are consistently engaged in a Sisyphean task of switching strategies, approaches and beliefs.

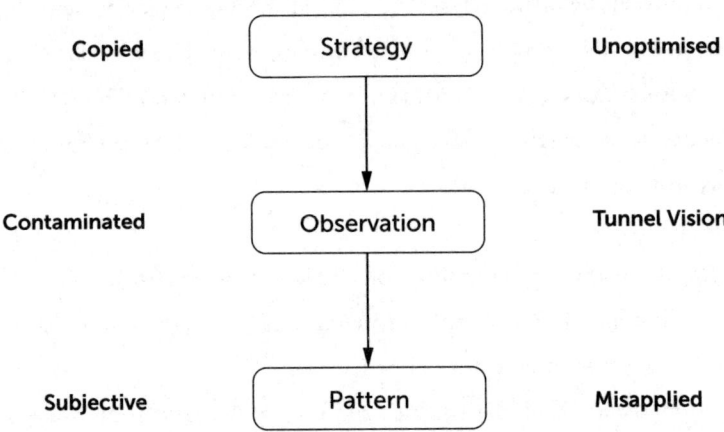

Figure 2.2 Example of a "contaminated" trader's framework.

Note the differences between the figures. A "contaminated" trader's strategy is implemented before observation, explaining why they might confuse a pattern and a strategy. In Figure 2.2, the trader's observations of order flow on the price ladder—the smallest, purest kernel of activity—are supplanted. And their chance to learn freely is lost too. Instead, it has been replaced by an emulated or 'learnt' strategy, which is optimised for another trader and is likely a product of an old or previous market cycle and conditions that are outdated.

Moreover, this contaminated trader naïvely observes market behaviour through the narrow prism of the 'rules' or mechanics of this strategy, creating a tunnel vision in their learning rather than "listening to the market." Instead of learning foundational principles of the market's order flow through the powers of their unfiltered observation, the trader only infers what they can from their learned strategy. *The indicator is crossing over, so the market must be bullish!*

Then, oblivious to whatever the market is doing *now*, the trader will simply apply the strategy and trade "whenever they can," as explained by *The Razor*. This leads to the sighting of a 'pattern' creating a Pavlovian response in the trader, to chase, as it were, every rabbit that leaps in front of them, to shallowly apply the same unoptimised strategy everywhere, no better than a simple and unprofitable trading algorithm.

For our readers who feel this to be an uncanny description of their trading—consider that your strategy has no edge as it has been misconstrued for a static pattern. Or perhaps, with good intentions, you have cloned your strategy to learn from others, but in doing so have never really experienced a week of simply sitting down and observing the market; just *watch*. Listen to the market and your innate observational ability will take you much further than before.

Purposeful observation is certainly more powerful and productive for the new trader than frequent, active market participation, which induces tunnel vision that draws the trader into minutiae, thereby missing what is really going on around them. A trader thereby keeps busy by replicating the strategies of others, potentially contaminating their fresh, unmoulded worldview, and the rare, fleeting chance to become an act of creation, not replication. Haywood asks how many traders labour for years on journaling, crunching statistics and visiting performance psychologists when they simply cannot sit, watch and *observe*. "Everyone from the early days knew they could not take *The Razor* off his screen, ruthless in his focus, blood in his eyes from staring at screens all day," he said. "He knows when the moment is right to strike by *not* trading; just watching—observing."

FINAL TOUCHES

We return, then, to the development of pattern and strategy inventory, understanding that before their creation comes observation. So, the successful composition of a trade only occurs with endless hours of observation. We put both together; recall our claim that each trader in this book is successful due to their observational powers and confidence in this ability. And so, from great observation is formed the great composer of a trade.

"To spot a good pattern is relatively fast—a few weeks can be enough—but it takes years to create the best strategy for it," *The Razor* said. That is because of the need to gain a deep understanding of market mechanics and experience the same pattern in different market conditions. "So, you build a unique strategy, and with time and experience, your aim should be to put the biggest size you can on it. But you do not need hundreds of strategies to become a successful trader," he said. "Develop the best strategy to fit your skills, to fit you like a suit."

So, the strategy must play to the trader's strengths and avoid their weaknesses in skill and behaviour. Weakness in skill can be rectified, yet behavioural patterns that lead to poor decision-making often stem from the misapplication of a strategy with practical burdens an individual cannot bear. Trading 'personality' is a nebulous, abused topic, yet we will define it as the willingness to take specific risks that a certain strategy requires, alongside personal behavioural patterns that reveal themselves when trading that specific strategy. Some traders, for example, are able to stay in a trade for a long time; others find this intolerable. Would the latter be labelled as generically 'risk-averse'? Yet, that same trader would also seem almost casual in trading immense size at a moment's notice. Risk tolerance comes in many flavours, and both of these traders can be highly successful.

"I am very patient and can wait for days for a pattern to appear," *The Razor* explained. Days is an understatement—consider weeks, even *months!* Other traders have failed with similar long-wait strategies as they do not fit their behavioural patterns. They are too burdensome.

"And I also think I can read the order flow. Let us call it emotional intelligence," *The Razor* continued. "Therefore, I can apply a strategy that takes advantage of unique market participant behaviour." *Unique* means the kind of stagnant, low-volatility market environments that feature very subtle shifts in the order flow. These opportunities are only visible on the price ladder—the kind that bewilders or entrances every new trader to the ladder, as if chasing ghost ships glistening on the sea's horizon.

And when placing a strategy upon a pattern, *The Razor* continued, "you then need the combination of proper execution technique, even keyboard shortcuts, if need be, of where to enter, manage the trade, exit—for both winning and losing trades. You must ask what could go wrong and how you are prepared to handle it. Having a strategy means being fully in control of the trade and of your mind at all stages. Leave nothing to chance." This is an interesting conclusion for a domain inseparable from chance—from probabilities—risk is our domain!

But *The Razor* is completely right, speaking to his worldview that ensures consistency. Yet, there are other traders in this book who will say they leave it *only* to chance and that there is no control. They are also right. Trading is indeed an act of contradiction.

"Either way, the traders that do not have time and energy to develop their own strategy will probably fail. It is likely they also do not know themselves very well," *The Razor* said. "It is easy to go onto the floor and see how people make money. *Look!* It is this and *that* strategy. *Ok! I will just trade those.* And you apply them without discernment, without knowing *how* to apply them, to execute them, without understanding how they fit your personality or the market conditions at that specific moment in time." That trader in question had a chance for creation and creativity, but it is now supplanted by naïve mimicking, never to observe the market behaviour with their own powers and talents.

Career constraints, too, will force further personalisation of strategy. Profitable traders who grow rapidly in size may have to change their execution methods or stop some strategies altogether if their size causes excessive "slippage"—the inability to get in and out of the market at a specifically desired price. The same applies to new traders, like those at the AXIA desks, who invariably have a limited amount of funds to risk on the day, a constraint that would mean trading a pattern through an altered strategy, or not at all.

Even so, determined attempts to avoid contamination do not excuse forgoing the collective creativity and input from peers on the trading floor. Preserving one's identity while learning through a community is another key skill and a very important one to make the best use of a high-performance trading floor. *The Razor* himself spent four painstaking years crafting his perfect trading floor in Wrocław because, among other things, a community is most valuable when the network effect of cross-learning between individuals is at its strongest.

Take *The Razor*'s experience at his former trading floor—Firm Y. "I was exposed to a lot of information and strategies. For example, the month-end trade, which has flows occurring within a specific window of time," he said. This market phenomenon was very potent in the early 2010s and purportedly driven by large institutional portfolio rebalancing. Many traders at Firm Y devised ways to trade it, which exposed *The Razor* to it. "It does not look like a bad pattern. Yet, there is no applicable strategy for the way *I* wanted to trade it." Even after recording and studying its occurrence since 2010, so exacting is *The Razor* that he has not found a way to trade it in a manner that fits *him*; nonetheless, he still studies it to be ready at all times. And this is one such example of many patterns and observations that were born from the trading desks. "He *only* watched another specific market move for five years before it eventually became one of his core strategies," Haywood added.

This is revealing of *The Razor*'s commitment to the long game—long-term dedication to what Haywood calls our trader's "R&D department," the most dramatic output of which culminated in the 'limit-down' trade.

A HOUSE OF TRADING

Eight years into his profitable career, *The Razor* was still living very modestly. The dreariness of his shared small-town accommodation, a lack of social life and a persistent culture clash made our trader feel he had put his life on hold. Sixteen years had passed since he had first redirected his life towards trading and he had now reached a level where he was comfortable enough to withdraw more money out of his account for greater expenditures, to enjoy the fruits of his labour.

Part of this quest involved moving to Poland, where Firm Y had opened a trading floor. "I was finally free and felt like my life was starting again. I was forty, and it was the best feeling," he said. Our trader melded with city life, revitalised his social circle and, finally, exited the waiting room of his previous years.

"Yet, I clearly remember this *other* feeling. Things were going too well—far too well—something bad was around the corner," *The Razor* said, having finally accumulated a seven-figure account by grinding it out and spending little of it over the past eight years.

And then it came—following his first large withdrawal request to buy an apartment, Firm Y refused a request of this size, thus starting an ugly saga that would reverberate into the stories of many other traders. Denying the funds that were rightfully his, our trader explained how he took legal action against the firm while fighting malicious rumours and misinformation spread by management in an attempt to slander him.

Margin calls were made, and trading was suspended company-wide. Our trader says revelations only came later that the company had mismanaged the trader's accounts, and the remaining funds could only cover a fraction of the cumulative size of all the accounts at the firm. The rest of it disappeared, and with it the totality of *The Razor's* trading account, which was just over seven figures at the time.

"Eight years of sacrifices were gone," *The Razor* said after a long pause. Having never made previous large withdrawals, our trader was only left with little funds to hand, and he would use the majority of it to finance legal proceedings. After years of patient and frugal living for a chance to bite the apple, fate had other intentions, swiping it out of his hand just as he was about to savour it.

"After that, I had only my knowledge and skills," our trader said, and he was now forced to restart at ground zero; in doing so, he reached out to an old friend. By providing a vital loan to our broke trader, he had once again played a critical part in his life, having once helped him finance the final part of his university studies following the complete loss of his mother's life savings. Simultaneously, the future team of the nascent AXIA–FCT partnership was still in development, a new team yet to re-emerge from the ashes until the Brexit Referendum night.

For *The Razor* to join the intrepid crew he had to capitalise his trading account. "My friend agreed on a loan of just under six figures but didn't have the cash on hand, so he offered a similar amount in gold bars," our trader said. With the dash of a Western in the air, the old friend drove the bars himself from Italy to Poland and to a physical exchange where our trader was located. As it turned out, the gold-to-cash conversion was a mere trip to the local shopping centre. *The Razor* was now recapitalised and back in business, as he described it, and reminisced of his immense gratitude to his old friend, who had always stepped up at critical junctures in his life.

It was a real crisis but also a testament to his consistency and strength of character, as the calamitous 2016 had, in fact, become *The Razor*'s most profitable year at the time. Total seven-figure account loss, legal battles and stress about an uncertain future with nearly no cash on hand all seem but a blip on our trader's return statistics. Back to trading in June, with nearly two months out of the game, he was already returning very healthy amounts. Describing the newfound mutual trust and respect with this new team, our trader and Kyriacou worked together to take advantage of Brexit, its volatility and various other unique opportunities, despite the relationship being in its infancy.

"I felt I could finally take flight without the weight on my feet from the previous prop firm," *The Razor* said. Aged like fine wine, this turned out to be his vintage year. Finally, unbottled and unbound, he would produce a consecutive personal record-breaking year alongside his first six-figure trading day within this period. "When Firm Y collapsed, it was a very painful and destructive situation; I was crying every day for a month," he recounted. "Yet, it turned out that it was the best thing that could happen to me. It took time to appreciate and process the whole event, but now I'm happy I lost that million. I made the same amount again in one year, whereas it took me eight at the previous firm."

Amazingly, our trader still proceeded with plans to purchase both an apartment and a new office. This pressure, he considers, helped him to perform even better in the following years, a very similar experience for other AXIA traders at the time. *No Plan B!* A reflection of this trader's belief in his consistency.

While trading from home, *The Razor* strongly desired a trading-floor environment. "I always wanted to create an office. One I wanted to trade in myself, a place where people are happy to come and trade. Not a workplace. A boutique. A *house* of trading," he said. And it would establish itself in central Wrocław, the city which our trader fell in love with. Brooding over the lack of certain facilities, support and control over the environment at Firm Y's trading floor, the time was now opportune to build his own, and, by extension, a legacy. "I personally took care of all the interiors," he continued. "Being a very precise and picky person, it took me much longer than it should have, but I believe the results were worth waiting for."

THE NEXT TRADE IS ALWAYS THE MOST IMPORTANT ONE

"There was still one thing on my mind, though, and that was *the* trade I experienced in 2008 as a spectator," *The Razor* pensively described. "I've done this trade in my mind a million times, thinking of the best possible execution and all the different scenarios in which it could happen."

The Razor remained on high alert. Should the S&P futures plunge on an ill-fated day in such a violent manner, it would need to catch participants off-guard; something *big* had to happen. And so, he always travelled with a laptop and itinerary bound to reliable internet connections to be one step away from trading at all times.

Yet, the universe did not conspire to reward his prudence when the time came. Historically, the trade would occur only once again in 2015, the exact time our trader was out of the office and country attending a funeral. Further occurrences of "limit-down" happened during the Brexit Referendum result and Donald Trump's 2016 Presidential Election victory, but it did not materialise in a way in which our trader could execute it. "I was afraid that during my whole career, I could have only one chance for this," our trader said. "And I knew that I must be at the desk for this trade. It has been a long time since a market crisis, and I felt that something would be happening soon."

So it did. *The Razor*, it turned out, had booked a long-awaited, long-delayed and much-planned "dream holiday" in the Caribbean. The date: March 2020. Market participants might remember how painfully unreactive Western markets were towards the fear of Covid-19 in February, with general opinion greatly divided on the significance of the new virus. Equity markets continued to rally, and volatility remained placid.

The Razor's instinct to cancel the trip was strong, but since he was not in possession of the marvellous ability called *hindsight*, he continued with his holiday after further deliberation and guarantees of internet quality.

The markets remained relatively stable for the entirety of his holiday until the last day, 9 March. But after clearing airport security and preparing to board the return flight, a quick glance revealed that the S&P futures contract had sunk nearly five per cent in one session, close enough for *the* trade to materialise.

"What do you do? After very stressful discussions with my girlfriend, we had the option to either stay another week, but I could have missed out on the new volatility conditions that were arising; the hotel internet turned out to be bad," *The Razor* said. "Or we could head back to London, where the layover was long enough for me to trade out of the AXIA office." It seemed there was just enough time to get to the office before the market opened in America, he said, and so the London team scrambled to set up a desk while our trader boarded the plane. "It was an eight-hour flight, yet it felt like days. Once we landed, I checked my phone and saw there was still a chance. We went as fast as we could. The fastest commute ever."

But it was too late. The opportunity for *The Razor* to execute this trade exactly as he had practised and prepared for countless times had gone. "I was painfully watching the trade I had been waiting for all my career happening in front of my eyes, and I felt powerless. All due to a one-week holiday." Having watched a recording of the S&P price ladder and realising the trade worked perfectly, our trader was stumped. "I cannot describe what I felt at that moment."

Slowly, *The Razor* made his peace, and like the events of losing his mother's life savings and the total loss of his old trading account at his previous firm, he would carry on. "I came back to the office like usual, there was not a lot I could do. I started to trade as if nothing had happened. As I like to say, the next trade is always the most important one."

Only concerned about his downside, *The Razor* would soon prove how truly he embodies this maxim. "That Wednesday, 11 March, two days after I came back from the holiday, I did what was probably the most important trade of my life," he assessed. The S&P futures had collapsed again to enter 'limit-down'. With a variety of other conditions met, our trader was engaged; he queued a thousand lots on the offer above the limit-down price.

But—*again*—not to be! As our trader waited to be filled short, the offers on the price ladder started to decrease in number. *Something was going on!* The way those offers peeled off suggested there was some new information, and likely something positive that would make those other determined participants angling to get short suddenly become much more hesitant. The queue dialled back, the thousands of orders waiting in line suddenly vapourised.

And *The Razor* needed the queue to get out; the protective barrier was falling away—*OUT!* In the decisive tenths of a second, our trader pulled his own thousand lots out of the queue—then the market screamed higher. "If I hesitated, laid back in my chair, or I had been distracted for that split-second, I would have liquidated the thousand lots at-market and would likely have lost a million dollars or close to it," he said.

Our trader was queueing but not *in* a position, as no one had bought into his offers just yet, so pulling or cancelling them ahead of time would suffice. If he instead delayed, and there was indeed a new development in the world to cause buying flow to enter the S&P, its participants would have filled our trader all at one price and have run through him; mere seconds into carrying a heavy loss offside before he could blink. And this would force his hand to liquidate *at-market*, an emergency exit.

Yet, even in normal conditions, the S&P would very likely slip and skid many prices if a sudden thousand lots hit the market. But now, to cover his short, the illiquidity would have meant punching through a gut-churning, eye-watering amount of prices, as the former triple-digit offers on each price diminished to mere single digits. But at-market liquidation is an emergency of a lesser evil than trying to "run" the position offside, which carries unknowable risk, variance or paths. It was not a trade *The Razor* would ever consider. *Hence!*—it was far better to cancel his orders ahead of time than to be filled and *in* the market if something adversely changed.

But did he? At the end of the day, our trader flicked through his trading history, fills and P&L. *Wait! P&L?* And he glanced at a particular row: *ESH20… 0.00.*

He traded the S&P! "A thousand round trips," he smiled. *The Razor*, in fact, *scratched* his trade, where he sold and re-bought it at the same price rather than merely cancelling his orders. The 'liquidate' order does what it says and exits the live market position at any best price but also cancels pending orders. The 'cancel' button does just that but does *not* liquidate or close existing positions. *The Razor*, certainly knowing this, as all traders should, had always planned to hover his mouse over the liquidate and not the cancel button, to catch all eventualities.

And the day proved him right, for he later realised that within the very second of trying to pull his orders, he was filled, then positioned short in the S&P with a thousand lots, and upon liquidating had bought them back at the very same price—just fast enough to buy them back from the queue of orders that remained behind him.

This all happened so fast that it seemed *as if* he merely pulled his orders instead of entering and exiting a position. Should he have clicked 'cancel' instead, then this chapter would have been written very differently—with his orders likely to have been taken by the market just before clicking, and the split-seconds needed to hit the liquidate button afterwards would have been too late—seven figures too late.

Yet, this is also a testament to *The Razor's* thoroughness—those biscuit factory bosses wanted him back for good reason! The protective barrier, or the offers that piled on top of the limit-down price, had tapered off from thousands to hundreds—to none. But somewhere along the line, there were just enough of them to let *The Razor* buy back his short at a single price, as had always been the plan.

Our trader, however, uses this story to caution others. Too many, he says, even those experienced, profitable and successful, hardly know the inner workings of their software, the price ladder, the mechanics, rules, inner workings of the exchanges, the minutiae of how these trades are cleared. For *The Razor*, this is flagrant disregard for what is, in effect, a racing car for the professional driver. And it is almost impossible for him to understand such seeming ignorance; it is irresponsible at best or the beginning of a horror story at worst.

And so, this is an example used by Haywood to show how capable *The Razor* is of applying immense size when the perfect trade materialises. *Not risk-averse, but variance-averse!* Even if a loss occurred on liquidation, it is far exceeded by the potential gain of many multiples; the trade is still asymmetrical—a multi-dimensional puzzle that is thought to be worth it, as *The Razor* demonstrated through his actions. This is also the same trader who would never consider putting a single lot on a market pattern he watched for ten years; it was never quite good enough.

The very next day *The Razor* carried on as normal—in fact, not placing a single trade. How many other traders would stay in control after giving up a trade for which they had been waiting for over a decade, to then use it to excuse poor, emotional trading for what they had just experienced? Too many, Haywood concludes, blow up their accounts for far less. *The Razor* offers no quarter to such excuses and trades as if it were his last. And it is apt since, for many traders, it proved true.

PRINCIPLES

The thrice-vacuumed carpet supports *The Razor* as he slowly paces between the rows of polished, lacquered trading desks as he simplifies *his* trading to their fundamentals. The building blocks, the principles, are far more useful and timeless to build, as it were, your own house of trading. This is what *The Razor* wanted to provide.

First principle: understand time decay. The more exposure your trade has to *time*, the greater the variance, as an increasing number of events may occur. Reformulated, the success rate of the trade decays over time. "I always feel you have the power to predict the next few seconds. So, the more you are exposed to the market, the more you have a fifty-fifty trade. Let's say you have ninety-per-cent accuracy in predicting the next couple of seconds. Then, eighty-five-per-cent accuracy for the next five to ten seconds. The longer you are exposed in a trade, the less power you have over it. I don't know where the market will be in three hours, but I can tell you with high probability where it can be in the next second or two. So, this is why I focus on trades that could give me just a tick."

The Razor has spent his career focusing on this premise. "Because I focus on the trades that ought to never put me offside; eighty per cent of the time, exiting a minute later will be better [more profitable] than exiting in the next few seconds," he continues. "I know that. Yet, I prefer the certainty of one-second loss or gain rather than one-minute exposure to the market."

All traders deal with the impact of time. Because the passage of time increases the variance of a trade. *The Razor* takes the most extreme approach as he refuses to deal with time in the first place or trades over the smallest kernel of time possible. Therefore, *The Razor* ensures immaculate consistency as he exposes himself the least to variance. *Not risk-averse, but variance-averse!*

Second principle: never underestimate a strategy's burden. Our trader is also acutely aware that different trading strategies come with their own special mix of stressors and are shouldered differently by traders. Stress, of course, comes with the territory, but traders handle it differently; some find different types more insidious than others. Spending a long time in a position with fluctuating risk can be a special circle of hell for some but tolerable for others. On the other hand, *not* being in a position when there is sufficient price volatility is either handled well or not at all. Many like to swing for the fences, they think, but are barely able to hold the bat by the fifth attempt, and of course, the trade will work on the sixth time just as they give up.

Understand, then, what the strategy really implies—what it will put you through in the practical sense. "If you are a news trader you need to be dead-right and be ready to hit at all times. For *me*, it is very tiring. It just erodes my energy," *The Razor* explained. Anticipation, as they say, can be far worse than the real thing. "With my strategies I know the engagement period, of when they are most likely to happen. I may only have to be stressed and intensely focused for two hours or less, and most of the time far less than that. When it is over, I don't have to be on high alert for the next twenty hours, waiting for some impending news or event like other traders," he said.

A trader must seek a deeper understanding of their (in)ability to deal with variance—the passage of time—and how they deal with *different* stressors of various strategies. Rather than trying to fight your natural responses and to make up for your weaknesses, *The Razor* asks, how do you place yourself in a position where your strategy does not expose your vulnerabilities? *The Razor's* ability to reduce time exposure places our trader in a position of strength as opposed to exposing his weakness: that he is *deeply* emotional.

Increased time exposure introduces a long chain of decision-making that can be corrupted by his emotions, therefore increasing the variance of outcomes and reducing consistency. Literally, as our trader says, he "does not have time to be emotional," or need to be. And with *The Razor* now in his late forties, his early decision to align his trading with the stresses he can tolerate is a testament to his foresight to help ensure longevity in an industry with a high attrition rate.

Third principle: glory in quiet consistency. The focus and mastery of *one* strategy permits consistency, and "consistency over a long period of time can lead to excellence," *The Razor* said. "Tick by tick, you can make millions. Step by step, you can go very far." And remember, *The Razor's* spiral staircase that ascends from humble rural Italy is laden with the gold extracted from the market's seconds, mined and smelted from a singular price.

"People will remember these big and incredible trades yet pay little attention to making two thousand dollars each day for thirty years." Both require superior skill and are paths to financial success, but there is something sublime on the overlooked, quiet path. "I find beauty in being up a little amount each day," *The Razor* said.

And we easily forget that most humans do not deal well with large variance. "What do you prefer to make—fifty thousand dollars at the end of the month, yet with a massive swing in the middle?" *The Razor* asked. "Or make thirty thousand dollars at the end of the month, yet with making a bit every day? I prefer that I bring home a few thousand, rather than experience a negative-twenty-thousand day, tomorrow plus-thirty, then negative-five the day after."

But there are further implications. "You can be at the point where you lose five. Then you lose twenty, then some more. Now, something is wrong. You can easily get into a loop of bad habits and lose confidence," *The Razor* elaborated. "It is difficult to go back. Losing trades is like a scab. One small scab, and it's easy to recover from. More than that, and you develop a scar; it's deeper psychologically and financially. Therefore, I prefer to be down one thousand each day for ten days rather than to be down ten thousand on one day. The financial result is the same, yet I know I can keep my losers tight, so it is easier psychologically to recover from."

Fourth principle: patience follows skill. In our trader's eyes, those who suffer from impatience do not understand or believe in their edge. "In trading, ninety-nine per cent of the time, you should just be observing. Doing nothing is part of the job—a big part of the job. A trader needs to be like a lion in the bush! You should only rarely expose yourself to the market. Opportunities disappear. If a gazelle sees you in the savannah, it will run away. You need to be there to observe the weakness of the animals, and then you attack."

Recall how *The Razor* spent only two hundred and forty seconds exposed to said savannah in 2017. And he feasted like a king. Yet, it is difficult to know what you are looking for if you do not know what it is. But a trader is assailed with worse. "It is hard to sit on the sidelines for so long, to sit, wait and *then* be incredibly aggressive when the opportunity is at its best," Haywood added. Doing so demands an immaculate understanding of trading identity and belief in edge; the trader has to reject all but one opportunity—*their* opportunity. The leverage, the firepower, involved in futures trading demands such precision. "A loss of focus, impatience in a single bad trade can destroy weeks or months of work. We cannot afford that. The market is already difficult and competitive enough; you cannot be unprepared and take a sloppy trade," *The Razor* concluded.

Fifth principle: To click is human; to refrain, divine. Trading action bears a hidden cost; successful trading offsets it, but the bad exacerbates it. Active trading drains energy and focus—a trader's ability to spot the forest for the trees is slowly chipped away. Trading outside of worthwhile edge depletes the trader before the real action appears. "You are either a talker or a listener. A talker says what he already knows. And if you constantly trade, you are talking and not listening," *The Razor* said. This would prevent a trader from doing what *The Razor* does best, executing large size at a moment's notice even after long periods of inactivity. He is fresh and ready and does not waste his time and energy by needless exposure to other trades he does not understand. "I don't take all the trades I would like, but I certainly don't take the trades I don't want to take," he said. And yet, this is a fraction of the real cost. Slack, imprecision and indecisiveness invite weakness and can turn into a deadly spiral over time—the opportunity cost of missed or blundered trades compound, mentally reinforced as if by habit, and over time can dramatically skew the outcome of a career in the decades that follow.

ARE YOU LISTENING?

What do you regard as the foundations a trader is incomplete without? To succeed, in my opinion, you need to have self-control, patience and method. Obviously, you also need a big desire for the job, respect for it, as well as humility and determination—a willingness to succeed. To have the ability to read the market and possess good money management. These are all in a circle of equal weighting. The market will eat you if you lack even one of these skills. It is going to destroy all the positives of all the other strengths that you have. You need to be prepared—mentally, technically, physically and emotionally. You need to be empty, like a white piece of paper with no ego. You need to let the market draw the painting of the day. And every painting cannot be the same as the previous one since it is always painting an amazing new picture. This is what I always say to the new traders: the market is speaking one language, and you want to speak another one. Are you listening to what the market wants to tell you?

You are famous in our small circle for your precision and consistency. There is no slack in your trading...
I do not have any slack in my trading because you need to go to the core. You need to be very practical. In life, there is a lot of unnecessary talking and a lot of superficial stuff. People don't go to the core of issues, problems, emotions and feelings. In trading, there is no room for that. You get to the point, or you lose money. There is no room for nonsense indicators or macro-economic news that cannot affect the market price. Sometimes, people ask me the same question every day in a row for one week. How can you expect to make money if you are not a quick learner? The market doesn't wait for anyone's learning curve. Often, people don't listen; they collect answers as if little pieces of information, but it doesn't mean these pieces will be useful for them. Instead, you need to be a meticulous observer to receive all the input and information the market is giving you. Every day, the market is giving you hundreds of inputs, and you need to see them. If you ignore the market and only keep asking other questions, you become overly reliant and are not in a position to receive from the market. At

the beginning of your career, you need to observe the market and ask the important questions; once you are ready you need to quickly cut what is not useful and rely on yourself.

What would you say to traders who admit to slack in their trading, who perhaps trade too much?
Constant involvement in the market is the result of an addiction. We are not here to be addicted. As I like to say, I think trading professionally is comparable to flying an aeroplane or performing brain surgery. You need to have that precision and meticulousness, and you cannot screw up; there is no room for emotion in this job. Of course, in the beginning, there are emotions because we're human. But you need to put in place tools that will set these emotions aside. For me, that is finding the trades that are successful ninety per cent of the time and applying them meticulously and quickly, with no room for my emotions to intervene. Yet sometimes they do, and when emotions come into trading, I know I am vulnerable, and I do not want to be so. That is why I don't stay slightly longer in my trades, even if I know I am extremely likely to make *more* money. Because in that extra minute or two there will be emotion involved and I could make different decisions. That is the right thing to do for *me*.

LEAVE THE GUN. TAKE THE CANNOLI

Fed cut rates… circuit-breaker… limit down… trading halt…
News headlines continuously flooded the background.

Twelve years! For our trader, it had been building up to this day. The lead-up of the past decade was not lost on anyone who knew him.

To work past the sacrifices and toil that this entailed, delivering on the trust those closest placed in him, to walk the emotional tightrope of his early career. To survive complete account loss, perpetual unfortunate timing, with the craftsman discipline to deny his own trade due to imperfection.

He did not come all this way to stop now. Six hundred lots—filled. *It began.*

Yet, margin and liquidity issues abounded. Exchanges and brokers were getting nervous. Phone calls demanded the millions of dollars needed to keep the position alive. Once again, so close but seemingly denied. *The Razor* could only bring himself to say one thing.

"If I can't take this trade, I'm going to quit!"

The phone rang again.

Kyriacou was back. "I've been in and out of phone calls with the brokers. I spoke to Roger too…"

Our trader remained still.

"He's going to do it himself. He'll put up the seven million as margin for the trade. It is a huge risk for him, but he believes you can do it. The position is safe. Just hope the margins won't keep going higher. You are close to the U.S. market open now."

Having spent the entire night managing the many traders, Kyriacou was still hard at work finding ways to keep *The Razor*'s trade alive overnight. And Kyriacou found the financing through FCT's very own chairman, Roger Carlsson. He did not know the trade, but he knew the people. To him, this was backing them—*The Razor*, Haywood, Kyriacou—and showing faith in the team. Such had been his craft for the past forty years.

But for *The Razor*, this had all been a preamble, a fifteen-hour turbulent ride of being trapped in stasis, limbo, with enough time for all manner of doubt, hesitation and questioning to creep in. Fatigue burned his eyes.

Yet! The S&P was still to open. But it was yet up to him to execute, to get it done. It was now a trade that chipped away at more than one soul.

15:25. *Five minutes!*

A most dangerous period: the order book—the price ladder, in effect—shut as the market began a five-minute auction. Other global markets picked up with even greater volatility; as if chained and trapped in place, the great serpent of volatility that stretched across markets whipped viciously. The tail of its greatest aggression thrashed and writhed, angered by this artificial suppression. Bond markets were roaring, commodities peaked and troughed at a rapid pace, and the currencies spasmed continuously.

The most important market open in years was about to take place.

But then! *Something* on the price ladder. The auction cracked; it was absolutely frantic. It skipped prices lower, lower and lower—the S&P was down another two per cent and had already reached the next floor price at negative seven per cent!

The Razor did not move an inch. He was still short. Hold.

And there it was. *Limit-down*—again—which meant a further fifteen-minute trade suspension. *Good news, bad news*, he thought. Now, *this* was truly the most dangerous period. Should any positive news happen now, it would undo the entire fifteen hours of waiting. And he would be at the complete mercy of the order book's closure.

THE RAZOR

But, it held… 15:32… 15:39…
15:44. *One minute.*
Sixty seconds felt longer than the past fifteen hours.
15:45—*Open!*

The S&P's bids and offers *disappeared* from the screen. It howled as it collapsed into an endless void of prices down below.

The Razor fought to keep track of the market as he recentred his price ladder again and again as the sparse bids and offers caved in and smashed any order along the way.

Our trader's positioned bids are filled with instantaneous speed, like the crack of a whip. His total market position was lobbed off as the S&P heaved lower.

600. 400. 100—*OUT!*
Done.

Our trader, Haywood, Kyriacou—everyone—*relief.*

All was still. Standing before *The Razor* was a long green line of numbers. Multiple seven figures glared from the screen.

The numbers? Meaningless.
The significance? Vindication.

For personal sacrifices and that of his family. All the toil to build a living that disappeared in a flash, not due to the markets but the pilfering of others. The near-misses, the stress and the uncertainty. Of a life on pause for so long. The desire to achieve greatness and reach one's potential. Delivering on the trust so many had placed in him.

This was cosmic payback.

HOMINEM TE MEMENTO

The most impressive part of *The Razor*'s triumph was *not* his trade but what came after: a complete lack of celebration. He was deeply aware that he was vulnerable. His past account growth was now dwarfed by the biggest singular trade of his life. And losing perspective while basking in the glory of success is as old as the seven hills of Rome. Hubris leading to downfall is an even older story, and the solution, as it were, for the ancient Romans was to continually remind the triumphant of their mortality; *Hominem te memento*, "remember that you are but a man." Only mortal, fallible and human. Traders more so; the stories of downfall after immense profit and success are persistent. Overconfidence and the ability to trade bigger size than ever before is a standard recipe for undoing the previous success, or worse.

"It didn't end with the execution of the trade," *The Razor* said. The planning must deal with what happens *after*. "I knew the risk after the trade. I could clip much more size, I could go crazy, I could throw away a lot of money here and there. My plan straight away was to come back to the office and take away a few ticks a day."

Beaming with admiration, Haywood added to this critical point. "Traders experiencing a day like this is similar to a tennis player winning against a great player and then losing the very next match. They are coming off a massive high, and it is hard to consolidate. Many traders have a big account push, but they are not ready for it."

Our trader agreed. "It wasn't easy, but that was my target. Yet, my dream career goals had been achieved, and I felt I was missing something. I made peace with myself and needed new targets and stimulation." One of these would be to perfect the execution of *the trade* on the rare occasion it happened again.

And so, *The Razor* doubled down on his consistency as a key goal in the upcoming years. Pointing at his return statistics, we examined the following month, April 2020, where our trader had made only a few *thousand* dollars. "This is not a lot, but I was already happy to be profitable the following month," he concluded.

The small return notwithstanding, the act of staying in control and preserving the multiple-seven-figure profits of the previous month was *the best trade*. "For me, it was crucial to total multiple six figures by the end of the year," our trader said. "That is, to not have had a losing month for the rest of 2020. That was also the target for 2021."

Yet, there is a finer thread that we can tie up. "The limit-down trade is the pinnacle of the *trend is your friend* concept; that was the supreme lesson I learnt from the Parmalat story," *The Razor* said. And so, the seeds were sown long before—a seventeen-year round-trip.

Following our interview with *The Razor* in late 2021, we noted that he had not had a single losing month since December 2019. And in fact, his streak continued into early 2023. The inertia and exuberance that would have made our trader vulnerable had to be ironed out, in so doing preserving the fine edge that earned our trader his alias. As *The Razor* says: "The next trade is always the most important one."

PRACTITIONER'S POSTSCRIPT

Explore resources derived from this chapter to further support the practicing trader.

axiafutures.com/
toot

Refer to
The Razor's
section.

LEARNER'S IMPRESSIONS

Below are some personal impressions *The Razor* made on us that we still discuss with other traders.

1. *The power of a tick.* Just restart here if all else fails. The market's smallest increment simplifies much, and it is a great way to master the key principles of this domain. Constraints are powerful liberators of creativity to aid learning and solve problems. Can you capture just a single tick from the market? *The Razor*'s answer forged an entire career. Power to those who master the first tick and then evolve to capture the second, then the third. Much can be done with so little.

2. *Consistency as endgame.* Our trader focuses on the downside *only* and forgoes the complications of maximising the upside. The latter is assumed to be the end goal of all traders, but *The Razor* shows an alternative. Sacrificing multiples of additional P&L is re-paid in kind by lifestyle stability, of predictability—words nearly anathemata to those who trade unpredictable markets, with the manic toll it entails. Yet, it is made possible by *The Razor*'s avoidance of large variance, prizing safety above all else. Our trader reminds us to respect the quiet craftsman rather than the glory trades. Yet another way in which constraints can be liberating.

3. *You are the trades you reject.* Our trader's mastery is defined by the trades he refuses and by the actions he does not take. Patience follows when one intimately understands their trading. *The Razor* refused to be vulnerable after the thrice-thwarted limit-down trade, as he also refused to trade on an immense high following

the eventual outsized success of the same trade. To abstain in the hardest moments unlocks the ability to consolidate gains and success. Consolidation is a marker of mastery.

What are your impressions? Write them down and converse with this book!

CHAPTER THREE

THE COLLECTOR

A winter morning along the English country road. Dark and damp, with lorries on their last runs—but then a grumbling in the distance—*louder!* Fog lights beam down the straight road, wide and low. An Aston Martin grates into the morning twilight; its engine rips into full torque, and it ascends and collapses in pitch. The revving echoes into your chest, and *there* it goes!————

————its red backlights shrink in the distance, blurred by the fog, and its sights and sounds dissolve beyond the trees. Twenty minutes later, or close to it, the Aston arrives at a parking bay. It is not the closest to the building's entrance, but it is parked in the most appropriate place… right next to the now very humbled car of the trading floor boss.

Not real trading! Or so the floor boss would say to those reprobates, those mere traders who scurried around picking up ticks in the wake of the *flippa*—whoever they are, or whatever *it* is, perhaps an algorithm that seemingly appears to push around order flow with large orders that never trade. Yet, figure out what the mystery participant is doing and a tick or two can be had from the market in the confusion. *A mere party trick!* But the driver of the Aston, a late-twenty-something sporting a hoodie, jeans and trainers, thought otherwise—a tick's a tick; all is fair—the scrappy tick trade is what took our hoodie enthusiast from broke and struggling, a laggard for two years, to the ire of the floor boss—*useless!* Now he had a burgeoning trading account, well-kept and deserved. But still at the ire of the floor boss. It is all very well, then, as the Aston's number plate is none other than *FL19PER.*[*]

And so, our twenty-something trader, who is so very English in his casual defiance, the good-old-lad type of the Home Counties—the pub-crawling, self-deprecating, sarcastic, dry-humoured shorts-and-rugby-shirt-upon-the-first-glimpse-of-the-sun—one of the lads, and, over a decade later, in our current trading world, it often feels he is one of the very last. This trader is a survivor, as all great ones are.

That was thirteen years ago. It was the beginning of our trader's circuitous path at an old and now-defunct prop firm that was far removed from the London scene: the very same Firm Y we encountered in the previous chapter. But then, along his journey, he would venture to London onto a different trading floor altogether at the beginning of a tumultuous time—that is, for the traders—as the financial world had instead experienced a quiet implosion, making history by having *no* story.

Overall, the market opportunities following the 2007–2009 Great Financial Crisis and the following European Debt Crisis had started to fade by 2013. Volatility, the lifeblood of traders, had crumpled under the boot of the *new* masters of the universe—central bankers. And so, near-universal zero-interest-rate policy became the norm in the most dominant economies. Seemingly endless quantitative easing, alongside a slate of other factors, was either hailed or derided for this so-called taming of volatility, depending on which side of the market you sat on.

---

[*] Or something to that effect, in the interest of privacy.

A whole generation of proprietary traders who grew up with the advent of electronic markets or those who thrived after being thrown into the maelstrom of the Great Financial Crisis would find their strategies losing potency at best, or become brutally loss-making at worst.

And right in the middle of this was our good old lad, expecting his new London trading floor to be bursting with vitality, the great next step in his career. They would not know it, but these traders would soon become the old guard, dogmatic: "The markets will become good again, we just have to wait!" But good *again* implies a normal state, and such a notion is dangerous in the markets. Boisterous optimism degraded into stark cynicism as the vast majority of traders refused to adapt their mentality and strategies.

"Then I saw all these dinosaurs die—the great extinction," our good old lad explained. "I was at the biggest prop house in London; at the peak, there were a hundred and sixty traders. But every month, there were traders leaving; by 2014, half of the floor had left, and soon ninety per cent were gone. They did not evolve."

Haywood, remembering his own beginnings as a trader at the turn of the millennium, reflected on this period. In the early 2000s there was enough opportunity for a trader to trade just one market. Outside trading hours, nothing else mattered. Traders lived the stereotypical fast lives in what we would now regard as poor personal discipline. One could arrive at the office late, trade and leave early. No market preparation, deep learning or constant improvement was needed. Volatility meant opportunity, but the death of it meant traders had to then fight for scraps. Only the most professional trader who improved every aspect of their game, inside and outside the office, would survive the change, comparable to the professionalisation of most sports over the twentieth century.

And so, our trader described something of an age now deeply foreign to newer traders. At times, it felt as if he were describing a drinking team who occasionally traded, but of course, the truth is somewhere in the middle. Said team was successful, with something of the strength of a local community, like the local sport team—the good old traders down at the pub. It was here, he says, where a new trader learnt the most.

The trading meta-game, the current optimal approach towards the domain, seemed self-fulfilling in nature as the culture came with the times. The trader's mentality was closer to a nine-to-five job. Come four-thirty in the afternoon, the majority of the prop traders in London wrapped up, regardless of what was potentially on the horizon in America. *Central banks? Why stay for that?*

More so, there was a try-your-hand attitude prevalent in the industry, where a trader would learn a few core skills and strategies and then effectively wash out once these stopped working. Even so, this could carry a trader's profitability for many years since the cyclicality, the pace of change in the market environment, was much slower than now. *Hence*—the mentality, the implicit meta-game, had not been challenged for at least a generation or two, long enough to become conventional thinking.

Another veteran of this era, *The Godfather*, explained that a trader was expected to identify himself by *the* market they traded. "I am a Schatz trader, a FTSE trader, an S&P trader, a Gilt trader, a Treasury-EuroDollar trader…" or, as it was, the division between a spread and outright trader. There was no multi-market, volatility-chasing trader—*no need!* You have all the volatility and opportunities with just one.

And so, the conventional wisdom was to wait for the markets to "become good again" to fit *their* strategy as opposed to evolving themselves. A trader's career *was* the strategy he was trading rather than viewing this strategy simply as a tool of a wider skill set, ready to be interchangeable as the market evolved over time. But the shift in the environment in the early 2010s was far more raw; fundamental—it would swallow a trader in totality. A trader's life is now closer to the demands of an athlete, of complete planning, of control of their daily, weekly and monthly routines: a controlled diet, strict abstinence from all that's entailed in an active social life, anything that can hinder focus and energy for long stretches at the desk. Such a monastic life would previously mark the odd trader out, but now these are the *minimum* demands for the novice.

Yet today, we meet *The Collector* as a man recovered from old wounds. But he made the changes where so many could not. No trading strategy is too strange, nor is he above any opportunity in the markets, nor too proud to entertain and absorb new perspectives. No method, diet or routine is too awkward to aid a body now sapped of energy and endurance. His mind, instead, is an assortment of trades, tactics and situations of these scrappy trades, as he describes it, all assembled in a mental toolbox, all to be pulled, mulled and thrown together to take advantage of anything the market is providing. His body is committed to routine and exercise; above all, he must endure as a trader—whatever it takes.

But his true edge, Haywood explains, is that he is exceptional at using the nature of the trading floor to learn optimally from those around him, repurposing this knowledge into his personalised ever-growing toolbox of trades. "His implicit learning is incredible," Haywood said. "He is the best I have ever known at this—the way he creates his environmental learning through observation, listening to it, and yet has the discipline and foresight of understanding what to filter out and what *not* to do." A procurer of ideas, curator of observations, *The Collector* of market experiences, and a student of all.

And the results! After taking flight, our trader has never experienced a down-year since, and he has long since ranked as a seven-figure trader. Even during a difficult decade, for many years, our trader experienced forty to fifty up-weeks in the year, and the loss-making ones were insignificant. So consistent, in fact, the only trader to best this record is *The Razor* himself. Yet, his first years were anything but controlled. They were a struggle, a near washout.

BACK IN BLACK

When *The Collector* got the call in 2007, he said it was a feeling bested by no other; Firm Y hired *him*, convinced, like so many others, that *he* would be the one to make it. But he became an anomaly, as instead of being placed on a graduate training course, he was thrown directly onto the trading floor—*Google the Bund and just trade!* "I had no real style or understanding of what I was doing. I was doing everything… just a junkie, and I had so much energy for it, albeit misdirected… I just loved the idea of trading and the process," he began.

And rather than sitting with a group of ten other trainees, he was already sitting among 'older' traders, interspersed with those at least a few years further along the endless learning curve. Absent the kind of resources available now, rubbing shoulders was his only real source of knowledge—perhaps why he is so strong in learning from the trading floor itself, remarkably so compared to other traders.

Alas! That trading floor boss pulled him aside and warned him that he was on his last legs. Thousands of pounds in the red, there was little rope left. And to send the message, the trader standing next to him was *The Sphinx*—a trader we will meet later—but at the time he had been fired and turned into an analyst. And to our traders, that is no better than being shot on the spot.

The Collector recalled this final warning as he experienced sudden clarity. "I was so scared of losing the opportunity, I couldn't take enough risk at the right time. I was snapping at small profits; I just needed an *up*-day! I was so desperate, so invested mentally and emotionally in *becoming* a trader," he said. "They told me I was standing at the edge of a cliff, and it was my last chance. Yet, as they said this it felt like the shackles came off. I felt as if I might as well just go for it now. It was liberating."

Paradoxes, contradictions and roughness are inescapable in the trading domain. The act of letting go, trading with an attitude where one cares yet seemingly also *does not care*, proved an emergent act for *The Collector*, a life of a trader is that of contradiction! An unapologetic drive and self-belief ensured our trader would claw out and breathe life into his career. "I just entered a mentality where I *had* to make it happen," he continued. "I needed to find ways to be successful. So, I started edge-hunting." Leveraging the knowledge of a collaborative trading floor and his personal connections to many traders, *The Collector* had created a process which would earn him his name. He explained how he had approached one of the most profitable traders on the floor. "I said to him, where are you making money? I haven't got time! That's when you started to get the 'Chicago PMI' [Purchasing Managers' Index] trade, where that trader and another were making amazing money. Four months later, it stopped working, yet it gave me enough to get off the ground."

Readers should note the nuance. Our trader asked, "Where are you making money?" as opposed to *how*. Recall one of *The Razor's* principles: "Your strategy has to fit like a suit." Our trader did not aim to emulate those around him verbatim; rather, this allowed him to focus on a lucrative, in-the-moment niche. His own research and homework permitted him to execute this trade in his personalised way: a subjective strategy upon an objective market pattern, as we reviewed in the previous chapter. That is, to use skills and abilities that are natural to him; to fit the burdens of strategy that are tolerable to him. "This trader was also doing very well with specific order flow anomalies on the price ladder in markets like Gold, Crude Oil and the Bund," *The Collector* continues. "Back then the opportunities in these anomalies were ripe just after the Financial Crisis."

And so, through a reductive process he had stopped trading all strategies other than his best. With total focus, with no energy or account risk devoted to anything else, our trader worked for each and every tick. Hunching over the meeting table, our trader emulated the stiffness and focus with which he looked at his screens. "I used to sit there all day with one lot in the DAX [German equity index]. I thought, I will sit here for hours, and if I can nick ten or twenty ticks out of the DAX… if I can make three to four hundred euros every day, that will be enough. It will get me going," he said. "After banking two thousand euros a month later, a few other order flow trades started working. I threw everything else out, all I traded was this specific price action and data releases."*

Standing at the cliff's edge emulated *No Plan B!*, one of the few repeat, common features between many of the traders in this book. It *forced* them to become profitable and successful. With reality now beaming down upon them, brushing so close to the stark alternative of their trading career, it forced these traders to cut through the fat, those whimsical trades to satisfy their ego or release psychological pressure.

Plan B is almost certain to manifest at the expense of one's trading career. Worse yet, this also unravels a strange trader's version of Parkinson's Law, in which work fills up the time allocated. If a compa-

---

* Traders often refer to P&L in different currencies, as various futures contracts are quoted in their respective currencies (e.g., the DAX in euros, the S&P contract in U.S. dollars). Further, each trader's account is denominated in a currency of their choice, and P&Ls are converted to that currency at day's end. How they reference their P&L often corresponds to their chosen account currency, or a specific contract they traded.

ny's project deadline is three months, it will take at least this long. If it were three weeks, it too would be completed in three weeks; such is the workflow of large organisations described.

But so, too, are traders who are not totally pressured by a timeline or other constraints. Those who have *no* financial or time pressures will likely take much longer to become profitable, if at all. Because they do not *have* to make it work. If they do, it is very likely they became successful when they have finally run out of time or other pressures become too great, making it work just in the nick of time. A deadline is a funny thing.

Consider the little rope afforded to traders like *The Razor*, and as we will see with *The Godfather*, whose career alternatives were so unpalatable and resources so few that they had to make it work. Too little time, few financial resources and relationship pressures ruin new and old traders alike, yet possessing too *many* resources ensures the same outcome. Going forward, let us call it the *trader's resource dilemma*.

Perhaps the only practical solution for aspiring traders is to ensure they are in a position of resource strength, yet facing immutable shorter deadlines, benchmarks and aims where learning is focused, purposeful and ultimately transformed into performance. The consequence of failure must be sharp and strict. The low barriers to entry in this industry make it too easy to return and drag out this process painfully for years, a far worse fate than those who maximised efforts yet left this trading domain with their heads held high and did not look back.

The Collector continued, "I was so incredibly focused. I knew that if I missed a tick, that could be the difference between surviving or not. I started capitalising on my momentum and consistency. I brought my account back from a loss of twenty-three thousand pounds to flat in three months. I have had three crazy happy days in my career, and this was one of them. I remember vividly when I got my trading statement to show that I was positive, I went to my desk and played AC/DC's 'Back in Black' on a loop. It still gives me the shivers when I play it."

As Haywood explains, our trader made use of "the extended mind," a more formal way to understand how a trader learns from the floor. We borrow the term from Annie Murphy Paul's book *The Extended Mind: The Power of Thinking Outside the Brain* (2021: 163), as she writes that the practice of "thinking with experts" is the practice of learning through *imitation*. And that is a time-honoured practice that has been a critical part of education since antiquity, with modern education as the exception. And that learning through imitation, she continues, is widely observable in nature and biological processes, most evident in babies and small children, who learn language, behaviour and gestures through imitation. But we agree with Paul—there should be no stigma about learning by imitating!

Superficially, it might seem we are suggesting that *The Collector* is superior in imitating or emulating the trading strategies of others. How can this be reconciled with *The Razor's* principle of "contamination"— the warning to avoid emulation, as the trader would live in the shadow of others, never to achieve "greatness"? Paul provides clarification on this issue, as "imitating… rarely entails automatic or mindless duplication… it demands a willingness to look past superficial features to the deeper reason why the original solution succeeded, and an ability to apply that to the underlying principle in a novel setting … imitating well demands a considerable degree of creativity" (2021: 173).

Where are you making money? takes our trader to the hunting grounds, the streams and rivers. The answer to the question is a mere signpost, but he will still have to learn to fish and hunt.

So "thinking with experts" at the trading desk was a mere starting point for our trader. Much effort was spent on developing and applying his personalised strategy, to trade it in his own way with his own constraints. And the constraints were tough! To *that* trading floor boss, being unprofitable ranked you low, even morally offensive, and getting *any* concession was a major victory, especially for our good old lad, who managed to justify trading a single DAX lot after losing money for so long.

But it worked! After two years of struggles, he gained traction, returning to flat on his trading account. "It turns so fast," *The Collector* recalled. "You do need a bit of luck; you need something to fall into your wheelhouse to get your teeth into and gain some momentum. These little price action events are what got me going; you have to just focus on one thing. I remember that in the next nine months, I made between one hundred and two hundred thousand, and afterwards several hundred thousand each year consecutively."

The Collector did not bask for long in his triumph, with the single exception of purchasing the Aston, which was symbolic. Perhaps a purchase for a kind of release, a relief. But with a shift in tone, he still sounded incredulous. "It was a wicked moment after everything you go through. The pain, the exasperation, the pressures of failing while others succeed, hard work amounting to nothing. When you first become a trader, you *assume* you will be successful. I celebrated when I got the call to join my first trading floor, but the arc of pain that followed for years afterwards..." *The Collector* shrugged in conclusion.

A SURVIVALIST'S TOOLBOX

We sense that it is good practice to learn from others; look no further than the biographies of every practitioner in any field. *And it is why you are reading this very book!* Yet intentions for many, as experience on the AXIA trading desks shows, remain only so. Somewhere, there is a disconnect. "A lot of new trader intakes become too insular too quickly. They are stubborn and are not supple in absorbing from their peers or seniors," Haywood said. "On the other end, there are those who copy *superficially* and do not understand the intuition or logic of why an edge is expressed in such a way." As explored before, the new learner has to navigate between learning and avoiding hijacking, as Haywood calls it, that is, being constantly dragged into trading different things, always restarting from scratch.

This problem is rife among retail traders whose main intake of (mis)information from the internet is either old yet promoted as new, of dubious quality, or simply written by those who are frustrated, jaded and have given up. "This is why *The Collector* is special. He still balances this well, even though most fail at it, including some more experienced traders at various stages in their careers," Haywood continued. "Watching the evolution of a new trade through *The Collector*'s interaction with the 'extended mind' of the floor, and the ultimate transformation of that trade, to make it his own, is incredible."

And like most things in trading, persistent *unknown* undercurrents can be too strong to allow a trader to get to where they need to be. And often, making them *known* is half the battle. Therefore, we formalise a common observation, an intuition of learning from others, or "thinking with our relationships," as Paul calls it (2021: 161), into a potent, conscious and *intentional* framework which permits a deeper understanding beyond common observations. It allows us to think cross-disciplinary; a trader on the cutting edge will always forge a *new* path ahead by drawing resources outside their field.

"Our brains evolved to think *with* people: to teach them, to argue with them, to exchange stories with them," Paul writes (2021: 189). One of these was "thinking with experts," as we explored previously, and another was "thinking with *peers*" (2021: 187). This is the strength of a trading floor, evidenced by none other than *The Collector* and *The Warrior* when they sat next to each other for the first time in their careers more than a decade ago. "This was a good thing because I was always a little bit risk-averse," *The Collector* began. "*The Warrior* was pretty fresh at the time, and I was already three years into my career. I explained a trade to him, and he did the same trade, with the same size as me!"

Not to be outdone by this newcomer, he traded more size—more lots—the next time. *The Warrior*, as if on cue, increased his size again in response—*and it went on!* Both traders credit how experiences like these helped to push boundaries. Countless exchanges of details, observations and different practices between the pair undoubtedly fit this horizontal exchange of mind-melding, combining the best of both.

The Warrior also recounted this period, describing how the pair experimented together in trying to best execute their trades on news headlines and comments that were frequently occurring during the newly developing European Debt Crisis. Interestingly, both traders took and learnt these trades together, but the style of execution was different, as it had evolved to fit the distinct personalities and risk tolerance of both traders.

Their learning was cooperative yet simultaneously competitive. And their experience did not completely replace or hijack the other's. The fruits of their labour became evident a year later. "There was this 'credit line' trade where we both whacked the S&P. We had both made just over thirty thousand that day, huge milestones in our careers. We were both delirious!" *The Collector* grinned. "We ran to the back of the office, and we just jumped for joy, hugged and ran around. We didn't know what to do with ourselves. I was shaking for two hours. This went far beyond our biggest up-day before. Like the day I had resuscitated my account back to flat, this was also one of the three crazy happy days in my career, even if this amount now seems small in comparison today."

By 2013, *The Collector* had logged several profitable years, his account saw healthy growth. His remarkable control of the downside remained.

But then the trading floor at Firm Y split; older and senior traders at the time, like Richard Bailey, moved away while others remained in the original location. In other words, *The Collector*'s ability to continuously learn from an experienced floor had vanished, and thereupon, our trader set to move to the "biggest floor in London, ready for the big leagues!" and a different firm altogether.

And that is where he would witness the aforementioned "great extinction." It would deeply colour his understanding of trading as a profession. Among the few that survived, *The Collector* had got to know one of the oldest traders on the floor, who is still active to this day. "He was the only one bucking the trend. He was a very natural trader; everything was obvious to him," *The Collector* explained. "Yet he is extremely hardworking and always tries to get better. He is in his fifties and still believes his best days are ahead of him. He is always trying to find new edges and new ways to evolve. He would always say, 'Look at this! Come over and check *this* out!' He was always excited to explore new things. He didn't rest on his laurels, to assume the market would always be there. However, that trading floor was very cynical. A lot of other people made fun of this trader, of his constant curiosity." Of course, true to his name, *The Collector* passed the correct judgement. "I thought this trader was making money and always would; the people gossiping about him were not. *They're screwed!* They were complaining, and asking, 'When are markets going to come back?' They had a mentality where they had a specific edge, and if there was no opportunity, they wouldn't trade. And all of those who had that attitude virtually disappeared. Very few people walk away from trading after they had their best year ever, like many had done on that floor in 2008–2009."

The experiences of the dwindling floor, in contrast to the older trader that *The Collector* held in high esteem, would drive home the need to constantly search for edge; assume it will one day fail, as it always does. "If you want to have a long career, that is the only way you can approach it," our trader said. "If not, the markets will change in front of you. Two or three years will go by, and you'll realise you have not improved as a trader. The markets will look almost foreign, and you will have nowhere to turn. It will be like starting again, as you haven't evolved with the markets," he continued. "And remember, over the course of the year, *someone* is making money, as there is always an edge somewhere. It might just not fall in your specific niche. Almost a whole year can go by with barely any news comments. So… you're sitting there waiting… just to hear a comment in 2014, yet for six months, there was barely anything. But then look at 2020, there were ten a week; it always comes and goes. However, in 2014, there were still opportunities if you were willing to learn new ideas and new strategies."

The Collector offered a reflection of what may come and where our profession is headed next. "I just have tools. That best describes my trading. You need to have as many tools in your locker as possible to survive. I can trade [bond] auctions, MOCs [market on close], and month-end flows. Those are just one type of trade. Next to that I have all my event trading." As he described his mental model, he gestured as if he was stacking multiple shelves. "I have *those* collections of trades, then I have my longer-term trades, which is a whole other, newly developed area."

The Collector's toolbox is a composite of trades discovered through judicious debriefing, of "thinking with peers" and "thinking with experts." He had separated the trade from the strategy and had developed his own strategy to overlay—in keeping with *The Razor*. "I was just an absolute scrapper. I always found these little trades and edges that you can leverage up. I wasn't good at what people would call 'classical trading,' I was still profitable, yet I still felt like I was underperforming." *Note—underperforming!* Even at this four-year stint at the rapidly shrinking London prop firm, *The Collector* bulked out his P&L to bigger and better numbers. He was still thriving, but in the *present*. To him, the future would catch up, and at this rate, he had to assume he was already extinct. And so, a new floor, for new skills. A new "extended mind" of fresh ideas, new trades, a different approach.

A NEW CURATION

Our trader joined the AXIA floor in 2017, a mix of new and old faces, like Bailey, *The Warrior* and *The Sphinx*, among others, whom he'd traded alongside at Firm Y.

But now, a new challenge. "I was exposed to so many new ideas, I was pulled from pillar to post! The previous trading floor was like a library; now, at AXIA, I was hyperstimulated," *The Collector* began. Becoming increasingly animated, and picking up the conversational pace, our trader continued. "My eyes were opened to my skill limitations. A lot of my old skills, the price action trades, for example, were no longer in play, and you had to be a lot more skilled to execute them. Additionally, I would be surprised if I had even made a dollar with 'classical trading,' I'd lost all the money I made. My knowledge was crude; back then, the only things I knew about [market] profiles were normal distribution and single prints." By "classical trading," *The Collector* refers to trading market patterns on a variety of 'technical' tools like standard charts, market profiles and more. "It was going to give me a great opportunity to evolve again and become a better trader," he continued. "Yet I still had to come to terms with the fact that I was in a new environment, and it took time to make progress," he concluded.

Nevertheless, the hyperstimulation of a new floor, its behaviours and energy alongside the pull of new ideas became comparable to the same effect observed earlier—where the development of a new trader's edge can be hijacked by others. Even for someone as experienced as our trader. "*The Warrior* was playing breakouts on Gold [futures]—I kept trying it too and lost money ten days in a row! The same with other ideas being traded around me," he continued. Health issues also made this sensitive learning period increasingly difficult. Yet, he drew the line. "All I need to see is one trader making money. If he can do it, I believe I can do it. When you are struggling, all you need to know is that it can be done."

Once more, pressure forced *The Collector* to reassess. He threw his hands in the air. "What should I do? I know *The Engineer* has been doing exceptionally well. I remember when he was in his early days back on my first trading floor, and now, he has grown into a massive technical trader. No one at my second prop firm would have believed the idea of someone trading hundreds of lots in the Bund on a *technical* set-up!" This sheer performance was enough to entice *The Collector* to dig deeper, providing the critical peer confidence, a psychological cornerstone that protects a trader's morale when it is tested by stalled learning progression and poor trading. And, most importantly, a sign pointing to where the best hunting grounds are.

Yet, *The Collector* still had his strongest card to play—the potency of his own connection to the floor's peers and experts, its "extended mind"—"I learned an awful lot from *The Hero* when he sat behind me. I picked up things through small chats," our trader said. "What I realised was that he was incredibly formulaic in working to understand the 'big set-up'—the technical trade—and how he prepared for it. I realised he prepares for them with the depth and seriousness like my preparations for central bank meetings."

Furthermore, as *The Collector* made deeper inroads, his consistent discussions with a *domain expert* were a real-time sounding board. This feedback loop served to develop his skills for "classical trading" by accessing the filtering system of *The Hero*'s expert perspective on market structure, profiles and analysis. This is the crux of the "transactive memory" of the trading floor, as Paul calls it (2021: 235). Where leveraging the nuances and intricacies of different trading edges allows us to access a treasure trove of collective expertise. This perfectly describes a high-performance trading floor, as the trick is to never impede the connective tissue between all these different nodes of expertise.

But that is still only part of the journey; making use of it is entirely different. *The Collector* has been proven to possess high levels of agency, to affect change, to follow through on intentions, placing him among the few. Our trader followed through with a plan when his career was at a cliff's edge, to relearn and then commit to developing his technical trading skills.

HARD EDGE, SOFT EDGE

A decade into his career, *The Collector* was a beginner once more, repurposing his daily routine to accommodate this learning period. "I began to look at the market from a wider perspective. I began to layer different time frames together and would dig down to shorter ones," he said. "Every night, I came home and analysed the markets in this new way. I cannot tell you how much that fast-forwarded my trading. For the first time in my career, I come into the office and actually have an idea of where markets might be going. Where is it more vulnerable, where is there pressure building up? I didn't have any of this understanding before!"

Yet, *The Collector*'s amassed skills were not supplanted—hijacked—by what he was learning from *The Hero* and the wider floor. Instead, he used what served him well throughout his career. This included an assortment of small-timeframe chart patterns, price action and specific order flow events. His 'scrapper' skills became repurposed with his new repertoire, drawing connections to what he had now learnt about "classical trading" to make it his own.

The Collector discussed how he would "layer" different inputs of information, ranging from market fundamentals, themes and order flow, alongside the interaction of correlated markets that can impact the behaviour of one another. At its core, this top-down layering approach serves to filter out the seemingly endless opportunities presented on the price ladder and highlights the most important to our trader. In other words, his layering of clues reduces the variance of a trade, in keeping with how he is able to remain so consistent.

Our trader collects and amasses specific repeated market patterns that occur within economic data releases or other phenomena like month-end rebalancing caused by large institutions and funds altering positions and adjusting portfolios. "There is so much edge where you can identify instances when flow *and* time are condensed," he said. In other words, if the trader knows something has to happen in a certain period, then this vastly reduces the variance of such a trade. Furthermore, if the right action does not present itself in specific instances, then the entire trade is avoided in the first place. In fact, *The Collector* possesses a long history of meticulously documented events from earlier in his career. He places the most recent event at the top of the pile—complete with the sequence of events and updated with the most optimal strategy to trade such a market move. A necessity, he says, as we underestimate how fallible memory is, of our overconfidence in it, demonstrated by how many traders on his previous floor would hit the U.K.'s Purchasing Managers' Index (PMI) economic figure "the wrong way." It was wrong because the market had traded in the exact counter-intuitive, seeming 'nonsensical' way for several consecutive instances. By the time of next PMI release, everyone forgot that the environment had shifted to this counter-intuitive state, that they must now trade 'illogically,' and instead the market burnt them once more.

The pinnacle of this is trading central bank meetings. In this case, consider *The Collector*'s outperformance relative to the trading floor during a European Central Bank (ECB) meeting. "In 2020, the Bund on ECB meetings was trading badly, yet it had already been so for four to five months, so it should not have been a surprise," he said. "Instead, the BTPs [Italian ten-year bond] were a pure play, directional and over a hundred tick range. If you were logging and breaking it down, you would have realised this. Yet we are human, and we still forget six weeks later." This enabled *The Collector* to produce a multiple-six-figure day solely from one market, a synthesis of everything he had thus far developed and breathing new life into the older aspects of his trading. He could repurpose prior, perhaps disused tools from previous market conditions to build up a latticework of trading tactics, analysis and more. This is how he "layers up" his view of the markets, more explicitly than other traders, as he intentionally has organised his skills or "tools" within a greater mental model.

However, the challenge at present is not directly monetary but energy related—*something* happened after that damned appendix removal. "I had to get on top of the energy issue. Before, I could go out all weekend and be fine by Monday, but now I would go a whole week feeling terrible on the floor, and I was frustrated," he said. "This would take another leap forward in my trading, and I tried so many things... supplements, diet, meditation and other things to find what works for me." But the key question was how to measure trading progress now. "You might not be at the best of your game, and you may not feel at your sharpest and you are tired, sometimes as if you are in the deepest hole," he said. "But you can be better *this* time in dealing with this situation and get the best out of yourself than you would have done two years ago. You are just trying to get the most out of what you are capable of right now. To improve the little things, the *soft edge*."

Consider the ease with which traders can give back much P&L after outsized gains. "You made fifty thousand—*oh well*—what's a five-grand loss now? But you would *not* come in the next day and just dump that same amount. Do that ten times a year, and that is just too messy," *The Collector* said. "You've allowed carelessness into your game; it will infect it, and it will grow. But if you can have discipline in the moments of potential weakness, then that is an opportunity to be better than I was last time. This is a significant soft-edge opportunity, worth a lot more than the numbers on the screen."

In keeping with *The Razor*, our trader stressed how good habits compound. You trust yourself, he says, allowing for greater consistency in trading more size. It matters more than the P&L outcome of a single trade. To "error prune," as Haywood calls it, is the first step to reductive mastery; to consolidate and hold on to gains is one of the first markers of an improved trader. Struggling traders often cannot end their cycle of committing the same mistakes and errors and, once again, lack the *agency* needed to effect change. This is why our trader's insistence on focusing on the soft edge is as important as all else, to shed errors as fast as possible.

But there is more to the soft edge of *The Collector*. "You also have to surround yourself with a support team, as athletes in tennis and golf do. You cannot take it all upon yourself," he said. *Agency!* A circular path of personal growth, self-discovery and headstrong dedication to the craft.

And so, our good old lad concluded: "Even though I may have my moments and low periods, I had never questioned that I would not be a trader this time next year or in the future. I still completely back myself. I absolutely never thought of, or discussed, quitting. It is not conceivable, even when these challenging moments occur and the results don't follow. This might be to a fault, but I love it, and I know I will always find a way. When it hits the fan, you either give up or pull yourself through. Everyone on the trading floor had to adapt and change. It is endless, and so many other people would not keep going. It feels horrific when you are in it, stomach-churning—it hurts. But if you keep going and fundamentally believe, then you will find a way. Eventually, some markets will come alive, something else will work and you will start connecting things. You move on. Everyone who's had a long trading career is the definition of a growth mindset. They keep pushing and never give up... those that do never realise what they're walking away from."

PRACTITIONER'S POSTSCRIPT

Explore resources derived from this chapter to further support the practicing trader.

axiafutures.com/
toot

Refer to
The Collector's
section.

LEARNER'S IMPRESSIONS

Below are some personal impressions that *The Collector* made on us that we still discuss with other traders.

1. *The trader's resource dilemma.* Too little time and money is the most common end for traders. Yet too much can also trap the trader in limbo, as they never really have to make it. The cure can be worse than the disease. Traders must still place lucid limitations and measure progress to prevent an ever-growing opportunity cost of a life lived in limbo.
2. *The "extended mind."* A trading floor's value can be assessed by its "transactive memory"—to reach different domain experts when required. So, too, must a trader assess his ability to learn from the floor and make changes accordingly. Do not assume this is automatic. A lack of action plagues many—the majority never engage in a trading community. And learning is also social. Find your team, share abundantly and leverage the power of "the extended mind." A trading community can only be as strong as the transfer of expertise between its members. That is how you create your own toolbox to survive the market's only guarantee: change.
3. *Soft edge, hard cash.* Soft-edge development is a visible marker of progress that will become increasingly important as the trader's career lengthens to meet many of life's challenges. Better behaviour now in the same situation can be far more valuable than the P&L to pay its dividends in the future. Because you now trust yourself to push boundaries, to handle more risk. Develop it as seriously as your trading edge.

What are your impressions? Write them down and converse with this book!

CHAPTER FOUR

THE ADVENTURER

Many dream of it, yet only a handful achieve it. A balanced life escapes the grasp of many traders, plenty of whom were attracted to the industry with notions of freedom and financial, spiritual and moral sovereignty to escape the leashes of corporate office.

But in reality, one exchanges a desk for another, often working longer hours than before with far less chance of success. *The Warrior* laments how he lives in chains and abhors what the markets force him to become. Others, like *The Sphinx*, are wholly swallowed up by the markets—absorbed, addicted—and do little outside them. Such is the price of performance. Yet, like all phenomena, the exceptions are far more revealing.

The Adventurer is that exception, for he is famed among his peers for often trading in locations which are, of course, exotic in comparison to a regular trading desk. *The Adventurer* traded the weekly Wednesday U.S. crude oil inventory data right off his scooter, parked by an empty country road in Majorca. You might find him briefly repurposing a night-train cabin as his jerry-rigged trading desk while backpacking abroad. He would manage his positions off his phone in the middle of the Palace of Versailles or initiate new ones from his laptop in hotel rooms in New York, Okinawa, Shenzhen and further across his travels through Asia and the Americas.

He is anomalous, not only as he travels while trading *successfully*, but he is different in trading style and worldview altogether. Profitable since his first year of live trading in 2015, *The Adventurer* has locked in returns of multiple six figures per year. And the centrepiece year of his returns rests in 2020, with a return of over seven figures. Yet, this description disguises his crowning achievement. While these returns are enduring and life-changing for any proprietary trader, these results are achieved with the *least* amount of time and effort invested at a trading desk and screens. If one were to plot an effort-to-reward ratio among all traders, *The Adventurer* is in a league of his own.

Nevertheless, our trader understands the long-term compromise. He knows that he is in the arena against obsessives and the unrelenting—the fiercest competitors. Furthermore, he is aware of his talent that could vastly push his trading results, a detail often mentioned by Haywood and Kyriacou. Yet this would require confinement, routine and structure, with far more time watching markets as they perpetually demand commitment. But our trader does not wish this, as his lack of confinement is a necessity and he lucidly exchanges a better trading performance in favour of maintaining his life away from the trading desk. Perhaps this is also part of what makes him great, a cornerstone of *The Adventurer*'s persona.

But! Abundant talent is required to achieve such a balance between trading and travelling, which many other successful traders cannot do while remaining a competitor in ruthless markets. Coldly introspective, *The Adventurer* admits he no longer possesses immense love or obsession for trading, but he still maintains that this is a critical *minimum* requirement for any new entrants to possess, as he once did.

"Initially, when we start trading, we all want financial freedom. Yet, at this stage, I don't feel that adding an extra zero to the end of my account balance will change my life," he said. "I would much rather ski with friends or read a good book so as to be better off the next day. I want to further explore the possibilities in life." The markets have become a means to an end; the income *now* provides freedom from the time commitments of most other careers, and in turn, this allows for time to be spent with family, to fulfil autodidactic desires, to travel and ultimately to give back to the world. Specifically, *The Adventurer* would often trade at his desk at home for three weeks and travel for the fourth. Sometimes he would forgo trading altogether on some longer, more exotic journeys.

And so, his story reveals what happens *after* a trader's "success," which is seldom discussed. But that is natural, for the volume of potential and struggling traders far outweighs the successful. Dealing with high-level traders is a different process. They are in a different stage in their career and financial status. They possess different goals, objectives and a philosophy of life that deals more with *meaning* than one focused solely on growing their income.

Caution ahead! This chapter will not redeem the naïve worldview that trading can be relegated to a three-hour, compartmentalised side-activity for a novice who just discovered there is a market other than the S&P 500. Those who argue that a certain "lifestyle" is possible will not find consolation here; remember that our trader is anomalous for a reason. His uniqueness is evidence of how rare and nearly unachievable his travelling and trading feats really are. The unfortunate salesmanship tactic of advertising trading as an easy lifestyle or "side-income" with so few hours of effort has done great damage to the expectations of potential traders. If our readers still believe these 'expectations' after finishing this book, then we have failed in what we set out to accomplish; the markets demand their pound of flesh, and it will be paid one way or another.

Also, consider an important detail in *The Adventurer*'s career path by understanding his equivalent in high-level athletics. All high-level athletes train differently from how they did as novices. But the novice who tries to replicate the training of a high-level athlete naïvely assumes this is how the champion always trained, that their current state is what made them become the best. Instead, their training evolves over time, as do their constraints and capabilities.

We term this the 'champion fallacy,' an easy trap for newer traders who try to emulate the strategies and behaviour of expert traders as they are at this very moment rather than understanding and learning from how they got there—often an entirely different journey. And in that transformational journey lie more valuable lessons and more relevant ideas.

And so, for many years, *The Adventurer* did not substitute deep focus and long hours for anything else. Plain living and complete dedication to the improvement of his craft, *The Adventurer* also reached the "darker side of trading," as he called it, becoming obsessive, possessed—addiction-like traits. Wholly immersed, our trader was always at his desk and doing little outside the office to make the most of his learning opportunity in the first few years, which is the minimum price for success.

Therefore, do not use *The Adventurer*'s story to eschew deep focus, immersion and hard work early in your career. Rather, use it to wisely understand how your career priorities eventually may change from *just* the bottom line—a positive decision if the compromises and opportunity costs are understood. Haywood compared our trader's

THE ADVENTURER

previous athletic ambitions to his current career. "In skiing, you went as far as you could; in trading, you went as far as you wanted." There are many professed obsessives profiled in this book, but *The Adventurer* is no longer one of them.

THE FIRST SUMMIT

The mountains are in *The Adventurer*'s blood. Hailing from a French village in the Alps, competitive skiing was his first love. Our future trader had a shot at the Junior Winter Olympics and won a college sports scholarship in the United States. This is important as several life experiences had prepared him for a strong start in his future trading career.

But in keeping with his realist streak, our trader quickly understood he would not make the cut for the Olympic team. The hard lessons he learnt through skiing would later allow him to avoid the same mistakes that so many other novice traders—his peers—succumbed to.

Like *The Collector* and *The Razor*, our trader also began his career at Firm Y, and he described one of his novice peers at the time. "He was always rewatching the same videos of price ladders, obsessed that he had found something. Yet he never progressed. I could see myself in the mirror. When I stopped skiing, I knew I could have trained in a more intelligent way. I brute-forced my training to get better, yet this is not enough to get to the top. Trading at the start is so demanding. Every minute you put in must be productive. If something is not working, you must move on. Often, I would lose trying to do the same thing. And so, each week, I tried to erase that trade."

By now, some readers are likely to protest that both of the above points—effective use of time and doing less of what does not work—seem obvious, but many traders and coaches would be quick to point out how rare it is to do the obvious.

We are sure that many would attest to long periods of missing the obvious, and entering messy, overcomplicated periods of their trading, lost in the process, lost in their identity and edge. Haywood highlights how this issue is not limited to novice traders. Those experienced and profitable can enter periods of working 'harder' as a psychological defence against bad drawdowns, to no avail.

For *The Adventurer*, there were other harsh lessons learnt racing down cold mountains. "It is fine if trading does not work out, but you cannot have regrets," he said. "It is the same in sport. If you want to become a professional, you need to try your best and push. I know many skiers who did not give all they could during training. Even ten years later, they are frustrated. They say how they could have done more; they could have reached the top—but it is too late. Give trading *everything*, and it is fine if it does not work. There are many other things to do in life."

The Adventurer's emphasis on the importance of perception extends to career direction, morale and reasons to continue. Our trader recollected a day when he was trading against a strong trending market and, with it, recalled a conversation with a legendary figure on the floor. "I was really losing during the day, yet by the end of it, I cleaned up like crazy. I had a debrief with this trader and he couldn't believe how I traded. He was amazed. My confidence just skyrocketed. I am sure he doesn't remember, but for me, this was everything. I looked up to him; for me, he was the god of trading." Even for *The Adventurer*, so self-assured that he would "make it," this affirming conversation was a perception shift, one of the "little things" that a novice trader forgoes when they trade in isolation, without a floor or community. The power of lineage within a community is profound.

All traders access the collective lineage, perhaps mythology, of the desks and trading community, to inspire, endure and even provide the seeds for the later blossoming of creativity to forge their own identity and edge. This mythology is *unique* to that community, built upon a network of shared personal and professional histories. One day, you will also recollect your own heroes and become one in the eyes of the next generation. And so, the cycle continues.

The Adventurer put well-earned lessons from ski racing to good use, dramatically so, as he became quickly profitable in his first year of trading in 2015 and consolidated in the second. But it was at this moment that the same events at Firm Y rocked the careers of many traders in this book, as it did for *The Adventurer*, with his account vanishing overnight.

Right on cue! Splendid timing! Our trader had just moved to Wrocław, Poland, and relied on his trading account to draw any semblance of cash flow. He was now jettisoned… no real savings, no account… abroad and alone.

But he soon became part of the inaugural team of the new AXIA–FCT partnership, and the loss was the gain of something else, a powerful shift in perception—*No Plan B!* If there is any pattern among these first few chapters, one that will continue throughout the following pages, it is that these traders become dangerously *excellent* when they have no choice. And, as we are about to explore, his true edge and talent lay in so much more.

"SOMETHING ABOUT THESE FRENCH TRADERS..."

The Adventurer, in many respects, is the complete opposite of *The Razor*. "I cannot tell you how I trade. I don't know what my edge is; there is no specific thing that I do," our trader said. But this is exactly what we expected him to say! His edge does not lie in structuring a trade like *The Razor*. Neither does he harbour a deep and documented understanding of the market like *The Engineer* or aggressively trade news headlines like *The Warrior*. Nor does *The Adventurer* limit himself to trading only some of the market behaviour like "momentum" or "reversals." "I never found one thing for myself, but I have many things that add up," he explained.

Indeed, he trades with all the approaches and tools previously mentioned, but his edge lies elsewhere and is noticeably twofold—a simple yet robust observational ability combined with masterful dynamic sizing of his positions. "It's something about these French traders," Haywood said, "who all seem masters in freestyling their trading, beautifully and dynamically managing their risk."

A common trait among these successful traders that can "dynamically" size their trade is an unbridled ability to trust their natural observations of the market more explicitly than others. *The Adventurer* is able to monetise his observational power as his frequent, intense trading creates a fast feedback loop. This ensures he is synchronised closely to the latest market behaviour, structures and environment. And identification of said environment is often half the game.

For example, a trader's edge that is predominantly "momentum"-based in a "range-bound" market environment might, at best, break even—and require considerable skill to do so. In comparison, a mediocre trader whose edge centres around "fading"—trading market reversals—would easily gain good profits while the market remains range-bound. An ability to correctly identify the environment overcomes average execution skill, explaining in part why novice traders might experience iterant periods of success yet remain inconsistent overall.

More so, the confidence these dynamic traders possess in their observational power is mirrored in their aversion to overcomplication. Our trader frequently discussed the *keep it simple, stupid!* principle and truthfully embodies it. Early in his career, our trader had listed every idea he had heard, seen or learnt. Through pure trial and error, he quickly found several trades that worked in that market environment and ran with them. The rest he'd figure out later. This is a refreshing contrast to many who overcomplicate the markets to justify a parchment hanging on their wall after years of studying more... overcomplication. As some say, perhaps they prefer to show they *know* markets rather than trade markets.

Haywood best describes what it's like watching *The Adventurer* trade. "He might be offside in a losing position for a long time yet be down relatively little. However, at the end of the day, he's cleaned up! He has a fantastic ability to wait for the perfect moment *then* attack with size when it really matters—when the trade turns in his favour." Thus, the dynamic trader is summarised.

And, to better understand why dynamic sizing works as an edge, we can explore the relationship between variance and 'adverse selection,' but we will splice, cut, retrofit and mould these concepts for our own needs, to better understand the purpose of intraday futures trading. In the theme of our trader, *KISS!*

Imagine that you are shopping for exotic fruits, and you find a trader who is selling them at lower prices than usual. *Exotic... rare... but how are they this cheap?* This price information should be sufficient to give pause as you assume this fruit trader, as the seller, likely knows far more about exotic fruit than you do, as you are a layperson and a buyer.

So, adverse selection is caused by the disparity of information between the buyer and seller, the lack of which benefits the exotic fruit seller if a transaction is made.

We can simplify to say that price alone is often *good enough* information to infer participant intent because of the knowledge or belief they hold. Price is inherently information; perhaps the fruit is much closer to expiry than you expect or is of lower quality. Perhaps it is not even exotic but a close, fake substitute.

You might never find out why the fruit is being sold aggressively. This information asymmetry is your reality as a proprietary trader. You are not a multi-national, conglomerate crude-oil trading desk tasked with hedging commercial clients with access to niche information flow. Nor a hedge fund with creatively expensive research and access to relatively esoteric markets. But it does not matter to a nimble intraday futures trader who is never obligated to hold any positions, who is flexible up to a certain point, permitting liquidity over a series of prices and seconds. You can be just as fickle as the market, and that can also be an advantage—*it has to be,* says a trader who manages positions dynamically.

And so, consider that the market price in a liquid, 'healthy' futures market reflects the latest action of the most determined participant. For example, if a participant hits the usually highly liquid U.S. Ten-Year futures and starts moving the price, then you know they are doing this for a reason. The firepower and aggressiveness needed to move a vast, liquid market so fast imply something is going on because a big participant never wants to move it otherwise. This might be a forced liquidation; perhaps there is rushed hedging activity or someone had the news earlier than anyone else. The reasons are different and endless—so wasting time arguing on the internet about it is futile—but the price moved all the same, and that is indisputable.

So, in a simplistic way, by dynamically managing your position, you can hope to turn someone else's knowledge into your own trade by piggybacking off their flow—you assume they know something you do not. And *unlike* the poker table or buying exotic fruits—a one-off event—trading a futures market is a continuous, infinite process permitting endless opportunities to enter or exit: fold, raise, buy and sell.

Roughly, then, it is using the fast, aggressive market efficiency to your advantage. But debating the nature of market efficiency is beyond our scope, yet for our purposes we can accept that it is *highly* but not perfectly efficient. You can *assume* the market is "nearly always right" and is trading higher or lower for a reason. This creates a truism for dynamic, outright futures traders—if you are in a winning position, there is likely a good reason for it. If you are in a losing position, there is *also* a good reason for it.

And so—act accordingly: size up! Size down! The greater the volatility and the stronger the momentum in the market, the faster participants are forced to make decisions in a compressed time period. This is when price information is at its most pure and easiest to observe. When markets are stagnant and non-volatile, the same effect plays out but on a much longer time horizon, thereby obscuring this behaviour of the market.

Each of the traders in this book has empirically observed the same behaviour and taken advantage of it. *The Warrior* summarises adverse selection when trading news or periods of high volatility in the markets—"I don't want to be the first guy to hit the news, but you always want to be the second." Let the market tell you what it wants to do.

So, the nature of adverse selection creates the basis for managing risk dynamically. If your trade is in a losing position—there is a reason for it, and you will never *truly* know why. But what you do know is that your risk and exposure should be minimal. Once that sequence of events plays out, and the trade is in a winning position, then something must have changed, and the trader should press their advantage alongside their trading size.

This is the essence of dynamic sizing, but the details of how it is executed change with each trader. These principles hold true for an outright, directional futures trader; other types of trading—hedged, spread trading or trading different instruments—blur the purity of dynamically managing trade in this way.

The Adventurer, then, enters and exits trades in much smaller amounts than most others. A standard procedure is to divide your maximum tradeable "lots" or futures contracts available to trade into "clips"—the usual being five clips.

These clips are a way to group your lots to enter and exit the market in manageable pieces. For example, one could trade a maximum of thirty lots on a specific futures contract and would then split these into six lots per clip. A single click on the price ladder enters the market with one clip or six lots. *The Adventurer* trades far more than thirty lots but still enters the market with one or two lots. He constantly scales in and out of his trades—*ClickClickClickClick*—and therefore adjusts to the natural *flow* and action of a trade. He would hold minimal size when in a losing position, but when the right flow presented itself, he would strongly and abruptly add to his trade to take out big chunks of profit.

This is the genius of his domain! He does not have to be an expert in various trade strategies; his self-adapting sizing allows him to circumvent the effect of *high* variance, an issue for traders who do not have full depth and expertise in a strategy to understand when they should not take a trade. In other words, the information and feedback he receives from markets by participating within them is paid 'cheaply' through minimal exposure.

'Variance' as a term is stretched widely within our own trading domain, and even more so outside it. But we will define and repur-

THE ADVENTURER

pose it sufficiently for ourselves, regarding variance as a set of potential outcomes of any given trade strategy. Each time we take a trade similar in strategy or objective, a different outcome may occur, adhering to a certain unknown chain of cause and effect, perhaps random but not quite. Different trades possess a range of outcomes, and most trades possess fairly high variance, so a large part of a trader's edge is to understand how they manage variance.

For example, certain niche trades possess very small or tight variance, and that is the domain of *The Razor*. He does not tolerate trades in a losing position—what price is doing is information enough—and so exits the trade. Others, such as *The Collector*, use a methodical breakdown and logging of market patterns to establish a potential cause and effect and place themselves in an environment of much lower variance. Therefore, they do not have to manage a trade *dynamically*. We can regard these traders as managing their positions *statically*. Entering only in periods of *low* variance permits static or nearly no management of a trade.

But *The Adventurer* is not a specialist in any trading strategy or environment and, therefore, exposes his biggest vulnerability—high variance. Figure 4.1, the Market Path Diagram, helps to visualise this point.

Consider that *The Adventurer* and any trader who manages his positions dynamically can be on any 'path' of a certain outcome of a trade. But he does not know what will happen next or know which path he is on. This is not important, as he adapts to the market through the order flow and price activity—the best singular piece of information. To our trader, the *only* piece of useful information.

Therefore, he is able to stay light and nimble in the market as the paths play out. When the right outcome presents itself, he will be in a position to increase his exposure and take profit. This high variance is countered by dynamic position management; take care of the journey, and the destination will present itself.

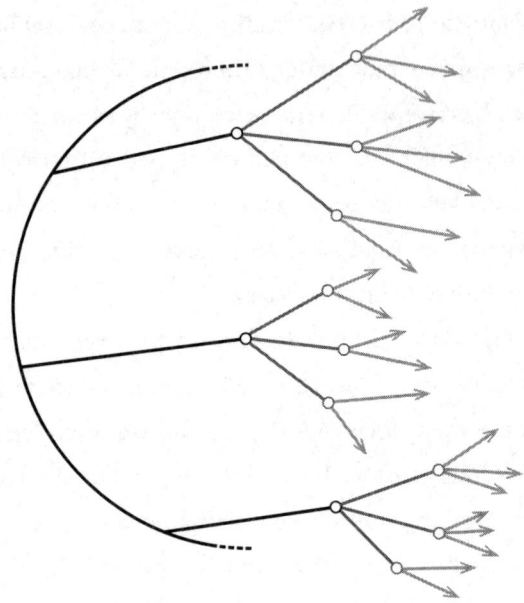

Figure 4.1 The Market Path Diagram.

The Adventurer describes the nature of this 'path' in his own words, built upon his confidence in his observational ability. "It is *never* one thing. It is always a mix of little signs. Let's say you have your 'ten traffic lights' of when you should take the trade, and you have eight that are now green—then you just go for it. It is not formally 'ten traffic lights,' of course, and sounds very silly to say it. Yet, in your head, you have a couple of signs that provide context, and that is enough." *Go for it!* Then figure out the rest with dynamic sizing.

The opposite of dynamic is static position management—all in, all out. Compare the highly structured nature of *The Razor*, *The Collector* and of others we will encounter later in this book. They deeply understand the *destination* of the trade and let the journey take care of itself. They do not need to be dynamic with sizing as they are only exposed to trades with very specific paths—subsequently sizing their trades as "all in, all out." For *The Adventurer*, his dynamic sizing is predicated on "scaling in, scaling out."

This is important for traders to understand, as too many novice traders mix risk management—an abused term—with dynamic management within a trade that is inherently highly structured, which, instead, is best served being managed as all in, all out.

In reverse, many other traders attempt to *statically* manage their exposure in trades that have too high variance, leading to inconsistency and frustration. In this situation, it is better to develop skills and tactics on how to best manage these trades dynamically, perhaps deployed in smaller and more frequent clips, like *The Adventurer*.

Nevertheless, many traders who size their trade dynamically fall prey to the usual mistakes—adding too late or early, not enough or too much. And certainly, this is a skill issue that is rectifiable through time and strenuous application. But there is also an undefinable part of what makes *The Adventurer* so effective in managing his trades, likely where *talent* plays its greatest role.

THE UNDEFINABLE

We can regard talent as the little bit extra that *emerges* when the component parts are aggregated. The ability of some traders to use their "negative" emotions in a purposeful way perhaps comes the closest to what we can tangibly designate as "talent," *The Adventurer* and *The Warrior* are both notorious for wearing their hearts on their sleeves.

The Adventurer recounted his own experience. "When I get angry at the desk, I think it is a way to tell myself, *Hey! Something is not working well. React!* I tried to be very calm for one year, and it was a disaster. I was going offside, onside and offside. I was just sitting there calm but not reacting. Then I started to get angry again, it was a lot better. I wasn't angry as much as before—since you feel stupid screaming so much alone at home." Nevertheless, this physical alarm created by these traders serves as this *undefinable* edge. Certainly, most traders can be wholly swallowed by sheer panic or anger-induced recklessness. Yet, as we will discover, *The Warrior* is at his best when he is the most animated, aggressive and loud. *The Adventurer*'s attempt to regulate his emotion reveals how important it was once lost or suppressed—his physical alarm seems crucial for himself, a trader who manages positions dynamically. "The more discretionary you are as a trader, the more you use your gut intelligence, or 'interoception,'" Haywood said. "Therefore, they have to create a physical trigger, an alarm to align themselves with what the market is actually doing."

Consider that the dynamic trader relies on adaptable sizing to "find their way" through the market variance—yet this undefinable, interoceptive edge helps them organise and define the current market behaviour. So, are all the traders in this book deemed "talented" because of their achievements? Or is it a product of each trader finding a way to play to their strengths, thereby making it look like talent in retrospect? Nearly every trader in this book will reaffirm the difficulty of predicting which new traders will be able to sustain a career, and finding "talent" early in a career is even more difficult. This is why we acknowledge that we can document certain attributes that could come close to explaining *The Adventurer*'s ability—to hypothesise on the fringes. Yet, we never fully bridge the gap due to the nebulous nature of *talent* overshadowed by the act of defining something undefinable.

PERCEPTION

Invariably, our conversations took place over food in cafés and restaurants in the market square, or *rynek*, of central Wrocław.

Speaking with purposeful pace and clarity, *The Adventurer* discussed the relationship between his high-level athletic career and trading, specifically within the context of perception, which is "very fundamental in how you see the game, maybe it is the most important thing."

How did you approach trading when you first started?
When I first went "live" as a trader [running a real money account], every day, I was losing more money than I had savings in the bank. When I think back, it was a crazy and scary situation, and at some point, I had twenty pounds left in my bank account. Of course, I could have eventually reached out for help, but I can't help thinking how precarious this was. But I *never* doubted for one second that I would make it. I was sure I would; I could see all around me how you could make money—and I just *knew* I was better than some of these other traders. In a way, no one had ever told me that it was impossible; I had no idea at the time the failure rate was so high.

How would you improve the success rate for newer traders or identify the reasons for a high failure rate?
A very difficult question. Maybe the low success rate is what it should be because for some traders to earn such incredible amounts, they have to be so few in number. I will still try to answer—it is hard since there are so many things in trading that can make you fail. You can have one big issue which overrides any strengths you may have. I have also noticed how many new traders who speak to me about

the markets seem to overcomplicate everything. Most of the time, after you talk to someone about trading for ten minutes, I can tell you if they understand trading or not. Sometimes, they just don't see *it*; they have no clue what you are speaking about, and you don't understand them either. It doesn't mean we all have to think the same of course, but it does feel like you are speaking a completely different language.

What is also very underappreciated at the beginning of your career is the ability to build regular yet smaller profitable days. Bring in six to eight hundred a day regularly. Even with a small trading size, there should be enough volatility to do this. But so many traders with potential can trade well for three weeks, and suddenly, in one week, they give it all back. Whatever happens, you need to do the right thing, and if you do this, you should keep the money you make.

How did competing as a high-level ski racer help you on your trading journey?
I think sport is such a good school for life. I think every kid should do some competition, so they learn to lose. To learn that it can be unfair. Some people run faster than you; some people are bigger and stronger. Even when you win, you learn to be humble without thinking you are the best in the world because in two weeks' time, you will see that you are not the best anymore. Like trading, every day is different in ski racing. The snow and the course can change. The inclination of the slopes, the temperature, the wind and the visibility change. Like trading, you can aim to reduce the impact of these variables on your race, and this is what the best do, to adapt to the snow and alter their turns. Traders like *The Warrior* or *The Engineer* can adapt to a slow day or a fast day, and this is why they are some of the best.

THE ADVENTURER

How did you learn to lose?
You don't win most of the ski races. Same with trading. You have some good times, but most of the time, you get punched in the face. For both racing and trading, it is very important to forget the day before. It is difficult to forget completely, but you must come back as a clean sheet and restart. I can be very emotional one day but I always wake up the next and be very positive. This is my strength. I remember others on the trading floor who would get so frustrated when they got stopped out by a tick. Trading is too frustrating? *No!* Imagine training for the biggest skiing race of the year, and you drive for ten hours to the other side of Italy to compete. But, by a small millimetre of error, you go on the wrong side of the gate during the race, and it is all over. You do not have a second chance. *That* is frustrating. You always have the option to get back in again if you are stopped out in trading.

How does this impact any drawdown or bad runs in your trading?
A trader doesn't need to destroy everything when they've had a bad run. Rather, calm down and be patient to come back into a positive cycle because, like everything in life, the profits increase your chances to make more. Losses increase your chance of losing. In skiing, it is the same; when you have a bad time and don't feel confident on your skis, you only wonder about when you will crash. When you have confidence, you are absolutely convinced you will not crash.

Do you have any tactics or processes that you use to get out of a bad run in trading?
It is very difficult to stop a bad trading spiral, but it is easier when you try to think longer-term. Imagining where your returns were six months ago compared to now, it does not look as bad. I was going wrong before when I was trying to change too many things during a

bad run. But that doesn't mean you should be passive. You should come back to simple principles and focus on the things you can control. Accept that it is unlikely you will make millions the day after a bad run and just focus on the trade ahead. Slowly, you regain confidence after a few small successful trades, yet it provides you the opportunity to hit a big trade, which gives you much more breathing space.

Therefore, the best thing sometimes is to do *nothing* and keep trading without doing anything too stupid. On the other hand, everyone tells you to trade the market and not the P&L. Yet at some point, if your bad trading spiral is bad enough, you *do* have to trade according to your P&L. Sometimes, you just need to pick a positive number out of your trading account and regard that as the new "zero," the hard floor. All of a sudden you will really trade like you mean it; like I say—it is always about perception.

Lastly, do not underestimate the power of just going outside to take a break. Look at other things in your life; appreciate spending time with friends. Maybe, you are lucky with your family life or passionate about something else. This is why it's so important to have a life outside trading. It is even harder if you have nothing else. When trading goes wrong, there is just so much more pressure.

How do you look back on some of the P&L milestones in your career?
Here is another example of the importance of perception. My first thousand-pound day was in the Bund, trading nine lots on some risk-off move. At the time it felt *amazing*, but that is now normal, mundane—yet that first day still feels special. Compare that situation to my first six-figure trade many years later. I could have acted like the king of the *rynek*! Instead, I felt very vulnerable after such a trade, so I turned off my computer and went outside. Maybe it *was* stupid to turn off my computer, as the trade that came after was very easy. Even

so, I knew to be careful because of the dangers of how you feel after performing extremely well or badly. I only focused on making a few thousand again the next day so I could consolidate.

◆ ◆ ◆

And shift perception he did. Not long after his first six-figure trade and having just restarted from 'zero' following a complete account loss during the debacle at Firm Y, our trader had rebuilt his account to just under two hundred thousand euros.

But then, within a short space of time, he drew down to just shy of fourteen thousand euros. However, that is when our trader came into his own, finding an inner consistency and resilience that Kyriacou frequently lauds as part of our trader's talent, a consistency only rivalled by *The Razor* and *The Collector*. "We cut the size and just restarted small," our trader said. "In a couple of months, I traded well and built back up to ninety thousand. Just by banking two- or three-thousand days without fail," Not long after, *The Adventurer's* account sailed right past its previous high.

But why drawdown so much and so fast? "I was a bit too easy with myself since I performed well before. And so, you give the first ten to twenty per cent back; it is only when you start being honest with yourself, and the earlier, the better; you can put a stop to it. Yet it is a very difficult compromise. If you can be extremely diligent in not losing like *The Razor*, that is amazing, but on some days, you *have* to accept losing," *The Adventurer* continued. "That two-thousand loss can easily transform into twenty thousand. All of a sudden, that two-thousand loss now looks much better. Later, you start to fight and fight, yet lose and lose—then you start onto the highway of loss. Instead, you can just liquidate everything and go outside. You will live."

KING OF THE RYNEK

"And not only did we do it, but we traded it with bigger size than we could have ever dreamed. Like every trader, you have so many instances of bad luck—like a toilet break just as the biggest trade of the week happens. Yet it is really amazing that in one trade, all the bad luck was made back tenfold." Such was the conclusion of *The Adventurer* on the 'limit-down' trade as it happened on the fateful night of the emergency Federal Open Market Committee (FOMC) rate cut in March 2020. We described that very same trade with *The Razor* and others in the Wrocław office and community that managed to pull off this series of trades. For *The Adventurer*, the returns of the entire month had nearly matched his cumulative lifetime returns. How about that for *perception*?

"I really compare it to a sportsman who has trained and prepared since he was ten or fifteen years old, and by chance, on the day of the Olympics, he wins the gold medal," our trader said. "If I was not experienced as a trader like this, I would have never managed to take this trade with the size I put on." *The Adventurer* would go on to consolidate the trade of over seven figures in the subsequent year. He would eventually resume many of the activities we described when we introduced him, exploring "the other things in life," investing in his family's future and diversifying outside of trading. Haywood highlights how successful traders can often be the worst investors, recalling stories of others mismanaging their personal trading fortune due to hubris or naïvety. Yet, *The Adventurer* is keenly aware of these implications; further success and security widen the gulf between those who enjoy the comfort of success and the bloody-hungry, the driven traders who possess *No Plan B!* The gulf becomes dangerous to fall into.

More dangerous in the context of our trader's worldview, who, by his own admission, no longer possesses his original love for the markets and only trades as a means to an end. As such, we return to the same question we originally asked: what comes *next* for our trader after "success"? Or at what point will he decide he has truly gone as far as he wanted?

"I bought a nice house, but I am not going to buy seven—what is the point?" our trader said. "We all know by now that this will not make you happy. It is still fascinating for me that humans are happy when we go 'above' us and help family and friends. Last year I met with my former schoolteacher in my home village and bought thirty books on French history to give to the kids. It is the small things like this by which you can influence the community around you, and it is better than having no money at all. It would be my dream, for example, to help out a friend with a talented kid to send them to a top school or university."

What followed was a deeper discussion between *The Adventurer* and Haywood. "Now that you are financially secure, could you have less stamina?" he asked. "During a tough day, it is easier to give up. If you had no choice due to a bad financial situation, you would not give up. Do you think this attitude creates a vulnerability? It is easier to say—screw this! I got my money."

"Yes and no," *The Adventurer* replied. "Like when we discussed that huge two-hundred-thousand drawdown previously, I had to restart very tight. I can't easily just give up, and I still see this as a career. But if my account goes to what I deem as 'zero'—it is over in my head."

"But it is still dangerous if your commitment to trading is different. A committed *Adventurer* is a different animal," Haywood said. "We've seen how amazing you traded after your steep drawdown and how consistent you became. You've also been able to get away with it because of your raw talent. Now, with your investments and security, you become a different person. At this stage, maybe it is worth focusing more on getting bigger as a trader…" he paused. "Do you even want to get bigger?"

"The way I see it, I first want to move away the bulk of my wealth and income from my trading account," *The Adventurer* replied. "Some traders have nearly eighty per cent of their money just in their trading account. I think the evolution from that point onwards is knowing I can still trade less but be very focused and committed when I do. I know I am going up against other traders who are on the floor all the time. But I personally do not want this type of life. There is an alternative, but also a compromise, like accepting that you will miss many trades and moments in the market."

"But I will probably have more stability in the future, being grounded in Wrocław with my family, and it is likely the way in which I will have to evolve again," he continued. "I hate routine, but I do need to add a bit more structure. As for returning to a trading floor, I never exclude doing so if it needs to be done."

◆ ◆ ◆

There is no conclusion but rather an open-ended possibility, as this reflects the reality of dealing with traders at this level. In the end, *The Adventurer* will have to find the answers himself. Perhaps he will never have to deal with the issues discussed above, and newer ones will appear in the future.

Our trader is acutely aware of the dangers upon his sense of meaning if he chases performance and money for its own sake. As we discussed in the beginning, *The Adventurer*'s abilities and worldview are a reminder that not all approach it in the same way.

THE ADVENTURER

And that has a profound impact. The cursory experience of some new traders embarking on their careers reveals 'narrow' goals, perhaps naïvety about their expectations of future fulfilment and no other sense of purpose beyond adding "an extra zero to your trading account." *The Adventurer's* story is a counter to this, reflecting a more mature, wiser expectation of what comes *after* a trader's "success" and its implications for their career. One day, this could become the most sobering and relevant chapter of all.

PRACTITIONER'S POSTSCRIPT

Explore resources derived from this chapter to further support the practicing trader.

axiafutures.com/
toot

Refer to
The Adventurer's
section.

LEARNER'S IMPRESSIONS

Below are some personal impressions that *The Adventurer* made on us that we still discuss with other traders.

1. *The power of perception.* This is as evident within an individual trade as it is subtle within career development. What happens after "success"? What of the blissful ignorance of the difficulties ahead for the new trader? What of the counter-intuitive powers of *No Plan B!* when it begins to force matters? *The Adventurer* is cognisant

that his desires no longer match performance maximisation and of the trade-offs that entail. Perception is inextricable from the life of a market navigator, lest they allow it to become their jailor. Those who reshape it in their favour truly win.

2. *Dynamic sizing.* Our trader's fine ability in dynamic sizing allows him to follow the 'path' or outcome of a trade without becoming a specialist within it. It requires the ability to scale in and out of trades to stay in the market for as long as possible until the trade plays out. Managing size—increasing or decreasing risk—in a trade must be contextually applied to the right trades at the right time. Some trades are hindered by dynamic size management; other situations demand it.

3. *Lineage.* This is one way to value a community and trading floor. Our trader described his strong confidence boost after being lauded by other "Gods" of the trading floor. Yet that generation had their own Gods, as those that came before them. Another exercise in perception. Some find confidence in their words; others find inspiration in successfully recreating their trading identity. Best practices are reinforced by the approval of the experienced. A small pebble with distant ripples; at the bottom of the lake lie thousands thrown by generations before.

What are your impressions? Write them down and converse with this book!

CHAPTER FIVE

THE WARRIOR: PART I

"Remember, the first to cut was the Fed, followed by a global coordinated rate cut by all major central banks. Equities just kept melting each day, and it was nonstop risk-off; financial conditions worsened, debt repayment questions, the…"

Ah, the '07–'08 Crisis stories. It was just before his time, but our trader remembered how he once sat there—dark, wavy hair, chubby-cheeked, fresh-faced—as the other juniors fantasised, glorified, mythologised the stories they heard. *Some of them lifted, like, I don't know! Hundreds, thousands of S&Ps! They were all up millions; only minutes after the headlines hit!*

By now, our trader had lived these stories for over ten years. He imagined them in the shower; he visualised it while eating dinner and dreamt about it in the car. The correlations that would come into play, the type of headlines to dominate all others, visualising how he would fire off maximum clips into the markets just before they fly off the screen. *The surprise big cut! Lift two year… lift Spoos… lift Stoxx… hit Bund*—everything, the order of attack; the clicks, the size; how much and how fast? This *is* visualisation, and our trader does it—but does it *more so*—he feels it, believes it, whips himself into a mania, a fervour—an unrelenting, violent display of *attack, attack, attack!*

He transforms and unleashes something monstrous… a warrior-type spirit, Haywood says, and for *The Warrior*, this is what he needs to execute, to push and drive, to squeeze every last drop out of the market—to trade as if it were the last day on Earth.

Then! A virus started to spread through the world. Some governments were already enforcing "lockdowns"—*will they work? Will it finally be acknowledged as a pandemic? How will other countries respond?* Now the financial markets finally started to take notice. The signs of stress were already there in the rates, the credit markets, commodities and then, finally, equities. A placid breeze in February was, by March, a gale. And the sense of occasion was burning on the trading floor. Yes—markets *were* moving, but we had not reached the twist, the explosion, the blowing off the top—the rupture, the tear—when the markets reach peak, absolute, unrelenting, heart-stopping, gut-spilling, soul-screeching *climax!*—and this was one of those times, a page-turn away.

And *The Warrior* felt *it*, the trade of trades. He was going to throw everything at it. The group on the first floor at 4 Endsleigh Street dispersed and sat back at their desks. Our trader rearranged his price ladders in accordance with the anticipated market correlations. Trading floor conclusion: *The Fed cut is coming, and they will cut big, maybe bazooka cuts.*

◆

The Warrior glanced around his desk. His entire semi-circle of monitors was perfectly aligned; price ladders were fixed. With one eye trained on the screens, he sped through the montage in his head—the play-by-play, short-end flows, long-end reacting... STIRs; the dollar, the equities... *The Sphinx* and *The Collector* recalled how central banks released statements exactly at the turn of the hour. Our trader set his alarm: *11.59 p.m., 12.59 p.m. and 1.59 p.m.*

But time ticked on. *12 p.m. Nothing. 1 p.m. Nothing. 2 p.m. Nothing!*

He spent the whole day hopping in and out of markets, trading them and feeling them. But his P&L slowly ground down into the red, getting nowhere. It was pointless, *and the Fed rarely acts after the market opens*, he groaned.

He leaned back in his chair in a state of general nausea, and unwell. And that is a rarity; *The Warrior* is known to trade turbulent, volatile weeks, to then hit the clubs on weekends, and then straight back into his chair by Monday twilight—*fresh*. "Supernatural stamina," as described by Haywood... *But now... this? Why am I so ill now of all times?* Our trader glanced left towards *The Godfather* and Haywood, who sat perched at their desks...

... He sank further into his chair, his body loosening up after trading all day. He sighed and glanced out of the window... *What if we have to lock down the office?*

University students were still wandering around, and takeaway drivers darted by on bikes and motorcycles. *I wonder what I will eat today. Maybe I will*—DINGDING!

FED CUTS RATES BY 50 BASIS POINTS – 15:00:00

The trading floor roars! The markets rocket off everyone's screens. *The Warrior* feels like he will explode—he does. He leaps out of his seat and dives towards his mouse, *No, no, no!*—the most valuable seconds in the industry are now lost, *What the fuc*—

Get in! Get in! GET IN! He throws himself all over the S&P ladder—*Any price! Any price! Just max it out*—*please, please, please!*

But then he sees it. He starts to feel trapped, bile churning in his liver, disbelief—his soul eaten alive. Because nothing appears on his confirmation window.

No fills. No position.

What? Why?

He shoots his cursor over the S&P ladder and tries to lift more prices. Nothing! *Why am I not getting filled?* Again! Nothing. Again! Nothing.

The Warrior is breathless—his fists slam the desk—his feet rumble the floor beneath him. An animal trapped in a tightening cage. He cries out—shrieks and yells—"I can't get filled! I can't get filled! W–what is going on?" *It's slipping away...* He is dizzy, faint, then—rage; terrible rage—he sees red.

"HOW IS THIS HAPPENING TO ME?!"
The frustration is unbearable. Agony.
It overwhelms him.

This moment! How has it been stolen from me? HOW? How did God allow this to happen... this—*INJUSTICE!*

His fist smashes the metal drawer next to him.

In eleven years! Nothing! Nothing like this ever happened—the unfairness! How could it have happened—

En ginete reee!

His heart is crushed. *Then!* His headphones play garbled, warped noises of order confirmation sounds. *I'm in! In! Filled, filled!*

◆

The Warrior has lost the first forty seconds of the move, and those seconds are everything. The system lag abates, and it finally displays the correct prices and positions. But he is filled at higher prices, *much* higher—the worst prices possible. He has paid up dearly.

Millions! I've lost out on millions! I've missed the easiest part. Thoughts race through his head, he seethes; the anger—*injustice! Cheated!* He splays himself all over the markets; he lifts five hundred S&Ps, a thousand Stoxx and a hundred DAX lots at terrible, horrible prices. *Loser prices.*

But the market is still bid, reacting as it trades higher and higher. *Okay, maybe I can salvage this, but it was stolen! I will never get out! No, no... I won't get out. Never. I deserve to get paid no matter what. It was stolen!*

The Warrior trades in a haze of anger; stapled to his desk, exasperated, injured, he fights. The S&P is now trading seventy handles higher—two hundred and eighty ticks higher! And *The Warrior* is in $700,000 profit. *It was stolen!*

All the years he has spent visualising and preparing for this trade, but the dream does not match reality. His guts boil. *What I could have made!*

His P&L is now $800,000... 900,000... 960,000—nearly one million! No, *I am not getting out.*

But then the markets begin to reverse. They wash back—and so too the P&L—$700,000… 600,000; 500,000; 400,000… *I can't accept this.*

Haywood has sat next to *The Warrior* for years and knows him well. He has seen him lose himself and give back enormous days. Even then, he rarely intervenes, only when our trader is in the darkest of places—but this is one of those times.

"Don't let this go red. Just don't do that," Haywood pleads softly. "Don't let it go red… you are up half a million on the day. You know it can reverse—we discussed it. Don't do it to yourself—cover the trade." *I'm not giving up on the trade. No matter what.*

The markets retrace their entire excursion.
The Warrior loses everything that the day has to offer; a day he has been waiting for over a decade.
He falls silent.
What have I done to deserve this?
He slams his desk for the final time, he screams; parts of his soul escape him.
Pain.

◆ ◆ ◆

This moment, the peak—the gyration of events, of positioning, re-pricing, narratives and themes that suddenly click into place and then *shatter*, a singular watershed moment is the entirety of *The Warrior*'s career. A trader of a sample set of one—of these tail events. Whereas others may trade the ninety-nine samples that condition the markets, he trades the—*surprise!*—the very next sample, to break all the rules.

To do so is to be a volatility-hunting global macro-news trader, and just look at his desk! The space is renowned in our small corner of the world, more akin to a jet fighter's cockpit with fourteen screens consisting of price ladders, news terminals, X feeds, charts and more that envelop our trader. Strewn across his desk are numerous mice and keyboards; underneath them lie myriad computers, audio equipment and power supply back-ups. For an outsider, this set-up may seem overwhelming, shrouded in mystique to leave observers stunned as they are watching *The Warrior* trade.

A spectacle indeed, but his trading engine is as blunt and straightforward as it is slick and precise. *The space reflects the man.* Thoughtful craftsmanship mirrors the intensity of purpose: built for speed, built to execute and built to conquer. The man who sits here is a trader's trader.

"His peers would describe him as the dominant force on the floor," Haywood said, "a showman—the nucleus of our trading desks." And he is the benchmark of *absolute* performance—P&L, size, conviction and soul in the game. He is the standard-bearer—and standard-setter—to constantly push the boundaries of what is deemed possible. *The Warrior* is one of the most frequently cited and positively credited traders by others in this book, and by more across the proprietary trading industry. Should you ever best our trader in *any* aspect, then you have become a unique and very dangerous individual indeed. *Ultra*-lethal.

And, readers, let us begin with a stand-off, for he is so good as a news trader because he is *not*—as one might expect—a news trader to be. Instead, he is a supreme, savant-like tactician of the price ladder and order flow, a shrewd operator within market correlations, in which he fights and presses for each and every tick, every last penny, pound, cent and dollar—a master of dynamic position management. As experienced and knowledgeable as he is in macro-fundamentals—

trading headlines, comments, central bank action, large repricing events—it just so happens, by historical accident, these market phenomena just fit his order flow skills; he is a master of momentum.

You have just read an account of the most painful event of *The Warrior*'s career, missing the Federal Reserve fifty basis rate cut of 3 March 2020 due to a system malfunction. A massive influx of orders hit various futures exchanges as the rate cut was announced, and this overwhelmed the front-end software used by many traders to execute orders and view live market prices. The software displayed outdated prices, behind by a few seconds. When *The Warrior* attempted to execute an order at the prevailing market price in the S&P futures, the actual market price was considerably higher. What should have been *at-market* orders were left behind as limit orders far below the market. Our trader has seen this occur only a handful of times in his entire career. *Sod's law*.

But this is only a fraction of events *The Warrior* has traded over the past fifteen years, including the Brexit Referendum results, national elections, countless central bank meetings, the Trump–China trade war, the Iranian retaliatory attack on U.S. bases after the assassination of Qasem Soleimani, the Covid-19 vaccine announcements, the beginning of the 2022 Russia–Ukraine conflict, the end of zero-interest-rate policy—at least for now—in the biggest economies and other historical, macro-economic and geopolitical flashpoints.

Through trading all of these, he's long since passed various milestones—eight-figure P&L years, a collection of seven-figure trading days—and he is still growing in trading size.

But! Forget the flashiness about his upside; what about the downside? In contrast to what observers and other traders might imagine, *The Warrior* combines aggressiveness with an unbelievable consistency, a steadiness relative to his explosive nature. Over the past five years

THE WARRIOR: PART I

The Warrior has experienced only two down-months a year. His biggest up-day is roughly three times his biggest down-day, and he has sustainably grown a £50,000 account from 2016 into eight figures by 2020. Like *The Razor* and *The Adventurer*, our trader's old six-figure account was lost in Firm Y's meltdown.

But his P&L curve, as Haywood shows, is steady from the first day of live trading in 2009. And this is what *The Warrior* emphasises the most, at times barely interested in discussing mere *upside* matters—the best traders, he said, are the ones that keep it all. To lose only two, when you make ten, as others lose twelve. Even at his darkest moments, *The Warrior* did not let the painful events of the missed Fed rate cut excuse losses.

Yes! An escaped opportunity, and for *The Warrior*, that is inexcusable, outrageous, a good reason to fire a trader—but the whole trade was scratched: break-even, of meagre P&L values, not in the deep and bloody red. And in the long run, as painful as it ever is, letting *that* position during the March 2020 rate cut come back was strategically—career-wise—the *right* decision in the right context. And we will explore why. Anyone can blunder into money, but keeping it is the real game. And he is one of the best to play it.

There is something compelling and charming about our trader, disarming visitors to his trading cove when the markets are quiet. Affable and warm, our trader—a Greek Cypriot—bears a trademark smile, eagerness and good spirits, his olive skin and pitch-black wavy hair in contrast to his gold-striped Real Madrid tracksuit and white trainers. There is a boyish nature to be found. Talk to him long enough, and you feel an endearing child-like enthusiasm for everything he does, no story too small or boring to uncover a new perspective.

Catch him in good spirits, and it is not unknown for lucky junior traders to spontaneously find themselves in our trader's (in)famous jet-black Taycan, en route to a private members' club in Mayfair or partying the Greek way—*Bouzoukia!*—where our trader is busy smashing dinner plates. "After a whole week at the desk, people think I would sit at home and relax, do yoga. This is not me. I am not the yoga type—I need to blow off steam." *Smashing desks during the week—smashing plates during the weekend!* He grinned—"Ha! That's good—write that in!" And like all big traders, he has time for the small ones. He listens to you, eyebrow raised, and the ensuing discussion guarantees you leave feeling wiser, a deep empathy lost on no one.

But! We cannot discuss our trader without trying to understand *"it."* Catch our trader on a volatile market day, and you will meet an entirely different person. A *Jekyll and Hyde*-like transformation—Stevenson himself stunned to see what hides within our trader. Once the volatility hits, the shouting, stomping, chomping and rage peak and trough with cries of pain, misery and desperation. Our trader's desk is only saved from the hail of fist-slamming due to the equally abused filing cabinet on our trader's right, which takes turns with his wooden desk as he relieves his frustrations. Like *rolling thunder,* as some traders call it, as the stomping vibrations reverberate throughout the building, serving as a signal for those meandering in the kitchen to run back to their trading desks; likely a surprise comment or headline has just hit the newswires.

Stranger still, as the new floor runner—the new kid—would discover by the ill-timed delivery of food or Greek frappe, our trader would sustain this mania towards his computer while trading, only to completely turn around to the new floor runner and instantly transform back to Dr Jekyll—the Cypriot's nice, endearing and calm self. Having thanked the runner and received his delivery, our trader would turn back to face his computer once more and resume his bestial, Mr Hyde-like mania, as he tackled the market volatility.

THE WARRIOR: PART I

Idiosyncratic, Haywood says, but our trader is very much *in control*. Outsiders would understandably be worried, imagining that our trader is perhaps experiencing an existential meltdown due to enormous losses or... *something*, rather. But the near opposite is true, and for whatever reason, the more our trader wears his emotions and enters this bestial state, the more he is focused. Because *everything* is a fight to the death, and it is a gruesomely morbid spectacle when the volatility has him whipped into a relentless fervour. Even when hugely profitable, he can be infinitely frustrated at lost opportunities—*Stolen! Injustice!* With an ultra-competitive mentality, he has the need to always outperform, he says, to always be the benchmark, and he cannot find a sliver of peace otherwise. But in this state, he is at his best to intuitively feel, to respond to the order flow and make instant decisions, cut positions or run them, to maintain tight risk management.

This is the experience of "dying at the desk," as Haywood calls it. Recall with *The Razor*, we examined the burden of strategy and the real-world implications that different trading methods and strategies have on your life. It will run counter to the glamour that veils the darker side of our sport. Because *The Warrior* is as addicted to trading as he passionately hates his trading desk, he feels caged and bound by it, hating the monster it requires him to become—not to mention the unrelenting physical stamina and presence macro-news trading demands.

However, this is not an open invitation for our readers to copy this mania and emotional outpouring to become better traders. *The Warrior* describes it as a "horrible habit" picked up from his early days, but it speaks to his savant-like nature to trade better the angrier he becomes.

Certain traits are double-edged—help your trading, hurt your life—and novice traders should note that emotions in trading are highly complex. A popular retail trading trope assumes that *all* successful traders must work towards shedding or discarding emotions to become paragons of emotional control, machine-like and "hyper-rational" in decision-making.

But empirically, the traders in this book cover the entire spectrum. *The Engineer* is librarian-like in comparison, but as he says, he just processes his emotions differently. *The Razor* is very aware of his emotional nature, and so chooses to shoulder the burdens differently to ensure he does not bear the unbearable weight of long exposure to the markets. *The Hero*, too, is expressive, loud—like *The Warrior*—a caged wild animal. But, as they all say, it never becomes easier. You do not 'ascend' your emotions. Traders just find different ways to use them effectively. Because the pain is a learning mechanism, Haywood says, and "this is similar to what Josh Waitzkin explains about Marcelo Garcia, who is widely considered to be one of the best grapplers in Brazilian jiu-jitsu. He is one of the best because he viscerally feels the pain of a mistake and so he never repeats it a second time."

The visceral response is precisely what drives *The Warrior* to adapt his execution to whatever is new in the markets; the intensity of feelings created by reviewing relatively poor execution becomes too much to bear. We go darker and deeper, as *The Warrior's* feedback loop from the pain, on some level, is intertwined with his intense and intuitive *feel* for the market order flow, the most common word he uses to describe decisions.

Now we shall investigate the nature of an event that blindsided markets, one that dissipated as fast as it arrived. In other words, an event that is unique.

THE WARRIOR: PART I

A MEXICAN STANDOFF, JANUARY 2020

She looked at him; having spent the better part of Christmas and New Year together in Tulum, it was good to see him muster the courage to be away from his desk. For once, he looked... relaxed. *Let's not jinx this*, she thought. *You know how terrified he is of being jinxed.*

The beach bar was alive, and music filled the air as the hotel guests made the most of their remaining time. She glanced back at him. With whisky in one hand and his phone in the other, his expressions shifted as he graduated from giggles to talking under his breath, smiling still. Strangely, in some circles, he is referred to as *The Warrior*. He is peaceful.

Then –

What?! His phone began pinging notifications. *Soleimani... U.S. strike... Iranian...* he managed to catch some of the words as they scrolled by. Get the charts! There it is—classic risk-off. Glaring from his screen, Crude Oil and Gold futures were hugely bid, and equity markets sold off.

He started to feel his heart slowly sink, feeling heated—sick. *Can't you just wait?* He leaned back into his chair and continued to sip his drink, ruminating.

"We are flying back tomorrow, right? On Monday..."

"No, remember, the flight was delayed, we will only get back on Tuesday night. On the seventh," she said.

Fysika! He sank deeper into the chair—*please God, can you just wait for me?*

◆

"So, that is how I started 2020," *The Warrior* said.

The new kid, Theo, sat adjacent. The trading floor was quiet for a Wednesday afternoon, so it was a good opportunity to learn from *The Warrior*. Our trader was happy to have newbies visit his desk; today, he was especially talkative.

"During that weekend, there was talk of potential Iranian retaliation to Soleimani's assassination by striking back at American military bases," *The Warrior* said. "Of course, the level of uncertainty would go through the roof if that happened." He retold further details as if top of mind, but these were, in fact, recollections of over two years ago.

"You need to see how the market *reacted* to understand where the sensitivity lies and what could potentially happen next on this theme. We are always trading on what is next, not on what already happened," *The Warrior* continued.

◆

Jet-lagged after his long flight, he flicked on his computer, and the semi-crescent of more than a dozen monitors lit up—an exact replica of his office trading machine situated in his apartment.

Just gone nine. The computer finished loading his price ladders; in front of him sat the world's futures markets—equities, bonds, currencies and commodities. She peered in; the glare of the monitors lit up the dark bedroom, drawing a long silhouette around our motionless trader. *I hope he doesn't have a long night.*

Then! The S&P price ladder jutted off the screen. *What's this blip? Unusual after the U.S. close…* He scanned news terminals and Twitter feeds, glancing at reporters tweeting *something* about some sort of attack.

THE WARRIOR: PART I

Eh… ask questions later. He sold S&P futures and bought Crude Oil contracts. *ClickClickClickClick.*

The prices bubbled up and down. *Tickticktick… going nowhere—Bang!* Reversal; the S&P ripped higher, and Crude Oil offers-in-kind—*Out!*

He printed a $70,000 loss.

Gamó!—he banged the desk.

He started to seethe. *The first trade of the year is a loser! I should have switched off my screens and gone to bed. Am I jinxed? Where did I go wrong? Am I wearing any red? Red clothes… red clothes… no… maybe it is that new runner on the floor;* he hadn't been unjinxed yet.

He lay down on his bed, writhing, turning and tossing as he replayed the events in his head. The anger overwhelmed his fatigue, and he stayed awake for the rest of the night.

◆

Our trader turned back to Theo. "In a fast-developing situation like this, your only choice is to trust the market reaction, and it is the speed that counts. Your risk–reward is often at its best if you can get those first prices. But in that specific case, it turned out to be a false alarm, and the market retraced. This practice depends on where you are in the *theme*—the start, the peak or the end. It is very important to *not* be aggressive when we are dealing with a theme that is past its peak, in other words, a well-known theme."

He shifted in his chair, readjusting his poker-chip-themed cushion. "Often in these situations, a loud bang or explosion will get lost in translation," he continues. "It will reach a Twitter [now X] account with a bigger following, which in turn will get reposted and so on.

Then it later impacts the market, even if it is unconfirmed, random news—anyway, you control your risk. You puke it. Try again later."

◆

Two hours later, he was still lying on his bed; the mix of anger and fatigue still plagued him. *What's wrong with me? Am I going to be like this all night?*

PINGPING! His phone glared into the dark room, vibrating with more Twitter notifications—news that American military bases were being fired upon. He leapt back to his desk. *Only a few minutes until the CME reopens...* He messaged *The Sphinx, The Godfather* and others. They agreed to go for Crude Oil, Gold, T-Notes and S&P futures.

Market open! But choppy flow. Muted. Nothing... our trader had mainly bought Crude Oil futures; *tick up, down, up, down... up... down...* He felt it; he lived every tick and every fluctuation. Making money, losing money. Making. Losing... slow and grindy... *am I right or wrong?* His breathing changed, the wait became frustrating, the anticipation—minutes felt like hours. *Losing fortunes in a tiny range. Chopped to pieces again... amazing—Bravo! Well done!* He stomped the floor. *God, please. Please don't do this to me again.*

But then the drift gathered pace. Momentum was starting to build—fast—then faster! The flow became strong and consistent, and an acceleration took hold. Already having worked other positions, our trader bought Gold, Oil and T-Notes and sold the S&P. There it was—*risk-off, finally.*

His cursor started to bounce and pivot around his screens, over his price ladders, flicking in orders and covering others—*DINGDING! RINGRING!* His headphones began to combine order sounds and confirmations into one massed ensemble. His mouse continued to weave around the desk—*DINGDING!* He frantically whipped around across his desk, as if holding a conductor's baton, the mouse cursor dancing around bid and offers—*bid, bid, bid; offer, offer, offer*—the market ebbed and flowed, he increased positions—a hundred and fifty Oil and Gold; three hundred in T-Notes—

ClickClickClickClickClickClick

Short two hundred S&Ps—long safe haven, short risk and long Oil.

Then! The news wires picked up the story. The Iranian Revolutionary Guard publicly confirmed they had launched an attack.

Markets are going nuts! He felt as if he'd been swallowed whole. His heart beat faster, feet scurried under his desk. His eyes darted around his screens, filled with price ladders and news headlines.

His body heated up, he felt it on his face, in his chest.
Come on!
His breathing was shallower.
The world compressed around him.
The pace of it!
His adrenaline surged.
No longer tired, it felt like he could go on forever.
Hours and hours. Time is fast. Time is slow.
Volatility as methamphetamine.
His mouse reached orchestral fervour.
His body danced around the conductor's baton.
DINGDING. DINGDING.
Bid, bid, bid! Offer, offer, offer!
He carried four positions across markets.
And they were screeching.
Maximum pace.
Now!

His P&L lurched higher.

$100,000—200,000; 300,000; 400,000; 600,000.

This is it! The last legs.

The Gold and Oil markets kept rallying,

Their bids and offers skipped higher off the screens.

Peak market fever. *Then –*

CRESCENDO!

He aggressively covered his positions—out, out, out!

The markets exhausted;

silence.

Two hours experienced as seconds,

a conclusion of tonight's performance.

An Ode to Risk.

◆

"There you go. Had I not taken that loss, which so enraged me, I probably would have fallen asleep and missed the first big move," he smiled. "As they say, God works in mysterious ways." He tilted back in his chair.

Theo always noticed *The Warrior*'s physicality in trading. His feet and posture, alertness. He put his soul into every market tick.

"So, Theo. Do you understand the events?"

Theo recounted the story. It was a classic risk-off flow due to increasing geopolitical uncertainty. Fast participants were already selling risk assets like equities, anticipating larger institutional players would do the same, and rotating into safe-haven assets like Treasuries and Gold.

Even if the large participants do not eventually do this, the market temporarily behaves as if they will. Though, as *The Warrior* reminded him, what's regarded as a safe haven depends on the market conditions at the time; should things get too wild, then even long-end bonds—the ten and thirty year—can get sold off as *duration* becomes a risk. In this particular case, Crude Oil futures were bid due to the anticipation of a supply shock should a large-scale war engulf the Middle East.

This created a correlation between markets—the real answer *The Warrior* was waiting for. If Crude Oil traded higher first, then the S&P would get sold in response, so the flow in the Crude Oil futures would have led the night. The key is navigating these ever-changing correlations. They can flip from positive to negative, powerfully linked or very loose, non-existent relationships.

"And once we had *confirmation* of the move, my style is to start increasing my positions and exposure very aggressively," *The Warrior* continued. "This one was a slow-burner, not an instant reaction, and that changes how you execute. Once I had built up positions in those four markets, I was still scalping around, adding and reducing my positions, which gave me a *feel* for the order flow. When I clip at-market, I feel the price action—the way it flicks me in and out. The sounds coming from my headphones provide extra bits of information' adding to the feedback loop as I scatter bids and offers."

But then, our trader paused. "Okay, but what is *next*? What we just traded is now old news; it is priced. At the time, we waited. Is the attack the beginning of something bigger? Are they going to attack elsewhere? If so, what's the plan? Are there any U.S. military casualties? The market reaction will likely be different depending on casualties—reasons to escalate," *The Warrior* said. "What will Trump do? Escalate, or call it an isolated incident, and everything dies down?"

You are operating on the cusp, mentally positioning for the imminent future, Theo thought, *five minutes ago is six minutes too late.*

The firehose of news information creates *minor* tradeable opportunities, *The Warrior* explained to Theo, but so too a lot of noise; *chop*. The skill is in retaining as much P&L as possible in this period—do not give it up on low-quality opportunities!

"Only then, you put on bigger risk on the *key* piece of information that dominates all others. As it happened, the Iranian foreign minister tweeted how they acted in self-defence under the U.N. Charter and stated they did not seek an escalation or war. *That* was huge."

As Theo listened to *The Warrior*, it dawned on him. *I was scared to trade at the start of the fast, explosive move when the market feedback was the most direct. Instead, I risked the most towards the end, when it was too unclear and too noisy, with the worst risk–reward.*

"Then it becomes risk-*on* flow; it is the opposite move, the removal of the war premium. And that is why we then *bought* risk assets, sold Crude Oil, Gold, Treasuries and—"

DINGDING!

The Warrior snatched his mouse, darted his eyes over his monitors and price ladders. Theo was caught off-guard.

ClickClickClick.

Our trader sold some clips in the Bund. "Is it big?" he shouted across the floor.

"No, it's nothing—rehashed ECB comment. No idea why they put it as a red-head," *The Sphinx* calmly replied, sitting opposite *The Warrior*.

He is right—Bund's not reacting. ClickClickClick—OUT.

"Eh… good job"; more sarcasm flowed through the other traders on the floor, some grunts, groans and cursing. And then, applause—to whoever at the other end of the newswires decided *that* was worthy of a critical red headline.

Theo glanced at *The Warrior's* P&L, tucked away on the far-left side of his screens for the purpose of video recordings. *His cost of entering and exiting the market is nearly the same as an entire trading month for me.*

The Warrior turned back to Theo.

"Anyway. The Iranian retaliation seemed symbolic rather than an escalation, and then Trump tweeted that all was well and confirmed the positive news. And so, the markets quickly shrugged off the bad overnight news; those positions I traded for the risk-*on* reversal made another three hundred thousand or so; I was up to about nine hundred by 3 a.m.," *The Warrior* said. "Let's just say I couldn't complain anymore about being jinxed."

◆

As reports of the Iranian retaliation subsided, our trader squared off the last few orders dotted around the markets, and he was already replaying the trade in his mind. *What a night! The markets make you feel like you are on the edge of a Third World War, but now it's already old news.* It was now 3 a.m., and everyone was to go to the office for the 7 a.m. European market open.

Then, he was greeted by the usual faces on the trading floor as he whipped around: *The Sphinx*, *The Godfather* and the new runner on the floor, who sat adjacent to his desk. He grabbed his chair—*ready*.

The dark London morning leans into the atmosphere on the trading floor. It does no favours to re-energise the team. Roughly twenty-four hours ago, he was still in Tulum. *Now this.* The markets were relatively calm and quiet. *Iran's limited response and no casualties make sense.*

He regrouped his thoughts. *What's next? The Trump conference at 4 p.m. London time. That's the next move. What's the market pricing currently? Based on the way they are moving and the general overnight narrative, the consensus seems that Trump will sound harsh on Iran but refrain from announcing further conflict after the latest attacks. If that's the case, then we would probably expect another leg of risk on, but it would be short-lived as that is mostly priced in.*

Later, President Trump walked onto the podium in front of all the news cameras, and the world held its breath. *Hands on mouse, eyes peeled.*

He began. The traders held firm. President Trump continued. "Iran appears to be standing down—"

ClickClickClickClickClick.

Instantly!—Long S&P, short Crude Oil and Gold. Buy risk, sell safe haven. *The Warrior* was already busy, flicking in and out of positions, jostling to stay onside. President Trump continued. "We must work together to make a deal with Iran... embrace peace."

This is it! He scrambled. *ClickClickClick—SmashSmashSmash. Add more, do more—sell into the lows! Buy into the highs! All this war premium will completely wind down after these comments.* Conviction was absolute. *We're going to overextend the other way as others are going to puke; I know they will. They are screwed sitting on the other side—full-size it!*

Keep adding, keep going! He glanced at his P&L. One million dollars for the first time ever. *Shocking.* Yet, he pushed on. *Everything is here, working. Push! Push for the world record!* Even as he scaled out of positions, he re-added again to reach maximum trading size. *Again—sell it!* Crude Oil and Gold futures obliterated any bid on the way down.

By the time the flows had abated and the trading day had slowed down, most of the positions had been squared off.

Done. *That is $1.3 million.*

Later—a message from *The Godfather.*

"*Ela malaka*—drinks at Mandrake then?"

Of course.

THE WARRIOR: PART I

◆

"So that is the important thing, Theo. There is no reason to be defensive or try to be reserved and lock in my P&L at this stage. I'm on a roll; it is one of those *rare* days when everything works. The stars are aligned, and you are going for the record. You must push to maximise as much as possible. It's on these days you need to expose yourself and put on more size than you ever have before," *The Warrior* said.

The day was winding down; some of the traders struck up conversations in the background. Theo sat listening intently. *He is right. That extra layer of P&L provides you the optionality to get in again and again for the outsized reward on these rarer instances. You pay cheaply to prevent missing out.*

Leaning on his armrest, *The Warrior* had spent a good afternoon talking with Theo.

"Trading is all about size; the results are a factor of what you clip. You can be the best trader in the world and clip ten lots and make salary money, or you can be a mediocre trader, but you can just do *it*—clip big size and make millions," he explained. "You can perfect everything else with regards to execution, consistency, right mindset, but if you do not push the size, then you will go nowhere. Or at least, you will never be a big multi-millionaire trader," *The Warrior* said as the conversation took a darker turn.

"But pushing size is always easier said than done. Yet, that's why you're doing this job. I'm not putting myself through all of this to earn a salary," he continued. "You can't get that feeling of relief and satisfaction on the floor. With trading, I rarely ever get a feeling of happiness. Never. You lose money and you want to jump out of a window because it feels like the world just ended. Or, if you had a great day and smashed it, then you just feel *fine*—'Ok, job done; nothing more to it'—and one day, you understand that your worst feelings will never be matched by positive feelings on the good days. Perhaps this is the fate of traders, the true price we pay. Sometimes I think I go through this pain to the point where good results should be a given."

"Were you always like this?"

"At the beginning of my career, I had ambitions of becoming a big trader," he said, playing with his armrest. "I had the drive to succeed, but I needed to prove it, so my motivation was stronger. Within the first weeks of going live, I had my first thousand-pound up-day. I felt like a millionaire, on top of the world. *I made it!* What followed was a roller-coaster of satisfaction, desperation, anger and fear. I don't think most other professions experience the range of feelings a trader experiences within a single day. *Every day.* It's truly immense. Comparing the first thousand up-day to the first million up-day, the happiness and overwhelming feelings I felt on the first don't compare to the second. I think it is because of the motivation you have when you are trying to prove yourself. Looking back, I wish I still had the same motivation now.

"Obviously, I still love what I do—at times," he grinned. "I still want to be bigger and push as much as I can grow. This hasn't changed, and it never will. As I said before, do you want to earn just a salary after all that? No, there are much easier ways to earn a salary. So instead, you push. You *must* push. Because the day I decrease my trading size is the day I quit."

Theo leaned back in his seat.

"But what do we always say?" *The Warrior* asked.

Theo paused. "Don't be meek."

Our trader suddenly stood up. "That's right," he said as he grinned at *The Sphinx* and *The Godfather*, both glancing back.

"You meek, you die."

THE WARRIOR: PART I

SUPPORTING MATERIALS

Watch a recording and analysis of *The Warrior* trading the 2020 U.S.–Iran geopolitical flashpoint.

axiafutures.com/
toot-flash

SUPER-SCALPER

The straight-A student, once an officer in the Cypriot Military Service, with multiple offers from top British universities to study computer science and a Fulbright Scholarship to complete an MBA at UCLA.

But also one of the neighbourhood boys full of mischief under the late-summer sun. With football as his only obsession, to end up playing for the Cypriot national under-18s team. Then he flunked exams for entry to the island's most prestigious school. Later, as a half-hearted university student, he moonlighted as a poker player, a gambling streak he carried over from his youth, when the kids paid adults to cash in their sports betting slips. *Which one is he?*

In fact, all these results are a front, a means to an end. From the beginning, *The Warrior* would go his own way. Those school entrance exams that he once intentionally flunked, he instead passed the following year with flying colours in order to remain at the same school as his friends.

National service tests were aced just to "guarantee an easier life as an officer and be closer to home!" He rejected the top British university offers in favour of a mid-ranking university so that he could enjoy life, hang out with friends and play poker. He spent little time studying yet he was the only student in his class to graduate with first-class honours.

And here is another of *The Warrior*'s idiosyncrasies: he has fantastic memory capabilities that translated into strong aptitudes—but damned he should be if someone should force him to use it! Our trader is not your strong-aptitude hoop-jumper, but he will use his capabilities to exploit that very hoop out of existence and revel in the process.

So, he had all the makings of a classic trader! But he discovered the game late, and any inkling of trading was cut short by 2009. Instead, he started working as an investment banking analyst.

"I hated it from the first moment. I thought, is *this* what I have to do to become a millionaire? But what else was there? I didn't know of another way. So, I stuck with it," *The Warrior* said. "But then we were doing the most boring tasks in the world, zero excitement. We joked about being jailed in the Excel *cell!* And for what? Money was never my true motivation anyway. I just wanted to do well in life. Surely there is another way than working like a dog for a decade to make a million, and I was going to find it." So, *The Warrior* quit on the spot after a manager made him pull several all-nighters to complete a project that was instantly redundant upon completion.

A proprietary trading floor followed soon after—Firm Y—which at the time already housed *The Razor*, *The Collector*, *The Sphinx* and Richard Bailey. "Working on the trading floor made more sense to who I am as a person. At the bank, I felt alienated. Everyone was so *proper*. The way they talked—you had to be polite for no reason," *The Warrior* continued.

THE WARRIOR: PART I

"But on the trading floor, I felt it was more of a battleground; people were shouting, and you could feel the energy. I loved it! The fast-paced environment fit with who I was. The bank was more about smiling and looking good, which was a game I had no interest in. It was constant excitement from the first day on the trading floor. I found it fascinating to figure out how markets work. I cannot think of anything that comes close. We sit and watch the markets moving on the back of world events. How can you beat that? How can it be more exciting, compared with working on a spreadsheet all day long, for example? You can't even compare things like that when you could be up close and personal with something like the markets."

And so follow the first few years of how *The Warrior* came to be. "Even from the early days I was developing my own unique style. There was no guideline on what to do; I was introduced to all the common tools, but it never made sense to *me*. I had to figure myself out," he said. "Instead, I started my career as, let's call it, a super-scalper, in and out of markets straight away. And that was *before* I traded news. I learnt it from pure observation. At the time, what made sense to me was scalping for a couple of ticks very quickly with a huge round-trip count."

Haywood added that this accelerated his visual learning feedback, which, like hitting the bat so many times, created an intimate understanding of order flow, or, as *The Warrior* says, of feeling it, that comes from possessing an immense repertoire of pattern experiences and strong visual memory.

"There was some kind of crisis kicking off at that time," *The Warrior* continued. "Back then, I had no idea what it even was. But I put the Bund price ladder next to the S&P price ladder, and on the market open, I'd take something like twenty trades. I'd see the

S&P go up, sell the Bund in response and get out. I'd wait again, and when the S&P went down, I'd buy the Bund for two ticks and get out. You feel the market so intensely when you're fighting for every single tick. I wasn't just putting on the trade and then getting coffee and watching the chart until the market went to some level. Many people did this, but for me, *every* tick mattered for that style I was trading; to do that, I had to watch the flow nonstop, every day, forever."

So, without knowing it, *The Warrior* had already intensely developed foundational principles that now form the core of his trading—intense risk management and a deep understanding of market correlations.

RISK AND CORRELATIONS

The first principle, a microscopic and intense controlling of risk, was best explained by *The Warrior* as he sat in front of a group of AXIA Career Course alumni. His preference, he says, is to control his downside by aggressively cutting and re-entering his position numerous times if needed, with the goal of ultimately being positioned for a likely directional move. He prefers to do this rather than letting the trade go against him. Other traders do not, or cannot, manage their positions so aggressively. These tactics—now reflexes—stem from his earliest days of scalping the market. S*calping* is a word of particular contention, as it has lost all meaning, abused and diluted over generations of traders, and is especially confusing for new traders who term nearly anything as "scalping."

But it is valid that in futures markets, there is *usually* a very tight bid and offer spread. Much of the time, this is just a single tick. A tick

THE WARRIOR: PART I

is the minimum movement of a single price, and the inside bid and offer prices are the best prices at which one can enter or exit a market.

As such, many traders who are "scalping" seek to profit off these small price changes, like *The Warrior*, who trades frequently yet only seeks to "take a couple ticks out of the market." They can do so due to this tight bid and offer spread. This has still allowed *The Warrior* to intensely micro-manage his positions well into his career, even as his trading size has grown considerably. You still can see these tactics more than a decade later in the video recordings of *The Warrior* managing his trades, ballooning his position when in profit or doing away with it altogether if the market is pressuring him.

The second, market correlations, is a deep topic yet is often unnecessarily overcomplicated when, really, the idea is intuitive. Understanding these correlations is fundamental to *The Warrior*. It is impossible to separate the two. We can view order flow not within *one market* at a time but across two or more markets at a time.

Recall, or know, that markets *price in* information. This is one of the key reasons why markets even exist—it is one of the least-bad methods civilisation has discovered to accurately value and place a price on assets, instruments, goods and so forth. This is why the term *price discovery* is used to describe such a process. It is in the market's nature to digest new information and re-express it as the 'correct' price once that discovery process is over. It is always curious to poke and prod in different directions to feel out the market participants. Watching this price discovery process is 'order flow'—*to us*. There is a vast array of reasons why a particular market is "pricing in" certain information differently from others. Each tradeable market pertains to a group of *asset classes*—equities, fixed income, currencies and commodities. A significant price move may influence others, depending on the context.

Recall *The Warrior's* trading a 'risk-off' scenario in the section 'A Mexican Standoff,' above. In that situation, WTI and Brent Crude Oil futures were leading the flow and correlations, as contextually it was the most vulnerable market. And on other entirely different days, themes and trades, there is other shorthand that describes correlations: risk-on, hawkish or dovish flow, bull flattening, bear steepening moves, equity index rotations and others. These denote the contextual news, or the thematic environment that drives correlations. And as *The Warrior* says, the skill is knowing and observing which market is leading the pack.

Through simple observation these correlations and flows among various markets certainly do exist, and the patterns are 'predictable' up to a point. *Lo!* The reasons for these moves are, of course, always opaque and debated. But it follows along these lines: many participants in the futures markets are not speculative. They can be commercial participants wishing to hedge 'exposure'—an airline company wishing to protect against volatility in the energy complex, for example. Others have interests in protecting their exposure to foreign currency, interest rate volatility and more. Other immense financial institutions, such as endowment funds and pension funds, have mandates and cannot sit on the sidelines to hold cash.

Therefore, they must rotate between various asset classes, perhaps seeking refuge in bonds as equities become too volatile. Other *speculative* market participants know this, so the market, being reflexive in nature, reacts in kind even if no immediate action is taken by large participants. Many times, the tail does indeed wag the dog.

In his early days, *The Warrior* confessed to knowing nothing of these concepts. He effectively stumbled upon them through observational power and later incorporated these order flow patterns into a tradeable edge. But, as fate would have it, that was *the* skill to have as an upcoming news trader.

"These flows worked more often than not, and I would never let the trade go against me too much. I was always building consistency. I was building days. I remember periods when I would scalp twenty-one winning trades in a row," *The Warrior* said.

And that is how we evolve our understanding of a strategy's burden into understanding the difference between 'cash flow' and 'wealth-building' strategies, a mentality which is perhaps seldom appreciated.

Consider wealth-building strategies as those that rely on lower win rates and higher payouts, which can work well *if* you do not need immediate cash flow. And, as we established earlier, *if* you can tolerate the burden of striking out many times in a row. Not many people can, and they do not have to. But the rare payouts can be very large.

But the majority of newer traders will often need the cash flow and *certainty* to even pay for cost-of-living expenses, including the costs of various trading tools, data feeds and software. As many traders know, the lack of cash flow ends careers, and it is not a coincidence that virtually all the profiled traders in this book found success and sustainability at the beginning of their careers because their strategies were *cash-flow*-orientated, and their returns were low-variance, even if the payouts were smaller.

The Godfather often discusses the importance of a trader understanding where they are in their career. If they are building or rebuilding an account, he says, then they cannot afford to "swing for the fences" as they will simply run out of cash, savings and career viability before a big payout happens, to *also* account for the losses along the way.

But as a trader grows in size, establishes financial security and grows a trading account, career opportunities can change and transform into wealth-building ones, like *The Warrior*, who trades to maximise days like 'A Mexican Standoff.' He is no longer trading for a salary. The biggest risk for *The Warrior* is missing *the* trade—not his rent payment.

But! This is different for a cash-flow trader, whose account likely cannot handle a larger hit, as the next opportunity may only resurface well after their insolvency, to adapt a popular J.M. Keynes quote. Likewise, should a cash-flow trader who needs to prioritise consistent daily positive P&L find themselves, for whatever reason, within an extremely outsized, positive P&L day, then their positions *must* be covered earlier. The place in your career determines the right decisions. Early-career traders who take on goals and decisions that are correct only for a late-stage wealth-building trader *contextually* make the wrong decisions at the worst time.

It has been proven, multiple-fold, on our trading desks that on these rare, outsized days, simply participating—*just click!*—can revive the entire trading careers of junior traders who are in deep drawdown. Ensuring survival at this stage is more important than thriving. That trader cannot afford for the entire, rare, outsized P&L trade to return to flat, as that is likely to have been the sole opportunity of their early career to prevent failure. A last chance wasted on ill-fitted "principles" or "rules"—*just take the money!*

To return to the *champion's fallacy*, which we introduced in the previous chapter, copying *The Warrior* in his current state is often futile. This is not only due to a lack of skills but also logistics, accounting and cash flow. *The Warrior* can take many hits and be in no danger of failing to pay for his monthly or yearly expenses.

But he also began as a cash-flow trader, as dictated by his career restrictions and objectives, taking sure, fast trades on the price ladder. Even as he no longer trades for "just a salary," the toll his mania inflicts on his body and mind can only be somewhat justified by the immense payouts.

But *The Warrior*, too, highlights the necessity of building consistency in the early stages. "In the first couple of years, you need to print green nearly every single day," he said. "There are opportunities each day, sometimes hundreds of them or just two. You adapt to the fast and slow conditions. You need to make money; it simply doesn't matter how. You need to find a way to do it each day at that stage." Since then, the scope of his objectives has changed, which in turn has altered his decision-making, but his intense micro-management of the price ladder and intuitive, well-greased groove of understanding and *feeling* market correlations have stuck ever since.

A ROAD NOT TAKEN

But now, a challenge. *The Warrior* was earning good money but not great, he says, especially in the face of a tempting graduate scholarship at UCLA, as endeared to him by watching too much *Californication*. So, the goal was set—*really* make it in the next twelve months or quit and take up the scholarship. Then the European Debt Crisis came knocking, and *The Warrior* was ready for it. He threw himself at every opportunity.

"Back then, it wasn't like someone had to tell you what to do. You saw something hit the newswires, and the market would move twenty ticks. I saw this and started to create a strategy for it. I couldn't believe how simple it was—very binary," our trader said.

Gesturing with his hands, *The Warrior* created two visual points, an A and a B on an imaginary price ladder. "Enter here and exit there. As soon as I saw the potential, I thought, *this is what trading really is!* Because of the volatility and these comments. We didn't have this after the 2007–2009 Financial Crisis. The edge was so ripe that there was *crazy* money to be made on these European sovereign credit downgrades. As soon as one country got downgraded, the Bund [futures] would explode in the most straight-line fashion ever. *No pullbacks*—for a good sixty ticks! Sixty! And it happened again and again as others were downgraded, including Greece, Portugal, Spain, Italy," he said in disbelief.

Moves like these would seem nearly unbelievable to today's traders. The environment has changed, and markets have evolved. It is now rare for the market to move in such a controlled fashion. The "clean" moves are few and far between.

But our trader evolved too. And now he's mastered the fine ability to navigate these meandering market moves, the squeezes and brutal moments where markets will try their best to force or 'trick' traders to exit positions, all before the real move is underway. Navigating this dauntlessly is a trait that Haywood identifies as the main reason why *The Warrior* has stayed a cut above other competitors and why he has continued to push his performance.

(1) OPPORTUNITY MAXIMISATION

"When *The Warrior* puts on risk, there is a whole new calculation that goes on," Haywood noted. And to appreciate what has enabled our trader to build this navigation skill and, by extension, illuminate potential skill development for ourselves as traders, we can examine two further concepts: 'opportunity maximisation' and 'pressing the initiative.'

THE WARRIOR: PART I

'A Mexican Standoff' and other 'one-off' trades highlight the 'tactical' imperative of obtaining the best prices, which is the purest way to understand opportunity maximisation.

But it can be a double-edged sword, as the market can react strangely just after the trader tries to hit the best prices—immediate entry—and they find themselves instantly offside or even forced to liquidate altogether. But this is the nature of the beast, and the opportunity cost of *missing it* far outweighs getting it wrong: a $70,000 loss paid to prevent a much larger opportunity cost, in this case, $1.3 million. That is what it is like to think as a wealth-building trader *at the right time*.

"I think what has always characterised me is that I trade with the mindset that tomorrow the markets will be shut forever," *The Warrior* said. "If *this* market move happened, and I missed it or didn't maximise it, then I am just stupid. Why am I here? This is why I hate leaving money on the table. Why would I be happy if I could have made more? It wasn't difficult. You don't have to be a genius to get in and try again," he continued.

And this is a learnt survival instinct. Recall the dearth of volatility following the European Debt Crisis, the doldrums around 2013–2018 that we explored with *The Collector*. The slivers of volatility on a rare news headline or theme meant opportunity, a time to eat. Who knew how long it would be until the next opportunity? It is not a surprise *The Warrior* embodies this obsession to maximise what he can, a product of the time. Compare it to what came after the 2019–2020 U.S.–China trade war, the pandemic and the subsequent years. In those older, dry times, opportunities were often at best prised from the limited and subtle language shift of a central banker.

So, the very risk of *missing* something due to simply being away from his trading desk is intolerable. In highly volatile periods, *The*

Warrior will never be spotted away from his desk, with the exception of entering and exiting the building or going to the bathroom. As *The Collector* said, traders will experience some of the most expensive bathroom breaks in history. And missing *it* because *The Warrior* is away from his desk is indeed his greatest fear and, therefore, his greatest pain. The lowest points of his career are always triggered by missing market-moving events; a sorry path strewn with *what if?* And his inability to accept these instances is what he admits to be his greatest weakness.

"If I execute badly, and lose a lot of money, it will hurt, but I will quickly get over it. However, missing an opportunity *tilts* me big time." Tilt—as per poker parlance—is a state of intense emotional turbulence: frustration and recklessness that threatens any deployment of a plan or proactiveness. "Especially if a trade escapes me for reasons outside my control—like a system issue—then it plunges me into deep frustration. These intense feelings take time to resolve, and often mark the beginning of a bad run," *The Warrior* continued.

This is also why he has replicated his trading floor set-up not only at home, but also in his other houses and apartments across various parts of the world, to minimise the risk of missing anything and to guarantee peak performance at all times. Irrespective of where he is, there can be no compromise on a seamless transition, except for having to message other traders when 'off-floor,' rather than physically speaking to them. *I'll bring the trading floor with me!*

Even if the Endsleigh Street trading floor is only a five-minute drive away, his London residence was chosen for its "strategic proximity" to the office, to minimise the chance of missing anything during the commute, and it has everything exactly replicated too. "And I mean exact in every aspect. Identical PCs, monitors, mice, keyboards—the exact same layout—the monitor size, their positions and angles," *The Warrior* explained. "Also complete with the fastest possible fibre-optic lines, back-up lines, 5G routers and other redundancies to cover all eventualities. If I change one thing in one of my set-ups, then that change is instantly replicated to all of them. You won't find anything that is different because *I* cannot afford to find anything different between home and the office. If something feels off, then it will bother me and it will affect my execution. The moment you worry about anything, even the internet stability, for example, then you will begin to doubt. Then you won't be as aggressive as possible. At that moment, you are meek, and you lose."

And as we know, there are the *burdens* of a strategy. *The Warrior* took a seventy-thousand-dollar loss in 'A Mexican Standoff' to not miss the next seven-figure opportunity. The premise with the *pain trade*—the missed March 2020 Fed rate cut—is the same, but the numbers are different. He forgoes a million-dollar upside for the opportunity to gain multiple times that amount. Sometimes you strike out—*miss it*—hence the burden and pain when that happens. But this lends to the all-important statement we borrow from *The Engineer:* the sole goal is to maximise wealth *over time*. That is, to understand what a real ultra-opportunity-maximising, wealth-building attacker really looks like, because, as we said earlier, he made the *right* decision at the right time in his career.

At this stage, would another 'mere' million dollars have pushed the boundaries of his career? Not so much. But now, the potential for multi-seven figures in one day? *That* is how you shatter boundaries.

"It might seem like a contradiction to readers," *The Warrior* added, "between my skills of intense risk management and this failed Fed rate cut trade. I was going for a home run, but it was not destined to be because of system lag and failure. I knew this deep down, but I did not want to accept it, and this comes down to my character and personality. If I find myself in a situation where I feel something was stolen from me, I take excessive risk. That is when I trade badly because of this 'injustice' outside my control, and I know it. But I also need that same aggression to achieve peak performance. At an extreme it can sometimes transform into: *what I could have made!* But it also allows aggression for perfect execution. I had the determination to defy the temptation to take the million and push for more," he said. Because in other situations in the future, it is exactly this mentality, this super-aggression, that will let him rip out *his* own pound of flesh; that multi-seven-figure trade is only a matter of time.

Help your trading, hurt your life; you cannot have it both ways. Whatever traits, personality or behaviours you have that help the former very often hurt the latter. And so, too, you cannot have the colossal up-days, our trader says, without having the stomach for the big down-days. Or, in this case, to risk leaving so much on the table every once in a while. *Sod's law* is an immutable force.

(2) Pressing the Initiative

Once *The Warrior* bites, seldom will he let go, due to a maniacal devotion in *pressing the initiative*. This is where we separate our traders from what people expect 'news trading' to be. Those who wish to begin trading the news often prepare in what they assume to be the logical way—deep research combined with a specific plan of action, *If A does B*, a binary 'set and forget' mentality. *If the Fed hikes, sell bonds. I've deeply researched it and understood A, so B must happen!*

But, of course, the bonds rally instead. Markets are rarely that easy, as we deal in a domain where '1 + 1 = 3' happens frequently. That is, the markets are a *complex* environment, a specific term we will explore much more throughout the book and then deeply with *The Sphinx*.

Blast! And when the markets truly react in a '1 + 1 = 2' fashion, many traders will miss this as they were so far behind the curve on the '= 3' reaction that they now attempt the '= 3' trade, just as the market moved back to '= 2': a classic double-bluff.

"I think one thing I do differently to almost all traders is my ability to keep adding to a position even if it has gone very far. It is super-risky and aggressive when it does not work, and you give back a lot of P&L," *The Warrior* said. "It is true I am not a news trader in the way people think of it—'smash-and-grabbing.' These traders would typically struggle to add to their positions once the move accelerates because they will be very mechanical and specific on how they trade the news, how much size they put on, depending on how 'big' the news seems. But for me, it is about trading *the flow*, not the news! That is why 'slow-burner' trades are the best for me, where the smash-and-grab traders struggle," *The Warrior* continued.

"Often the market has gone ten to twenty ticks on an insignificant headline, and most traders will argue why it wasn't worth hitting: 'How did this move?' or 'Why is this moving?' Sometimes, if the market has not moved, that just means you can get the best prices. So why *not* do a few big clips and see what happens? If it doesn't go, you are ready to puke it—quick exit—for a small loss," he said. "But if it does go, then I can build a core position and patiently sit and follow the correlations and story development. Feeding the size in and then running the trade to exhaustion. These are my favourite trades, where the source of news is not obvious—an obscure tweet, for example—but sometimes the market will start slowly then crescendo into madness."

And why else does it seem like *The Warrior* is just *there*, on the cusp before the news? "I realised early on it is all about speed. That also made me realise that if five headlines drop, I won't have time to read them," *The Warrior* said. "I am going to rely on the first person that hits the market and I have to be the *second* one in." The speed of our trader's reaction to President Trump's announcement that "Iran appears to be standing down" in 'A Mexican Standoff' was also guided by the market flow supporting risk-*on*—equity bid, bonds offered, Crude Oil sold, as the probability of war diminished. The markets reacted as fast as the words hit the microphone, and they seemed to pre-empt the broadcast, but for *The Warrior*, the instant, aggressive market reaction *before* the broadcast reached his ears was good enough.

"Nine times out of ten, the markets will point in the right direction," he said, and the trick is to manage and navigate the meandering path until they get there. *What is this sixth sense?* It is not from analysing what the market *should* 'logically' do—based on new information—but from trading what the market is actually doing. Flying in the face of logic. To echo *The Razor*, "Are you listening?" Let the market tell you what it wants to do, or, in the case of our trader, *feel* what the market wants to do.

◆ ◆ ◆

Consider, then, the tactical implications of trading a binary, one-off but very *anticipated* event. This is different from 'A Mexican Standoff' as the U.S. airstrike, to the markets at least, was a complete surprise. Not so for the release of the Pfizer Covid-19 vaccine Phase-Three results. The race for the vaccine was on for months!

"It won't be a slow-burner; it won't give you time to think and analyse," *The Warrior* said. "Speed is everything, milliseconds matter. This is what we trained for all these years again and again; when you see the words hit the newswires, everything goes absolutely nuts. Instantly. And visualisation plays a huge part in a trade like this. In other trades, you improvise in the moment, and you lean on order flow and correlations, but anticipated events are more 'structured.' We plan for what are the best markets to hit and what we are looking out for, to *perfect* execution—getting in as fast as possible, hitting as hard as possible, and running it!" he continued.

"Adam, a trader on the floor, pointed out that Pfizer normally reports studies on various drugs at exactly 11.45 a.m. [GMT]. We confirmed it, and seconds before 11.45 a.m., we hovered over the S&P price ladder, ready to go absolutely nuts. We leaned towards 'risk-on' because results from earlier studies were very encouraging, so we had to assume Phase Three—the big one—should also be positive. How positive? Unknown," our trader said.

Pfizer Reports… Ninety-five per cent—Huge! Huge! Go nuts! And *The Warrior* offloaded size into various equities, the Bund and more. After a momentous day—seven figures—he was not done. Because the market flows were still there, and he was ready to rinse all of it.

"After all of these huge moves, of this risk-on play, instead of packing up like most traders, I then attempt a *short* on equities by leaning on the NASDAQ (NQ) sell-off and a long position in the Bund retracing an over-extension," he said. After such a positive event for the markets, they take another look because "the so-called stay-at-home stocks, like Amazon and Netflix, which had been outperforming due to lockdown orders, are now expected to sell off on the potential reopening of the economy," our trader continued.

The market was looking forward. "So, I am not done as order flow and correlations will still dictate my actions. And I just *cannot* be out of the markets when they are moving. If I am not long, I need to be short! This is what makes me as a trader. It doesn't mean I will take the same risk as before, but until the dust settles, I will squeeze out as much P&L as possible—to print the best day ever—it's there for the taking," he said.

But such a mentality underpins all of *The Warrior*'s trading. "No matter what headline just came out, you will hear my mouse clicking nonstop and hear my headphones playing 'order filled' sounds, dinging hundreds of times, because I always throw in bids and offers to feel the market," *The Warrior* said. "I would get in with a five-hundred lot and constantly scale out with two lots to keep feeling it."

Readers who watch the video of "A Mexican Standoff" will spot this immediately—the constant, manual scattering of tiny limit orders to chew away at his core position. This is insignificant in terms of P&L yet doing this across markets creates an almost kinaesthetic audio-visual feedback, a feeling, a synaesthesia of activity of the mind–mouse market that emerges from the screen and comes alive.

"So, this feeling provides me feedback on what is happening, to add or exit more aggressively. It goes back to my earliest super-scalper days—constant fighting for ticks, feeding the markets with bids and offers on massive volatility," *The Warrior* said. The sixth sense is a physical act of overcoming the barrier of the monitors.

There can be other one-off events that are either blindsiding or completely anticipated, like the U.S.–China trade war tweets in the former and programmed events like ECB or FOMC interest rate decisions in the latter. And these are just "headline"-determined trades! These are lone injections of volatility. But then there are whole other developments of themes *over time*.

Note how overtly inextricable our trader is from personality to methods, style and approach. As if he could not be any other way, and thereby has become unique. An act of creation, a *0 to 1* moment that so very characterises *The Razor*: both men are such maximalists in both personality and trading, to become an individual on the trading floor, as *The Engineer* sees it, or to feel as if "they are on a journey," as Haywood calls it.

THE WARRIOR: PART I

SUPPORTING MATERIALS

Watch these tactics and principles in action as *The Warrior* trades the Pfizer COVID-19 vaccine announcement and other key headlines in our video gallery.

axiafutures.com/
toot-one

WHATEVER IT TAKES

Your obsession with maximising opportunities far outweighs your fear of losses. Does this stem from something deeper?

In trading, as in life, I have a tendency to always overestimate the likelihood of winning rather than losing. I often come up with the reasons why the positive outcome will happen and ignore the chances of things going wrong. In trading, this lets me click first and ask questions later.

Growing up, I was always really impatient. If I wanted something, I needed it right away! I just couldn't wait. And if I didn't get it, I would cry and demand it. They say patience is a virtue, but unfortunately, it's impatience that characterises me.

So in trading I have always been over-trading since the first day. I just cannot sit there and wait until something happens, or until my "perfect set-up" comes into play—I always have positions on. The greater the volatility, the more I keep clicking my soul away—long-short, long-short—thousands of trades every session. And once the adrenaline kicks in, any fear of losing tends to fade away. The thrill takes over, and I become aggressive, constantly reacting to order flow and price action.

The unpredictability of this game is another reason to maximise. I do not take anything for granted. At [Firm Y] I saw my account disappear overnight and I had to start all over again. That was a huge loss at the time, yet I had no choice but to go again. This incident prompted me to trade even more aggressively, as it made me realise that if I could lose it all—just like that—then I better make boatloads more going forward. It made me aim much higher. So seize every big moment; make the most out of it—achieve something great. You don't know when the next opportunity will happen, or if your edge will continue. Over the years, this industry has evolved from the pits to screens to algorithms—who knows what's next?

Trading is best comparable to a professional sport because of what you described that goes on "behind the scenes." What do you mean?
Trading is not just a job, because like any performance discipline, if you want to be at the top—at the peak—it requires your heart and soul. Day in and day out. There are no shortcuts, no easy way of making it. I don't know of any trader that figured out an easy way of making money. And it is a performance because you have to go through it all—the extreme roller-coaster. The peaks, the troughs, the glory days, the annihilation days, feeling invincible, feeling defenceless, on top of the world and hitting rock-bottom.

We also see it as a sport because it becomes an enormous part of your life. It affects my feelings, my mood and my lifestyle on a daily basis. And when it affects it negatively, it just sucks. On the bad days, I sit there getting chopped up nonstop, losing trade after trade, coming home exhausted as if I was running a marathon all day, absolutely destroyed with large negative P&L. The feelings of anger, desperation, agony, despair. It can suck—it can really suck. This is the darker side of trading that people don't see. It is what goes on behind the scenes. What I actually go through in order to achieve what I have. Like I said, life on a roller-coaster.

When you are on a bad run, it does feel that you will never make money again. No matter what anyone tells you, you just feel hopeless and helpless. What if this is really coming to an end? How can I walk into the office every day and take losing trade, after losing trade, after losing trade? Whatever I touch turns bad—*red, red, red*. What can I do? How do I stop it? In those moments, it feels like it will never stop. But in reality, you know it eventually will. Yet, it doesn't stop you from doubting yourself, your process, your methods. Am I still bulletproof? Have I changed something?

You have to experience all of it. And expose yourself to it. Because if you want to have enormous up-days, then you need to know how to stomach the large down-days. That is part of a trader's journey. That is what it means to have the *will to perform*.

What do you do after a big down-day?
So, I have taken a hit, and the damage is done. And after a cigar and several glasses of whisky… discussions with God… I'm fearful, you know, that this was an act of retribution. But then I really start to get over it, and I think more rationally. How do I make something positive out of this? I *have* to learn from this. It must have happened for a reason. I use days like these as a wake-up call.

Maybe I have been losing focus recently, caught up with other things in life, and not being properly up-to-date with everything. Maybe my routine is slipping: going to the office later than normal, not keeping up with big themes, not visualising and not being excited enough. The moment I feel that enthusiasm has dropped and I am not completely present and focused, then I know something is wrong. I use it to make sure I have everything in check again. I will make changes to my set-up—price ladders, newswires, alerts—and make sure everything is streamlined. With different market themes taking over and interchanging, sometimes you forget to adapt quickly enough, which means you are sub-optimal. Everything should be streamlined to the extreme degree to give me the best competitive advantage for the next opportunity. I will run through my head the themes in the play and start visualising different scenarios and how I execute them. Who are the next speakers? What is the next big event? This big down-day *must* serve as a check to get me back on track.

So, when the times get tough, that's when the main learning takes place, both for skills and psychologically too. How do you mentally manage these big down-days? What effect do they have on you? Do they make you defensive? How quickly do you run out of confidence? What are your trigger points? All these questions only surface when you *struggle*. And the big down-days, that's when you struggle the most, as that is where the pain is the greatest. So instead of falling into despair, be ready to use these questions and insights as weapons to improve your performance. Turn them to your advantage.

And after the pain fades, a big down-day also serves as a reminder to look at the bigger picture and reflect on life. It reminds me how fortunate I am—grateful for what God has given me: my beautiful family, who have supported me, and my health. A shock like that puts everything into perspective, so that stress and worries of daily life become insignificant compared to what truly matters.

THE WARRIOR: PART I

What do you think about trading on the floor versus remotely?
The traders who surround you all play a key role—their strengths, the things they say, the way they react, even their weaknesses, their screams, their shouts—all contribute to a feedback loop that shapes and defines you. Everything that happens on that floor is an input for your development, especially the competitive spirit of the team motivates you to excel—to push. These dynamics are very powerful and hugely important in developing a career. All the big traders I know grew their size on a trading floor. Yet most of them struggled or retired after they changed their environment.

But I'm not implying that successful remote traders do not exist. I understand that not everyone has the opportunity to be on the floor. However, what makes a remote trader successful is the ability to interact with other traders in real-time. To share views, ideas and trading scenarios as market events unfold. To help stay on top of themes, to update news sources, to discuss which are the best and latest markets to hit, and so on. It is crucial to be in a team environment, whether it is on a physical trading floor or through a remote system where information is continuously shared throughout the day.

And consider my environment, because it is the one that made me. Looking back, it was a blessing in disguise that I lost my entire account when [Firm Y] went down. It catalysed AXIA's birth, and this is where I grew exponentially as a trader. I'm truly grateful for having all these top traders—top people—around me all these years. I always feel on the floor we are one—all of us, the junior traders, the seniors, the "management," and the people behind the scenes are the most important in keeping this ship going. "Super Mario's" [Kyriacou's] support in every aspect from the birth of AXIA has been hugely important in the success of this team and particularly in my own achievements. We wouldn't be here without him.

♦ ♦ ♦

So, *The Warrior*, once embryonic as a super-scalper of market flow and correlations, used these skills to trade news comments with the advent of the European Debt Crisis. At first, a very tight, controlled, consistent player, a cash-flow-priority trader.

But then, a dramatic shift to wealth-building; the time had come. The way forward was due to maturation, a graduation from trading sole news comments to understanding the long-term market themes, narratives and, ultimately, *the story* that grips markets through time.

"But it also started becoming impossible to increase size and extract the same kind of scalp-flow trade from the market. I had to adapt. Getting in and out of three hundred lots is a different story than trading ten when the order book is thin. It is like poker—at low stakes, you can be the best, but at high stakes, the players are better, and the game is tougher. And then you move the market when you get in and out, which means you are effectively losing ticks in the process. So, I had to run my trades further," he said.

Necessity, then, to escape the bounds of liquidity on the shortest temporal and smallest prices of the market—a fast spike, a few ticks—drove *the Warrior* to the bigger picture, in fact, the *biggest*, of market themes, narratives, the story arc of the markets.

And, as Haywood identifies, the very special part of our trader is understanding, knowing, feeling and *believing* when the risk is worth it, of when to match it with exposure—a master of trading the peak of the theme, the plot twist, of when the markets shatter.

"Unlike others who might not really excite themselves, I keep pushing, hyping myself up throughout the day," *The Warrior* said. "I constantly visualise which market to hit, in what order, and how to react to every possible scenario. Once I see what I want to see, then I have one job—to go absolutely nuts and max out risk. When conviction is there, when I really believe in it, anything short of maximum size is disappointment and failure."

Such is the will to perform. And so, the tension, the painful duality of top performers with unique traits—help your trading, hurt your life—for all the emotional outpour, *The Warrior's* attempts in vain to overcome it is perhaps a tragic story—the old Promethean, chained-to-a-rock, eagle-pecking-away-at-the-immortal-liver-type story.

It is too intertwined in what makes him unique, too entangled with his abilities that allow him to dominate his niche. This *monster*, a Mr Hyde, forces him to put on the size, to take the risk and push for more, demand more. And to do so is to believe, with utter conviction, down to the bones.

"Those few seconds, where it all happens, are worth more than the next three to four months of sitting in front of the screens. How can I let myself miss that? Or how can I let myself *not* be aggressive?"

PRACTITIONER'S POSTSCRIPT

Explore resources derived from this chapter to further support the practicing trader.

axiafutures.com/
toot

Refer to
The Warrior's
section.

LEARNER'S IMPRESSIONS

Below are some personal impressions that *The Warrior* made on us that we still discuss with other traders.

1. *The trading persona.* We notice how attuned *The Warrior* is with his career choice—dare we say it is a calling. He is inextricable from his niche trading approach, his Jekyll-and-Hyde persona and his outlook on the markets and life. This is a trader who has shouldered the correct burdens. A successful trading persona will always look different from what you expect. Because if you can predict them, are they really unique? Feed your idiosyncrasies.
2. *Cash flow to wealth-builder.* Yet, even with this all-or-nothing approach, *The Warrior*, like all traders, prioritised consistency, cash flow and a "green-every-day" mentality at the beginning. *Just take the money!* Where traders are in their career determines the right actions and choices. Novices or those rebuilding an account cannot be opportunity-maximisers and risk giving back what they have in their hand. Yet those already with a sizeable account and personal finances secure *must* push boundaries and risk giving back smaller opportunities. And risk the large down-days to have the titanic up-days. Be wary of mixing up priorities.
3. *Trading as a sport.* The analogy extends further than the physical toll. Our trader is all about presence—physically dominating his domain—*feeling* it. To harness the fighting spirit, the will to perform. Trading is not just an art or science but a bloody sport of financial violence. Do not risk intellectual, bureaucratic detachment. Because presence at their desk and in their space, Haywood

observes, is starkly evident with the trading greats. Wielding emotion, can you also bring yourself to it in totality? Is there something preventing you from doing so?

What are your impressions? Write them down and converse with this book!

CHAPTER SIX

THE WARRIOR: PART II

Trading is an act of continuous, infinite problem-solving in financial markets, which requires an inherent act of creativity. And that is your moat! To go with your best guess. A defendable *human* edge if nurtured appropriately. Beyond preserving an unassailable edge from "the algos" and artificial intelligence (AI), it also applies to other human traders—competitors. Creativity is a vast skill 'ceiling,' *infinite, arguably*, and climbing higher than other traders allows you to outperform them, to become exceptional over the great. But we venture into the AI domain only to reflect on our own; forays into this topic have served to further reveal the power of the *human* trader. The contrast is to illuminate our very best: how the few pounds of matter between our ears will endure.

Specifically, if we lucidly understand the hard limitations of these approaches, specifically rule-based algorithmic trading and general approaches to developing AI, then we can work our way to understanding the *human* advantage and, therefore, *The Warrior*—so we can double down on how to improve ourselves as discretionary, point-and-click traders.

THE WARRIOR: PART II

Current AI based on current computer processor designs or algorithms and systemised strategies are built off *inductive reasoning*. This is a sample-set approach, where the observer infers rules and develops the optimal playbook for their environment after many repeated samples. This works fantastically well in "complicated" and static environments, where the rules *never* change, like Chess, Go and *StarCraft*. If you iterate millions of games in a fixed environment, the general approach of machine learning, then you can slowly dig towards the 'optimal' concurrent action and reaction to the game. It is calculable and iterative, the domain in which the computer reigns supreme. So, in a complicated but *calculable* static environment, the trial-and-error creative operator who needs to figure it out is trumped by the best-practice, optimal-playbook operator who has already figured it out. And these days the latter has become your friendly neighbourhood server rack.

Yet for a computer learning to play a game over time and processing many samples, changing even seemingly minor variables—or just one—dramatically reduces its win rate. It has to now relearn the slightly altered game with many more sample sets to improve its win rate.[*] So, an inductive approach is always behind change.

And financial markets are not static. They are an unending storm of conflict that elicits change. They are a wily, dynamic and complex environment! They love to trick myopic participants into imagining the rules are as static and rigid as a chess board. To not realise that you are, in fact, in the eye of the storm. And then—*surprise!*—the rules shatter, and so too the best practices and 'correct' actions that were learnt in the previous market or economic environment.

---

[*] " ... dramatically reduces its win rate" as explained by Erik J. Larson with the game 'Breakout'. See (Larson, 2021: 127)

Your derived general optimal practices supported by facts and rules—the inductivist process—were just rendered obsolete. So, you better get creative, because the playbook just went out the window.

Creativity, then, wins in *complex* environments. To pivot, adapt and change on a sample of *one*, not a thousand. And this is termed as *abductive reasoning*, going with your best guess—the exact type in which the AI field has made very little progress, as explained by Erik J. Larson—computer scientist and technology entrepreneur—in *The Myth of Artificial Intelligence* (2021).* And not for a lack of trying; their very hardware design prevents them from doing so! Which is what we are about to explore through *The Warrior* himself.

Change, in other words, is both a maker and a breaker of the human trader—the very reason you can continue to exist in the trading domain, and often the very thing to get you in the end!

But, as they say, *or should say more*, in markets, a once-in-a-lifetime event occurs monthly. This is where *The Warrior* and others thrive, where the inductivist, sample-set-taught algorithm or systematised strategy flounders. *The Warrior*, then, is an expert navigator of these tail events, an operator who is comfortable with a sample set of one, not a thousand, who, by utilising the strength of human *abductive* reasoning, can use his best guess. And have the conviction to *go big* on his best guess. That is the art of speculation and getting it right places you in very select company.

---

*   In this chapter, we are much indebted to Angus Fletcher on the "understanding of time … which is simply ignored by computers", "rhetorical functions" and how the "symbolic logic of the [processor] … ignores such components" (Fletcher, 2021c: 1–28); Erik J. Larson on "abductive reasoning", "inductive reasoning" and current AI (Larson, 2021: 120–126, 157–189) for their materials and work surrounding AI and its limitations; and David J. Snowden and Mary E. Boone (2007), whose classification of complicated and calculable vs complex environments and guidance on navigating them are key elements of the 'Cynefin Framework'.

THE WARRIOR: PART II

It is also about placing the clues in their *evolving* context! *The Warrior* puts this as the "three phases" of a market theme: emergence, peak and post-peak. These phases may have the same input of clues, headlines or causes but with very different effects. What was strongly market-moving in a *peak* theme becomes a loss-making trap in *post-peak*. And that is because the context, the story, has moved on; the complex, dynamic market has moved on. And so the following section explores the nature of the three phases of a theme with the outbreak of the Russia–Ukraine War in 2022.

THE ARC OF A MARKET STORY

Interview and discussions compiled between winter 2021 and summer 2022.

Can you explain how you understand market themes, with an example of a period that you have traded recently?
Identifying where you are in the lifespan of the theme is critical to your operations as a trader. I think a clear and recent example is the Russia–Ukraine War. It was a hugely sad and horrible event, but it sparked massive volatility and powerful market moves as the situation kept evolving, which meant big trading opportunities for global macro-intraday traders.

At the beginning of the theme, it will create strong straight-line moves that go far as the market is faced with a new macro-economic and geopolitical reality. Let's call the beginning *phase one* of a developing theme that involves pricing in the risks of the possibility of a Russian invasion of Ukraine.

In early February 2022, there were reports of a Russian military build-up along the Ukrainian border, but Russia denied any invasion plans. Russia had been demanding that the U.S. and NATO deliver a satisfying response to demands for security guarantees, but there was no concession. The U.S. then warned that Russia might invade Ukraine, but this was still met with denial.

At this stage, a Russian invasion is nowhere near priced in the markets. But as it happened in the months to come, the Russia–Ukraine War became the main theme that dominated flows and price action of all asset classes across the world.

The first market-moving "news" occurred on 11 February—a tweet late in the day sparked panic in the markets. Until that day, the market was not reacting much to the Russia–Ukraine headlines. Markets tend to ignore such geopolitical flashpoints unless the possibility of it happening increases significantly. And that is exactly what a tweet by a PBS reporter had done. It snapped the sleepy markets awake to the possibility of an invasion and its repercussions. It was the taste of what was to come.

How did you trade this tweet? What was your thought process then?
The tweet said that Putin had made the final decision to invade, according to U.S. officials, and that a full-scale invasion was expected to begin the following week.

I had a look at the markets, but there was not much of a reaction initially. I bought some WTI Crude Oil and some Bunds. Oil began to react and gathered within a few minutes. I bought more Oil as it accelerated, and then I sold the S&P. Risk-off started creeping into the markets, and everything was on the move now.

I held a big position in the Bund as I knew there was room for a big safe-haven [risk-off] move on this. The Bund had also been selling off on a hawkish ECB meeting. And there was a chance for position unwinding as there was a lot of short positioning after the last ECB meeting. So, the more it went up, the more it accelerated as stops were getting taken—forced short covering. And then, the S&P had also started to sell off harder on this. I sold some Russian Rouble futures as well. At the time, they were liquid and tradeable, but all liquidity evaporated after the invasion. The majority of the P&L here, multiple six-figures, was made on Crude Oil and the Bund.

Then, thirty-five minutes later, Jake Sullivan, the U.S. national security advisor, held a press conference. He said he did not believe the final decision by Putin had been made. It wasn't exactly a denial, but we will keep it simple and regard it as such. As soon as Sullivan said it, I reversed and sold the Bund and Crude Oil and bought the S&P. As the moves on the original tweet were quite large, I expected a decent market pullback on the denial. They did so, but the reaction was short-lived. Nonetheless, I managed to capitalise on the denial as I executed it as a smash-and-grab trade. I did not expect a huge trend out of this denial—more of a fast and short spike that eventually faded.

These "denials" are very common when a second source comes to contradict or play down the original source of the story. Markets tend to react very quickly to such news, although in most cases the market reaction gets faded [traded against] as participants know such denials are just political jawboning and that the original source is probably true. Nonetheless, it creates an opportunity.

What is the nature of the market reaction, its patterns, at the start of the story—at "phase one"?
The market moves tend to be straighter; they actually follow through and are slower. The market is asleep, and it takes a while for the theme to ignite. A slow-burner, as it was for 'A Mexican Standoff'.

When a theme starts to dominate, it is crucial to quickly identify the best risk–reward opportunities by trading the most sensitive markets to this new theme. As the Russia–Ukraine War theme evolved, so did the dynamics and market correlations to adapt to the new realities that the war had brought to the world.

However, at the time, at phase one, it was straightforward. Any hint that invasion was closer would lead to risk-off. Gold and bonds bid higher, Crude Oil bid and risk assets—the equities—sold off. The opposite would occur if there was an indication that an invasion was less likely. Within that narrative, you would expect European equities to be more sensitive to American ones, so during the European session, the focus would be on the DAX and the Eurostoxx.

Later, when the Russia–Ukraine War disrupted supply chains, we could see that bonds started behaving *differently*. It wasn't just a case of risk-off, with the bonds bidding higher, as before. Prolonged war meant more supply disruptions with higher commodity prices, which led to more inflation. Higher inflation prints, and bonds futures would trade lower.* It is key to identify that narrative change within a theme, to adapt to the markets you are willing to take the most risk on. But this only came at a later stage, months after.

How did the remainder of "phase one" play out?
So, after this first pivotal day on 11 February, the Russia–Ukraine theme had ignited. Markets were now "switched on" to the possibility of Putin invading sooner rather than later. But was it actually

---

* To simplify, the supply side was impacted as a result of the war and other pre-existing disruptions. Demand-side factors, like prevalent fiscal and monetary stimulus during the pandemic, had caused inflation prints to lurch higher. Notably, inflationary pressures began emerging before the Russia–Ukraine conflict, which then intensified existing trends. And central banks must respond as per their mandate to control it. Bond futures traded lower (yields higher) on implications that central banks may have to now increase or maintain interest rates higher and/or for longer. This period marked a significant shift from the preceding low-inflation, low-rate environment that had shaped market expectations for years; another—*Surprise!*—as stable rates of inflation conditioned the markets, and it participants, for well over a decade.

happening? Or was it just some fearmongering, false reporting? I came in very early to the office on 14 February, alert for any developments. I set up my news terminals to highlight any keywords related to the themes, alongside new alerts on the newswires to notify me instantly as soon as news dropped. I started to scan Twitter to make sure I followed all the right people who could break the news, from reporters on the ground to politicians to newspapers like Kyiv International and RT News. I also moved all my price ladders with the theme-sensitive markets in focus, so they would sit in direct line of sight. I kept the DAX, Eurostoxx, Bund, Rouble and Euro price ladders in this main area.

Around midday, Sergey Lavrov, the Russian foreign minister, struck a de-escalating tone by noting he proposed continuing talks with the West and was committed to diplomatic measures in solving the crisis. As soon as headlines dropped on the newswires, I sold Oil futures and the Bund and bought DAX and S&P. As an intraday trader, you are looking to offload size as soon as the news breaks and capture the move. Sometimes it goes ten to twenty ticks, sometimes fifty or sixty and sometimes more than a hundred. But because markets are very sensitive to themes at this stage, at 'phase one,' the opportunities keep coming, and the risk–reward is there to keep taking those trades.

There was a fast reaction in bonds and equities. However, [WTI] Crude Oil was choppy and never had a clean move. I made good trades on the Bund and equities—several six figures—but lost sixty thousand dollars on the short Crude Oil position. This is one of the reasons I tend to spread my risk across several markets. Some of them might react in a strange way, or there might be something else driving that market and preventing it from doing the move you're aiming for. In this instance, Oil did not react well; I went onside with over a hundred and fifty lots but ended up liquidating the losing trade.

In this instance, I was trading Oil to unwind some war premium on the comments. As the theme was in its infancy, it might have been a case where the big risk-on, a positive sentiment, eventually dragged Crude Oil up with it. Or it simply could have been something else.

Nevertheless, the *feedback* from the market was there, so next time I was ready to take more risk in bonds and equities and *instead* observe how Crude Oil futures would react. On the same evening, I remember there was a tweet by a CBS correspondent citing a U.S. official saying that satellite images showed Russian troops leaving assembly points and moving to an attack position. I traded this as the S&P sold off within a late-session risk-off flow, and the bonds and Crude Oil bid into the close of the day. Trading on just 11 February and 14 February, I totalled seven figures P&L.

On the night of 21 February, Putin signed decrees recognising the Ukraine Separatist Republics, and after a televised address, he ordered his troops to enter the Donbas region. This was the unofficial beginning of the invasion, although the main military operation started in the early hours of 24 February, when a full-scale attack was launched by Russia. All of us traded the overnight session on 24 February, and although it might have seemed straightforward, it was one of the toughest overnight sessions.

We were following all these people on Twitter who were reporting that the invasion had effectively begun with attacks stretching all the way to Kyiv. But the markets were not responding to it much until Putin gave a speech officially announcing a "special operation." I remember the market was very choppy, I kept selling the lows of the S&P and buying the bonds and getting chopped to pieces. Eventually, after quite a long time, the market released. But the losses from the very choppy price action meant this was not a career-making day for me. This was closer to an average up-day. Then, the following day, all markets reversed their overnight moves. The S&P rallied hard to finish positive on the day while Crude Oil, having bid over seven hundred ticks overnight—seven dollars a barrel—ended up closing unchanged on the day. This was a similar story in the bonds.

This phenomenon of such massive events is quite common. A large reaction overnight and an unbelievable reversal the day after. It happened with President Trump's 2016 Presidential Election victory and with the Brexit Referendum result. The initial reaction is to shrug off the event. However, the reversal rally in equities did not last long. In the next few sessions, as Europe and the U.S. started implementing aggressive sanctions on Russia and its banks, risk assets took a hit again while Bunds and Crude Oil futures bid aggressively once more.

What was it like when we started to reach "peak" theme? The middle of the story? Would this be 'phase two'?
Yes, in 'phase two,' we were close to peak theme, when it became the only market driver for a period, and everything else was second-order. This is where the big money is made; it is now *the* story of the markets. The market will mainly respond to anything related to the theme; any headline that pushes probabilities to one or other side will move markets accordingly. And the reaction to news becomes completely different than in phase one. It happens much faster, and it is all about speed. It doesn't require as much patience as things resolve one way or another very quickly. It is less subtle, and you do not have the luxury of time.

Importantly, hit a comment *late* in phase two with size that doesn't play out as it should, and you get killed. Generally, the equity markets love to find a reason to rally, so any resolution to a situation that made them sell off will cause a very aggressive move the opposite way when the 'war premium' is unwound out of the markets.

On 16 March, I remember a senior trader shouted out about an article in the *Financial Times* regarding a peace plan. It reported that Ukraine and Russia had made significant progress on a tentative peace plan, including a ceasefire and Russian withdrawal if Kyiv declared neutrality and accepted limits on its armed forces. It was, of course, important—if true. I instantly bought the DAX and S&P and sold the Bund, Crude Oil and Gold. As soon as the markets started drifting onside, I scaled into big positions. I lifted a hundred DAX and three hundred S&Ps while selling two hundred Crude Oil and five hundred Bunds. That was one of the biggest cumulative positions I ever built across markets up until then.

So, the markets started to trend and gather pace. The news had yet to hit the wires, and we knew that once it did, the market reaction would accelerate as the news became widely available. I sat tight and tried to run the big size, and the trade worked out. In the end, the peace plan was not confirmed by either side, so the news and the market moves ended up fizzling out.

What were you thinking as we hit the intense peak, phase two? What was it like?
So, the possibility of invasion increases—war or no war? The invasion then happens; will they only go into the Donbas region as a minor incursion? *What?!* They are bombing Kyiv now. This is *unexpected*, at least by the markets. How long is this going to last? They agreed to hold peace talks. *Huge!* Market rallies. On the first day of talks, the market rallies. If no outcome on talks, it pulls back. The second day of talks, the same.

Okay, I start giving up hope on peace talks. The French president, Emmanuel Macron, intervenes to set up a meeting between Putin and Zelensky. *Huge!* Market rallies—*buy, buy*. The meeting never happens—*sell. Wait!* The peace talks are back on again. The *Financial Times* reports that they are devising a fifteen-point peace plan—large market rally. The report gets denied by both sides—the market backs off. Agreement to stop military operation around Kiev… and the list goes on.

This was the intense phase of the theme. The peak. In the two-month period of February to March 2022, when the Ukraine theme was at its "peak"—*phase two*—I had my best-performing months. I netted several seven figures in those two months.

But then, from April onwards, the market realised that this would be a prolonged war with no possibility of a fast resolution, and hence, the theme-related volatility eventually died. That was the end of *phase two*; we were now going towards post-peak.

These are comments that I remember trading and having big days on. There are countless more; the same goes for any theme. But after a while, the market gets exhausted.

The theme goes into the background while another theme takes over. If nothing dramatic happens to change the status quo, then the markets won't react that much to it. And if nothing changes because we priced in everything already, that is when we move into *post-theme* or 'phase three,' let's call it. This is why constant adaptation to themes, understanding where the sensitivity is, picking the right markets and being up-to-date with developments and news are key to success as a global macro-news trader.

The last potential for strong performance was on 29 March. There were reports that negotiation teams had reached an agreement that involved Russia sharply cutting military operations near Kyiv. They also announced that talks were very constructive to the point that this ceasefire in Kyiv would potentially make way for a Putin–Zelensky meeting. Markets cheered the outcome and I also managed to offload big positions in this volatility. This was the last tradeable opportunity of the peak theme.

Even with the intense peak, would you regard post-peak or phase three as the most important part?
Yes, because phase three is when *most* traders lose money. At this point in the theme, the market is distinctly tired of moving on every headline. The market has made up its mind about where we stand, the status quo, and will only move if something significant comes to change it.

However, traders are still stuck in phase two. They are used to aggressively trading every comment from when the market was super-sensitive to the theme, and they do not quickly accept the new reality. They hit comments, but the moves do not happen. They hit the extremes of the move, and it bounces right back in their face—this is the defining feature of this third phase.

This is because the market has lost its sensitivity to the theme. I have seen many traders giving back everything they had made in phase two. Understanding the price action and order flow quickly when the theme has started to 'die' as we move to phase three is key to consistency and overall performance.

It is not to say that a theme cannot experience a second peak once more. We experienced multiple peaks in the 2019 U.S.–China trade war. During the pandemic, we experienced two short and sharp peaks in 2020—the outbreak at the beginning of the year and the Pfizer Covid-19 vaccine announcement in November. The summer months in between had certainly become a dormant, almost dead, post-peak-like environment in the middle of it.

This is why phase three is *the* most important. Because it is where the biggest differentiator of performance between traders occurs, not in the money they make, but in what they keep.

SUPPORTING MATERIALS

Watch a recording and analysis of *The Warrior* trading Phase One: the PBS tweet and the Sullivan press conference.

axiafutures.com/
toot-phase

THINKING IN NARRATIVE

'A Mexican Standoff' in Chapter Five, 'The Warrior: Part I,' demonstrates real-time adaptability as human creativity over a short period of time—a single day or night, never to repeat again. A dramatic, visual display of abductive reasoning. But 'The Arc of a Market Story' reveals the navigation of a theme as it develops over a period of months. These sudden real-world events do not conform to a schedule. Or, more importantly, the market's reaction to them does not conform to a schedule. There are no samples or time to train an AI model, to rewrite and adapt a systematic trading strategy, or an algorithm—it is over before you have your samples! And if you do, that implies that we are within phase three already, with far greater risk and pitiful reward.

But there is a deeper factor. Any algorithm or AI that is built off *existing* processor design will never be able to understand 'narrative' because to do so requires an understanding of time, which is simply ignored by computers. That is what story scientist Angus Fletcher argues in his paper "Why Computers Will Never Read (Or Write) Literature"

(2021c: 1–28), as he twins neuroscience and literature. And subsequently, we argue, it is why computers will never trade like *The Warrior*.

Fletcher argues the rhetorical functions that support narratives or stories within *meaningful* literature can only be conceived by the human brain, which is capable of *causal reasoning* or thinking in terms of cause and effect to understand "past–present–future components of a narrative." The headlines within a theme—the causes—have very different effects depending on where we are in the market narrative or theme.

Instead, the "symbolic logic of the [processor]… ignores such components… acting as though they do not exist," Fletcher writes, and symbolic logic can explain where two things are correlated—linked—but it cannot explain *why*, as "mathematical equations [symbolic logic] inhabit a perpetual 'now' where there exists no cause and no effect, logic cannot ever prove causation."

So, if computers cannot read or write literature through their very design, they will also face limitations in trading—application of dynamic risk-taking onto a vibrant, complex, story-driven world—regardless of whether a "simple" *if–then* algorithm is used or other models and approaches, like machine learning, that fall under the widening term of "AI."

All market themes, even simple one-off events, have their own beginning, middle and end, their own past-present-future. Emergence, then peak, and then post-peak. To navigate this successfully, you need to know where we have come from and where we are about to go. And that requires an understanding of time and of context to permit conviction and aggressive risk management that answers the *peak theme* in kind.

But as with many stories, there is a plot twist. Where everything you *think* you know or have come to expect suddenly shatters, and a reassessment is needed. That is to *think in narrative*—to leverage causal and abductive-based thinking. To understand cause and effect and time and to navigate a new environment with your best guess. That is the fusion of human creativity—connecting the dots—with gut instinct. And then understanding that this *is the time*—more than any other—to go big. Some may trade more 'accurately' than *The Warrior*, yet he will outperform them by several magnitudes. He will do ten times the size, and that is because *he believes.*

That is not all! Because, as our trader says, it is about who keeps the most when the dust settles. The transition from phase two to three—peak to post-peak—is where an inductivist approach, a market participant who is used to getting it right only after many repetitions, machine or human, is once again behind change. Staying ahead of change is a unique and enduring *human* faculty; that is the very best of our ability. We have identified it, so use it! Accentuate it, work to trust it, figure out how to unbury it from your trading approach, which is potentially saddled with too many self-imposed rules and methods of operation, and work it to the centre of your trading edge.

FORGER OF WORLDS

A deeper way to understand *The Warrior* is summarised in one word—*worldbuilding*. We will borrow from its overt use and analysis in science fiction and fantasy genres. Effective worldbuilding serves as a container to facilitate multiple stories that overlap or relate within that specific world. The act of worldbuilding creates a rich tapestry of details, depth, richness and colour in that world and, importantly, its rules and limitations.

No matter how fantastical that world may be, like the use of magic, for example, it is still governed by its own rules and logic to make the world believable, to allow the reader to immerse and suspend belief. It allows readers to appropriately weigh the realm of possibilities and to appreciate the context of information. This is a human abductive reasoning ability to *weigh* the realm of possibilities in an entirely fantastical world. First-rate worldbuilding weaves together as if a pyramidal-like superstructure, which determines the course of how the narrative and stories flow.

Consider how the rules of physics, geography and biology act as fundamental pillars and limitations of an imaginary world which in turn sets the course of its histories, laws, culture and other products of civilisation. From these, other aspects emerge, for example, the architecture of its cities and the appearances of its citizens—their behaviour, speech and beliefs. Within this superstructure is where the protagonists of a story operate, their own story arc progressing and weaving through that world.

Often, multiple stories and characters develop within that world. Each level of the pyramid structure strictly dominates the level above it, like the course of a river running against the valley rock. Visually we can draw this as Figure 6.1.

We will then take what we learnt about *thinking in narrative*, in *The Warrior*'s conception of "peak theme," and expand it in scope. Our trader does not simply engage in understanding a single market theme, story arc or narrative. Instead, he is actively worldbuilding himself.

Observe how worldbuilding is recast for financial markets in Figure 6.2. The immovable base, from the perspective of financial markets, is things like the economic backdrop, interest rate and business cycles, demographics and geopolitics. The base of the pyramid shapes the 'container' of this financial market world like the hard rules of physics, geography and biology upon a literary fantasy world. Upon these pillars rest secular market trends, which are dominated by the structure underneath it—the immovable economic activity, interest rate cycles, demographics and deep-seated behaviours also drive these trends.

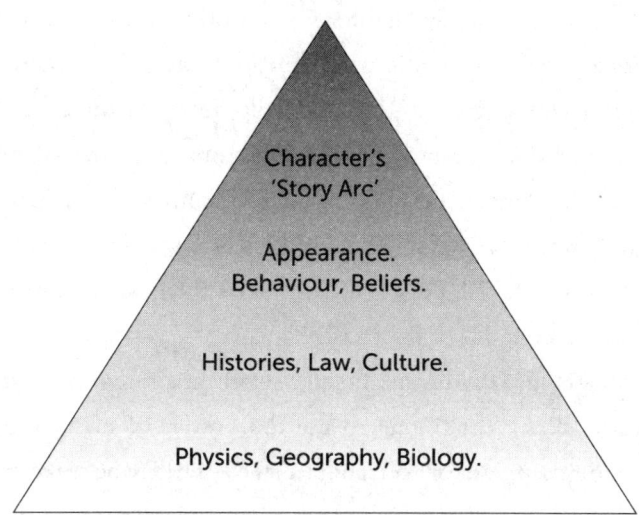

Figure 6.1 Fantasy worldbuilding.

Figure 6.2 Financial and economic worldbuilding.

We venture up the pyramid to discover other factors like market positioning, asset class rotations, correlations and expectations that emerge and recede like the tide upon the shores of the economic superstructure. Like the protagonists of a story in a literary fantasy world whose behaviour, motivations and appearances are shaped by the 'container' of history, laws and culture, so too is the market narrative shaped. Its story arc will peak and diminish as the market participants digest and act around it or discount it.

Immersion into this financial market world at a moment in time is what really allows *The Warrior* to use the powers of his best guess. Consider the discussions of avid fans of a fantasy series who try to anticipate how the story will proceed and what actions its characters will take. Plausible and likely theories of a fantasy world can be debated even if it is filled and governed by magic, monsters and mysteries—things that ostensibly do not exist in *our* world. Yet, successful worldbuilding permits this, and the context and framing of the 'container' allow its fans to use their causal and abductive reasoning to anticipate what will occur, even to be able to tier the most likely and least likely outcomes.

So too for *The Warrior*, who stresses to Theo in 'A Mexican Standoff' to always ask, "What is next?" Our trader is thinking of the 'shadow' future, the branches of how the world can evolve, yet it is rooted within the 'container'—the pyramidal superstructure of the market world and *its* reality.

Thus, he can never truly be surprised like an inductivist trader, no matter how rare and novel the sudden appearance of a news headline or theme. Immersion into this financial market world permits faster reasoning and decision-making, a shortcut, as the background work has been done before, and *The Warrior* understands its rules.

Confounding, then, as we have spent much time with *The Warrior* talking about how rules and the inductivist approach always have an expiration date in financial markets. Yet it is the strength of this worldbuilding perspective to imagine each of these worlds floating in the realm of possibilities, which are quick to become the singular reality, only to be shattered and discarded as needed as the rules change.

In its place: a new shadow future, a different world with a new pyramidal base and rules. *The Warrior* is just as quick to destroy these old or potential worlds in his mind as he is to create new ones, as many different iterations of the world are waiting on the fringes of his imagination. *That* requires creative faculty, so wholly prohibited to algorithmic or AI-related participants.

By understanding the financial market world context, surprise news headlines like in 'A Mexican Standoff' are navigated by asking "what is next?" *The Warrior* is building multiple story arcs, future copies of the current world in which one of them will eventually become the real world. In each of these story arcs, there will be a plot twist that will occur—the crescendo, the singular piece of news that will decide the course of events, a miniature watershed moment, and our trader is on the constant lookout, thinking, visualising *how* this will look.

That is where *The Warrior* will strike with maximum force, commitment and risk. Importantly, the clues to navigate this unfolding world could have been entirely different had the context of the 'market world,' its pyramidal base, been different. If it had taken place in a world with different geopolitical factors, then the correlations between markets may have played out differently. If that market world was contextually in an aggressive rate-hiking cycle—compared to placid and stable interest rates at the time—then this would have also affected the course of the river and, therefore, the reactions of market participants.

NAVIGATOR OF WORLDS

For *The Warrior*, creating these future paths inside the 'container' of the financial world will help to remember, on cue like a shortcut, the immediate plan of how to trade these different paths. This approach is akin to using a memory palace—a mnemonic technique where information is mentally associated with specific locations in a familiar space for easier recall. Each shadow future of the 'financial world' in *The Warrior*'s mind is created from his own memory palace, if you will, and he can refer to similar situations of the past *as clues* as to how he should operate in future ones.

For example, if one can remember the context of the Eurozone economic situation in 2012, a snapshot in time of other factors like the general interest rate environment, the European political situation, long-term economic and market trends, it becomes easier to recall the broader market narrative. Just as remembering the layout of physical halls and rooms allows one to navigate a building, recalling these interconnected factors helps reconstruct the financial world of that time. In turn, it is much easier to remember your own trades and activity during that period. This is likely why *The Warrior* has the overt ability to explain his trades in such detail as if they were recent occurrences.

The Warrior recalled in detail the context of the financial world surrounding a specific Bank of Japan meeting, the "three arrows of Abenomics," and the narrative leading into the meeting, the phrases he was anticipating and his subsequent trading of Yen futures, with *The Sphinx* sitting close by. But these events and trades took place a decade ago! Story is that context; worldbuilding is the container for it.

Yet, accurate recall presents another interesting phenomenon. *The Warrior* is noted by many for his prodigious memory, but so too is *The Sphinx*. What happens when you put two of these minds next to each other? "We have quite a unique relationship," *The Warrior* said. "Having sat next to him for years, he is the first person I go to whenever something happens. He has unbelievable market and macro-economic understanding. I completely and utterly trust him in whatever he says. I discuss the markets with him daily." Another instance, then, of the "extended mind" at work, as we explored with *The Collector*. It goes beyond the simple compensation in potential gaps in knowledge or depth in understanding. The two minds working in concert help with world *navigation*. If *The Warrior* is missing a piece of his worldbuilding, his utter faith in *The Sphinx*'s own world allows him to leap into his and take trades directly in this way. He has done it before. There is the trader's personal worldbuilding—the container of the market—but there is also a shared one communicated and updated in real time by the very trading floor, a lattice of interconnected worlds.

Moreover, the branches created in *The Warrior*'s mind do not simply contain one story, like a peak and post-peak news theme or a single trading day. This market worldbuilding contains numerous concurrent stories, weighed in relevance at any one time, and it affects each market participant in turn, as their reactions allow for further information gathering.

The Warrior's reflections on the performance of others on the trading floor allow him to piece together further clues to navigate the dynamic world. Different traders experience performance peaks and drawdowns by the nature of their trading edge. For example, our trader says, *The Collector*'s forte lies in trading economic data when it becomes contextually sensitive. Knowing this, *The Warrior* has additional clues that the market theme of interest rate hikes has entered a new phase, thereby allowing better navigation and risk-taking decisions.

Further still, the emotions that transpire across the trading desks contribute to this growing patchwork of information and clues to colour *The Warrior*'s worldbuilding, all working towards what happens *next*. The arc of most stories provides clues to give a semblance of where we are in the story, the beginning, middle or end. Often it is working towards a *plot twist*, and so too for the market theme. Witness enough of these market "story arcs" in their correct context, and you start to anticipate these plot twists—the sixth sense!

THE FATES IN RATES

Consider the following context. For over a decade *The Warrior* has been trading central banks in a zero-interest-rate policy environment, which featured the FOMC's few abortive attempts to raise rates. But as we speak to our trader in 2022, interest rate hikes have come globally and fast. The rules have changed, and already *The Warrior* has adopted new modes of operation, dealing with different market correlations, flows and behaviour.

"Understanding our place in time within the central bank narrative is no different. In many respects, it is *the* most important narrative. But it is a beast of its own," *The Warrior* said. "After twelve years of trading ECBs, my 'repertoire' of experiences is diverse. Yet, until February 2022, what I have *not* experienced is inflation. Since 2009, G7 bonds have been in a long-term bull market, not to mention a bigger, generational multi-decade Western bond bull market. The absence of inflation and enormous quantitative easing by central banks meant there was only one long-term play for the bonds, and that was bid. First, it was the U.S., Canada and the U.K., which saw their central banks pivoting hawkishly towards the end of 2021," our trader continued.

"Then the ECB pivoted in February 2022. Trading the first stage of the hawkish pivot—phase one, let's say—in late 2021, early 2022, is different to the later stages when the market and narrative are already expecting prolonged hawkishness, and we've had many 'big' rate hikes. So, the months from April to September 2022 have been dominated by central bank action. This became the dominant market theme peak as the Russia–Ukraine War theme was well into *post-peak*, phase three, and the markets reached a status quo on the war—for now," *The Warrior* said.

"It feels like the central banks have failed to guide market expectations. Forward guidance—the bank's publicised path ahead for rates—failed to the extent that it was dropped altogether, and instead, central banks have become 'data-dependent.' And that has created a lot of economic data trading opportunities. But after some time, as is always the case, the risk–reward in trading the economic data will fade away; this data, too, has post-peak-like effects where the market is tired and retraces all the moves very quickly, but many traders still trade this data aggressively like before and give back what they made in the first phase," he continued.

"During the Fed's June 2022 meeting, after the seventy-five-basis hike, Chairman Powell said that seventy-five basis—an extra-large hike—should not be considered as the *base* case going forward. But in July, the Fed hiked by seventy-five basis again! The market was very quick to settle and price in around Powell's words but *then* aggressively moved once this reality was not met. So, understanding where we are in this narrative is as important as anything else."

SUPPORTING MATERIALS

Watch a recording and analysis of *The Warrior* trading the ECB pivot in February 2022, and a collection of other central bank meetings over the years.

axiafutures.com/
toot-bank

BELIEVER OF WORLDS

We explained how *The Warrior*'s outperformance can be attributed to the distinct human ability of creativity to navigate events of a singular occurrence, not of a thousand. His ability to connect the dots and operate in real time allows for this kind of trading. Furthermore, we developed our understanding of our trader's skills from discovering the nature of "peak theme," thematic trading and "thinking in narrative" into an encompassing framework labelled as *worldbuilding*. Now we can address the fusion of all these elements—the part where gut instinct, emotions and dynamic risk sizing allows him to outperform by a large margin because *The Warrior* believes in his worldbuilding.

And for our trader to believe, to sincerely buy into the future, the shadow worlds he creates, to possess the entrepreneurial vision of the future, he summons complete emotional and physical conviction through the *power of story*. "Or how can I let myself *not* be aggressive?"

This is where it all matters! Because he has understood where we have come from and where we are going—the beginning, middle and end—the dimension of time in literature, of narrative and of story. That is how he summons the mania, a pent-up energy that is only generated by deep, sweaty, intense physical visualisation to create the belief, the faith, to operate within his own worldbuilding.

As we read with the missed FOMC rate cut in March 2020, in Chapter Five, 'The Warrior: Part I,' this worldbuilding and intense visualisation can take place over years to prepare our trader to take maximum risk in what will likely be the most important opportunity of the year and a handful over an entire decade. *The Warrior* repeated, emphasised and pushed hard throughout our interviews to ensure readers understand how much importance he places upon visualisation, rooted in the worldbuilding discussed above. *How will the headlines drop? Where? What will it sound and feel like? What will my price ladders look like? What size? What correlations? What will it feel like in those correlations?* "To achieve the biggest days, you need to properly expose yourself like never before," *The Warrior* said. "You need to feel uncomfortable, imagine and feel how you would hit the market, add to your risk by adding more size in the first seconds of an announcement. Visualise the surge in your P&L, which will enable you to keep taking risks and not freeze." This is a "pulling at your gut" sensation, as Haywood calls it, and it is a physical experience, akin to the locker-room warm-up of a boxer who is about to enter the ring. Or the ground-spinning nervousness before a big speech or public performance, because you know what it *means* at the intersection of where you come from and where you are going.

That is the power of story and understanding that the markets have reached a tipping point, a plot twist—the key watershed moment allows *The Warrior* to unleash himself into the markets. And it would not be a stretch to understand the power of story, as Fletcher says—narrative, its rhetorical devices affecting our mental states—to elicit feelings of excitement, healing, remorse, and to overcome fear, anger or struggle. To understand *what it means.*

And while we remain in a world that assumes calculations and processing are the superior answer to all domains, you, too, join a crowded race against many, trading notwithstanding. Left in your hand are the very things your competitors try to ignore—emotions, story, meaning and purpose—and those are the very foundations of an *enduring* and creative navigator of a complex, dynamic world whose only law is perpetual change itself.

So, *The Warrior* intertwines the story of markets, his own world-building and his journey to find meaning in the events about to happen and reach that level of *meaning* that will allow him to viscerally commit to whatever is about to occur.

That is the fighting spirit, the *will* to perform. And because computers do not understand meaning, as they do not understand narrative and story, or other traders who do not engage in the creative, dynamic act of thinking in narrative, will they ever experience a trade *pulling at your gut*? The rare moment where everything is aligned to *push! Push for the world record!* of absolute conviction. That is why *The Warrior* will do more size and hold it further. To consistently outperform. *The Warrior* does not out-think you. He will out-*believe* you. Because he must.

PRACTITIONER'S POSTSCRIPT

Explore resources derived from this chapter to further support the practicing trader.

axiafutures.com/
toot

Refer to
The Warrior's
section.

LEARNER'S IMPRESSIONS

Below are some personal impressions that *The Warrior* made on us that we still discuss with other traders.

1. *Creativity is the unassailable edge.* Our demise as human traders will be forever predicted. Yet it will only remain a prediction if we harness deep creativity to navigate change, to relearn and recreate. Systematic and rigid rules-based approaches—machine or otherwise—will always break rule-resetting financial markets. Make sure

to never entrench your trading too rigidly to risk recycling optimal practices as markets become seemingly static and temporarily reward you for it. Work on creating new ones. Push the meta-game. Nor is creativity restricted for the "news trader"—breaking away from that label and thinking is an act of creativity too!

2. *Denying the narrative.* The sublime thematic trader reveals themselves in the post-peak trading. The manic peak trading has all the intensity, yet the skill is to understand where we have come from and where we are about to go, to stop doing what every other participant has been trained to do after many repetitions. That is to navigate change once more. This is where *The Warrior* will keep most of his gains. Like *The Razor*, his ability to consolidate is a marker of mastery. To deny the action after so much of it.

3. *Worldbuilding.* But what of other themes? *The Warrior* will visualise possible future alternatives of this world, entirely new ones with different conditions. Because one will come true and he will be ready—not just intellectually—but he will be manic, fervorous, foaming-at-the-mouth ready to put on more risk than ever before when his world assumptions shatter and form new ones, across a depth of understanding with an infinite well of what this all means, the power of *his* story to elicit maximum conviction. *The time is now!* Humans understand this contextual sensitivity, but not the inductive, symbolic logic-based algorithm or AI.

What are your impressions? Write them down and converse with this book!

CHAPTER SEVEN

THE STUDENT

"Yes, mate, how are ya?" So entered *The Student* into 4 Endsleigh Street's Risk Room, now repurposed for an interview on a leafy August weekend. Tall and fit, despite welcoming two children in recent years, *The Student* has maintained a great physique, on top of what is demanded by the markets and other matters of daily life. When we met him in his late thirties, he still had a youthful look, with a lean face and a trusting and relaxed demeanour seemingly untouched by the easy cynicism that can mark a trader. And our Englishman, a London native, is too easy to talk to! Nothing off-limits, *The Student* was frank, honest and direct, sometimes, in fact, known to be *too* direct, therefore all the more charming.

Conversations with *The Student* felt as if between mutuals, with him as eager to discover and learn from us as we from him. He never pretended to give all the answers. While this is true for all the traders in this book, it was especially pronounced for this trader, whom we will aptly call *The Student* because of his pronounced learning ability. But consider the Latin origin—*studium*, "painstaking application." "How will you be a better student of the markets?" Haywood always asks the junior traders. Now simply *how will you better apply yourself?*

Our trader answered in kind: faith in the act of journaling. That is how he became the best listener to himself, to preserve an intentional state of self-awareness in the markets that will try to push this mindful state into oblivion.

And that is rooted in his fundamental trait of enduring humility. It has given him the world, at least, a professional one, for this trader reached a level of skill and achievement he once imagined to be God-given talent, only to find it was a question of nurture.

And wedged under his left arm was a hardback leather-bound tome, which he placed down on the table. *This year's journal.* Within are daily entries that follow the market's activity and calendar. His handwritten script rolls and swells between patient cursive, and hastened scratches on the page reflecting the market's volatility, and that of his mind. But what is really going on is *The Student* transmuting his pronounced ability to listen to himself, to diagnose and orient. His journal is the vehicle to monetise this ability.

"*The Student* has weaponised his mind, in effect, through journaling, and used it to build real-time awareness," Haywood said. "It is a mechanism to create a feedback loop, to deepen his self-awareness, to learn how to track himself and know when *not* to trade, to save himself for when it really matters. Others can develop technical skills and market awareness, like *The Student*, but there is always *one* thing a trader needs. And that is to summon from within and take risk at the right time," he concluded.

Conviction is context, and context is the power of story—the market story, and the personal story—as we have seen with *The Warrior*, to know where we have come from, and where we are about to go.

And *The Student* has come from a place of continuous year-on-year growth as if each year, a different trader is being studied. He closed 2022 with a multi-seven-figure P&L and remarkably low volatility in returns.

❖ ❖ ❖

From the outsider's perspective, *The Student* eventually evolved into a "hybrid" trader who consciously embraces trading news, events and technical trading. We have repeated throughout this book, in various ways, that the division between news or events and technical trading is rather crude; the market is too complex and dynamic to be divided into these neat categories. After all, we all trade the same markets, the same participants and the same flows regardless of approach. Nevertheless, we will still use these terms as a starting point to understand our trader.

Consciously, *The Student* strove to become an "all-seasons trader," one who could profit in a macro-dominated market environment and just as well in a technically driven one, absent any real news flow. Yet, this requires a vast accumulation of skill, experience and sheer market knowledge—far more than traders who focus on a deep 'silo,' who embrace depth over breadth. And that takes time. But there are many component parts in which understanding *one* aspect of the markets will transplant into understanding ostensibly unrelated ones.

For instance, as we will later read in *The Hero*, his intimate understanding of the price ladder led him to conceptualise order flow on a longer timeframe. This is how he perceives the market profile and uses it that way in kind; the same principles apply. By first understanding the dynamics of order flow, an entirely *new* world and possibilities suddenly reveal themselves.

Many readers have likely experienced the same in other domains, reaching a "critical mass" of experience intertwined with knowledge and skill to make what seems to be an evolutionary leap in their performance. The same is true in trading, as we have been feeling around the edges thus far in the book.

THE STUDENT

To explain it, we can introduce a concept—the "adjacent possible"—to formalise our understanding and permit a deeper appreciation of the entire process. This will help other traders reflect upon their career trajectory and journey.

In *Where Good Ideas Come From: The Seven Patterns of Innovation* Steven Johnson writes of the adjacent possible as "a kind of shadow future, hovering on the edges of the present state of things, a map of all the ways in which the present can reinvent itself" (2010: 31). And this reinvention occurs by recombining what Johnson terms "spare parts." These are nodes of information, concepts, skills and experiences taken from everywhere and anywhere.

A massed web of connections between these spare parts usually resolves into an idea; often, good ideas are simply viewing the same parts in a different light, Johnson explains. He concludes that "good ideas are not conjured out of thin air; they are built out of a collection of existing [spare] parts, the composition of which expands and, occasionally, contracts, over time" (2010: 35).

We can partly assess the quality of a trader's learning by the process of amassing these spare parts, and it is the knowledge, experience and skill filtered by reality of markets that sticks. We can then use the concept of the adjacent possible to understand how *The Student's* career evolved, and thereby our own.

THE WAY OF THE TED

Rewind to 2010. After a whirlwind four weeks of training, *The Student* found himself trading live markets—straight into the fire!—to trade only the European "TED spread." The Treasury-EuroDollar (TED) takes its name from its counterpart in the U.S. markets. While this spread can be constructed differently, in this case *The Student* traded the relative difference between the Schatz (the German two-year bond) and the Euribor futures contract derived from the Euro Interbank Offered Rate.

The Student's career began quite differently from many traders in this book, not least starting at a different prop firm altogether, but also as a different kind of trader—a 'spread trader.' Its counterpart, 'outright trading,' is the type you have been reading about so far in the book. Spread trading involves the simultaneous buying and selling of one market against another, like spreading the BTP against the Bund, the Italian ten-year bond against its German counterpart. Or trading the same contract but of different expiry dates against one another, like buying December 2024 WTI Crude Oil futures, and selling December 2025. The relative price *difference* between those two contracts, or markets, is the P&L, creating a *synthetic* market or 'product.'

This involves different skills, attitudes and approaches, a problem for *The Student* later in his career, as spread and outright trading are like the difference between squash and tennis. Some skills and knowledge are transferable, yet many practices, reflexes, muscle memory and approaches from one domain can hurt high-level performance in the other. It is as if one is about to compete at Wimbledon tomorrow having only played in a squash court for an entire career!

The orthodox approach—*read: meta-game*—to spread trading, at least as it was a decade ago, is to view the spread as mean-reverting. Traders seek to trade against, or "fade," the spread when the markets that compose it are out of line from each other for no tangible reason, as the prudent mean-reverting spread trader must assess. If a five-year sovereign bond trades far away from the rest of the "curve"—away from the pricing of the two- and ten-year sovereign bonds—then the five-year bond is like the knot in a piece of thread that has come partly loose. The further away it *relatively* trades away from the curve, the chances increase that the five-year bond will "mean-revert" and fall back in line, presenting a potential opportunity for the spread trader. That could be selling the five-year while simultaneously buying the two-year bond, for example. Often, outright trading is directional—not mean-reverting—going *with* the price excursion, though not exclusively. The other difference, of course, is that outright traders make a profit or loss through price changes in just a single contract rather than profiting from relative differences between two or more contracts like spread traders. *Squash and tennis!*

"There were eight of us in total, and they simply told us to figure it out," *The Student* said, "and it was the first time they put a new group of graduates to trade the [European] TED because of the way everyone had blown out of the TED in 2007–2008. They just wanted a fresh pair of eyes. We were complete virgins, and we made money from the outset, but we were wonderfully ignorant." A clean run compared to the previous intake group, of which *The Student* had originally been a part, only changing intake groups due to a last-minute opportunity to join a backpacking trip to Southeast Asia. This previous group had been assigned to trade Natural Gas spreads. "It so happened that it had been the worst time to trade these gas spreads; within six months, all of those new traders were gone," he said. Synchronicity, perhaps as *The Hero* would see it, or a routine divine intervention, as *The Warrior* would deem it. But shifting sands are a facet of life for traders. While *The Student* partly admonishes this as "too early of a start," the group of eight were competitive yet cooperative, especially in their bid to reverse-engineer and hopefully learn from their disastrous "blowout" days.

Our trader reflected on the nature of this early period. "The whole spread strategy was that you always trade to mean-revert. If it goes fives, you sell it. Sixes? Even better; sell more. Sevens and eights? Sell more! Nines?! *Bloody hell*—too far! *Puke the whole lot!* Needless to say, after we realised the way the TED moved, and after many blow-outs, we essentially had to trade it like an 'outright' and take a directional view on it. We became more deliberate, but with just a few of us left, we were not as fearless as before. But then we expanded our view and looked at other markets, at how they can impact the TED. For example, we wouldn't have sold the spread because of the activity in the peripheral bonds. We started to think a bit more about the implications of the macro-economic background and developed our view of the correlations between markets."

Two years on, our trader inched towards discovering his real "core fascination." That is, a phenomenon or a feature of the market that personally draws us to it. It provides as much creative inspiration as it does *motivation*: "We sit there and see the world markets moving on events. How can you beat that?" *The Warrior* says—and it suggests what your natural market observations are, the cornerstone in personalising your trading strategy. Our trader was fascinated by understanding and trading macro-economic themes. The issue, however, is how to get from *A to B*. If *The Student* in the present had met himself a decade earlier and sought to teach and unload everything he knew onto his younger self, it likely would have been a futile attempt. *Why?*

Because at this point, our trader's career had been more defined by *limits* rather than anything else. But "the strange and beautiful truth about the adjacent possible is that its boundaries grow as you explore those boundaries," Johnson writes in *Where Good Ideas Come From*; "Each new combination ushers new combinations into the adjacent possible. Think of it as a house that magically expands with each door you open. You begin in a room with four doors, each leading to a new room that you haven't visited yet. Those four rooms are the adjacent possible. But once you open one of those doors and stroll into that room, three new doors appear, each leading to a brand-new room that you couldn't have reached from your original starting point" (2010: 31).

The older *Student* had unlocked so many prerequisite skills that would be completely inconceivable to the young *Student*. It would be too many doors down, to continue with Johnson's analogy. The young buck would have to go through it, meanderings and all. But this tells you where to go next! These boundaries, these limits in skills, knowledge and experiences are a target: which door to open next.

And to our readers, those novices who simply feel overwhelmed by the developmental journey that lies ahead, it is prudent to *trust the process*, to not stare down the hallway at the infinite doors of the unknown. And that trust is based on understanding or discovering your "core fascination" and sticking to it, to never be far removed from it. It can answer the question of what skills to develop next. Then you will eventually remerge as something fresh, new, wholly recreated.

None of the traders in this book knew, anticipated or predicted what kind of trader into which they would evolve in the upcoming decade. If you can predict it now, with so much undiscovered, can it be that innovative? You cannot know the path ahead. Jumping too far ahead, with concerted vision yet lacking all the skills that must be picked up along the way, is to act in vain.

Rather, these traders became ardent explorers of the adjacent possible, the edge of *their* known world, and pushed, in their own ways, to continuously expand it and have succeeded accordingly. If you can target your limitations and identify current skills, then you have *something* to work with as you push boundaries of what lies ahead in your field of vision and slightly outside it. What lies on the other side of the mountain is unknown, but you can survey its foothills from where you stand.

For *The Student*, this came in the form of discovering the correlations between markets, of how their activity pulled and tugged one another. This opened the door and pushed his possibilities slightly further into trading news and events, the domain he now identifies as *his* core fascination. "I remember hitting the Bobl [German five-year bond] on an LTRO [long-term refinancing operation by the ECB] that was hugely oversubscribed for a six-tick winning trade. I got a lot of satisfaction from that," he said.

If traders doubt the validity of their framework—if the core is rotten—then how can they ever build conviction to trade size with purpose? How could they scale their business on a premise they do not believe? What, in the end, is the point of it all?

But then a problem. "We started to trade news. Yet I felt my knowledge about market fundamentals was still lacking, frustrated that when a headline came out, I didn't understand it, but it would send the TEDs *flying*. I discussed it with some of the senior traders. "Where do I go; how do I learn this?" *The Student* said. "I was still making money in the TEDs, but they were getting harder to read and more compressed. I was frustrated and I saw what *could* be made on trading news, but eventually I also wanted to make the transition from spread trading to outright. I wanted to head in that direction, yet I felt I had no one to follow or to help me. No one on that floor traded outright or news in that way. They had their own spread to trade and didn't care for much else," he recalled.

In other words, our trader could now see down the hallway, yet did not possess the spare parts needed to unlock those doors. As we explored with *The Collector*, the value of a trading floor can be assessed, in part, through its "extended mind"—a location with diverse domain expertise that can be drawn onto to tackle challenges, learn, to simply put more of those spare parts on the table. We propose that the more diverse and accessible the extended mind of your trading collective, community or floor, the faster and further you will be able to push the boundaries of your own adjacent possible.

In the case of *The Student*, he was starved of these spare parts, curtailing his adjacent possible through the lack of a strong extended mind at his initial prop firm. Such an environment "was part of the reason why much of my education in markets happened much later on the AXIA floor," our trader said; "it was just too stunted early on." By 2013, a change was needed. And this was not born from the regular reasons—losses—but from an enduring prophylactic mentality that we noted in our trader. Change now while you are ahead.

HOME TEAM

"So, I joined *The Godfather* in 2013… it was all Greeks and me, but I felt at home with them," our trader said. "*The Godfather* was already very established and had evolved from trading the TEDs to the Bund–Bobl–Schatz fly, something I would eventually learn to trade and move away from the TEDs. I respected him, and it was a positive step for me." This specific *fly*, or a butterfly spread, was composed of the relative value between three different bond maturities: the two-, five- and ten-year German bond futures.

This was a positive change for *The Student*, who would still perform well as a fly trader over the next few years. Yet, his mind was still fixed on the need to evolve, to change into an *outright*, not spread, trader, to continually expand his adjacent possible. That, he discerned, was how he could best reach his core fascination.

But, at the time, there were not many places he could best identify to do just that, and the invitation from *The Godfather* to join his team was too strong to turn down. Yet, *The Student* was still amassing his spare parts of a deeper understanding of the relationship across 'the curve' of these German bonds with different maturities and their interrelationships, further developing his knowledge of market fundamentals, correlations and subtle price ladder tactics. At least, now he was not *just* a TED trader, and he was still experimenting with outright trades in the Eurostoxx and a few other markets, yet not finding sustainable traction. "There was a gradual progress in trading these spreads, yet it wasn't enough, it wasn't exciting," our trader said.

And the universe would conspire still; then came a shock that some traders like *The Razor* and *The Warrior* know all too well: account loss through business mismanagement. But this time, not related to the events of Firm Y!

While the sordid details are too personal to share, *The Student* would eventually leave that trading firm, which provided the catalyst for change, to finally become an outright trader. It would take him across various trading desks in Dublin and Richmond, a London suburb. However, *The Student* could not find a trading floor without steep compromises, especially one that would realistically develop his desired *outright* news trader skills. And that was fast becoming the most relevant skill, just as what turned out to be the second part of the Greek debt crisis was rearing its head.

The Student eventually made his way onto the AXIA floor, just as the firm outgrew its initial small space—the "shoe cupboard," where traders jumped over each other to get to their desks. But this time, *The Student* ostensibly committed to transitioning to an outright trader, a seemingly straightforward transformation. What could be so hard?

As it turns out, it would take another four years for our trader to regard his transition as complete. "I had a plan to trade spreads in the morning and outright markets in the afternoon. I quickly found out

THE STUDENT

that was not possible; it's very hard to transition doing both. No one trades these at the same time. It resulted in executing both badly. A news headline would come out and mess up my existing spread position, and I would trade the comment late via outright markets."

His past success in spread trading, he said, had become a crutch. While the desire to transition was strong, it would take our trader another year until he stopped trading any spread strategies altogether. And this is how the adjacent possible can be used as a *diagnostic* tool. *What is impeding the exploration of your adjacent possible?* In the case of *The Student*, we can regard this crutch as just that, even if the spare parts are being accumulated from input from the new traders around him.

That is why we deem humility, a very pronounced trait in our trader, a positive because it enables him to listen to others. In reverse, for example, many newer traders show remarkable stubbornness in really integrating with the "extended mind" of a trading floor or community, invariably limiting their adjacent possible. But it applies to veteran traders too! Often a lack of humility or pride will prevent a lucid reassessment that the time has come for reinvention and of how long and painful that process will be.

Note the lapses in *The Student's* humility. "My ego got the better of me. I thought I would be different, to be the one to trade outright and spreads," he said. "It took me a long time to throw in the towel on spreads, even though it had been leading up to it for years." As discussed with *The Collector*, evolving by necessity once a trader's edge has stopped working is one matter, but changing direction while a trader's core performance is *still* viable and profitable is another challenge altogether. The trader not only has to intentionally forfeit income but is likely to contend with steep drawdowns—the cost of learning something new. Our trader struggled to navigate the contradictions of performing as a spread trader and learning as an outright trader.

THE ANTAGONISM OF LEARNING AND PERFORMING

The Student's struggle in embracing the transition from spread trading to outright is reflective of a great progression trap that many newer traders, or veteran traders reinventing themselves, experience. And that is the meeting point between learning and performing, a crossroads that some traders never leave, and they often regress in both endeavours. Awareness of the crossroad helps them to deal with it, but it *cannot* be circumvented, only traversed.

"I wanted to trade outright full-time, but I couldn't leave the spreads as they were paying me a living. Yet it was a juggling act between devoting time to learning to trade outright while balancing the intensive time needed to manage my spread positions. There was a source of frustration blending the two."

These two modes of operation require opposite habits, conflicting rules of thumb and best practices. *The Student's* need to trade, to *perform* on his spreads, while switching to trade to *learn* outright is an alternative way to view the source of his frustrations. Put simply, you cannot do both. Table 7.1 lists examples of the antagonistic requirements a trader has to adapt to.

Often, a beginner will not know what the best learning practices are to maximise their chances of success. Later, the same trader will strongly improve their learning ability, only for these very practices to be challenged as they need to start *performing*. Because success in 'performance mode' demands that the best practices and habits in 'learning mode' be supplanted. Worse yet, the very best practices in learning mode can be the worst and the most loss-making in performance mode. *Worse yet!* Spending two years or more in deep learning mode also engrains the best practices, which are very difficult to change while traversing into performance mode.

Learning Mode	Performance Mode
Mind is a sponge	Mind is a filter
Trying all trades; trial and error; expanding "competencies"	Restricted to trading only proven "competencies"
Participating to learn (P&L preservation does not matter)	Not participating in order to perform (P&L preservation is paramount)
Changing strategy, method, style frequently; experimentation	No dramatic change, itinerant adaptations; commitment
Listening to other traders; adapting what they say	Listening, yet going your own way
Humility to learn	Confidence to reject
Journaling to learn	Journaling to reflect
Outcome not measured by P&L	Measuring outcome by P&L
Progress measured by understanding	Measuring progress by error-pruning
More "spare parts"; more is better	Less is better; focus; reductive mastery
No "residue" of activity; current trading day does not impact the next	Strong "residue" of activity; current trading day impacts the next
Process of finding what prompts repeated "negative" emotional reactions and decisions	Process of managing what prompts repeated "negative" emotional reactions and decisions

Table 7.1 *Examples of the best practices in learning and performing mode; entirely antagonistic.*

Then the crossroads transforms into an insidious trap. Often, the trader observes their initial progress was underpinned by improving their learning best practices and habits. Seemingly, the logical response to underperformance would be to double down on the best learning practices once more. But the stubborn insistence on preserving a mentality of learning mode while trading to perform will likely only accentuate an inevitable drawdown or ensure account loss.

Participating to learn, for example, is an essential best practice in learning mode. A trader must try it all, experience trial and error and throw eggs at a wall. What sticks becomes a central focus, just like *The Adventurer's* simple approach. If the trader justifies *not* participating due to preserving fictional P&L on a simulated account, or a small trading account, then they must realise there is immense opportunity cost in experiencing and learning from what might be a rare opportunity. That singular experience might later be converted into a real substantial edge, far more valuable than fictional P&L or the insignificant remuneration from a small account.

However, once in performance mode, with real risk and a P&L to manage, justifying losses as a "learning experience" can become a vicious downward spiral. That is why traders are really defined by what they reject. Over-trading, revenge trading and other traps can be camouflaged as excuses for what had previously been a legitimate best practice: *But I'm participating to learn*, the trader says. *Correct!* if they are still a novice who has seen little. But this trader must refrain from doing what his job description says to do. Instead, they must *not* trade. Because they are long supposed to be in performance mode.

So, central to this concept is the balance of managing these two antagonistic forces. A trader cannot be stuck forever in learning mode, as it then squarely remains an intellectual exercise. Likewise, a trader cannot shut off learning altogether as it is guaranteed that the markets will change and render the trader extinct.

Instead, it is a different weighting on the same principle, depending on needs. For example, 'learning' in learning mode is experimental,

THE STUDENT

entailing accidents, discovery and boldness to enact large changes to create a raw edge, while 'learning' in performance mode is iterative; careful adaptations build over time as the trader is 'learning' by observing the market's evolution and studying their own performance. The 'learning' here is understanding how to scale, and to refine and perfect that edge. Experimental and iterative learning are a different weighting of the same process, appropriate for where a trader is in their career.

Beware! A trap can become an infinite death spiral if a trader continuously but erroneously responds to learning issues with the best practices of performance mode, or addresses performance issues with the best practices of learning mode. Still experimenting wildly rather than prudently iterating. Let us provide a few further examples of various traders who are stuck at the crossroads trap, which we have personally observed in some traders in the wider community.

1. A trader is dutiful in creating a database or a log of personal observations, thoughts, market patterns and reactions, macro-economic developments and more. At this stage, this is what a "journal" means to them, and it has been a useful framework for *learning* about the markets. Later, they transition to trading a real account, but then performance is lacking. Therefore, they answer the issue by doing *more*: further tracking of more market patterns, reactions and analysis. This saps energy but also confuses the trader, and they lose their very identity or their framework of how they understand the markets. Their pattern logging efforts do not evolve to performance mode, where the journal—a concentrated effort of logging information—instead needs to become a tool for reflection and "understanding where they are relative to their process," as *The Hero* said. Their journaling best practices in learning mode become a hindrance in performance mode.

2. A trader develops a credible, well-built framework, edge and personal understanding of markets. They amass "spare parts" by extensively discussing and experimenting with the suggestions of other traders. As they transition to performance mode and inevitable drawdown occurs, the trader overweighs the advice and feedback of other traders. It seemingly worked before! But instead of making small iterative adaptations, they quickly switch approaches based on the latest conversation, only to switch once again following another bout of drawdown. The once-proven and useful input now serves as a conduit to confusion and loss of confidence in the very existence of their edge. Their mind is still stuck in funnelling advice and feedback rather than filtering it.

3. A trader needs the best practice of participating actively; they take *all* the trades via simulation regardless of the temporary daily swing in P&L. Yet, at this stage, the measurement of progress in learning mode is not assessed by P&L. Moreover, the market conspires to mask their simulated trading activity as a profitable and successful performance. In reality, the risk taken to achieve this performance is unrealistic in live trading but this is not significant in early learning mode, and it is never addressed. The trader then goes live, and their performance collapses, as the outcome is now measured by P&L, and various "good-sense" risk management limitations are suddenly in place. Now the trader cannot take *all* the trades and is not carefree of the risk this requires. The 'residue' of the emotional drain and the impact on morale from previous days now all matter. The P&L of the previous day and week is *cumulative*, and not 'forgotten,' as it was in learning mode.

THE STUDENT

Much of what exists in the body of knowledge of our trading domain must be taken as *highly* contextual, but that is seldom mentioned. And you likely have come across much of the above in Table 7.1 already—*but!*—it is now filtered through a more appropriate context. All the above "good practices" are valid depending on the situation, but they can *also* be the worst practices. It is a matter of applying the right thing at the right time and then weathering the difficult adjustment period of traversing the crossroads from learning to performing, undoing much of what became habit.

Yet, *The Student*'s story reveals more. Spending too little time in either can be detrimental, which is the reason why he assessed his first-year trading as something that "stunted [him] as a trader." That is, being forced to perform too quickly, to the detriment of wider learning, which yields better fruit in the future. A trader transitioning too quickly risks lacking real depth and understanding of the wider world, the context of their edge and their place within the market. Overemphasis on performance *now* forces a trader to learn by rote, and that is only sustainable until the market changes.

But the reverse is far more common yet just as dangerous. Traders stuck in learning mode, who never permit their amassed learning to make contact with reality, will often find themselves on a lonesome road of pure fantasy; years wasted on something that simply isn't feasible when trading with actual participants.

And *when* is it the right time to traverse? Your judgment will be the best candidate to decide on the best time. It has to be: your observation and judgement are the two things you must trust to find your way back to shore. Getting this part wrong *is* part of the process—such is the circuitous route of invention. And that is why the crossroads cannot be circumvented, only endured. Believing you can ignore them is also part of their trick!

FAITH AND THE CALL

Viewing our trader's path, progress and, ultimately, P&L in *reverse* makes his journey that much more remarkable. That is, where he was in 2020 would leave you astounded compared to where he was two years prior, and so too as we meet him in 2022. Now, he trades multi-dimensionally, as comfortable with a market profile as he is on the price ladder. He is as successful in trading news headlines and events as he is trading larger market moves off 'technical' reasoning—all as an *outright* trader, thereby closer than ever to becoming an all-seasons trader. *The Student* now trades any market as relevant and suited for the environment, across all asset classes.

Yet, in his first year on the AXIA desks, 2017–2018, our trader had lost the *entirety* of the account he had initially funded through regular trading. So, what occurred in this initial three-year period, up to 2020, to allow such a steadfast transformation? For our trader, this first amounted to a profound mindset shift—in fact, the simultaneous act of holding on and letting go. *Trading! An act of contradiction.*

"What do you really want? Trading spreads was a crutch. I was scared to give it up as it was making me money; especially if I never made it as an outright trader," *The Student* said. "I would have told myself years ago that I have the ability to do it; I just need to take that *leap of faith*." And faith extends further. "I had lots of conversations with Kyriacou and Haywood to hit the issue on the head. In the end, I was simply *forced* to give up trading the spreads. I have to credit Kyriacou too; he was very supportive; he believed in me, and gave me leeway on the account. That was on pure confidence to keep going." Faith is a team effort.

And that can be as simple as sitting in the same sphere of influence. At previous trading floors *The Student* recalled "looking up to

THE STUDENT

these other traders who were next-level, and that is just how it was. They were the superstars." *The Student* thought these traders to be abnormalities, touched by the Gods. "Yet, with *The Warrior* and *The Engineer*, I could see first-hand what they did, and how they did it, as they shared so freely. *The Warrior* had his video recordings, and *The Engineer* had his debriefing process, his weekend work and the way he reviews his trades. I was never exposed to this; I simply thought that if I matched that approach, then I would give myself a good chance." And so he did, revealing to *The Student* that it had been a question of nurture all along; the superstars sitting on one's left and right are mortal, human—a product of process.

Likewise, the ability to trust the process, to possess a vision and eventually manifest it, is central not only to every trader in this book, but seemingly the case with high performers in every field. As we explained earlier, the process cannot be circumvented, yet awareness of it helps to provide clarity on the journey ahead. In other words, it helps to *keep the faith* when there is no seeming path ahead.

But then, the act of *letting go*. "For various reasons, I realised I possessed the guilt of being a trader. Ten years now passed, and part of me always wished to do something else," *The Student* said. Even in 2013, when our trader was still profitable, he questioned the nature of his profession. He was in two minds about changing jobs.

"I told myself I needed to get to a certain level of profit, and if I did that in a set amount of time, then I would quit trading," he said. And the setting of this monetary target, for deep-rooted reasons, became a significant barrier. But, as in trading, and in life, this was not obvious at the time. "*The Student* outperformed in early 2020, yet still settled into prolonged drawdown," Haywood said. "There was a large amount of pent-up skill that had been built in the previous three years, which was not released."

But then came what our trader regards as the most important trading conversation he ever had with Haywood and Eric Jousse, a senior mentor at AXIA. They recognised that our trader's specific profit and time goals, in order to quit, were the very things limiting his progress. "It was important as I now realise how strong that time pressure was in the back of my head," The Student said. "Every change, positive or negative, took me closer or further away from my goal of quitting and doing what I *thought* I wanted. It forced me to trade what I wanted rather than what was in front of me. Discussing this had made it obvious what was going on." Jousse himself is highly credited for helping to develop The Student's technical trading skills, as he works with many across the experience curve. This is typical of his involvement. "When a new trader completes our training programme, Jousse takes charge and takes them to mastery," Haywood added. "He is the lifeblood of the coaches, meticulous and detailed, with his own long and interesting history as a very successful trader."

Following this juncture, The Student embarked on his most consistent run ever, which ended a prolonged six-month drawdown that began in the middle of 2020. The role of acceptance was important in this. "It turned out I was getting in my own way. After discussing it with my parents, they had always been supportive about trading. Perhaps I misinterpreted how they felt about it, and it's partly why I always thought I would trade for a while and reap as much monetary reward as I could, before doing something completely different," he said. Compared to the journey of other traders, The Student had come to trading by near happenstance—certainly not the usual story of deep passion for financial markets—it was "originally further down the pecking order," he said. And our trader had to find a way to let go of the rest.

The period 2017–2020, then, can be reviewed as our trader amassing the "spare parts," and connecting those existing parts he picked up as a spread trader, to make use of them as an outright trader.

Nevertheless, while our trader had been profitable in this period, with a six-figure trading month in 2019, he still regarded it as a period of inconsistency, still troubled by his underdevelopment and progress, traversing the crossroads of learning and performing. But then came March 2020, and the pandemic fuelled the volatility. It would take the act of letting go of guilt and meaning to fully unlock what was to come, realisation and acceptance of what it takes to slowly consolidate into a deeper performance mode. That was 2021, a period of extreme consistency and growth in technical skill as much as P&L. This prepared the stage for 2022, where he accumulated multiple seven figures before the year had run out. Beyond acceptance and an answer to *the call*, Haywood attributes the "pent-up skill" of 2017–2020 as an ode to the *power of journaling*.

THE DUAL TRADITION

It is somewhat telling of humankind, so steeped in war and conquest, action and energy, to yet also remark upon the importance of religion, reflection and observance. This tension between the martial and religious traditions is similar to that of *action and reflection*. Ineffective when disjointed, yet holistic when these seemingly opposed states are twinned. It is action that prepares you for reflection, and reflection that prepares you for action.

And *that* is the nature of journaling; its power is a space where we twin these traditions. This is the sense of how we will be viewing *The Student*'s relationship with journaling, not simply to learn—a glorified database—but rather to build a "self-awareness engine" that mobilises our trader into action.

"With *The Student*, we cannot underestimate his *humility*. He looks at you deeply with a non-sceptical look and allows you to bring the best of your presence," Haywood said. "The space to bring across your message in a non-hurried way."

And this self-awareness engine is predicated on the ability to *listen to oneself*, in the same way our trader listens to others. And seldom do traders do any of this. Typical culprits are those who write long essays about their trading each day to debrief "rote"—to go through the motions—and never take the time to reflect, to re-read and take the necessary steps to elicit change from the most valuable feedback they could have read. This period of reflection, born out of action, highlights their important coexistence. Traders who cannot reflect, cannot listen to themselves, forgo these incredible learning opportunities. *The Student* describes his approach.

"I am trying to dig deeper and ask myself questions, neutrally and with no self-judgement. It is to bring awareness of *where* I am in the morning and throughout the day. I ask myself, how am I feeling? What is my energy like? What is my predominant emotion? Am I angry? Why and what has triggered this? It is to reduce the intensity of these emotions if they are somewhat out of control. This works just by getting it down on paper. For example, *I am feeling anxious about Bunds since it has broken a key level, and I missed it since I came in late to the office and had a terrible sleep. My urge is to get into this trade without considering objective technical data. Do I have an entry? What is my risk?* By doing that, I'm slowing myself down, as *The Engineer* would say. I am becoming more synchronised with the market and with my emotions. And I understand the fear of missing out is so strong in that scenario, desperate to trade and click. Two years ago, I would have lost a considerable amount of P&L at eight-thirty in the morning."

THE STUDENT

Moreover, "the physical practice of journaling, of pen to paper, has created real edge," said Haywood. That is no metaphor. In *How to Take Smart Notes* (2017), Sönke Ahrens highlights a study where a group of students wrote their notes by hand while others typed. Handwriting slowed the students down. It forced them to grasp the core ideas of the lecture first and to write their notes afterwards. In contrast, the students who typed their notes circumvented this immersion (Ahrens, 2017: 78). It was a low-effort regurgitation that resulted in less understanding and diminished learning compared to the hand-writers who learned on a far deeper level.

The concept of "slowing down" will resurface with *The Engineer* and *The Hero*—both strong advocates of this physical practice who provided the seeds of inspiration for *The Student* to do the same. Because it is all too easy to write by keyboard! Too easy for the trader to get it all down in some note-taking software and never look at it again.

Next, take for instance a specific way our trader directly improved his performance via error-pruning. *Action to prepare for reflection.*

> Anxious and embarrassed. I wonder what others would think if they saw what tiny size I used on the trade. I question myself again on how I could be so fearful on a trade with a great technical and macro-set-up yet so scared to lose. What is this frustration and anxiety about? Is it a feeling of failure and emotional discomfort that every loss brings? My measure of success is in P&L and my P&L is in direct comparison to my colleagues. I keep considering how much better they must have done compared to me. Why does that matter? It makes me feel inferior as a trader. It leads to anxiety and frustration as I ruminate on the trade and then take on an impulse trade that leads to a spiral of bad decisions and trading.
>
> *Extract 1*

The Student explains the context of this entry. "Prior to writing this, when I had executed a news trade badly or made a small amount, I conjured up this idea of how *perfectly* others did and would beat myself up about it and eventually stop out for the rest of the day. As crazy as this sounds, this was common behaviour," he said. "Getting it down on paper brought awareness to these feelings and reduced the intensity; it stopped me from clicking too much. Instead, I banked a profitable day there, however small that may be. This is a lot better than going home with a loss on the day. This is how you notice this behaviour, no matter how odd, and that was the beginning of the end for that specific pattern of behaviour." This is a trader who *listens to himself*, what he calls the ability to self-coach, a step closer to building his self-awareness engine. We can regard Extract 2 as a way to "download" his thoughts onto the page. That is, to help get them out of the way or simply acknowledge that they exist. Which, to our trader, is already a great step indeed.

> Feeling anxious, not committed to trades. Not done prep for events today. Feel nauseous and unsure. Little energy and motivated by loss avoidance rather than confidence. Looking for a freebie rather than engaging in the process. Thorough process and checking criteria is the only way around this. Pointless for me to be here with this mindset. Need to refresh process and criteria.
>
> *Extract 2*

But it had been easy for our trader to be "too judgemental" of what actually came onto the page. So, he now aims to be increasingly observational. But the judgemental behaviour was learnt behaviour, a bad habit. *The Student* specified how, in fact, his journaling did not purely start with stimulus from *The Hero* or *The Engineer*, but as a product of his spread trading era—a simple way to keep track of his spreads. In turn, he began to write down his thoughts and emotions in real time but in quite a detrimental fashion. "My wife once read these journals and saw how abusive I was towards myself," our trader recalled. "That was not a force of good. Yet, I didn't notice it in that way until she mentioned it. So rather than blurting it all out, I rather 'state' that *these* are my emotions. You are more observant and factual rather than feeling it out too much on paper." These entries were profanity-laden, negative and messy, a disorganised stream of consciousness. This explains why our trader specified that he has repurposed this into writing "neutrally with no self-judgement," as he aims to tether his questions and self-talk to objective market information and real-time activity.

This process was specifically designed by *The Student* to incorporate technical and "clue-seeking" information within his writing. Earlier in his journey to develop his technical trading skills, he had been deliberate in writing down the relevant market information with a specific template he had designed. The template itself, basic in nature, was more valuable in forcing the habit of returning to objective market information. Our trader elaborates. "I would write down to assess market profile factors, the tempo of the price ladder, the activity of correlated markets and where we are with respect to long-term structure. When I felt the desire to trade, it would make me reassess. Have I got four out of seven factors in play? Ideally, I would mark off the seven. This is when I was at my most structured, to avoid too much bias, impulse and over-trading." In effect, *The Student* created this structure to reduce the variance in the outcome of a trade, another method to "slow things down."

Importantly, this real-time notetaking does not supplant the practice of the "cold" dissection of markets and performance that takes place in an end-of-day and weekly debrief, as per the process of *The Engineer*, which we will explore further in that trader's chapter. But know that *journaling* and *debriefing* are not interchangeable. The former is the intersection of real-time thoughts, emotions and observations. The latter is an organised breakdown of performance, market patterns and a record of events. And *The Student* certainly revisits his journaling; it is implicit in the process!

So, this free-flow journal with little structure allowed our trader to navigate the learning and performance crossroads. Consider Extract 3; *reflection prepares for action*, and so too the pause gives a chance to arrest bad action.

> Ladder very thin and bouncing from absorption points. Delta is still increasing despite two-way flows. High RVol but low auditioning at price and very low book quantity. The seller still present and still big absorption at prices preventing the market from accelerating... Lack of clear price action and order flow keeps letting me out of Stoxx. Twice I added into poor areas and paid the highs due to a lack of focus and conviction where I had to reposition and hold from the sell area. I didn't check my criteria and was too attached to my P&L and the thought of giving it back with no focus of process and awareness. Refocus and reset.
>
> *Extract 3*

Journaling practice reduced the friction between these two antagonistic factors of learning and performing. Like a pendulum, it can swing freely to investigate a lingering emotion, record an important market profile observation, detach from the morning's trade, note odd market correlations, and so on. We can track *The Student*'s evolution as he traversed the learning and performing crossroads, as his real-time journaling became less structured over time.

"Structure had been useful [in my journaling] but I feel over the past six months it had become less structured, and the same with my trades. This is where I've gotten better," *The Student* said. "It is more intuitive, but this is very hard to define. Before I might be quite black and white on a trade—when I was trying to learn—and wait for my entry where it would either work or not," he continued. "Now, I try to access a broad idea and focus on getting in sync with the market over the course of the day. This happens in tandem with my notes on what I am thinking and feeling about the market."

And that is the "natural progression of a novice to expert; framework dissolves into intuition and flow," Haywood added. "All that grafting and framework has resulted in the flourishing of *the artist*. But you would not have come this way without the structure," he continued. "The intuition is trained this way. Taking the concept of change—by tracking how you are thinking and feeling each day, not blindly writing, but an active journaling of your flux, you are *navigating* change. Without journaling, something else might change in your environment, yet you would remain stagnant; unresponsive," Haywood concluded.

Many traders *retrospectively* record more information than was available at the time of a trade or market move. So, reviewing a timestamped record of their actual thoughts reveals a far different assessment in the moment than remembered. It is why Haywood went so far as to ask *The Student* if he had effectively "journaled and written himself into an edge." What was to follow our trader in the upcoming two years would provide an unequivocal: *Yes!*

SYNTHESIS

The Student's final acceptance of his trading profession unleashed the "pent-up" skill by the end of 2020. The coaching powers of his self-awareness engine were born out of a practical journey that transformed into a watershed moment in November 2020—the day of the Pfizer Covid-19 vaccine announcement.

But our trader had underperformed! "I had a good trading day but compared to the opportunity, I made only a small fraction of what I could have in the right frame of mind," he explains. "However, it was a relief. I had gone from April to November from either flat to drawdown, losing money, month on month." March 2020 had been, as for many other traders, a month of the biggest performances of their careers until that point. *The Student's* drawdown during mid-year was exceedingly painful and testing, but to remind readers, this does not mean calamitous account destruction. And our trader only drew down a fraction of his March gains—nearly eighty thousand pounds drawdown, at the worst of it, following a profitable multi-six-figure month in March.

But it was the return of inconsistency and the difficulty in finding traction which frustrated *The Student*. As all traders know, there are periods when it feels impossible to string two performing trades together. And a drawdown is a drawdown. So, putting an end to it, no matter how, was an immediate relief. "Even though I knew I really underperformed, I still was not as angry as I might be now. Instead, I was just relieved; the pressure was off, and I had some breathing space," *The Student* said. "From that point on *I just got consistent*. I got back into a proper routine. I focused on learning; I wasn't trying to force a big day out of the market and making back losses. I got back into the groove of trading and of following a process."

THE STUDENT

If 2020 cleared the way, then the following year had set the stage: "2021 then became the most consistent year I ever had as an outright trader," *The Student* said. "I didn't have *huge* growth, no massive up-days, just very consistent fifty-thousand-pound months through the year. But it was what I needed. I knew that without being consistent I would never be able to push size, I would never have the confidence within myself to increase it. That was the year I finally proved to myself that I can be an outright trader, I had those returns with being very tight on risk," he said.

This was the product of four years of learning, relearning and navigating the crossroads of learning and performing, now solidly within performance mode. "The year 2021 was the manifestation of the experiences of 2020," Haywood added, "but that year was a culmination of all the work in 2017–2019. Now *The Student* has the foundation for 2022, where he can start pushing himself. And there was a trade specifically where you can see this, his first singular trade of multiple six figures," Haywood continued.

And this trade was precisely what *The Student* had been working towards: to become an "all-seasons trader." It is a synthesis of complete technical market understanding—positioning, market profile analysis, long-term structure—combined with price ladder navigation, acute perception of the market narrative and a mountain of preparation, journaling and visualisation. What makes this trade especially relevant is that it had set a new personal benchmark for our trader. His personal blueprint of composing and executing these trades had marked a new era.

ADJACENT PROFITABLE

Before we discuss your new "benchmark" trade, how would you describe your trading style or method?
What is most important to me is the market profile, price ladder and, of course, the simple candlestick chart. With profiles, I lean on them when preparing for a news event or central bank meeting. Where is positioning? Where is the biggest vulnerability? My biggest conviction comes from understanding longer-term balances, breaking out of balances or a failed break and a move back into range. Long-term structures… weekly profiles and so on. Much of it is learnt from *The Hero* and *The Engineer* and extrapolated from them. And then, I combine this with the news. While I am trying to move away from needing news to instigate a *technical* trade, it still provides the most obvious catalyst. Even so, with the news, I am still reading deeply, looking for facts and points of view that create a narrative and where it can break down. So, synthesising the news is part of my edge too. And the news—macro-economic developments, geopolitical stories and how they interact with markets—has always been my keenest interest.

Describe to us your thought process in the WTI Crude Oil trade of summer 2022, your new "benchmark."
It was a trade I had utter belief in. It was a combination of news and technical trading, and these are my best trades. I understood Crude Oil technically, and I was sure a news headline was impending, perhaps that very day. I mapped it well over the previous couple of weeks, especially over Sunday. By watching it each day, I built the trade in my head, I knew where the targets were and what the key market prices were. It just needed a news trigger. And this was the only trade I deeply visualised. Ever. I did it since *The Warrior* always says how important it is. I knew the

technical set-up was there—the structure—I visualised it, watching it build up, and had planned out each scenario of the outcome of the Ukraine–Russia negotiations at the end of March 2022. Even of *how* and *where* the headline could come out. I trusted the set-up so much, even if the final headline was not conclusive. The execution was all pre-planned, and that is what let me feel calm and patient with it. The build-up, the execution and the culmination of what I was working on rank it as the "benchmark"—aside from the P&L.

If this is your best so far, what was your worst?
My worst day was actually a few weeks ago [August 2022] on an ECB meeting. It was a narrative and trade I understood perfectly. I was so convinced that my ego was attached to the idea that they *would* hike fifty basis, but the market priced only twenty-five, with a small chance of fifty. And structurally there was good downside in the bonds, from a technical perspective. I was so adamant they would hike fifty, I didn't plan enough how I would execute, the size I would hit and where I would get in and out, and what the headlines would look like at the 12.45 p.m. newswire release. That was where the edge was on this trade. I was executing too late, hitting prices which were actually targets, trading too much size. I took a massive loss as the trade reversed. I was *right* about the outcome of the hike, but that is irrelevant since I didn't plan enough. I couldn't accept not doing well on this trade. But instead of trading it smaller, I did the same size and turned a normal losing trade into a worst-ever day. I get so much conviction in an idea that if I don't keep it in check, I can take it too far.

Would you say your journaling efforts repurpose your strong convictions in a better way?
Completely. It keeps me objective, and I do not get caught up in my own thoughts. Without journaling, I can just get lost and lose under-

standing or awareness of how I am feeling and, in turn, *how* it affects my behaviour. I get lost in the moment, even with things outside of trading. I need to take a step back, and that is what the journal does for me, to keep me in check. I can also be risk-averse, at other times extremely risk-seeking, at times impulsive and other times very disciplined and controlled. You can make the case that this is true for everyone, but I think it's especially true for me. Because of these contradictions, and how I execute as a trader, this is why *awareness* is so important for me. Without the journaling process I would never trade as well.

◆ ◆ ◆

Note that this was the one trade which had been deeply visualised, the importance of which we had covered with *The Warrior*. This is the difference between a trader who would be overly interfering with his position, one of shallow preparation, compared to the conviction of *The Student*, who steadily built and held his position with calmness and purpose. "This is what *The Engineer* often considers," Haywood said, "if you take just these kinds of trades, the synthesis of deep preparation and conviction, you only need to trade twelve times a year. If you do just that, then you will have an *incredible* year." A new benchmark and direction, then, means to eventually direct all attention, emotional commitment and risk onto these kinds of trades—the next evolution of *The Student*.

FLOW

Since the summer of 2022, *The Student* has gone on to achieve similar P&L feats that set a new benchmark, which is why Haywood regards our trader as the most improved of that year. But where does our trader go from here? We meet him as a study of one seeking to go from great to *exceptional* without yet having all the answers.

"The vast majority of people, when they're struggling, look for certainty," he said. "And in the markets, they want a sure winner. They want a clear news trade or a perfect technical trade. They want to create certainty out of an uncertain environment. They're constantly overthinking things and clamouring for that information to lead to that 'perfect' trade, and in doing so, they miss what is really important." So then, more work to gather and piece different information together eventually becomes an act in vain. We've therefore decoupled the idea of more work contributing to improved performance at this *specific* stage in a trader's career. The subsequent question then becomes: how do you make the best of what you've got?

Yet, *The Student* is no stranger to a mentality of seeking sure winners. "It becomes self-perpetuating when going through a tough period because it feels like I am moving out of that *flow state*. Rather than coming in and being synchronised with the market, instead, I'm trying to look for too much and trying to make things happen. I get too attached to ideas." Identification of the flow state, then, is very much in the crosshairs of both Haywood and *The Student* regarding how to enter said state as much as possible. This provides our trader with an area on which he can next focus his efforts.

Flow, as a concept and term, entered public awareness through Mihaly Csikszentmihalyi's extensive publications and work like *Flow: The Classic Work on How to Achieve Happiness* (2002). A person experiencing "flow" enters a state of intense concentration and focus on the given moment, a loss of the perspective of time and *satisfaction* gained from the act of experiencing flow.

This is now cutting-edge for our trader. At the time of our interview, he was still trying to understand, to grasp around the edges. And it is valuable for us to see how a high-performing trader of his calibre deals with something new.

"What triggers my flow state, I think, is down to market conditions," *The Student* began. "It is easier to enter it when there is a market theme or volatility. Or there is a clear technical structure on which I have high conviction; I know it will play out for different reasons. Therefore, when I come into the office, I am not reactive. I know what I am looking for: technical, news or economic data. I am clear and committed to the idea. I intrinsically accept the risk. If I come in and lose a large sum of money, I accept it. That is the key difference, as losses don't seem to bother me. I am understanding, and I am not so far removed."

Therefore, the flow comes with the territory, and *not* experiencing it suggests something has come between the trader and his process. "Since I am not so far removed, I am able to sustain focus, even if I take losses. Consider the markets at the moment—August 2022—the markets are very stop-start," our trader said. "You suddenly have the Pelosi–China theme for two days, and it disappears. Then, the gas story disappears. I am not clear on the overall macro-picture. I think bonds are massively overstretched yet bullish on the day due to other variables. So, I am *scatterbrained*, and every day is quite different. It is hard to structure what exactly is going on. My attention is everywhere. The question then is how do I get into flow in these conditions?"

Further discussion with our trader suggested that perhaps the "scatterbrained" feeling is a strong sign to avoid significant market interaction altogether. The formulation of a trade idea is yet immature and undigested, and no real conviction can be built out of it; the scatterbrained feeling reflects this.

Nevertheless, there is no clear path ahead for our trader as there is no *best* path. But he continues. "Compare that to the days of April

THE STUDENT

and March 2022, where I have a clear technical idea. It feels effortless and I'm utterly absorbed by it. I am able to take on risks and win or lose money. It does not matter to me either way. But out of flow, I am frustrated by the smallest things and always thinking about P&L. It's a world of difference."

We can regard this as the exploration of the adjacent possible in terms of *performance* rather than solely in terms of *learning*. The Student's exploration of flow, of understanding and consciously framing it, is an extension of his own history of working with performance coaches, clinical psychologists and others, amassing the "spare parts" of performance that can be recombined to create better ideas about improving performance. As our trader sits firmly within the confines of performance mode, this becomes increasingly important and relevant. Not so much, contextually, for those in learning mode. It is too early! Often, the novice learner is too quick to focus on performance psychology, practices and habits that solely seek to enhance *performance* rather than learning. Once again, navigating the antagonism between learning and performance demands the application of the right thing at the right time.

FAMILY

A certain threshold was crossed during the creation of this book throughout 2021–2023. The traders who are now parents or married across the global AXIA trading desks outweigh what remains of the eligible bachelors. And so, of course, family and children are an important topic to discuss—on a long enough timeline, *the* most important.

The accepted notion, then, not limited to trading itself, is that family and children render the *end* of a trader's career, perhaps out of increasing financial burdens, which might hamper risk-taking mentality, or due to the pressures of time. *The Student* himself is no stranger to these pressures as his family welcomed two children in the past three years, right in the middle of the pandemic. And right in the throes of our trader's reinvention.

But *The Student* stands firm. "You can tell yourself whatever you want in terms of family and its impact on trading. It's just an excuse, and we know how much people love excuses," he began. "Take *The Godfather*. He had a family from the time I first met him, but it never impacted him, he never complained about it and always made it work. He works harder than anyone in terms of the hours he puts in." It felt as if our trader had had this conversation many times before.

"I do not see it as a disadvantage because I have kids now. It has never crossed my mind that I now *somehow* cannot compete with other traders who do not have children. It doesn't put me in a negative place in any way. Having kids means I can't get away with being inefficient. When I am at my desk, I don't mess around with conversations; I keep them to a minimum—I am here to work. Otherwise, I miss out on time with my kids and my wife," he continued. "But it would affect me if I tried to carry on with all the other aspects of my life, such as socialising and hobbies. If I tried to do all of this *and* be a good father and husband, work would suffer, so it's important to understand your priorities. It's a blessing to have a family, and I always wanted one. I was never worried or concerned about how it would affect my trading. I understand that I will miss market moves and events. Before, I might have stayed late for a potential comment or headline. Now I have to leave to put the kids to bed. But that *also* means I will miss times when I could have taken losses on those very comments or headlines."

But our trader also concedes, "Of course, you are sleep-deprived, and you still have less time to review, debrief and so on; I would love to spend a full weekend doing just that, and it would likely make me a better trader. Yet, I am a better person for spending that time with my family, which, in turn, will also make me a better trader, as I am happier and more content, and I trade better as a result. You will never stay upset for too long after a bad trading day when you are playing with your kids," he said.

"Before I would try to push and power through; now that I am older, I am more respectful of my body, I know I can't survive on two hours' sleep. So—trade smaller, trade less and be even more specific about what to trade. Be more patient and understanding. It's not realistic to push and trade at full capacity every day. Sometimes I feel like I am at quarter-capacity and trade accordingly. I accept it and do not lose my mind by expecting the results of a full-capacity day," he concluded.

A note on *perception*. This is the hallmark of a trader who *has* to make it work, rather than wishing to. Having less time can be viewed as an opportunity to use what time you do have more efficiently. Pressures and responsibility outside the trading floor led to an opportunity to reprioritise. In the case of *The Student*, or *The Godfather*, they also possess a different card to play, which provides an extra meaning to their career—purpose. If nothing else, at least a means to an end to support their family.

THE STUDENT

Friction is the experience of creation, as to create the unique is to navigate a path forever shrouded in obscurity, dead-ends and circuitous routes. Too smooth a path is much too trodden. In order to thrive, all traders must eventually become an act of creation, as markets and society reward acts of creation, and so traders *must* experience friction. And the power of journaling is the navigation of friction, a trader's permanent companion when searching the fringes of their known world—the adjacent possible. To make their unknown *known*. To leverage the creative human faculty of connecting the disparate dots together in a new light in different ways.

And power, then, to *The Student* for his steadfast application to his journal, for possessing the humility and foresight to navigate his adjacent possible—to evolve from a stunted, one-product spread trader into an all-seasons trader, a synthesis of the best of news and technical trading as effective with themes and macro as he is with the market profile. To be able to dissolve the past, thereby allowing himself to become the best learner and transform into the best performer, all while navigating change, professionally and personally embracing *family* and using it as a source of strength, rather than an excuse. To then reveal that the path of friction to reach the lofty Pantheon of *select* traders is built on the process, of nurture and endurance. And on the ascent to become "the trader I always wanted to be."

PRACTITIONER'S POSTSCRIPT

Explore resources derived from this chapter to further support the practicing trader.

axiafutures.com/
toot

Refer to
The Student's
section.

LEARNER'S IMPRESSIONS

Below are some personal impressions that *The Student* made on us that we still discuss with other traders.

1. *Limits are targets.* A trader needs to add more spare parts—experiences, new stimuli, a trading floor network—to develop. Limits are then a map for where to go next, to push *just* over your current boundaries of skill, knowledge and perception of what is possible. Sometimes, pushing too far puts you too ahead of your time. But sometimes, the calamity of exploring just beyond the pale fosters creativity in order to make it work, to electrify all you've worked to develop and experience all you have accumulated. And so the trader emerges further away from the masses, thereby enduring within the markets. What can enhance or impede your exploration of your adjacent possible? How can exploration of it be improved or, at least, not impeded? How can you push performance boundaries where one cannot do "more" work?

2. *Antagonism of learning and performing.* All traders must painfully traverse the crossroads of learning and performing. Best practices in the former can be the worst in the latter, and vice versa. Career reinvention often necessitates performers to become learners once more, a task that requires supplanting perhaps a decade of habits and practices.

3. *The candlelight of self-awareness.* The market will do what it can to snuff it out. But *The Student*'s journaling practice prevents this from occurring. His practice allows him to dynamically survey lingering emotions, control or emphasise action, make note of observations as a learner and *elicit change* to become a better performer. That handwritten leather-bound companion is space to prepare for action and, in the aftermath, to prepare for reflection once more.

What are your impressions? Write them down and converse with this book!

CHAPTER EIGHT

THE GODFATHER

"Now is the time to call it a day and get a job."

All traders will be tested. There are times when it will come down to the survival of that trader, a test at the cellular level. But in that moment, some are caught in perpetual headlights and fizzle away. *The slow disappear.* Routine breaks, beliefs erode, defences are jaded; cynicism remains as the last marker of self-worth. Others disappear instantly.

This is not a test of strength, or smarts, passion, or persistence. It does not care for bravery or sacrifice. It does not assess pain tolerance, endurance, spirit or valour, nor is it a contrived test of masculinity, humanity or other "ities." This test has felled the strongest candidate and preserved the most unlikely. Because in every trader's head, there is a key, button or switch that must never be pressed, tapped or flipped, or the gas that ignites the fire will go out. Forever. The markets will test this, hunt for it, like a shark seeking blood, to do what they can to push that button, to flip that switch. The job, then, is to prevent this from happening.

Some may not know it, but their switches were flipped long ago; everything else just has to catch up. The switch hides well; it often does not affect other parts of life, only survival within markets. Some have protected it; others possess rare talent because they lack one at all. At any rate—do *not* get flipped.

Whatever the reason our trader walked out onto the floor those fifteen years ago, that was the moment, if he knew it or not, of *the* test. Will he flip? Because now, four years into a promising career, our trader had lost his trading account within months and then some more. His house, car and, in reality, stability and independence were at serious risk, always just a tick away from bankruptcy. A few months prior, he had returned to his old trading floor, his original haunt. On the first day, his fiancée had called to let him know that in a few short months, he would become a father. "It is fine," she said, "three months to make it work." Cooler heads prevailed.

And now, the European Central Bank meeting of November 2008, a fifty-basis-point rate cut. *Sell the Schatz—what?*

This was the defining trade of his career. In short order, our trader hatched a plan only twenty minutes prior to trade in a manner that was completely alien to him—on fundamentals, to trade a central bank statement, then a nascent art on the London *electronic* proprietary trading scene. He had done so with maximum trading size and conviction to go against what the textbook says—that is, selling bonds futures on an interest-rate cut, not buying them.

It was '1 + 1 = 3' thinking, a step ahead of the crowd. Most traders at this point would and *did* fumble, especially those with so few years in the arena. For others in his situation, the sheer pressure of impending bankruptcy was dwarfed by the weight of real adult responsibility. Their switches *flipped*.

"I was eighteen when I saw a documentary about the London LIFFE [International Financial Futures and Options Exchange] trading pits and was fascinated by the jackets and the noise. The narrator said that it is the closest life experience, other than war, to chaos. And that all those traders learned to manage themselves within chaos," our trader said. "I wanted to see how *I* could handle chaos."

And chaos he received.

This would not be our trader's first test, nor his last. In fact, this trader, too, has survived the erosion of time upon his skills, physique and energy. Trading since the time of Greenspan aptly led *The Engineer* to christen our trader *The Godfather*, as he predates nearly everyone in this book and is known and *connected* in various ways to the entire London proprietary trading scene. Incidentally, he is also a superfan of the film trilogy!

During the last two years of Greenspan's tenure, *The Godfather* has been in survival and reinvention mode, *the* critical skill identified and necessitated by *The Collector* and his story. Later thriving—both philosophically and technically—his mastery led him to pioneer various aspects of his craft. Now at age forty-three, with a nearly twenty-year career behind him, *The Godfather* trades at his best and looks at his best with a lean, athletic physique cultivated over years of *getting it right*. And that comes from the iron discipline required to trade as committedly as a young trader should, persistent training for Brazilian jiu-jitsu like a man two decades younger while juggling his responsibilities as a husband and father of three. He is, then, the benchmark for senior and junior traders.

A North London boy, *The Godfather* walks with suitable swagger, cruising around the floor in his trademark look of sharp tracksuits and expensive trainers, more dapper than some *malakas* appear in suits. Certainly *not*, if asked, a result of a triangular fashion rivalry between *The Warrior* and *The Sphinx*. Our trader's strides are long and wide, of the athletic kind. His hair—crew-cut, waxed and combed—the stuff of fighters. His temperament is easygoing, jovial yet instantly focused, primed and impassioned when the market volatility hits. This *snap* to action is the hallmark of a veteran trader. As a natural storyteller, he rolls his intonation and pitches his speed to a captive audience. The North London accent, with its replacement of "...th" endings with an "...f", permeates his speech and mannerisms. The discerning ear would pick up a dash of a Cypriot accent. *Correct!* The Greek blood also runs deep, and the trend to go with it, as he is also a global macro-news trader.

Together, these aspects create an allure and persuasiveness that saved him from getting cut due to a bungled test during a recruitment drive at his first trading firm, as a result of a speech—a pitch—so good, the recruiters said: "You could sell it."

Seldom would you find a junior trader who has not excitedly joined a huddle and conferred their anecdotes of *The Godfather*. One day, a junior recreated the scene—*He used his belt!*—"Focus on your weaknesses," *The Godfather* reportedly said to the junior, as he stood on one end of his belt and tugged the other, "and then you can move forward with strengths. Otherwise, the belt will not move. Both need to come with you."

No doubt it is easier to add to your anecdotal collection of this trader than others from the first floor at 4 Endsleigh Street, as he frequently glides around the building on phone calls or towards the kitchen to fuel his evening grappling sessions, with wild portions of meat and salad.

The Godfather's career is punctuated by three distinct periods of different trading strategies of perspectives and, as we will see, radically different philosophies and expectations. And unlearning them was perhaps harder than learning from scratch, yet ultimately thriving in all of them. Following his third transformation period of 2016–2019, this trader had since broken through the barriers of his own perceptions and personal performances. Long since a seven-figure trader, he now punches in multi-six-figure days, one of which we will examine later in his chapter. By the time of writing, his career growth is the fastest ever, increasing in both trading size and the scope of possibilities, yet never compromising on quality or consistency, as he has come too far for schoolboy screw-ups.

FUTURE(S) TRADERS WANTED

The year is 2003. The early *noughties* still rode off the tail end of the pull, the glamour and the pervasive pre-millennium siren call of *the City* that still held its all-or-nothing allure for young graduates; get a job—any job—but make sure it is a *City job*. Miss your shot by a narrow few months then... *eh?* What is that paper hanging on your wall, or lost in the attic, really for?

Bank and institutional proprietary trading still held strong until the Great Financial Crisis would come knocking a few years later, but the pit trading scene—open outcry—was dead in London. Instead of sporting a coloured jacket, *The Godfather* was now a middle-office investment banker—*a job, any job!*—as the LIFFE floor had shut down physical trading. "The *Evening Standard* printed a massive ad that turned out to be a graduate training programme. So, I applied and turned up for the interview," *The Godfather* said, and rolled a grin. "I thought it would be just *me*. Instead, it was nearly fifty guys, all my age, getting ready for a group interview! It was when *The X Factor* became popular, so they decided to get rid of ten a week." The electronisation of trading, from pit to screens, created a diaspora of ex-pit traders, *The Godfather* said, and many veterans did not adapt, so this new firm recruited fresh. The age of the point-and-clickers had come. And our trader was there at the dawn of a new era.

THE GODFATHER

A compelling pitch later, and after reassuring conversations with family, our trader had actually become one of the handful of new recruits now relegated to an experiment to trade the Bobl, the German five-year bond. The twist, however, was that this futures contract was to be traded *outright*. It was not a happy twist, as the entirety of the floor and their expertise lay in spread trading, the simultaneous buying of one contract and the selling of another, a different business than outright trading, and, in that firm's view, of the sordid kind.

Like *The Student*, who would roam the very same floor in the years to come, the firm liked to experiment in this way, at the cost of new trader careers, and within six months it was time to wash out; no one had made any money. This is unsurprising if one were to value and understand the knowledge-network effect of a trading floor. Recall the "extended mind" concept we picked up in *The Collector's* chapter. In the context of *The Godfather*, it reveals how these new traders had no expertise to plug into—it was a firm of spread traders—mainly of the Treasury-EuroDollar (TED) spread, which required a different style, and mentality, as it was altogether a different product.

"But instead of washing out, we went up to the main trading floor for an interview with the big traders, with a chance to join their team," *The Godfather* said. "Before I ever saw the *Evening Standard* ad, I saw another article discussing these new point-and-click traders: these young guys—twenty-three, twenty-four—coming in to trade this product and that product! They specifically mentioned the name of one of these traders, who was just shy of a million-pound year. I was so inspired that I cut it out and stuck it on my bedroom wall." *The Godfather* began to whisper as if in respect to the conspiratorial universe he was about to describe. "Guess who I was interviewed and taken on by? I wound up sitting right next to him."

OUT OF THE BASEMENT

Yet there was no sunset to sail into, and time wore on. After a year there was no headway, financially or at least of lateral skill development, which our trader felt was lacking on the floor. It was like hitting a brick wall, as *The Godfather* said; a trader sometimes simply may not stick, find traction with the right elements of the floor at the right time. But our trader *was* ready to change, and willing to risk radical change and do so at the right time.

Time for a new trading floor, then, and this one was full to the brim—298 souls with two seats remaining—one of which was to go to our trader. "So, I walked into this new heaving and buzzing trading floor. *Loud!* In with the big boys, screens everywhere—it was like a bank! Whereas I came from this dingy basement, a bucket-shop-style floor," *The Godfather* said. He proceeded to list off well-known names in the industry who were trading at his new floor at the time, and he talked about these massive traders with veneration. And this new firm gave him a shot after only a year of trading the TEDs. But the others to do so were his mother and brother—lending our trader five figures—to fund his trading account and to buy time. A chance to make it work.

"We've got an issue with your original seat. But you can also sit with the Bund outright traders. Is that okay?" the floor manager asked, yet it was the universe that conspired. *The Godfather* walked towards the new row of seats he was about to call home.

"What do you trade?" the traders asked.

"I'm a Tedda."

"What's that?"

"Euribor! Schatz!"

"Euribor versus... the Schatz?"

THE GODFATHER

"They didn't even know!" recalled *The Godfather*. And wedged between these heavyweight traders was the freshest-faced, innocent tree-hugging, globe-trotting troubadour, dandy do-gooder, skinny schoolboy—*a certain Alex Haywood!*—who, the management decided, was promising enough to throw onto this part of the floor to learn from these big, talented and ultimately legendary generations of traders. It would be the first of many times *The Godfather* and Haywood would find each other by happenstance. The last of which, of course, is now on the AXIA trading floor, and a far more intentional decision. A small world, and smaller still in *prop*.

So, these *were* outright traders, as opposed to "spreaders" like *The Godfather*, yet highly successful outright traders that ensured a healthy, valuable knowledge network for *The Godfather* to plug into. "At the time I didn't even trade on a price ladder," he said. "Instead, I was using software where prices scrolled horizontally, and the bid and offer were printed like they are on spread betting platforms."

The career move shortly paid off with our trader's quick evolution to spreading the TEDs via an *actual* 'vertical' price ladder, which was a pioneering act itself, *The Godfather* said, within the London proprietary scene at the time. "Now what happens? I start to make money!" he said. "These exceptional Bund outright traders—*outright trading!*—I was raised to think that outright trading was pure gamble, *a punt*. Insane! It didn't even exist at my previous floor." Our trader would watch with disbelief as some were placing triple-digit Bund outright positions. His old floor colleague too, who he instant-messaged, was certain it was a mistake—*must be only ten lots!*

"But it was correct," *The Godfather* said. "And that's a thousand euros a tick! So then if it goes ten ticks offside? To me, at the time, it was inconceivable." Those same traders later grew to trade a couple thousand lots in various markets.

And so, *The Godfather* attributed a shifted state, a focus, that became the reason for a turnaround. "My *only* mission at the time was to give my mother and brother their money back and then to build my own account. I used the experience of these traders to develop my skillset to become more professional, like researching and understanding the U.S. Non-Farm Payrolls data release and preparing well for central bank events. All of this did not exist in my previous world. No one understood fundamentals in this way. I used all of this to my advantage in trading the TED." By the end of his third year in the business, *The Godfather* was finally making multi-five-figure months and hit a year P&L of just over £300,000. "The risk team loved me," he said. "I took thousands of round-trips a day, made several thousand pounds a day and would go on long stretches of consistent up-days; I had a very low-risk profile. Everything was going so well…"

Hold the cliff-hanga! When things go *too* well—not least in financial markets—as we ought to know, is where the story really starts. But we must first ask an important question: what got *The Godfather* this far in the first place to finally break through? First, we have an attachment to real group expertise, Haywood said, reusing the "extended mind" concept. These traders are successful and growing, but unlike the traders at his original firm, these ones were doing it *differently*.

And so, *The Godfather* became an act of creation, of creativity in adapting and borrowing these foreign concepts into his own mix. He did not let this trading group hijack his process and trading. In fact, he remained a TED spread trader, but he took the best from a high-value, diverse environment rather than recycling ideas and processes from the monotone, uniform, groupthink-like environment of his first trading floor.

In doing so, he became a far more unique, niche TED trader than the rest of the market. What he learned about the Bund, from an outright, non-spread trading perspective, led him to improve his TED spread fills and trade better prices due to the correlated nature of the two products. Understanding market fundamentals filtered out traps and adverse situations, and much more, as we will explore later. This is why the lack of human interaction is, unfortunately, the very dearth of healthy idea generation, a recurring issue for those who came to the trading industry desiring solitude. A trader who assumes they can sit alone at their desk to think big thoughts to invent future trading methods or strategies may lead them to the same circuitous route. A copy of an original trading idea, formally your own or the product of others, will likely degenerate into mere copies, as there are no new, fresh and foreign, even random, inputs. The random element of a diverse trading floor helps to connect things together, an act of creativity.

This explains why traders *disappear*. Once they leave the floor to trade alone, they forgo these random elements of inputs, no longer connected to the extended mind. We hear the same story, anecdotally, of traders beyond the pale of proprietary trading, those in institutions, funds and banks. As we ought to know, no one is an island; traders seldom too—nature does not tolerate inbreeding, and neither do successful ideas and practices.

VIGILANCE

"Everything was going so well…" and well it was. Our trader was able to buy a house and a car and maintain an active social life with the costs that come with it. This was of real note to a twenty-five-year-old who had previously lived "like a pauper," as *The Godfather* puts it, following university and the first few years stuck in the new trader's limbo—losing money, losing time. But the market *tests*.

And chaos he received.

Then came an ECB meeting in April 2006 in which the president, Jean-Claude Trichet, did *not* say "vigilance." As with all central bank mandates, price stability *à la* inflation must be controlled at a certain level—targeted—by the control of specific interest rates, the very, *very* "short end" of the rate curve. And the ECB responded in kind by a rate-hiking cycle that began in December 2005, in which Trichet's tenure was marked by a consistent message of "strong vigilance" over inflation. So consistent were these expectations, in fact, that the markets became conditioned to expect a rate hike the very next meeting upon hearing these words.

But now, its absence? *My God! The rates, the rates! What a bonanza!* A trader who sat four seats away from *The Godfather* had immediately lifted two thousand lots in the Bobl—the German five-year bond—as it bid higher on the implications that the ECB may *not* raise rates as much or as fast as previously accepted. At least, not at the next meeting. The expectations have changed, and therefore, market pricing should too. The Bobl lurched higher, and that trader had made well over half a million euros. "He was the only trader in our circle who understood what *not* saying 'vigilance' meant," *The Godfather* said. "This was the first time someone really revealed the power, the edge of statement science," added Haywood, especially within the intraday futures proprietary trading space.

"But I took that home with me; all of a sudden, everything I achieved felt *this* big," *The Godfather* said as he held his index fingers facing each other with a tiny gap between them. "I promised I would go into the following year and strive to be *that* trader, maybe even outdo him, that I would make the numbers he did. I was already making thirty to forty thousand a month, but that was no longer enough. So, I started to push."

THE GODFATHER

But by pushing harder, *The Godfather* traded more aggressively to enter the spread sooner, but at worse prices and with more size. A spread trader *wants* the market to go further *offside*—against themselves—within their mean-reverting strategy. As more clips or positions are added to the trade, a bigger P&L awaits when the spread reverts. A spread trader can improve consistency by trading at 'extreme' prices yet miss out on average spread fluctuations. But *The Godfather* now wanted to trade at every opportunity—to push—even average risk–reward situations with increased trading size. But what if you trade at poor prices, with more size, and the spread never comes back?

As the world sped into 2007, the tremors were already being felt in credit spreads, exemplified by the now-erratic TED spread. The EuroDollar part of the spread derives from the London Inter-Bank Offered Rate, and while the futures contract is a proxy for interest rate expectations, it also bore the credit risk of banks as it was a form of overnight, unsecured lending, that is, there was no collateral to back up the lending. "Usually" is a dangerous word, but *usually*, that type of credit risk was deemed negligible. Yet, if the banks were deemed to be in danger, and they certainly were later, then the EuroDollar future contracts go "ballistic, and the TEDs become impossible to trade," *The Godfather* summarised. "The market changed *drastically*. Within days to weeks. Everything I knew and the strategies I learnt stopped working, I believed I could make money with the TED spread for the rest of my career—*Bam!*—blowout day, then another blowout day. Within six weeks, I lost my entire trading account. The demise was so quick—a blink. And I was in pain, *big pain*," he said.

The following months—a blur: further losses, amped market volatility; frustration, negative account, further losses, savings dry up;

mortgage now under question, the car a forgone conclusion; months pass… more pressure, drowning—*change needed!* Back to the old trading floor, sit around surviving spreaders; opportunities about. And the first day back —soon to become a father—*quit!* No—give it time; try new things— different spread, styles, rules. But, more lost time, further losses… keep trying, keep going— and now the ECB. November 2008. Cut fifty basis; sell the Schatz—*full size!* Bid, bid… *collapse!* The bids in the Schatz get hit, and hit, and hit, sucked into the void below, off the price ladder screen itself. *Shock!* The dust settles, and the floor manager walks over, grins and throws our trader a sweet—one of those dentist *good boy!* sweets. Relief. Maybe the house is saved; it had been a very dark eighteen months. *The Godfather* walks out and calls his heavily pregnant fiancée. The market test, he—*they*—survived.

"Babe, I just made seventy-five grand." She bursts into tears. Their son is born two weeks later.

◆ ◆ ◆

The markets received the fifty-basis cut lukewarm. *Whatchumean only fifty basis? Not enough!* It had been expecting more. Hell! The Bank of England cut their base rate a hundred *and* fifty basis that very morning! "But the bonds traded as if it were a hawkish reaction," our trader said, and in a 2007–2008 world of big-bazooka cuts, a mere fifty basis was a triumph of the hawks.

THE GODFATHER

In the context of his career, *The Godfather* remarked how important it was to stay in the game, to survive as long as possible to have the "chance to participate," to capture the optionality that transforms into opportunity. "After that I decided to break from the TED completely; that ECB rate cut trade provided the confidence to open another door," *The Godfather* said, closing the chapter on the most significant trade of his life, and it is meaningful because he survived *the test*.

It is a great example, too, of the importance of the support of those around you. The lack of moral support is one thing; but active rebellion against the trader's career is another and has served as the last talking point in the many obituaries of a trader's career. *Correct!* Our trader said as he described a promising talent—a protégé—who arrived in the following years and grew quickly in the initial stages, yet soon quit once he entered a drawdown period that had only lasted a few months. The real, active pressure from his family reached its limit; his switch flipped.

The Godfather's career, then, had been saved at several critical junctures by those around him. His mother and brother who lent him money to change trading floors, with little at the time to show for it. His stepfather, too, proved a supportive figure when *The Godfather* risked his investment banking job for a mere chance in a trading graduate programme. His wife, as we will see later, unfailingly, and routinely, appears in our trader's story at critical times to encourage, to provide perspective and the all-important support. To say, *we trust you*. At the eleventh hour, when others like *The Godfather*'s mentor figure had told him that "now is the time to call it a day and get a job"—instead, his wife had told him what he needed to hear: *keep going*. No trader is an island.

After five years, *The Godfather* ushered in a combination of skills, tools and philosophy that would become distinctively his, a real "0 to 1" moment. "I don't fear change. After the ECB cut, I had an account behind me, with the freedom to express myself in the markets. I had great ideas, trades and skills I just could not permit myself to use when one tick made the difference between bankruptcy and walking in the next day," our trader said. Following the return to his first, now evolved, trading floor *The Godfather* had been experimenting with various new spreads to trade: the 2s–10s, 5s–10s, the Bund–Gilt spread and others. Yet, he had settled on the (in)famous Bund–Bobl–Schatz butterfly spread; the relative difference between these three futures contracts would emulate the German bond curve.

The Godfather picked up "the fly" from others on the floor but he quickly became *the* fly trader, due to the first of his three pioneering acts—charting and trading the fly with the market profile. "Why not? The market profile, after all, is devised from a normal distribution; in a way, this is even more relevant for mean-reverting spreads. No one was doing it in the prop space at the time; the profile was associated with outright trading, and people represented the spreads via line charts. Once I charted the spreads as a profile, I never looked back," our trader said.

"Why was I better at trading the fly? Because of all my experience sitting next to the Bund outright traders for three years," he continued. "I took that experience and applied it to the spread. I learned market fundamentals and the way they saw the profile. I would fade the market profile tails on the fly and use other things, like the nature of correlations, to anticipate better fills on the Schatz. The fly would trade fifty, and people would buy it. *No! Hold.* And I only started to enter at forty and was out by fifty—the others would only scratch at fifty."

The other two acts followed quicky—the queue and open strategies. The queuing strategy involved joining the back of a bid and offer 'queue,' as nearly all futures markets operate on a *first in, first out* principle; our trader would do this on the more liquid, or 'thicker,' Schatz and Bobl, so to trade better prices in the fly. The intuition, then, is that if the queue is long, you'd better get there first, fresh and early, before everyone else!

"At the time, no other fly trader was doing this," *The Godfather* said. "You decide you are about to take a trade. You either pull it, fill it or hedge it. Sometimes, you could scalp it outright, and you would be up several thousand *before* the fly was even on! Others would fail at this since you needed immense discipline, too tempted to get away with a bad fill price with a hedge. The focus was a religious practice, a routine ritual, and I would be glued to my desk." *The Student* noted *The Godfather's* innovative use of this strategy. It enabled him to trade the fly for far longer in his career than others, as the spreads became more compressed and less profitable with the advent of a zero-interest-rate policy environment.

The third pioneering act, then, was not the creation of the "open strategy" directly—it was picked up from a colleague, the extended mind in action once more. But *The Godfather* got creative. The open strategy had actually required a trader to monitor the close at 9 p.m. each day as there was specific action to look out for. And then present himself ready at 6 a.m. to trade the market open the following hour. If the bonds were deemed to be "out of line" relative to each other, mainly due to the artificial market opening and closing, then there was potential in a trade. Combining this with the queuing strategy, our trader had been executing like no one else at the time. And so effective was this that the "day's money" was often made just on this trade.

Freedom of expression indeed. *The Godfather* would go on a seven-year run of ultra-consistency, more than enough to earn *The*

Razor's respect. This period features *no* down-months with some long periods of no down-days. This was creativity and risk-taking matched by *getting it right*—of discipline and focus—a duality attributed to our trader's two fathers. "My father and stepfather were both active in my life. Both taught me valuable things. My father was an absolute gentleman academic, worked and studied hard. He was a structural engineer and was always employed in a corporate role. My stepfather was a consummate gambler and a nightclub owner. Everyone knew him, and he was very charismatic. He could make money anywhere *but* never keep it; he was a big spender but also possessed a big heart. At my wedding, I thanked my father for teaching me to be a good man and to *be* a father. I also thanked my stepfather for teaching me to take risks in life and to never be scared to fail because I saw him do that endlessly, and he always got back up again."

It seems, then, *The Godfather* has manifested the best of both, of proactive risk-taking but of dutiful consolidation of gains. And this seven-year period was of consistent, very-high-six-figure years. A period of strong vigilance, if you will, over his family's finances, household and future as two more children arrived along the way. "I never wanted to go back to that position," he said. "I was in a dark place at my second trading firm. I did not want to let success get to my head; the fear of bankruptcy and losing the house stayed with me. So, I became the most consistent fly trader at the company." And *most* consistent was no small feat, as the firm was soon absorbed by another, and a whole new several-hundred-man trading floor was created in London. Yet our trader ruled the *fly* roost, growing a team of fifteen traders under him, teaching and funding them—but as we know, the markets *test*.

And chaos he received.

THE GODFATHER

0.00

There is always a cost, the burden of a strategy. In the case of spread trading, it was getting caught in *the big one* or "scary moments in which I had to wear it," as *The Godfather* describes it. An intense focus on the queuing strategy was needed as our trader had constant market exposure within the German bond curve. And the 2011 Fukushima nuclear disaster was one of these moments. "I was nearly annihilated; the market just *went*, and I had no chance to pull my limit orders. I was seventy-five thousand euros offside immediately."

The Godfather's losses soon flashed double that amount, and the problem was exacerbated due to a particular reason. It had been common spreader practice to keep the trading account at a specific low amount and to withdraw any surplus at the end of the month. Even if the trader had more funds in the bank, as *The Godfather* did, it was not in the trading account at the time to allow leeway for a trader to withstand such adverse and, *hopefully*, temporary market moves. There was no spare ammunition to keep fighting. The margin between survival as the best-case scenario and obliteration was hairline; an opportunity to counterattack would be lost.

"I was caught short on Bobl via a safe-haven scramble. I lifted the Bund against it—hedged and proceeded to scale in and out; *in, in, in! Out, out out!*" our trader said, as he gesticulated in the air of selling and buying with his hands as if he were a lone ranger in a Western sporting two revolvers and engaged in a high-speed shootout. "I traded my way around it like a demon. I came back to negative-sixty thousand, but I kept trading. By the end of the day, I was *flat*; that doesn't mean slightly down or slightly up—my P&L was exactly *0.00*." *The Godfather* found this to be the closest he had ever come to achieving the "ultimate flow state" in trading, of the athletic kind.

Such situations would occur again with the likes of the S&P flash crash in 2015 and other white-box volatility-illiquidity halts. And that is not an easy burden to shoulder. But these existential risks were one thing, yet the persistent, compressed and dry market environment was another. The range and volatility compression in the fly and placid yield curves during the mid-2010s had forced many out of the industry. For *The Godfather*, the risk–reward of the fly had become nonsensical, drawing blood from a rock, and his consistency started to slide. After all, spread trading inherently had—you could say, to sound chic—a *concave payout*. "You make, make, make and—*Boom*—big down-day," *The Godfather* said. And the payout had now become more concave than ever. Spread trading in this way, of mean-reversion, is a short-volatility business, and the spread always has to come back, *or else*.

Then came 2016, and perhaps it was time to leave the spreads for good, our trader thought, and so the universe conspired. The AXIA trading floor was taking its primordial state, and Kyriacou called our trader, offering him a spot as promised if a team were ever created.

And so, it was. "At the time, it was a massive gamble to move. I am leaving a big floor with a large and reputable clearing firm to join a new five-man team that trades out of a cupboard," *The Godfather* said. "More difficult, too, as I had been one of the last remaining profitable *fly* traders. But, again, I was never scared of change, some traders never leave the same floor they started on." Despite the doubts, *The Godfather* had once again made the right move at the right time. For all of the messy, start-up nature of the embryonic AXIA trading floor, it possessed one thing our trader desired most—outright traders—and to become one himself. A new environment, then, for new skills. But, the transition, as we saw with *The Student*, was unexpectedly difficult. *The Godfather* would spend the first six months in "no-man's land."

THE GODFATHER

Because by mixing spreads and outright trading, he began to lose his identity. These symptoms, as we have seen in the previous chapter, are a result of the conflict between *learning and performance mode*; their antagonistic demands frustrate and confuse the trader as they stand at the crossroads. Harder still, our trader says, as many things had to be unlearnt. Transitioning from the TED to the *fly* was one thing, but transmuting spread trading philosophy to outright and directional trading was another. Outright trading, to double down on chic, pertains a *convex payout*: to endure many small, failed trades and small papercuts, to catch the *big one!* This is a long-volatility business and requires a mentality that foregoes immediate profit, unlike the consistency afforded by the short-volatility business of spread trading. *The Godfather* could spot trades all over the fly, and even on other spreads, as the temptation to eat is great when one has been starved.

"I was a very consistent fly trader and now I was back to not making any money again," our trader said. The first step of progress, then, was to take one step back. "To all spread traders in my position, I always tell them to choose either spread or outright trading. It was very difficult to cut loose, but there was no future in the spreads for me." Following a conversation with Kyriacou, our trader removed his spread charts altogether, or anything that would tempt him to slide back into the well-greased spread trading groove; to forget about the short-term temptation, the cookie jar had to go.

Sitting close to *The Warrior*, as our trader does to this day, he would slowly morph into a news trader. But this was not intentional in the beginning; the dots happened to reconnect in different ways. *The Godfather's* skills, experience and knowledge were overwhelmingly based on macro-fundamentals, asset class correlations, understanding central banks, geopolitics and more. What better place to learn these factors when trading a yield curve, specifically the Bund–Bobl–Schatz fly? But all of this had to be recast into something new, repurposed for the times and what lay ahead.

"I eventually wanted to be the trader who hit different markets, and not be afraid. For five years I traded the Euribor and Schatz *only*. After trading the fly, it would be eight years until I ever traded the DAX," *The Godfather* said. "The idea to be this volatility hunter excited me; the only way you can trade across more than ten markets is to follow the volatility. On Trump's election victory night, I traded the Peso and the Yen for the first time and did very well in them. We watched those markets in the run-up as it was where the bolt of volatility would likely come from," he continued.

Importantly, this strategic decision to be "market-less" was necessitated by the very market environment. "In the early days you could ask, 'What do you trade?' It wasn't 'macro'; it was always just *one* market—I am a Schatz trader, a FTSE trader, an S&P trader, a Gilt trader, a TED trader and so on. These days, it is very hard to do, especially in a low-volatility environment. This market ultra-specialisation is a thing of the past," our trader said.

The 2016 U.S. Presidential Election served as a soul-branding, deep-in-your-bones-eye-opener to see how creative this burgeoning volatility-hunting business could be for *The Godfather* to become a "market-less" volatility supremo. And the AXIA floor was the right place to be, as our trader said, especially thankful to sit next to *The Warrior*. Yet, it was not an *easy* place to be. It would take, unknowingly, another two years of a long, sandpaper-like version of *the test*, of snakes and ladders as *The Godfather* called it, and the worst of it is *always* yet to come. Because it is the lowest point a trader will dig themselves into before they decide to climb out. If not, then…

MERCY, MERCY, MERCY!

It is May 2018. And in-between sauntering to their desks, with quick exchanges in Greek, *The Godfather* and *The Warrior* had sounded out the overnight premise. Giuseppe Conte is Italy's new prime minister, and he is forming a new cabinet. But—*ah!*—it was just announced that Paolo Savona is in that mix. The media reported Savona was apparently in support of withdrawing Italy from the Eurozone; *Eurosceptic* was the branding. And he is now seemingly picked to be the new economics minister! More fuel to a raging fire of what this all means—Italy's budget and spending, future policies in the context of the anti-EU Lega Nord and Five Star Movement, a hung parliament... all just two years after Brexit, what of the EU as a whole? *Anyway! Big news!* It has to be—no one likes a down-player.

But for the traders, the BTP futures—the Italian ten-year bond—was closed for trading overnight, as regular. Yet a deluge of news still covered Savona's potential appointment. An opportunity, then, to capture the next leg of the move at the 7 a.m. open.

And the BTP futures opened sixty ticks lower, following yesterday's close.

"*Only* sixty? Whack it! This is nothing!"
The traders sold the lowly BTP bids where they would expe—
Drrrrrrrrring! "*En ginete reee!* S–Stop!"
And then the BTPs rocketed higher.
It vanished off the trader's screens—the *wrong* way.
It did not come back.

The Godfather knew he had taken a big hit. The world slowed down; a chill crept over his back. Behind him, *The Warrior* rattled on, his foot-stomping indicating his violent refusal to acknowledge this *cheating, sonofa—unbelievable!* market. *The Godfather* slowly glanced to the left of his screens—a splash of red: –€110,000.

Whatever his small account had to show for in the last two grindy years, it had just taken an ugly hit—a full-on seventy-four-gun broadside, leaving it listing and helpless. The arduous climb to plant the smallest of flags—a sign that he's still *got it*, had now vaporised. *The Godfather* left the office late that night, his train was cancelled and diverted, his phone battery—dead. *Of course.*

His walk back home took him to parts of the endlessly variable London scenery. The townhouses, glass offices, interspaced parks and pubs—gnarly brutalist flats and depilated tenements—then back to thriving high streets with new restaurants. As the culinary nightlife dropped away behind him, the roads widened, and the ground gave life to the grass and trees, interspaced with beautiful mansions, gated, neat hedgerows; trimmed. Our trader chanced upon this affluent neighbourhood. This was the place that any North London boy dreamed of moving to one day, and it had always been his dream, too. Yet this now suddenly felt impossible. *Delusional!*

The following day, our trader and his wife drove through the neighbourhood. "I always thought that one day we would get here," he said, "but it's never going to happen now."

"Why does it sound like you have given up?" she replied.

"Well—"

"It's not over, is it? Hasn't *this* always been your goal?"

"And I will never forget that drive and walk back home," *The Godfather* said. "The next day, I walked into Kyriacou's office and told him I am now fully committed and will do *whatever* it takes. When I had my first career crisis, a performance coach at the firm asked me, 'What are you willing to do to make it work?'—I didn't understand it then, but I do now." Our trader had been toying with *Plan B*, and as we've seen from much of the book so far, the market will certainly give you it, as our trader was sounding out the possibility to leave the industry and try other business ventures, and he nearly made it so. Instead, he tore up his business plans that were lying on his desk the very same day.

"I realised I did not fulfil my potential," he said. "This was unfinished business, and I would *not* go out like that! I decided right there I had gone too far to stop." It was as if our trader rejected the *rudis*, the symbolic wooden sword rewarded to a gladiator in ancient Rome to acknowledge his newly earned freedom. But some chose to stay. *The gladiator was who they now were, what they had become, and they would leave this mortal plane like one.* After a fifteen-year career, with finances still secure, it was all the more tempting to bow gracefully at the curtain close.

No! "I am a trader who stands at the forefront of news, handling chaos, where a day can change your life for better or worse. I wouldn't change that for anything else," he said. *The Godfather* took the BTP blowout in May 2018 after two years of struggles to become an outright trader. Yet in the following three years, he would rebuild, grow and reach new career heights: another *test* survived. The neighbourhood dream of every North London boy? He now lives there with his family. What changed?

His perception of the *meta-game!* The length of *The Godfather*'s career is long enough to be interspaced with both market and proprietary trading history. And that includes the evolution of the meta-game—the optimal practices, the dominant strategies; the *do's* and *don'ts* also change over time.

A trader's problems begin when they fail to adapt to the new meta-game, which is forced by the market environment—or worse, the trader is drawn to what sounds to be a good idea, but this was the old meta-game from twelve years ago. Or perhaps the meta-game is only relevant in a specific niche, like spread trading, for example, and transferring that 'meta' was the wrong thing to do. But certainly, there are timeless and transmutable principles in trading—especially in understanding risk; *never say never!*

Consider how *The Godfather* astutely observed how the market cycle and environments loop faster than ever. "In the early 2000s, you could give a trader one spread, one market, and they would be good for at least five years or longer. They didn't need to know anything else. It took that long for the market and the edge to change. Later, you could get away with a couple of years. In 2022, it is as if the cycles last only a few months."

The speed of change in the meta-game varies, too, and it extends much further than the surface-level strategy. Such is the case with our trader's old practice of withdrawing all funds above one hundred thousand pounds from his trading account at the end of the month. Because it was what everyone at his firm did and was told to do. "What? You are not happy with thirty or forty thousand a month?" the floor manager would say, especially to those who did not want to withdraw profits and grow their accounts to trade more size.

"*At the time* this made sense; the spread trading P&L upside was capped," *The Godfather* said. To trade more size, you would need more funds in the account, but if you cannot grow past a certain limit—another old meta-game belief—then it is nonsensical to keep more in the account while being exposed to the risk of firm bankruptcy or a trading execution accident, he explained. The P&L upside cap became a self-fulfilling prophecy, hardened because everyone else practised and preached the same of never growing the account past a certain limit. Little was explored beyond the pale. Yet, *The Godfather* carried on this practice well into his outright career, hurting growth and progress as more funds needed to be kept in the account to scale proactively, and to grow in size as an outright trader. To take advantage of the convex payout with more firepower—with size—to match the reality that opportunities are non-linear for events or news-macro trading; really any outright trading.

And once the meta is outdated, it is old enough to become market historiography. In our example, the spread trading belief that outright trading was a "pure gamble" had created many self-limiting beliefs for our trader. And it would take a new environment, a new floor stimulus, to crack them. The big trading floor that Haywood and *The Godfather* first found themselves on in 2005—the one with burgeoning outright Bund traders—had shattered our trader's limiting beliefs over outright trading and how much size can be deployed consistently within markets. *A whole new world!*—to crack these old beliefs. The same again with his arrival on the AXIA trading floor.

"That walk home made me realise the importance of perception. I finally accepted what was possible," *The Godfather* said. "The floor cracked so many beliefs. At my old floor, a trader of fifteen years asked me, 'Do you know how much money I lost trading an FOMC meeting? *None!* Why? Because I never stay.' He no longer trades. Someone else, too. 'Why would I come in at 11 p.m. for the Scottish referendum?' But then Cable futures [British pound] moved three hundred ticks. But on the floor, we cracked these beliefs: to do what we need to do to succeed. A 2.30 a.m. headline? We've done it. A 9 p.m. S&P close? Done it. Turn up at 11 p.m. for days at a time? Done it too."

The former traders from *The Godfather's* story worked from *outdated* meta. The health of a trader and their environment—the floor or community—can be assessed by how well it refreshes itself to the new market meta-game. If you are listening to angry social media accounts or niche detailed, overly planned, step-by-step approaches found in trading videos or books, you are not updating your meta; you are reading a thing of the past. This is a reason why we focus on principles in this book, as opposed to overly detailed trades that will become old "meta" before the book is even published. Studying trades, though, is valuable when one gets into the head of that trader to learn *how* they think. Anything else is only of value for avid fans of market historiography, which can be as entrenched and argued over as politics. And it is where—unknowingly, as an innocent new trader—you find and believe in people telling you that *this* is what real professional traders do! Maybe they were right, ten years ago at least.

Notice the singular drive and purpose of *The Godfather* to focus on and repurpose his objectives in his earlier career. "My *only* mission at the time was to give my mother and brother their money back," he said, finding consistency soon thereafter. Within his second career crisis, *The Godfather* said: "I vowed to myself, I do not care about the person on my left or right. My singular focus is to make it *work*, earn a living and pay the bills. I've got a baby coming soon." Both times this occurred at the lowest, most dangerous points. The real *test* periods. And the punishment had been enough to solicit change. But the reaction was *not* to quit, to instead find what he needed to do to "really make it work."

Hence! our trader did not truly transform into an outright trader until he literally tore up *Plan B*; the distraction was too great. The vow to ignore others around him proved an important topic, as Haywood always raises attention to this decision often becoming the bane of a trader's progress. Yet this is precisely what *The Godfather* needed at the time to leave 'learning mode' and enter 'performance mode.' That is, the ability to listen against the ability to filter, the confidence to reject.

The Godfather agreed, in fact, that his experience with the trader who had made over half a million euros on the ECB's "Vigilance" moment would have been beneficial had he "channelled it correctly. Instead, I took it the wrong way and tried to get bigger before my time." The same, our trader said, was how he used the fear of bankruptcy to refocus his priorities to become the best and most consistent fly trader at his old firm. It did not cripple his creativity nor his exploration of the adjacent possible, which pioneered a different use of the market profile, and the open and queueing strategies.

Instead, it brewed a maturity and responsibility to prevent reckless trading within the "one-man hedge fund for your family," as our trader calls it. Reframing can also help to bring into focus a trader's constraints. The ambitions to become the best trader in the world, *The Godfather* said, would require sacrifices too great. So instead, he resolved to become the "the best *dad trader* in the world." Suddenly, the burden was lifted, and he could become consistent and play into what it means to *get it right*. Different and better expectations were now set.

The Godfather's career, then, is one long example of a trader's slow transformation from 'cash flow' to 'wealth-building,' terms which we first introduced with *The Warrior*. His old spread trading 'meta' had created the ultimate cash-flow trader, taking everything out of his trading account over a certain limit. But excising this practice was part of what unlocked his turnaround in 2019.

"I also struggled with consistency, but what helped was to stop measuring my progress as *daily* consistency. Kyriacou was important for this; he told me about the P&L curves of some of the traders and how their whole years are built on three months due to these outsized trades. The rest of the year is virtually flat," *The Godfather* recalled. "For the first twelve years in my career it involved looking at your daily P&L, especially as trading the fly necessitated it as you always had to know your position in the spread. When I was becoming an outright trader, I started to look at the end of the week instead of daily to assess performance. I started to see what it *meant* to become an outright macro-trader and how a career is built on these special moments.

Then I started to only look at the month, and now I only assess every financial quarter. This made the difficult job of building the account easier." That was the process of 2019–2021, in the middle of which he had traded his first six-figure day on the U.S. drone strike upon the Iranian General Suleimani, the events chronicled in 'A Mexican Standoff' with *The Warrior*.

But by the end of 2022, our trader was firmly in the wealth creation camp. His account had grown enormously and was now ready to push. "It is a process that has to be done at the correct time. Many fail, trying to get big before their time, before the account can handle it, or they just do not have the cash flow to pay the bills. Now it is time to build the bullets, grow and scale. I studied how *The Warrior* broke through the numbers. He did not achieve a twenty-thousand-pound day followed by a million. He went from the twenties to sixty-five to a six-figure day. Then a quarter of a million, then half, six hundred thousand, then a million-pound day. The process is always organic."

Similar, then, to businesses and entrepreneurs who prioritise growth, some famously maniacal in reinvesting everything into further growth. *The Godfather* reflected on his first success as a TED spread trader, in which he bought a house and car and spent the majority of his account's cash flow. Nothing was left to reinvest for growth. In our trader's defence, this was partly a product of the old spreader's meta-game of taking out the surplus cash; yet our trader is still critical of this period. "I wanted to reward myself and start living after so many years. I lost sight of the priority of building an account," our trader said. "Instead, the ECB 'Vigilance' trader was building at the same time. That was his mentality, of growth from fifty to two thousand lots in six months. That is how he could go for these kinds of trades—he had the account behind him and could wear whatever risk was to come."

THE GODFATHER

Haywood took a more forgiving stance over the mistakes of youth, yet still hammers a battered wooden sign—*Beware all ye who enter here*—into the ground. "The majority of traders, as we all know, fail before they even consistently make money," Haywood said. "But the next bloody culling stage is the struggle after *some* success. I have seen so many traders go out this way, too. They have an account, feel the relief, their routine and life changes too quickly; the 'I made it' attitude takes over."

Getting it right, then, has so far been an element of perception, reframing events and understanding the implications of real-life constraints that impact trading. You cannot sit in a chair for six months to hit the "big one" with two lots—*you've got to eat!* Cash flow and trading frequency to pay the bills; the stuff of glory is for the big-account club. Yet, with consistency and an account to go with it comes the time to push and take your pound of flesh: growth at *nearly* all costs. *The Godfather* and *The Warrior* will sound this message until the end of days.

And getting it right is the trader's way to navigate chaos. It comes down to the very basics—of showing up. "If anyone knows *The Godfather*, they will tell you about his religiously consistent schedule and routine. He is a ruthless professional, a role model, *and* that is now the minimum attitude a trader needs to compete," Haywood said. There is no amateur league in trading; the markets do not wait for late risers, the confused, rushed, rolled-out-of-bed rambler. You should chalk up your competition with a trader who can successfully juggle the demands of a family of three and maintain other areas of his life, notwithstanding intense training to compete in Brazilian jiu-jitsu, all as a minimum before we even consider the all-consuming nature of news trading. And in *that* he absolutely performs.

"Other fresh twenty-year-olds can't even stick to a real routine for three weeks—how will they ever rise to the level of *The Godfather*?" Haywood continued. A six-to-six schedule was born out of the demands of trading the fly open strategy, requiring the trader back at his desk for the 9 p.m. close. And this routine has stuck ever since. But there is yet a deeper benefit. When traders have no routine, there is no diagnostic ability to understand what is wrong or right in their game; there is no baseline. There are a few things in our control, yet routine, habit and rituals are part of *getting it right*.

A BIT OF THE OLD SUMMER DEBACLE...

So, a rigid baseline routine of professionalism, with the right approach at the right time, and smart use of what you've got—the spare parts accumulated over a decade of trading—supported *The Godfather* well.

But what about the street-fighting tactics? Like *The Godfather* says, being a news trader is all about having access to the relevant markets at the right time. This should be a given, but the real differentiator is trade execution and management. Over those years *The Godfather's* news volatility trading was always underscored by one principle—stay in the game for as long as possible. And this is as true for an individual trade as it is for a trading career. "The longer you go, the more doors open up," our trader said.

What he began to describe is what we will call an 'elastic' approach to managing a trade. That is, elasticity defined as the art of managing an offside position. "If I have conviction in a news comment and I go all in, yet the market drags me offside, then I zone in on peripheral markets," our trader began. "They should be correlated; if they really are, then I will hold the position. I will never liquidate it all in one go. If the correlations are not going my way and the market is choppy, I will scale out to leave a core position. Instead of a hundred and fifty lots, down to seventy or fifty. If you go onside again, then you scale back in as fast as possible. I am always objectively re-evaluating the unfolding events, finessing the position to stay in. Only if the next comment tells me I am dead-wrong, then I clip out quickly."

Next, *The Godfather* described a wealth-building-like approach that forgoes increased consistency in order to maximise any opportunity—*the right thing* if you are in the right place in your career. "If I am onside and the correlations are working and I have conviction in the comment *yet* the market stalls and chops, I then scale out some of the position too. I am 'buying' staying power—extra P&L—to never be forced out of the trade. You do not want to be the weak hand over seven ticks." You are a small, individual prop trader, even with hundreds of lots, in comparison to institutions, but you are also *nimble*; use it to your advantage.

Managing a trade in this way is part of the skill repertoire of a trader dynamically managing his position, as we discussed with *The Adventurer*. Recall the 'path' a trade could play out into the future. *The Godfather*, *The Warrior* and other dynamic traders do not know how these paths will play out—but by staying in the market as long as possible, your chances of finding the 'right' path increase. These tactics did not come easy for our trader, as much of it was a reinvention act involved in *un*learning. Executing a spread involves entering the spread as it goes offside, never too early or aggressively. But we consider this as 'bad'—in this context—because of a different meta-game, but when trading *outright*, the exact opposite must be done.

"With trading outright news comments, I originally wanted to see confirmation in the price action and enter five to ten prices *too late*," *The Godfather* said. "Many traders do this; they see the news—hesitate—and wait for the ladders to tick up. *Oh, I must be right!* Then, they enter one clip. If it goes higher, then two clips. But your average entry price is much worse, and then after ten ticks of washback, you are offside and have ruined the trade. I learned this from *The Warrior*: there is no hesitation; you cannot wait for confirmation. It is far better to go offside on four clips immediately than whimper slowly into fast moves. Best-price entry is so important to trade execution." A differentiator between *The Warrior* and others, our trader saw in his early days, is that he would see through the 'chop,' the market indecision, because he entered at best prices—earlier prices—*with* most of his size. He can wait it out.

... AND THE GILTY

Now follows a trade breakdown by *The Godfather*. The context was the U.K.'s Mini-Budget crisis of September 2022, instigated by proposed unfinanced budget cuts by Liz Truss' government. This led to aggressive, liquidation-type selling, and the long Gilt futures (ten-year bond) offered about a hundred and twenty points, or one thousand two hundred ticks, in four trading sessions.*

This was a seminal moment for our trader as it was his first trade of a quarter of a million pounds. As a spread trader over a decade ago, *The Godfather* would earn just over this amount in a year. But he now earned that in a single day.

What were you thinking going into the situation?
I knew what was about to come would be significant. The bonds,

---

* As measured on long Gilt futures (December 2022) on the Intercontinental Exchange (ICE) from the close of 21 December and to the lowest price traded on 22 December, the day before the Bank of England response. Roughly 120 bps.

equities and Gold futures had traded in a way that reminded me of a "bond vigilante" move. The newswires started to discuss the return of the vigilantes after they were deemed "dead" following zero-interest-rate policy. So, I started to get really energised and focused on the days ahead. I was in the zone and was trading extremely well, reading the flows, and I was up to date with the news. Once the bond vigilante narrative really began to develop, I started to trade other bonds because the narrative can spread quickly, and panic even faster. Suddenly, there was talk that even the Dutch pension funds could face the same issues as the ones in the U.K. due to the large bond market moves. As a result, there was a correlation between the Buxl [German thirty-year bond] and the Gilts. They moved together, as funds holding U.K. and German debt might have to liquidate the latter to meet margin calls in the former.

How did you prepare for what you thought was to come?
The trading floor expected some kind of intervention, so we followed all the relevant institutions closely and prepared for how they could release information to the press and newswires. Would they backtrack first? We did not quite expect the Bank of England to step into a high-inflation environment and start easing—buying bonds. Either way, I am always quick to move my ladders to have the most relevant in my line of sight, even if I've never traded them before. If they are prime opportunity markets, they are always in front. So, I moved the Gilts and Buxl to be side by side due to their correlation. Next to them, I placed the Cable [British pound] ladder. Then came 28 September.

What happened on the day?
I was actually *short* the Gilt and Buxl at the time and was handsomely

onside in profit. Then there isn't much to it. The headline hits the newswires, *but* it just said: "BoE Takes Action." That was it, the first headline. It was not highlighted as an important headline, just random and standalone. But *what* action? As soon as I saw this, I covered my short immediately as both markets were at their lows. I went long *only* one clip in the Buxl, and one clip in the Gilts.

Is this actually counter to your usual tactics of clipping big and early?
Absolutely—you have to know when to drop the usual plan. I did not clip a low amount because I was waiting for price confirmation, which would be a mistake, but that "BoE Takes Action" headline could have been anything. So, I was just ready with my mouse, and my other hand was on the spacebar to recentre ladders. Eyes on newswires. I wanted the optionality to be in, yet not to be caught on a deadly move if the "action" turned out to be something completely different.

What happened next?
So, I glimpsed the next headline: "BoE to Buy…" and I just lifted [bought] the Gilts. I did well on this day since I was tuned onto the Buxl. It was on its lows, and I lifted roughly a hundred Buxl, nearly a hundred and fifty Gilts, but I only got eighty Bunds away. And, really, *that was it!* The markets went strong bid and accelerated. I started to scale out, eventually over half my size in Gilts, and kept my whole Buxl position. Eventually, everything was down to half. I had no idea what my P&L was because I do not look at it—it will *always* force you to exit because you either made so much, or it makes you trade again because you did not make enough. And these are the worst reasons to trade. But, at one time, I had Buxl, Gilt, Cable, Bund and S&P positions on.

THE GODFATHER

How did you manage all these positions?
I am very cautious about size when I have this many markets on. I prioritise attention—with my eyes and mouse cursor—on the market I have most size on. Cable was not playing ball and was being offered; it interpreted the Bank of England action as dovish. So I got rid of it. At that time, it was a forty- to fifty-tick loser, yet it went another two hundred ticks lower after, so it was a good loser to take. Eventually, I worked down to be flat in Buxl and Bund. The S&P didn't go anywhere, and I got rid of it too, and focused on my remaining thirty to forty lots in Gilts. It had a vicious pullback, so I scaled out, but I always wanted to stay in regardless. I got back in again after it went bid on the second leg. That was it; without knowing it, I was up two hundred and fifty thousand by the end of the day.

That was an interesting chain of decision-making...
I will always scale out of some. As soon as you leave the core position, I work on offering small lots like *The Warrior*, so you know the market is going your way. I looked at the daily market levels, and the event is big enough that I did not care about one-minute or fifteen-minute candles. Look at the bigger picture—I had so much conviction in the Buxl—I knew this was right; it was a *shock* for the markets.

I know I am very fast on the news, and when these comments come out, I always think what everyone else, every other trader or fund will do when they hear this. *What is paper doing?* I try to operate like this even if something comes out at 5 a.m. and the market is going nowhere. Just hold it—the news still has to spread. There are other traders who will "smash and grab"—and if the market is not instantly moving onside, they will liquidate. *Well, it didn't move for thirty seconds!* I try not to do this in order to maximise the opportunity. That is why it helps to put yourself in the shoes of others. What will each participant do with this news? It helps to wade through the noise. And I think the markets changed over the pandemic; it's slower in different ways compared to before. There are thousands of locals—small, independent traders like me—who hear the news just as fast, yet the markets take time to digest it. We need "paper"—banks and institutions—to come in and start placing positions that will start to move markets.

What were you thinking when the Gilt gave back half of its move at one stage? You held it in a two-point or two-hundred-tick pullback!
It comes from managing size—always. If I feel a pullback is emerging, I scale out. The conviction means I am willing to get back in again, full-size if it goes the correct way. I am never flat, but I am never going to sit there with my entire position. *Of course*, I sometimes leave money on the table, this is because I do not smash and grab. I want to maximise the trade; I have a target and will push for it. This is because of the difference in trade execution between "cash flow" and "wealth building," I am now firmly in the latter.

When you scale out, how do you do this exactly?
I throw around tiny one or two lots like *The Warrior*. I picked this up from him. This is to feel where I am getting filled. If I am in a triple-digit position, I know these lots are meaningless. So, when I *do* scale out meaningfully, I will do it in quarters. If it's a two-hundred lot, then it's fifty lot chunks. Yet the first few one to two lots are an orientation exercise.

Finally, how do you think of adding even more size on the next big trade? As you are now looking to grow more than ever.
Yes, I am now looking to push. Outright trading has shown me the way to push boundaries. It just has to be done at the right time.

Kyriacou always said to me, *Back yourself! Trust that you are going to do it, that you are capable of smashing through the numbers.* It is not a scientific formula; you just become obsessed in growing the account. As I grow, I increase my default daily clip size in all markets. I work backwards—what amount am I comfortable with losing? Then, you find the default size that will give you enough leeway to trade throughout the day. I've now worked towards risking £50,000 in a single non-eventful day. Then for big, *important* trades like this Gilt–Buxl one, you just crank up the numbers each time, a hundred and *eighty* lots of Buxl instead of a hundred and *fifty* Buxl or whatever is relevant to the narrative in the future. This is just the new arena you find yourself in, and even in my eighteenth year of trading, you reach a new level with different stakes, objectives and players.

STILL HERE

The Godfather sat with us on a December weekend. The London weather was typically undecided. He started the interview by reading out a message from his Brazilian jiu-jitsu "professor," as he called him.

"'Morning… I want you to know how much I appreciate you and our friendship. And I look forward to the many years ahead. I woke up this morning and wrote this down: I am going to heal, rebuild my body and skills and turn myself into a monster. to destroy everything put before me…' and then he titled and dated it," our trader said. To us, it was as if *The Godfather* wrote this manifesto himself.

"He is fifty-four, and to the outsider, he already looks phenomenal. But he still wakes up and has goals and visions like this," our trader said. "That is inspiring. I am going to join him on this mission for my health and my trading, to improve it further. Why? Why is there a limit on your age?"

"Well… you're still here."

"Exactly, I have done what I set out to do and I am proud of this. But I still work to have the best years ahead. Out of the five on my graduate training programme, I was the one lagging behind. I could not explain it; things always seemed to take me a bit longer. Maybe my journey involves having to go through pain first to have major breakthroughs. Look at some of the superhero traders I looked up to from ten years ago; I was nowhere near them, but now…" *The Godfather* trailed off… he realised he had surpassed most of them. He slowly cast his gaze out of the cold room, and that newspaper stuck on his bedroom wall twenty years ago stared back. The boy read, and now a man writes. And so too will another sit next to him.

We said in 'Beyond the Disclaimer' that dematerialisation of one's entire life effort is the market's standard operating procedure. So, what of it? Our trader navigated this dangerous aspect of the markets better than most, resisting it. We focused on his reinventions because survival necessitates it. Success is but a mere shrug, and the failures are where we learn. *But don't get it wrong!* Our trader is not merely keeping his head above water, but he has built an entire village next to the shore. That is, a long-lasting foundation for his family, to give them the time, space and finances to travel the world. That boyhood dream house was well acquired. None of which, he said, could have been possible without his wife.

But *The Godfather* is proud not of a multi-six-figure day, or eventually a seven-figure one when it will come. Why? It is but a high score, he says, and he has seen others hit far higher numbers on the screen... yet it never left the confines of those pixels. What was the point of it beyond some back-slapping? You just burn up at a stratosphere higher than most but come back to Earth all the same. Instead, he took a career and made it material. It changed his life. *That* is the true goal and achievement.

And it allows for agency, for sovereignty! Is that not what we want when we become traders? Others would not get married or put off having kids, our trader says, because of how much they want to push that high score, and give *all* their pounds of flesh. Thus echo *The Adventurer* and *The Student*. A career made material meant his wife could quit her job and become a *present* mother, he said, and so a family of five came to be. He paused, pensive. That is what he is truly proud of.

"And I am sure it has gotten to the point where others would say, *damn*, he is still here; after all this time, he is still clicking away and trading."

Because *The Godfather* knows of the chaos to come.

And chaos he will endure.

PRACTITIONER'S POSTSCRIPT

Explore resources derived from this chapter to further support the practicing trader.

axiafutures.com/
toot

Refer to
The Godfather's
section.

LEARNER'S IMPRESSIONS

Below are some personal impressions that *The Godfather* made on us that we still discuss with other traders.

1. *Risk reinvention.* What are you willing to do? *The Godfather* has always managed his career well. Never settle on one environment, floor or community which you outgrow. A far bigger risk is to remain static in market environments that are changing faster than ever. Make sure never to be the best trader on the floor. Otherwise, it is time to change. How well is your trading environment staying ahead of the meta-game? Do not confuse current practices and ideas with what is, in fact, market 'historiography' that seems relevant only because it is still talked about. It can still be a thing of the past, not of where we are going.
2. *Measure up.* *The Godfather* sets the minimum bar for a trader wishing to stay in the game, junior or experienced. First, evaluate your routine if you cannot diagnose where you are failing. Routine is your tether within chaos, both a diagnostic tool and a shield from its effects. New traders desire a career and decry their hard work, yet *The Godfather* has already wrapped up the morning's trading by the time they wake up.
3. *Snakes and ladders.* Experience and P&L milestones absolve nothing; there is no guaranteed minimum floor a complacent trader can slide back to; they will crash right through it. And then some more. The markets turn strengths into weaknesses—experience and time risk the illusion of safety; demand for greater remuneration risks killing the golden goose. Such were the instigators of *The Godfather*'s career shipwrecks that followed his most confident sailing. Hints of vulnerability are too subtle until they

become manifestly irreversible. So, to climb is to prevent sliding, as our trader is still pushing boundaries in his second decade, to say that the best always lies ahead.

What are your impressions? Write them down and converse with this book!

CHAPTER NINE

THE ENGINEER: PART I

S tern, piercing, sceptical, princely, confident... *No, no!* Perhaps unperturbed... austere... *Nay!* One struggles to summarise our trader's expression, his presence, the way he carries himself to impress a certain eminence upon the room. Perhaps one can... *ah! Composed* is the word. A man of composure is a man on a mission. And if our trader would walk into any other place, one might equate that composure with deadly intentions. Perhaps that is the point.

Observe him silhouetted against the London twilight as he retakes the path to his trading desk with a leather briefcase in tow. Eschewing a hoodie or sweatshirt—as is the temptation—our trader is fitted with a sharp blazer, brown boots, a jumper and a striped shirt to complete the set. Moving with purpose, his expression—the one so hard to qualify—barely alters while exchanging the morning greetings... *ah! Laconic*—the perfect description.

If one can stretch the definition, his entire demeanour is laconic. All energies and focus are directed towards the sharp tip of the spear to embroil the markets. Should we crack open a dictionary: "laconic—of a person using very few words; *Lakōnikos*, from *Lakōn*, 'Laconia, Sparta,' the Spartans being known for their terse speech."

THE ENGINEER: PART I

And how refreshingly terse he is! One of few words and many pauses, and to do so comfortably pitching his head to really process your question. Composed. Up the stairs, turn left and find the L-shaped desk cove that nestles our trader for the rest of the day; seldom moving—and seldom speaking—that Lacedaemonian!

But let the numbers do the talking, for within this quiet cove resides an eight-figure trader, sitting upon his hundred- to thousand-lot clips, with enough firepower to haul in multi-six-figure trades, and, on a particularly auspicious day, a seven-figure trade. And this is a one-way relationship; the market is to only prick our trader, only with some occasional bloodletting. Consider 2018–2020, which featured no down-months, and outside those two specific years, our trader could often experience $25,000 down-months yet experience up-months of a million dollars, or more.

In 2022, our trader pocketed these six-figure trades and returned nothing to the markets, culminating in a four-million-dollar month. And these returns are not the result of financial alchemy, that is, a type of concave payout, the infamous carry-type trade rife throughout the financial world that often works long enough to earn the title "genius," before we, shockingly, discover that the very maestro was sitting on a leveraged thousand-pound bomb. *The Engineer's* well-honed consistency allowed him to rebuild as he restarted from scratch in 2016 with a $20,000 account. Yes! His account too went down with the ship that was Firm Y. And since then, he has accumulated lifetime profits in the low-eight-figure range.

And how, then, does one become an eight-figure trader?

Routine. Framework. Process.

That is it—*fin*. Let then our trader's form, style and approach develop the conversation—a covalence of the price ladder, Market

Profile and the occasional footprint chart, the type of trader so many struggle to become and later deem impossible, that is, a trader whose edge is overtly *technical* in nature. He is rooted, however, not in patterns with clunky, replicable, shallow rules, indicators and obscene charts but an entire framework—as he calls it—that is a modus operandi, a mental model deeply rooted in market auction theory. Understand the auction, our trader says, and you will not only understand *what* works but *why* it should. The difference in asking and answering those two questions creates a chasm between a failing "technical" trader and a successful one, eight figures wide.

And we shall start there, at his framework's core. *But first!* Our Lacedaemonian needs a name, so we shall christen him *The Engineer*, as Alex Haywood has done in honour of his former profession and due to his precision, thoroughness and ability to build, construct, calibrate and manipulate the market profile into a competitive advantage.

DO I HEAR FIFTY?

James F. Dalton et al. begin *Mind Over Markets* (2013: 9-10) with the imagery of a regular auction to form an intuitive base for understanding the market profile. And it is apt, for the financial markets, when stripped to their bones, are exactly this—a continuous set of auctions that domino or cascade into each other.

Begin an auction for a piece made by the hottest artist, and all the hands or paddles will scratch the roof at so-called bargain prices. And they will keep doing so until it is just too much for some, and eventually tolerable for just one. *Higher prices... fewer hands... higher prices... fewer hands... higher!* Each bid takes initiative over the previous bid until the last solitary bidder pays up. If those hands bid

THE ENGINEER: PART I

because they love the art, or they need to park their QE money somewhere, that is a whole other matter; we can infer endlessly about motivations. But the auction provided you with cold, hard, indisputable information—a range of prices the majority were willing to buy and *the* highest price that was paid. A belly and a tail, in other words, a bell-curve.

But throw in a continuous market auction where higher prices might suddenly entice the entire room to bid again—or alternatively *drop* in price to find a reactive buyer—as in a Dutch auction, then you end up with all sorts of skewed, warped, thin and fat, twisted and mangled distributions that look anything but normal. Thus, picture a horizontal bell-curve. But now hoist it vertically, dangling from the ceiling, with the market price on the y-axis and time segmented by thirty-minute intervals on the x-axis, and you have the market profile.

James Dalton, and indeed his early-career counterpart J. Peter Steidlmayer, proposed the profile to view the facilitation of trade over a whole day. Yet, with the advent of pit-to-screens, the market auction must be intrinsically tied to the price ladder, *The Engineer* says. At its core, order flow is just the hands and paddles in the room, or, as it was, traders in a pit, and now in our time, this is represented visually on the price ladder.

And liquid, exchange-traded markets are mostly fractal. That is, the processes that cause a certain market behaviour or phenomenon over the next few minutes are the same mirrored over the next few days or weeks, just different in scale. And so, to understand the auction intimately on a price ladder a trader can adapt these first principles to the different scales of time—a footprint chart as something intermediate, and, on a longer horizon, a market profile.

Because at their core, markets are driven by *initiative*-taking buying and selling, and *reactive* buying and selling. These are the four types of participation. Understanding their interaction is as relevant for thirty seconds of action as it is for thirty minutes and thirty days. And for everyone between a one-tick trade scalper and a value investor, it is always a question of price. With the exception of the fine purveyors of formerly negative-yielding European debt, not many want to pay full price, but many want a twenty-five-per-cent discount—until that becomes fifty per cent, then, *hell!* Even your central bank will hopefully take it. Your initiative-taking participant, the determined fellow with their auction paddle who is willing to pay anything, is really who drives the auction and the market.

Just think of a forced seller; that participant is going to take the initiative with extreme prejudice and will take all of your damn bids until they are done. Tick by tick, price by price, it is reflective of the latest action taken by the latest participant, and *always* by initiative. A bid and offer never cross; there are no "more buyers than sellers" that move markets, but there are determined, initiative-taking buyers and sellers, who most of the time are the minority until the last of the time—that, then, is your market high or low.

Frame the behaviour of the price ladder, this order flow, to the context of the skew, structure and shape of the market profile, and it becomes a universal language. A syntax, as *The Hero* said, that he and *The Engineer* choose to speak, and a framework into which all market information is thrown—central bank action, an order flow anomaly, fundamental market news, observations of sticky, unhealthy order flow, chart patterns—and it *is* a language because it speaks back. To answer what is happening and *why* it is. Tie the profile and its syntax to the "personality" and behaviour of order flow on the price ladder, and it infers critical information for the quality or the *health* of the auction, as our trader calls it.

"And it has purity," *The Engineer* says, "I fit my observations within the profile and auction theory, to think through it. You need a framework or principles that provide you with a lens and parameters to put things into. Otherwise, it becomes messy when you have no mental model. I lean on technicals a lot, but basic chart patterns are inconsistent. You need to skew probabilities in your favour by adding more layers of disparate information together. And then you must always understand why it should work *this* time," he continues.

Unfortunately, the majority of new traders seek a technically driven edge before all things, which does not force an overt framework or mental model to operate within markets. This, in turn, leads to traps like confusing a pattern and a strategy, an issue directly addressed with *The Razor*. That is, the faulty assumption that a market pattern can only be traded one way—a singular strategy—when a market pattern can be skinned many different ways, each requiring different strategies.

Understanding a clear framework, like the market auction theory, precludes the trader from falling into these traps. "When I started, the market auction theory made sense to me; as an engineer, I wanted to understand the mechanics of the markets. For example, how well are we auctioning? What kind of buyers and sellers are present? Each observation was clearer within the context of auction theory. Market moves made sense when understanding mechanics like this," our trader concluded.

Technical trading is often disparaged, and many times rightly so, but what the detractors really are attacking is a type of trading that permits too easily shallow thinking and shallower action, and that is why many new traders attach fervently to it. It is difficult to falsify and easy to obfuscate, as there are no obvious parameters to consistently test it against. Throw in the fund–institutional–academic complex born from mainstream economics and finance in the past seventy years, and your jaded spreadsheet-crunching analyst or quant trader has enough righteous mud to throw on all the plebs and proles below who have only discovered *the* head-and-shoulders pattern five minutes ago—it is also a status game, after all.

For the bourgeois above, understanding matters like portfolio management, balance sheet analysis, market fundamentals and valuations mostly works because these are inevitably rooted in what constitutes a framework, even if it is not explicit. For technical traders, overtly identifying a framework is of critical importance.

But *The Engineer* just as much considers recent economic data prints, recent central bank comments, the current macro-environment, the yield curve or other minutiae-like subtle changes in the order flow. So where does the sordid chartist stop and the *legitimate* market approach begin? A technical trading approach does not deliver inferiority or superiority by picking up the tool, but, as a truism, it depends on how it is used.

THERE'S A STORY IN THESE HILLS

As *The Hero* says, the market profile is but order flow on a larger time frame. And we start there because the market profile is a time-gated slicing of the cake. A separator of a deluge of data. Why then, is it so indispensable? "It is for context," *The Engineer* answers. "The market profile frames the auction process… to find asymmetry in the market. What is the probability skew one way or the other? The way the TPOs are distributed on the profile will allow me to look at how much time it needs to spend there to suggest a trade or to look elsewhere."

TPOs are *Mind Over Market*'s acronym for time, price and opportunity, the three facilitators of trade (Dalton, 2014: 10-15). They can be drawn visually as letters, starting somewhere in the alphabet and

THE ENGINEER: PART I

developing consecutively, with each depicting a thirty-minute period of the day. Amalgamate these together to draw a bell-curve-like diagram, and this completes the visual look of a market profile. Operating within the distribution, or shape, of the profile is a crucial difference between *The Engineer*'s approach to the majority.

A decade ago, at Firm Y, many sought to "pull metrics out of the profile," he recalled, and this is exactly how *The Hero* recollected such practice too. This would be just a binary recording of "things like volume point of control and the tails… there is not much more information in that than a candlestick. It doesn't tell you vulnerabilities, where is the skew in the auction? That misses the true value—the *context*. For example, if the profile is skewed higher, through initiative buying, then very generally you would shape your execution to buy more support than sell rallies," he explained.

The distribution of these TPOs and, subsequently, the structure of the day, once more, arise from the quality of the auction and its health. "The market may be rangebound, yet it is flowing with real two-way trade smoothly, and participants react naturally," *The Engineer* continued. That means, for example, the presence of initiative-taking participants who take price to one "extreme" to spur on reactive participants.

For example, aggressive sellers take the initiative and hit the best bid—400 lots clear out the price of "10s." These sellers wanted to transact with that market *now* at that price. *Take 'em!* But no buyer reactively adds to the bid at 10s through limit orders and the price is cleared. We trade lower to 9s, as that is where the next best bid is. The sellers hit 382 lots and clear out 9s. No one else "reloads" or adds back to the bid at 9s. The sellers clear out all the limit orders sitting at the bid at 8s, and so on. The price trades lower and lower until a big buyer(s) is found to snap up all the offers at discount prices! As if the market trades and digs lower and lower until—*Thunk!*—the shovel hits something big and metallic. *A huge initiative-taking buyer!* The buyer roars out of their slumber and then aggressively lifts the best offer, takes all the orders sitting there and clears out that price, and the next price and the next. They really wanted that discount and wanted it *now*. And so, we trade back higher. How fast this process occurs depends on volatility, which is inextricable from the greatest controller of all: *time*.

This kind of action leads to "tail-like" structures, long and tapered—an aggressive trade lower and reactive buying back. Other times, the profile can be perfectly bell-curve-looking. This suggests market balance, an agreement on price of temporary "value," over a period of time, which is, by default, for the day.

Depending on how the puzzle pieces are laid out at the time, there may be no real opportunity for the trader; there is no asymmetry. "Other times, the market is not auctioning well, the ladder looks churny and flippy, and it visually leaves a blocky-like structure or a ledge," our trader added. In other words, this visual inventory is termed as "poor structure." For a trader like *The Engineer* this can serve as much as an opportunity as it is valuable information to contribute to the puzzle.

SUPPORTING MATERIALS

Explore a gallery of different TPO structures.

axiafutures.com/
toot-tpo

THE ENGINEER: PART I

Auction health, then, infers participant type. Ledges often form with a large buyer "sitting on the bid" at a series of prices—or just one—and letting the market sell into him at large quantities, and this often takes time. The most extreme and simple example of this, and somewhat morbidly comic, is provided by the grindy bull-flattening days of 2013–2015, in which *everyone* sat on the bid in the European debt markets. Comic in the absurdist sense. Mario Draghi's "whatever it takes," and the later *QE-max* moment, guaranteed that behind your bid was that of the European Central Bank. An elevator to greatness, as long as the music lasted.

This formed the "super ledges" to the downside in markets like the German ten-year bond—the Bund—as any offloading of positions would meet an infinite bid. The dry, low-volatile days continued a grindy uptrend with very "unhealthy" auctions. Imagine throwing a jelly-like ball against the floor—the infinite bid, that is—and for several frames, your camera can capture the ball squished, nearly elongated and horizontal, before rebounding higher. This is an extreme shape, yet the market profile visually infers the same, to clue in a trader about the environment and participants.

Of course, the trader would not have been ignorant of the ECB's QE commitment at the time, but it is not often that such a binary and static environment emerges, as markets are usually in flux as ever, especially across geographies and asset classes. Compare a market profile of the Bund during QE in 2015, which represents one extreme, and the rate-hiking cycle of 2022–2023, another extreme, and you have a full spectrum of what the auction process can look like.

But the market profile does not instigate trades directly! Just as a liquid takes the shape of its container, so too does it shape a trader's execution. The profile, then, identifies the container. We have walked through the process of the market profile as an investigative tool to view the "technical landscape," as *The Engineer* famously puts it.

And a landscape it is. The presence and interactivity of market participants create a situation familiar to the sciences—we cannot see certain processes, but we know that they exist. And we most certainly experience the *output* of these unseen processes. The visible interaction of participants hides the mostly invisible *positioning* and thereby infers something akin to a hyper-speed geological world, helped by the likes of ice, rain, water and wind. Some participants can still be in the market with committed positions, as fickle as sand dunes or as stubborn as ancient glaciers and tectonic plates. The valleys and the plains and the cliffs are formed and reformed through participants of all sizes and intentions entering and leaving the market. And the order flow, like water, starts to trickle through the embedded valleys and marshes and river deltas, only for the geology to change once more, and the gentle stream becomes a raging torrent, the market landscape upended by the arrival of new positioning, new information, by the revolving door of participants with their new intentions. But every once in a while, an immense asteroid will hit and wipe the slate clean, shattering all. Market geology for context—a map for orientation—and, as it were, white-water rafting for the intraday trading.

"*The Engineer* creates a narrative of the technical landscape, of building a story," Haywood continues. "He considers the evolving profile structure in combination of how it auctioned the area. How the price ladder and flow behaved to create that profile shape allows you to notice a changing environment very fast, whereas a mechanical or algorithmic trader's system is likely to underperform since it was created out of a now outdated environment. He can sow the stories of different profiles and carry the information forward, as we say." Not all too different from how a geologist would use the power of story to convey information about the evolution of a landscape.

It is critical, then, to observe *how* the market auctioned out an area because market structure is not created 'equally,' as market participants and their operational reasons are not equal. One 'ledge' is as definitive as steel, another as strong as paper; another is porous or elastic before it snaps back violently. Yet, on the surface, they look nearly identical to a trader who did not watch them form in real time on the price ladder. But do so and you can "locate these sweet spots of volatility," Haywood said, "and this is why knowing when the price ladder looks different from last time is so important. It gives us clues when to leverage. And when to leverage is the whole art of trading," he concluded.

And as our trader puts it, when to leverage is a question of the balance of probabilities, and that is where the extremes of the AXIA traders' edge spectrum converge. *The Razor, The Warrior* and *The Engineer* are so different in approach yet overlap in one area—when to load the boat with *maximum* risk. That is when they have placed or found themselves in a market flow or structure of very little variance. *The Razor's* infrequent trading rests on opportunities provided by the market to enter a split-second, inter-temporal environment of a binary outcome. The trade wins or loses instantly.

But *The Engineer* "layers" various pieces of the puzzle—profile structure, order flow, news comments, macro-environments—to find outcomes of low variance, where the market will only and *can only* do so many things. Or, to use the same vocabulary, a balance of probabilities skewed highly in his favour.

In the words of *The Engineer*, this means to define where you are "dead-wrong," so a trader can make the decision to liquidate as fast and in as binary a way as possible. In reverse, then, this also means to be "dead-right" with as much trading size as possible. The hardest trades are of high variance, where the market can play out in so many ways; there are too many paths it can take. This is a grey area, a limbo where you are neither wrong nor right, making it emotionally draining and increasingly harder to separate noise from signal. And yet, this is where the majority of trading takes place, at every level of skill and achievement.

A SELLER? A SELLER!

The Engineer, in a presentation, walked up to a board bearing the daily Bund market profiles of the current and previous week. In those past weeks, our trader explained, it was important to have understood where the last participant *initiative* had come from. This was observable with the frequent tail structures, as can be visualised in a bell-curve. Any selling in the Bund was met with initiative-taking, dominating buyers. To the upside, there is instead no "selling tail" over the past five days; that is, no sellers were spurred to react dramatically at "too-great prices" and, therefore, sell aggressively and opportunistically.

By its nature, a market will search and prod until it finds a concerted response. The story so far is that any price seems 'cheap' to the downside and invites a flock of buyers, but not expensive enough to the upside to sell so flagrantly—yet. Pointing to the profiles, *The Engineer* said the balance of probabilities was that we were still poised to trade higher; therefore, not much risk, if any, should have been given to shorting the market.

Over the past few months, the valleys, mountains and cliffs have been formed, embedding participants, committing positions and conditioning others on how it should move. *North to south, a river always flows!* Sell this kind of a market with wild intentions, and its electric-shock response will eventually domesticate you.

THE ENGINEER: PART I

That held true until an Italian election in which *something* changed. "Until the election on Monday, in which we had the Bund spew up and then put in a nice rejection... that market high on Monday was really different than any since the end of January... months ago," he said. The plot twist, as it were, was now in play—and no one had realised this subtly *obvious* implication. That is, the "spew up" and reaction to it had created a beautifully tapered, healthy-looking "selling tail" generated by initiative-taking sellers.

A seller in the Bund! A seller in the Bund! This type of profile shape inferred a rare type of participant—endangered, many believed—the likes of which certainly have not been seen at least for months. "The market was much more complacent to the downside, so you can be much more accurate on the shorts," *The Engineer* continued. Because those already positioned long in the Bund had found themselves in an ever-crowded train, a self-reinforcing cycle that created a sense of safety for those positioned long, notwithstanding demanding more risk for less gain as it grinded higher, and thereby ensuring a serious underestimation of any alternatives; just ask your friendly options trader how frequently and gregariously the markets and participants under-price so-called very "rare" events.

The downside move, then, came hard but *not* fast. The skill was "mapping this and watching it trade," Haywood said; "maybe you watched the market for one week. Your greatest conviction happens five or six days later, shifting gears and putting on size," he concluded. The balance of probabilities now favours the market trading lower, our trader said, and he was much more willing to add size to a short trade *should* it develop.

The market story via the profiles no longer "forecasted" or "predicted" that the market would soon liquidate the next day, only to imply that the landscape has changed; the river was now poised to suddenly change current and direction and reveal its viciousness to those rafting on it. Our trader, then, is ready by the riverbank to paddle as soon as the river is abruptly forced to flow south-to-north instead.

As it happened, this came soon enough, and executing the short trade was then relatively no more complicated than selling humble market levels, or "blocky" profile areas. 'Simple' since few others were doing it, and many others were busy liquidating. An observation attributed to our trader explains it well: when the idea is obvious, its access is difficult; when the idea is subtle, its access is simple.

This is an instance where the strategic strength of the trade overrode any need to finesse entries or to find suitable "access." While the finesse, pirouette-like entries are critical to some trades—where the idea is fairly obvious to the marketplace—order flow tactics, tricks and tools, like a footprint chart, are needed to time entries that permit the trader to *access* the trade with identifiable risk, to know exactly where a trader is wrong, as the important adage goes.

Yet there are also times when a trader should not use a lack of access as an excuse to avoid the trade. The overwhelming market move can be strong enough to make up for a lack of access, *The Engineer* said. So, for a trade months in the making—market geological processes take so long—especially within a world of placid volatility: *just get in!*

The case for the market profile should also be made for non-overtly technical traders, especially those trading news headlines and comments. "Let's say you get a small and qualitatively insignificant dovish comment from a central banker, and the market flies off the screen," *The Engineer* said. "Other times it sounds like big news, yet the market will not budge. I believe it is due to participant positioning, and it will help macro-traders if they understand where the path of least resistance is, where the anomalies are on the profile," he continued.

THE ENGINEER: PART I

To conclude in his language, understanding the balance of probabilities going into a macro-event can make all the difference. "Your risk–reward is far better and allows you to size up further," our trader said. An example, then, of the innate transferability of the market profile for traders focusing on a different edge, because it is a framework and not a tool. The profile is a framework, to structure and frame thoughts, to contextualise trades. Because "the trader needs to remain a speculator. To have ideas yet to *monetise* them; a speculator understands uncertainty well and does not adhere to rules—there are none—or cannot expect a neat world when it is messy, to expect perfectionism," *The Engineer* said. A tool is brittle as it demands neatness; a framework is only to be updated and improved, strengthened by the messy.

900,000 WAYS TO MONETISE

Transmuting grey-matter deliberation that hangs in the air into red-blooded risk-taking, the gap between a talker and a doer, is, as we have addressed with *The Godfather*, partly a matter of street-fighting tactics. And they are virtually infinite, a product of expertise and thousands of hours of dealing with the market. A hundred people may watch *The Engineer* trade and find two hundred ways our trader subtly manifests idea to risk to reward.

Consider that to link the conceptual to the practical usefully is a by-product of thousands of small daily decisions, feedback, revision and further decisions to examine how that trader understood a concept, say, *strategy*, and brought it into the world. Individually, these small decisions are not enough for you to study or give importance to in isolation, yet we intuitively understand that collectively, they amount to much more. And that the sum of these parts does, indeed, form a greater whole.

Therefore, a trader's ability to tie the conceptual to the practical is what we will term *trade sense*. This is the ability to pivot in dynamic environments to evaluate new information lucidly. Trade sense can be split into two parts, and one such view is *top-down*. It is an orientation of how markets and their participants change through the trading day, week and month to hear their rhythm and tone. A "sense of occasion," as Haywood calls it, a feel for the significance of the times, the world around you—to know when to conserve or to go all out—to adjust. This is not intuition per se, but, as *The Razor* said, it is the ability to listen to the market. What good are other-worldly skills in reading order flow, or infinite risk-tolerance, to have the guts to trade large sizes if the trader dogmatically and statically treats each market move as if the same? How is that trader better than an algorithm, a trader whose binary and static approach ignores the tiering of opportunity? To not understand that the smallest of today's market moves will pale in comparison to the potential in tomorrow's FOMC meeting. All traders who have failed across the AXIA desks have lacked trade sense, and this has likely also been the case in other trading floors and communities.

Never underestimate how far failed traders can go in putting their head in the sand, to resist real-time decision-making. Some could not cultivate trade sense or were uncoachable in this regard, no matter how in-the-loop their trading floor or desk mates were. Top-down trade sense is to pick your fights, to possess a sensitivity of time and place—to contextualise the opportunity around you, and to spot a superior one when it arises.

The other part of trade sense, then, is bottom-up, which is to understand how the probabilities shift dynamically in the trade, and then to manage risk as a response proactively, and finally to evaluate the outcome of your actions and reorient again during a trade, while exposed to risk. The last point is where accomplishment ends and mastery begins: to understand how your own activity—adding, cutting, scaling size—has re-shifted the risk of your position while the probabilities of the market move have never stopped changing in the background. One can assess the quality of trade sense simply by evaluating how well a trader preserved their intentions within the market, to execute their trade in accordance with a framework or a guiding set of principles, while never being a slave to them.

Remember: a trader finds traction in a framework yet ensures success in bending but not breaking the frame. That is what we mean by trade sense, we are about to illustrate in the trade below.

◆ ◆ ◆

| Access supplementary resources to reference as you read the following section. | 18 September 2020 / S&P 500 December (Z) Contract (CME). 15:45–18:30 BST. axiafutures.com/ **toot-sp** |  |

For the context of this trade, consider the economic and market world at the time, which was roughly six months after the first government-mandated lockdowns and the Covid-19 outbreak. Central banks had cut interest rates hard and fast. Summer was dominated by future questions on how many more lockdowns and of what length to endure, answered in kind by dramatically different situations across the globe. Mainstream markets were now relatively quiet following the manic spring, with the S&P breaking all-time highs in August. The forward guidance of the summer FOMC meetings aged well, as they suggested for rates to stay close to zero through 2023. "Transitory," if readers remember, was yet to be the Fed's line. And the rest is history.

However, following the break of all-time highs, the S&P's march higher turned into a grind, with lower intraday volatility and smaller daily ranges. Lower volatility reinforced lower volatility, and the auction health was anything but, as there was little concerted selling pressure.

In this environment, *The Engineer* says mere cracks need to appear for the environment to convulse and suddenly change. The stale auction unravelled at the beginning of September, as two large downside days broke the back of the grindy trend, and eroded half of August's gains. One is reminded of Wall Street's most succinct obituary—to "eat like a bird and shit like an elephant."

This fast two-day selling transformed into a range in the next fortnight, yet in doing so had embedded poorly traded lows, and "so the seeds were planted days before," Haywood said as he began his dissection of *The Engineer*'s trade.

That structure, then, various shelves of prices—poorly traded lows—caught our trader's attention, as the market can powerfully break and liquidate through those poor lows, should the environment and other puzzle pieces align.

But then the market flow drove the S&P to its range highs—likely enticing fresh long positions—following a dovish FOMC meeting. Yet, it quickly collapsed those range highs. The following scene, the speculator prepares for, is now of a run on those series of poor market lows towards the bottom of the range, where those new long positions—now trapped—will likely unwind to add to the *oomph!* as the market auctioned lower.

There was nothing particularly special about the lead-up to the trade on 18 September that would suggest the kind of P&L *The Engineer* was about to make. He hoped, perhaps, to make only what was now average—a $100,000–$200,000 trade—if he could get away a hundred lots before the market slipped lower. Yet, by the end of the day, our trader would haul in $900,000 and offload some eight hundred lots into the S&P. What was the difference, then, between standard and masterstroke? *Trade sense.*

Recall the first attribute of bottom-up trade sense to understand how probabilities dynamically shift in the trade. Our trader had been watching the S&P play out the above auction process and was already interested, which would slowly evolve into conviction. Other U.S. equity markets, which are highly positively correlated to the S&P, also looked vulnerable to the downside. Often, more-volatile and less-liquid markets like the NASDAQ can be the first few rocks that roll down the hill, blow over the top and instigate a full rockslide with boulders to follow.

Moreover, these equity markets had closed meagrely above the lows of the previous night. Should the structures of other equity markets have comprised some nicely tapered buying tails, well auctioned with strong closes towards session highs, this would have tilted the balance of probabilities *against* a realistic, well-intended short trade. But as the day developed, it increasingly favoured the downside. Put another way, the market variance—the numerous paths it could play out—was being reduced.

Coincidently, it had also been the day of option expiry in the S&P, and this itself can create powerful flows, which some traders have exclusive strategies to deal with. Yet for *The Engineer*, this tilts the probabilities even more favourably, as OPEX order flow hits the market at certain times due to participants adjusting around the specifically timed expiry of these option contracts. These factors alone—a weak close, poor lows in correlated markets and OPEX day—had elevated the importance of what was to come next. An auspicious afternoon, a "sense of occasion," a trader should realise that this is not a day to take mere trades but to fry, as it were, the biggest fish.

Throughout the day, *The Engineer* identified his area of operation and where to start scaling in his clips. He identified a fifteen-handle or a sixty-tick range above a level that is often termed as a "ledge" on the AXIA floor. That is a market-level or concentrated series of prices, which the market revisited multiple times but had not traded below because the bid was strong and thick at a seemingly singular price.* Should that buyer no longer "step in" then the market can slice through abruptly. This "effort zone," as Haywood calls it, allows our trader to frame his risk by knowing where he is wrong. Framing it means quantifying it to a risk of $150,000. Should the market instead *bid* higher above this zone, then something has likely changed for the worse: a position *The Engineer* would regard as "dead-wrong." Easier, then, to take the trade as the exit is defined.

Ten lots *sold!* Fifty lots… one hundred… two hundred, two hundred and fifty—*sold!* Within ten minutes, our trader had already scaled in two hundred and fifty lots at a very tight range of prices. But to be able to do so implied new information. *There is a bid!* But there should not be none. *What next?*

"Should the market have sliced lower quickly through, then *The Engineer* would have likely had only one hundred lots on the trade," Haywood said as he continued the debrief. Yet the market had not even attempted to trade to the first raft of the poor lows. But then *The Engineer* did more. *Fifty… sold!* Even as the market re-bid five handles back to its original price, our trader kept selling, now short three hundred lots.

Why? *Trade sense.* The probabilities are now, in fact, *better* than ever. "Sizing into a trade is a matter of calibrating with the synergy of the day," *The Engineer* says. The balance of probabilities has not tilted *against* our trader but actually improved further. Even if the market is somewhat bid against him!

---

* The ledge is at 3317.75 on ESZ2020 on the Chicago Mercantile Exchange (CME).

THE ENGINEER: PART I

While watching the price ladder, *The Engineer* noted, "the bid floated up, it did not squeeze—so the trade got even better as time evolved. I did not expect to be in the trade that long—three hours—but as it got better and better, I built more conviction." This type of buying action is a "wafty bid," as our trader calls it. "He knows the difference between a temporary low in the S&P and a strong one that is a sharp and fast reversal," Haywood continued. "But this one was instead lazy—or floaty, to describe it another way. So, the market is likely to test the lows again and trade lower."

This is the inflexion point of the trade where you can separate superior trade sense from the rest. Other traders may have cut, reversed, re-added, covered, re-entered, chopped and changed. And only then to watch as the market trades abruptly in their favour while on the sidelines with a loss on the day, a repeat frustration every trader is doomed to experience.

Consider again the second principle of trade sense that builds on the first: to proactively manage risk as a result of the probabilities shifting during the trade. The way it traded this area, *The Engineer* said, is like other experiences with S&P order flow—a pattern, if you will—of constant accumulation in an area before a final release. And in real time, the market is letting our trader offload more and more size without negatively affecting his average entry price—why *not* do more? When to leverage, as Haywood says, is the whole art of trading. Too many trades lose potency as its execution is skewed by numerous entries at worse and worse prices, forcing the trader to become a weak hand as the market washes back. Yet *The Engineer* can add to his size, and not only keep his risk proportionally the same—as opposed to scattering his lots at adverse prices—thereby ensuring a bigger P&L should the market finally flush. The answer to the question of size management can sometimes be answered by what you can afford to risk, rather than isolated market analysis. If you can suddenly add more size, for the same amount of risk, why *not* do more? The sense of occasion pulls at your gut. You *must* do it.

Indeed, the "wafty" nature of this bid allowed *The Engineer* to sell up to six hundred lots while dragging his average price down just a few handles lower, as the market ranged over fifteen handles. Good execution, but then a mistake! The selling of the last two hundred lots followed an aggressive offer that forced the S&P to new intraday lows. It made our trader sell at worse prices that weakened his hand by dragging his average price lower.

But over the course of an hour, *The Engineer* had worked up to eight hundred lots, and kept his average entry price above and out of the pitched battle raging between participants in that fifteen-handle range. Now, at a skewed entry price, he had to endure the flow bobbing up and down between a negative- and positive-$250,000 position, the potential loss far exceeding his intended risk for the trade.

Thus! an opportunity to examine the third and most difficult part of what constitutes trade sense: to evaluate the outcome of your actions and reorient again during a trade, while exposed to risk. The most complex task, as it forces a trader to be multi-dimensional, as if constantly solving the market's infinite Rubik's Cube in one's mind.

What differentiates *The Engineer* here is what he and Haywood identify as the practice of "reciting the idea." Skimming through the long recording of our trader's S&P position, Haywood pauses so the duo can answer a question about how recital works. "If you can define things—risk, for example—then you can stay much more objective. You are not consumed by thoughts of 'where will I actually pay up and exit this trade?'" And *The Engineer* answered. "Recite your risk and why you like the trade; this keeps you more level-headed. Rather than thinking, *this really needs to go*, or *I need to make my money back!*"

THE ENGINEER: PART I

In the early days, our trader said this would be difficult as it is hard for a beginner to 'define' due to lack of experience, and so the difference between self-talk and objective thinking will be wildly different. "In my head, I always recite my idea while in the trade, then sit with it. Remind yourself what you are actually seeing, go through the charts and other information to reinforce why you have a probability skew in this trade," he continues. "If you tire out, your self-talk becomes unobjective, for example. You are frustrated and lost. You feel like you don't know what you are doing when the market is not doing what you think it should. *Re-frame* it. Well, what is it telling me here? Has it changed? If it is breaking this big zone, why is this not collapsing? Is this not what I expected? When it comes back into your face, and you just think: *What the hell—just go!* Or is there something you can interpret? Reframe it as positive. Does this allow me to put more size on? Reframe it in the moment, and you can circumvent this reactionary feeling, allowing you to think objectively and be proactive in your decision-making. Otherwise, you will just feed the emotional side of you."

"Imagine two traders of equal knowledge and training," Haywood added. "Yet one of them asks emotional questions and the other recites his original idea against what he experiences. That recital—those questions asked in the moment—are debriefed later, and the next time those questions are asked they are even sharper, more refined and stronger." Trading, when in the moment, is where most people fail in the industry, Haywood says—failure due to a *lack* of trade sense.

Specifically, that is the third part of trade sense—the inability to reorient once the trader has instigated their first position and their risk inevitably changes, alongside the probabilities of the trade. Concluding on this failure, Haywood equates it to a mental block, as "we become emotional when we do not see what we expect to happen." Addressing his decision to allow more risk for the trade than originally planned was a matter of intense conviction, as the market had simply not proven *The Engineer* wrong. Should he have worn a bigger losing trade due to bad execution of his last two hundred lots, then so be it. A trade where everything aligns only comes so often—that is a sense of the occasion.

"As I was spending more time in the trade it made even more sense to stay short, it confirmed my idea repeatedly. It just took longer than I thought," our trader said. "There was not good enough buying, just accumulation—and I still knew what price I would cover and pay up, but the market never went there. It was close, but never did. And so, I wanted the market to prove me wrong. You should never talk yourself out of the trade, only do so when it does not make sense anymore," he said.

But as it transpired, it took two hours for everyone else to talk themselves out of the trade. The S&P would tickle new lows and immediately bid higher, just enough to tease late-comers into selling the lows and to force them out, to constantly cover and try again. A trade, Haywood said, the whole floor was attempting and, by definition, was now part of the crowd. As *The Engineer* discerns it, the edge, then, is in the access of when the idea itself had become much too obvious, as the S&P was constantly sitting at the lows for a good part of the session. Accessing the trade now was a matter of holding on, simply to wait for the crowd to disperse. And this was not a trivial matter as our trader's six-figure P&L tumbled and flashed between green and red over this time. A trial, if you will, of conviction.

But then, the "accumulation"-style bid finally ceased! The market sliced lower through the raft of poor lows and structure, an aggressive offer *The Engineer* had initially expected yet which materialised late. The rest of it was a case of holding all of this size, which is difficult, yet that is the reason Haywood called that fifteen-handle range the "effort zone." *Get paid for it!* This is the area in which a trader takes all of the risk but never takes all of the trade once it comes good, he said.

Stamina, then, is a cornerstone of trade sense. And a precious resource it is, requiring a trader to constantly re-evaluate their situation while under the emotional yoke of trading considerable, perhaps maximum, size. That is another reason why we have written about this specific trade; it is an example of great trade sense and even greater stamina.

And it is trainable! It is a matter of repeated experiences, of stress exposure. Haywood says this exposure to greater discomfort while remaining objective is where the growth happens. Forgoing an opportunity for stress exposure and growth was far worse than a quarter-of-a-million-dollar loss, which our trader demonstrated through his actions.

This singular idea, intentional exposure to pain and discomfort, is not to be taken lightly; we end on it as it is the most important. It is where *The Engineer* begins and where he ends, the one factor he believes makes him the trader that he is, which he holds in "militant-like belief," as *The Hero* described it. And we are about to observe that in full.

PRACTITIONER'S POSTSCRIPT

Explore resources derived from this chapter to further support the practicing trader.

axiafutures.com/
toot

Refer to
The Engineer's
section.

LEARNER'S IMPRESSIONS

Below are some personal impressions that *The Engineer* made on us that we still discuss with other traders.

1. *Profiles as framework.* The market profile provides this explicit framework for all information—order flow observations, technical, fundamental—and understand it through the "purity" of the auction process. This permits him to infer participant type and, therefore, auction health and understand *why* something works. It is context and that suggests trades. If the markets are an expansive landscape with numerous, simultaneous processes, then the profile permits *The Engineer's* navigation of it.
2. *Trade sense.* It is all about bridging the gulf from the conceptual to application, bringing a plan into the markets and doing what you set out to do. "Top-down," the trader understands the sense of occasion and summons conviction and meaning at the right time. Opportunities are not equal. "Bottom-up" trade sense is the real-time calibration of risk in a live trade, understanding how probabilities shift within the trade and managing your risk in response—add, cut, exit, re-enter. And then evaluate this outcome and reorient again. The latter is where mastery begins.
3. *Conviction to enter, stamina to stay.* For the latter, our trader keenly asserts the need to "recite" the reasons for being in the trade and to remind oneself of cold information that supports it—a dose of level-headed logic when it is too easy for self-talk to hijack a trader, thereby becoming impulsive, reactionary, making the worst decisions at the wrong time. Are there adverse situations where a trader can "reframe" the problem that provides additional opportunity? This is trade sense at its finest. *The Engineer's* September

2020 S&P trade was just this—an adverse bid against his short was an opportunity to add more size, turning an ordinary trade into a near-seven-figure reward in which most others would have been hijacked by the market's constant retracements and squeezes.

What are your impressions? Write them down and converse with this book!

CHAPTER TEN

THE ENGINEER: PART II

Then, the fertile land with fruit-bearing trees and plentiful crops transformed into barren, empty plains. Volatility, our sustenance and the creator of opportunity, was sucked out of the markets after 2012. Gone, too, were the hundreds of traders who could not adapt to such a dramatic change in the environment. A leap too far; too sudden. The opportunity is now so remote that it demanded ruthless professionalism, immaculate patience and boundless persistence and destroyed the remaining notions of a typical job, forcing new styles of trading, frameworks, tools, abilities and strategies. As if now, a settled farmer could no longer tend to one place, forcing instead a brutal raiding culture over mere scraps. And right in the middle of this *The Engineer* was born as a trader.

To him, there was no other environment—this is all he ever knew—and as far as he could tell, it was all he would ever get. There is no better environment a trader could ask for on their entry into the trading world. Survive this, and you can thrive in anything.

♦ ♦ ♦

This environment also demands countless hours of sitting in the watchtower and staring at the placid, barren wasteland. Survival also means dealing with implacable boredom while being just bloody hungry. Yet, one cannot abstract only "framework"—*the action!*—and leave out the *boring routine* to which it is intrinsically tied. As routine and process are of equal importance, both of which serve as the high-water mark for what "professional" means as a trader, *The Engineer* competes with *The Godfather* in this regard.

And we mention "boring" specifically. "Why are you so particular about routine and process—about structure?" Haywood asked our trader. "Because as a person, I also change from week to week, month to month, so the challenge is to keep me ruthlessly consistent. And that is so boring! To have so much discipline and be resistant to so much," *The Engineer* answered. And Haywood agreed—keeping in mind the immovable *Razor*—and asking the determined new trader, "How bored are you willing to be to experience success?"

As such, we will convey their importance though the perspective of our trader's career history. The conversation below addresses his early career, which started in 2012 at Firm Y, the same firm at which *The Warrior*, *The Collector*, *The Razor*, *The Hero*, *The Sphinx*, *The Voyager*, *The Adventurer* and Richard Bailey all found their start at various times.

What were your initial experiences at Firm Y?
I felt there was so many unknowns. There was so much mystique about trading, a riddle in working out the environment and who were the successful players. To also understand what this trading game really is. Was it easy to just come in and make seven figures? How hard is it, really? And then you started to realise how many people were struggling and not making any money. For the majority struggling, it was easy to be negative and to get together and start to console each other.

We would always go down the pub, everyone would get around each other when they had a bad day or week, and almost subconsciously tell each other that it was fine that they lost, because *I* lost too, as if they were really fine losing and were not serious. And as I started to understand this dynamic, I could see how a lot of these people always did things the same way. Anyone who was doing well was instead an *individual*, and unique in what they did, and they had certain traits that were different than everyone else. So, I thought it would be interesting to look at the people behind the market instead.

What do you mean by "looking at the people behind the market"? And who did you look at?
I just tried to understand the players that were doing well, rather than the markets. You can learn quickly just by understanding their performance and then how to tackle the trading. To understand the traits that make a successful trader. Why are others losing? It gives you some confidence once you figure out the types of personalities who are doing well. I heard and figured that *The Collector* was making good money, *The Warrior* was coming through. *The Razor* was another one, but he was just so unique, yet they were my reference points. I also referenced off *The Veteran*, where I was lucky since he did a talk one day about his early years of printing out the market profiles and spreading them across the floor. He mentioned how his start was no different than anyone else, but you could see he had a real desire in the beginning to learn and build a really strong foundation. And he had a hell of a lot of trust in it, he was the type to throw everything behind it because he believed, but he wasn't reckless. He had deep trust in what he was doing. That had to come from somewhere, so obviously he spent a lot of time developing his core strategy, understanding and edge. That resonated with me. Luckily, I sat beside him for three years after that.

THE ENGINEER PART II

What did you learn from him?
His successful traits were not too hard to find, as a few things carry the most weight. If you find them, it cuts out a lot of faff. However, I hardly ever spoke to him. You could just learn a lot since you knew exactly what position he had on. You can understand what he was thinking and his motivations, and other times he would talk to us, and we would ask questions… but he also made and lost a lot of money and he made bad trades too, of course. I learnt a lot by understanding what he was doing wrong. I could see how doggedly he would get into positions, and his emotions and attachments to things. You learn both sides of what gave him pain as well. Then ask: if he had such success with what could be seen as, perhaps, bad traits, then what were the good traits that outweighed the bad? Well, if I just take those and add my own method, creativity and deeper understanding of those trades, then there is no telling what can be accomplished.

So, how did your own early trading and learning experience look?
I went live in April 2013; after four months, I was the *last* to do so in my intake group. I was very conservative with my risk, I never stopped out for the whole year. I was also lucky to be exposed to the price ladder and the market profile, which was due to *The Veteran* introducing it to the floor. He believed in it a lot, but others did not use it much. Before you understand how much of an art trading is, it takes a lot of observation and a lot of time. But you still need to make some money to keep you going. So, a lot of us found these little scalp plays or tricks, like patterns that would come and go on data releases. Now, I look at it more holistically, but back then I just used these little scalping strategies to keep going. There were some opportunities, but then came 2014, and it was the year where they started to price in QE and every day, the Bund was bid. The volatility was sucked out of the market. I didn't drawdown on account, but I stayed flat with few withdrawals.

Then it *really* died towards the end of 2014; you couldn't get any momentum to get the account off the ground. People were dropping out all around you. It wrecked my entire grad group and the one after me. They were saying you can't trade the Bund anymore, the game is finished. There was so much negativity, but all I was thinking of were these stories I was told of the Global Financial Crisis where everyone made so much money. So easy! I thought of how it must have been back then. I thought, maybe one day we will get inflation once more and we're going to make so much out of this Bund! Peak negativity ruled nonetheless, but I didn't like buying into it, even with all the evidence.

At this stage you had the beginnings of what define you as a trader—the market profile, a system of debriefing, routine and process coming into focus. Did you have detractors?
Certainly. The battle in 2014 was that I was not performing. I believed in a certain way of doing things and was not getting the results and being challenged by the management at the firm. I was putting in a lot of work but felt like I was getting nowhere, but I still believed that I could. I felt like I had come so far in that I *had* to become successful. I couldn't bear failing and going home with my tail between my legs. As the volatility died I learnt to scalp the market to death, just to make a little bit of money here and there. It was quiet, yet the good thing is that I stuck to a routine at my desk. *The Veteran* was always at his desk at 6.30 a.m., and I did the same. I never slacked off—ever. I felt like I was crazy for a while to come in every day when it was so quiet. It was really only ever me and him that early, and an extra hour a day, every day, pays off so well later. Then in 2015, it got dramatically worse those first few months.

How so?
It was crazy—unbelievable. Every day, the Bund would have four TPO lows and then still close on the high! It began to feel impossible.

However, the Eurostoxx then started to move, so I started to trade it, and then all of a sudden, it began to auction phenomenally well, but I still had to learn it as it was different. So instead, I actually started to haemorrhage money in trying to learn it. Then many more people left, more pressure, and then I went to negative-fifteen thousand on the account after keeping a flat account for two years. Every day, the yield curve would flatten and flatten and flatten, but then the Bund dropped ten points in two weeks! Everything broke after that, and I had no notion that markets could trade like this. But then, from spring 2015 until the end of the year, it was just *phenomenal* trading. That volatility lasted as we moved into the second Greek debt crisis. Funny that—some of the older traders left just the month before all this happened. Then, all of a sudden, in the summer of 2015, I had a positive-thirty-thousand month.

How do you view this period now, overall? It seems as if you were biding your time.
I couldn't have picked a better environment. I was very lucky. I started at Firm Y, when it was hard. The timing of 2015 was perfect. Because I was at a point where I could sustainably take volatility. If you are given a lot of volatility, you learn a lot of bad things as you cannot see what works or doesn't, a lot of bad stuff works temporarily when it is so volatile. Yet only later will you realise this. In a hard, slow environment you get to understand things at a granular level that you do not have time for when it is volatile. So, in 2015, I gained a lot of confidence. Because of all the things I had seen over time and reinforced, I did not have that anxiety or fear. As I was trading more comfortably and loosely, combined with better markets, it *just started going*. Building momentum is such a powerful force in this game, yet it starts off so slowly. It can go such a long way once you have a bit of it, and you tap into some market asymmetry and have a healthy level of confi-

dence. You start to stitch all these things together—that is the non-linear part. I had come from two years of grinding it out to see all these profile plays, and I was now executing them without hesitation or reservation. The year 2016 was when I really started to grow, from negative to up sixty thousand in a few months.

◆ ◆ ◆

Yet these foundations were to be tested not long after, as his account resurrection in 2016 came to naught following the collapse of Firm Y—his trading account shared the same fate as those of *The Warrior*, *The Razor* and many others in this book.

But the momentum, it seems, never stopped, and *The Engineer* found himself on the embryonic "cupboard" trading floor of the new AXIA–FCT partnership, with a fresh twenty-thousand-dollar account. This proved to be a true inflexion point, the start of a rapid growth to finally become the trader he is today. "The $50,000 and $500,000 milestones proved to be a ten TPO ledge to the upside," *The Engineer* laughed—a rare occurrence for this Lacedaemonian—and soon his account all-time P&L morphed into the low-seven-figure range. "Partly, it was also the market environment that kept me there," he said.

Through this entire decade his routine and process had never degenerated, only been adapted and improved to fit *The Engineer's* emergence of trading edge. And our trader proved this, by possessing a strong enough routine and process to differentiate himself from all other new traders on the floor, nearly all of whom did not survive their initial years.

And that is all a new trader can really do, as both our trader and Haywood stress. In the absence of screen time and experience, the duo state that the closest a trader can come to a holy grail is a trader's "learning architecture," an iterative feedback loop of process and routine. A lesson now from *The Engineer* in creating a robust eight-figure feedback loop.

ITERATE, ITERATE, ITERATE

Once upon a time, when the day was long and the London summer was particularly ablaze, the office's basement training room bore the brunt of it as it was packed by traders ready to hear *The Engineer* speak. Casually, he braved the heat and the focus of the crowd and wrote "Routine. Framework. Process" across the board. Then he paused, with a blank expression, as if to say, *That's it! Do you want more?*

Indeed, more was desired. So, he first began to discuss *Framework*. Pointing to the board—"This builds thought structure within me. Otherwise, it becomes messy. And it flows into my trading," he said. Framework is deconstructed into "idea, access, management," as our trader calls it, and *then* a trade review—a debrief.

This framework was true, relevant and powerful. But that was five years ago, and *The Engineer* iterated once more. What is revealing, then, is to see why and how this changed.

"You have small changes to your framework and sometimes larger structural ones. This has been my biggest in the past five years. It is always a product under review. So, I felt that my 'idea, access, management' was a bit too simplistic and suggestive," our trader said. "I got onto great runs in my career but tripped up for all the classic reasons: I stopped being dynamic and became over-confident. The signal-to-noise ratio I am good at separating, but I still collect too much noise—it's like a 'tax.' Sometimes, the noise trades work; that is how markets are, but it will always catch up. And that is the tax! Then you have deficits—energy, account, psychology," he continued.

"I figured that I compete in depth, not breadth. My signal-to-noise ratio can be higher; it must be. Many people talk about how you 'only' need fifty-one per cent of successful trades, a positive expected value and all the rest of it. It is true, but as your skills evolve you can be *really* accurate with your risk. And always improving this has been my goal. But with 'idea, access, management,' it biases you to action. It starts with 'idea,' *so go on, think of one!* You fabricate a bit too much; you start to anchor to those assumptions and thinking. That derailed me somewhat," he continued. "So, I have repositioned and redefined it to better fit *my* skills and edge, and it has improved my accuracy and clarity.

"Consider that trading is really broken up into two parts: the 'static' part—where everything is known—a profile, a trade that happened there, a comment said over there, data said that, inflation is *this*. And then you have to digest the static and make an inference from it. But you need the ability to do that in a *unique* way. The second part is dynamic observation, and that is where you really control your risk. The application of it is *never* static. I never take my static analysis and say, 'I will take *x* amount of risk.' You can never figure that out ahead of time, it never plays out the way you would think. Your risk must be dynamic; that is how sometimes a small edge can be very powerful," he continued, so evidenced by *The Engineer*'s S&P trade in 'The Engineer: Part I,' an exercise of trade sense.

"That is where static analysis and reality meet. You need to control it through an intuitive, faster mind. It is about channelling what is known in a better way. Once that triggers a trade, the dynamic takes over. You should never have your dynamic, 'faster' brain *suggest* the opportunity," he concluded.

And this is our latest instalment to one of the longest threads that run through this book. To understand that markets are a *complex* environment. A non-linear world that is prone to big sudden changes; one small change unpredictably leads to the large. And so, we witness *The Engineer's* latest approach of dealing with incompleteness of a methodical, static analysis and yet navigating in real time around the rough edges of this complex world that changes over time.

"So how do you blend those naturally? You do not want to be so static that you shut off the dynamic part of your brain, and that is the biggest part of our edge. Static analysis in a large group often gets to the same conclusion, but a tiny amount of them will make money. So, you need to separate yourself from the crowd, that is how you consistently outperform. The strength of your static analysis has to be *unique*. But your dynamic observation has to be *accurate*," he said. And that, our trader explains—unique static analysis, accurate dynamic observation—is the encapsulation of how he has iterated the concept of "idea, access, management" over the past five years.

"In the September 2020 S&P trade [in Part I], there was a probability skew in that range. Over the period that I am *in* the trade the probability of it working actually increases. It justifies more risk and different execution methods. So that dynamic part is really important. If you were static, you would have been stopped out four times over; after the S&P traded lower, you would have never put as much size on it and would have been lucky to get back to flat! You need the dynamism to cut when the asymmetry is gone, or hold on, or even add as probability has improved. These are the subtleties."

So, that is the key to "process," one of perpetual iteration. But what of "routine"? "It *must* be shaped around your edge," *The Engineer* continued. "Building the correct one for you takes time—four to five years. If you generically map and record levels, and look simply at the overnight market, you are not building anything special around your core edge." Traders often do the reverse, choosing their routine first to fit their lifestyle, or they do not work to remove their constraints before trying to find an edge. There are no such luxuries for the novice.

"What you do at the end of the day feeds into the next—you do not just rinse and repeat—you have a closed loop," *The Engineer* continued. The most important time, he says, is the period in-between arriving at the desk and putting on a trade: exactly why *The Engineer* writes by hand in the morning. In turn, *The Hero* and *The Student* started this practice. To slow oneself down—to remain composed—in contrast to the "hijacked trader," blasting away daily risk and losing half of it by breakfast.

Because to write is to "prevent me from being reactionary," *The Engineer* said. That is, to prevent "thinking with your fingers," as Robert Caro once called it in *Working* (2019: xiii). An author of political biographies, Caro compared his business of writing magisterial and complex thousand-page volumes every decade against his former profession of daily newspaper writing. Even today, he resolves to write and rewrite by hand first before continuing on a typewriter, echoing a truism of how conditioned one can be to *trade with their fingers* by the fantastic ease of doing business on the price ladder, or, as it was for Caro, the frantic pace of daily newspaper writing. Technological smoothness, convenience and speed can do much to erode depth. And *The Engineer*, as we've observed, is not here for quick business, but *big* business. That takes thought, time and a purposeful way to slow down. Thus, a pillar of his daily routine.

That, too, becomes key in supporting deep conviction, as we have seen with *The Engineer*'s stamina in his three-hour-long attrition S&P trade in 'The Engineer: Part I.' Because conviction often serves far enough only to enter a trade, but then it emerges as paper-thin, fickle and capricious. Conviction to take all the risk but never to see it through. Yet the ability to proactively stick with a trade is rooted in "clear thoughts, well understood," as *The Engineer* said. A clear idea enables calm and slowing oneself down permits clarity of thought. Conflicted thoughts, he says, drive the impulse and bias.

"A beginner requires more debriefing and reviewing and experimenting—more research put into his routine as he is expanding and building edge," *The Engineer* said. "Routine has to reflect your edge, and if you do not have edge at the beginning of your career, you need to work on that—so that *is* your routine."

"The more experienced trader should know his edge quite well and knows exactly when and where he wants to be in the markets, so his routine and practices are tailored towards his edge," *The Engineer* continued. The full-day routine already starts the evening before, the debrief to support the morning preparatory work, then into a conscious shift of *watching* markets, gathering information and watching flows; it is not a time to create "busywork" and overly refine journaling software or database logging when a trader should be focused on their actual business.

Finally, at the end of the session, the debrief becomes the focus once more, and the loop continues. This is how "routine" bleeds into "process." Routine is not overtly mechanical but should have guideposts, our trader says, so you can have enough flexibility and trust the process. That is the trader's ability to debrief, diagnose, learn and relearn, to strategically access their trading from a career-wide perspective all the way down to the minutiae of order flow patterns in reviewing the latest trade.

For all of this, *The Engineer* has a structure and a plan in place—yearly, quarterly and monthly reviews. For himself and *The Hero*, "process resets" help if stuck in an extended drawdown or if the trader feels there is too much slack in their trading. However, if the trader wishes to refresh themselves or reorganise their routine, it must be structured around his edge. And always in a "closed loop" to provide continuous feedback—a product of review and debriefing. This enables "process"—a structured approach for the trader to fall back on—an immovable pillar of their trading to enable consistency in a hyper-dynamic, complex world of markets. To "build a great foundation, so when you have a bad run, you can take the stress," as our trader said. Hence, when assessing the quality of the process, it is a question of how well the trader has succeeded in slowly becoming an "individual," separating from the majority who are likely trading uniformly and failing all the same.

Underpinning the vast topics of process, routine, debriefing and self-coaching, *The Engineer* cautioned that it is very often a skill issue and *not* performance psychology—as in sport—where traders go wrong. "Psychology is a function of your depth of understanding," he said. "If you really understand something, the trade won't suddenly have a better chance of 'working,' but you have clarity on the market. You are proactive, rather than reactive, and you are not hijacked. When you are unclear, you don't know how to weigh information from the huge stream coming at you. You can't organise or put it in its place; you are 'stuck in the static' and don't know how to be dynamic in real time. The latter is a function of clarity, of truly understanding something. If you understand, you are clear, which permits calmness. And then you're almost an unstoppable force. You will proactively deal with whatever the market throws at you. That is why it will come down to the person who knows the play the best, who knows the technical side of it the best. You have belief and confidence because you understand it," he continued. "And your psychology eventually changes and evolves as your career objectives change too. For example, in the beginning, you have 'hunger' to prove yourself and have an income. But how do you continue after you 'make it'?" he asked.

Or consider the nature of psychology intertwined with the application of discipline. "You always need discipline, but it is applied in different ways. In the beginning, you need to be disciplined with showing up—being at the desk—and consistent debriefing. Yet this shouldn't apply to avoiding trades. You *need* to make mistakes; you need to experiment. But once you've progressed and you have an edge, the risk is that everything then looks like a nail when you have a hammer. That is when you need discipline in *not* taking trades," he said. If form follows function, as a principle in design, then psychology follows precision.

Within the wider retail trading world, there is an obsession with discipline and general trading psychology—often a vain attempt to shore up a lack of deep understanding or edge. "You can have no routine and terrible 'psychology' but trade a massive edge and *still* make so much money," *The Engineer* said. "You obviously cannot make money without an edge, but people forget or ignore this." Like *The Student* says, the desire to seek certainty in an uncertain environment is very strong, and it can manifest in different, perhaps odd, ways. "But after that, as a trader *with* an edge, discipline becomes everything… to stay on track, not execute biases, to not run away, to not permit trading 'style drift'," he said. "It is easy to drift when money is no longer much of an issue." *How bored are you willing to be?*

THE ART OF THE DEBRIEF

The power of *The Engineer*'s business is none other than the debrief. All the work, and the R&D, as Haywood calls it, is done here. It is an extremely powerful process to allow for such conviction and precision to permit *The Engineer* to take some trades as if it is a done deal. And this is what let him *emerge* away from the mass, to become an individual. This factor alone was enough to convince Haywood to support our trader in 2014 when the management of Firm Y became doubtful, and where *The Engineer*'s unprofitable career was, at the time, precarious. We will now explore this very special debrief, this singular thread, in full.

First, note that the debrief is *part* of the overall process of "journaling." Often, the terms are used interchangeably; indeed, they are much intertwined—but they are different! The debrief serves to contribute, sort and connect pieces of the puzzle. We overtly began the thread of journaling with *The Student*, and with Steven Johnson's concept that good ideas are born from adding "spare parts" to the table and connecting those very parts in novel ways. The journal is that table, and the debrief, then, is a systematic way to organise what rests on top of it.

The debrief can be viewed as a tool for learning and a tool for conviction, one that stretches across the trader's skill, experience and accomplishment spectrum. This makes it indispensable, a lifelong companion that forever pays dividends the thicker and bulkier it becomes as it fills with the trader's career experiences.

Take *The Engineer*'s experience. After diligently logging and then actively debriefing eighty consecutive European Central Bank policy announcement meetings, our trader converted some longer-term patterns created by the meetings into immense opportunity, a case of a subtle idea accessed simply, a non-crowded trade. Entire seven-figure trades were spotted, learned, developed and refined, *then executed* from powerful and subtle patterns like this. That is the calling card of a 'strategic' trader, one that *creates* opportunity—as opposed to waiting for the market to provide it, like a 'tactical' trader.

"I always felt unsettled if I did not put things together," *The Engineer* said as he started to explain the origin of his debriefing practice. "But it is hard to consolidate and process the trading session during the week after long hours of focus and waking up at 5.30 a.m." Yet it was also the start of a delicate career, our trader said, and so he had to make the best use of time available—but how to make it effective for trading?

The weekend! What our trader does on the weekend is the real differentiator and our main focus. "I had no money anyway, so there was no partying or going out. More so, you are in a better state on the weekend. Compare it to the trading floor, where you are tired and cannot really *reflect*." And this closed-loop process is mostly scalable; the weekly debrief gave rise to the monthly debrief, then to the quarterly. But they all seek to give *pause*, to ask wider, near-existential questions—"What am I doing?"

And so, for the yearly review, "it gives you time to pivot, to think hard and reflect. Solutions can be very simple but if you do not take the time you can fly through the whole year. Dramatic changes can come through these simple solutions," our trader said. That is to *think upstream*.

The first proto-debriefing efforts—really, data-logging—began in 2013 as our trader lost money on a U.S. Non-Farms Payroll data release, yet he remembered the same sequence of events, a pattern, play out a few months prior. He recorded it, learnt it and turned it into a tradeable opportunity for the next occurrence. If it worked for the NFP, then why not do it for other events, perhaps even central bank meetings, and a bigger-picture or more subtle market pattern?

And so, our trader began to build momentum with this early debriefing. Because they became so potent three to four years later, Haywood noticed the weight and impact of *The Engineer*'s journaling effectiveness on his P&L, as if the 2016 inflexion point marked a critical mass in our trader's "spare parts," electrified and come to life, connected together when the market volatility jolted everything alive.

This practice has never stopped, but to call or regard journaling or debriefing as mere "data-logging" is cynically reductive, as it is so much more, and has come on in leaps and bounds since the innocent days of 2013.

The Engineer allocates three hours on Saturday to review the week and its trades. "I review and break down my own performance and my decisions, to ask: why did I do this? To keep track of my *own* patterns as well as those of the market," he said. The information that is gleaned is then fed into a closed loop to impact Sunday's session. Iteration makes it possible to discover mistakes, improve the current process and discover patterns, and the endless possibilities continue.

The Sunday session, then, is also of three hours and serves as preparatory work for the week ahead. "It is, once again, to slow it all down. It is also critical to be prepared for Monday," he continued. The minimum goal here—for all traders—is not to be caught short and to maintain awareness of all events and potential developments of the upcoming week. Yet, as ever, preparation will follow the nature of the trader's edge. *The Engineer* and *The Hero* could be found on a late Sunday morning piecing together various market profile structures and positioning in response to a late Friday move.

"All the money is made here on the weekend. All the leapfrogs I have experienced in my trading," *The Engineer* explained. As our trader says, the routine has to be built around our trader's edge. The weekend practice serves the same purpose. "This is so you understand what you are doing well, and this is where I understood and learnt the mechanics of *my* trading… I agree with Jim Paul's book [*What I Learnt Losing a Million Dollars* (1994)], that there are relatively fewer ways to lose money than the limitless ways to make it," *The Engineer* said. "So, the weekend debriefing is, in part, to figure out the bad." That is how debriefing efforts through an overall "journaling practice" serve as a learning tool.

THE ENGINEER PART II

The edge in *The Engineer's* process is the way he captures market observations and then processes them, Haywood says, of how he debriefs, assimilates and distils. "Learning one pattern is difficult since you have to record it so many ways," *The Engineer* said. And then he revealed one of many rabbit holes, which can arise early in a trader's career, like attempting to implement mechanical trading strategies. "Mechanical just got too frustrating, I couldn't stack the probabilities in my favour any better," our trader continued, "because I lacked the depth of understanding of *why* it worked. I started to believe you could look at something and use the price ladder to improve your probabilities for understanding *why* it should work, rather than a mechanical 'stop and target,' where you just keep crunching numbers to somehow improve these." The art of *The Engineer's* debriefing, then, is to spend time on the weekend to ask why it works and then answering it in kind during the week.

So, then, the tool for learning becomes a tool for conviction. The outcome of the debriefing practice is to build *trade sense*, and if readers remember, the one key trait of all successful traders in this book and the one lacking in all failed traders who have come across the AXIA floor. Those same failed traders, too, resisted any meaningful work or development to their debriefing process, practice or generally applied approach to markets. They could not develop an adequate trade sense in time; not least, they could have made use of debriefing to improve it. "Preparing like this at the end of the week is more powerful, and I have so much belief in where I am going," *The Engineer* said. A simple sheet is the final product of the Sunday preparation. "I keep it in front of me. Where are the big trades of the week? This is what I do. To remind me to only trade *this*, or significant news comments that cause repricing. Otherwise, I only care about the trades that can go seven figures, the low-frequency trades, which are my biggest plays."

THE SLOW BREW...

The notion of purposefulness to enable depth has not escaped the bounds of the trading domain. Trading is a craft like any other; depth surpasses the shallows, yet it is the multi-dimensional interaction between breadth *and* depth that forges something rare and highly valuable—and that takes time. The "slow brew" trader is preferred over those whose appearance on the trading floor is but a flash—quick achievements but then an even quicker disappearance due to little experience in withstanding the inevitable trials of the market. And *The Engineer* was no different; starting off *slow*, like *The Hero* and *The Godfather*, he too was the last to be promoted to live trading in his group, and as it turned out, also the last survivor. Slow learning is effective learning, even more so in complex, dynamic, evolving environments like financial markets.

David Epstein discusses the nature of learning in *Range: Why Generalists Triumph in a Specialised World* (2019), examining how child prodigies thrive in "kind environments"—with consistent rules and permanent patterns, such as chess, music and golf. Rapid progress does not occur in "unkind environments," where there are few rules, and those that exist are often broken, with shifting environments and open-ended goals. These unkind or "wicked" environments, as Epstein calls them, we have also encountered throughout these chapters as *complex* environments.

Specialists triumph in kind environments, while generalists succeed in unkind ones, those built on shifting sands. These complex or "wicked" environments at least ensure one thing—an element of *surprise!* That wily old market created an environment that, temporarily at least and unknown to its participants, fostered something like a "kind" environment, where a trader can stumble upon some easily accessible or a learnt trade that works—until it doesn't.

THE ENGINEER PART II

What else can I be—the trader asks—*but a genius success? Ha! Boring, futile debriefing and journaling are for the mediocre traders. Look at all the money I just made!* And then the market changes again, and the trader disappears alongside the money that never left the paper confines of their monthly statement.

The solution then, like the debrief, is to foster "conceptual reasoning skills that can connect new ideas and work across contexts," Epstein says (2019: 53), mirroring Steven Johnson's analogy of "spare parts": that a generalist survives over the specialist. And, in this case, a generalist survives change when the markets become "unkind" again. Yet, connecting the dots will take time, as "deep learning is slow," Epstein continues, "the slowest growth ... for the most complex skills" (2019: 97). And today's nuanced markets demand such skills of depth *and* breadth as a minimum. Which is why the best learners on a trading floor are ostensibly "the worst" if speed to reach a certain level of performance is the primary assessment. Because "the most effective learning looks inefficient; it looks like falling behind," Epstein says (2019: 11). And it seems like a prerequisite: the slowest growth for the biggest traders, and *The Engineer* is the classic example. Maturation to operate in a complex environment takes so long, and one needs to be wary in cutting seeming stragglers from a trading floor. Because, as Epstein says, "doing poorly now is essential for better performance later" (2019: 90), as he highlights volumes of research into this topic, and notes it is too often ignored.

The adage that good things come to those who wait, to sacrifice now and reap the rewards later, that patience is a virtue, is a truism, which is not limited to the bounds of our biology—the delay of immediate gratification, of the long game—and it has not been lost on Haywood, who often uses *The Engineer*'s career to exemplify the power of the "roundabout route."

Jutting out from stacks of paper, perhaps cracked open midway through, is *The Dao of Capital* (2013)—Mark Spitznagel's book is a reoccurring sight on the AXIA desks, and is also a favourite of Haywood's, who regards it as required reading, and often quotes it in order to explain the roundabout route—immediate loss, for a greater win in the future.

What glints in our conceptual mirror, then, is none other than Steven Johnson's term of the "slow hunch," as he calls it in *Where Good Ideas Come From* (2010: 78). Johnson explains that classic *Eureka!* moments rarely happen as innovative moments in history. Rather, disparate information, nodes and notes build and grow until they reach a critical mass—and the solution, the idea—emerges. That is why Johnson advises to "write everything down," to keep, as many scientists and thinkers did over centuries, a "commonplace book" (2010: 83–84). *A journal! A scrapbook!* precisely describing the delayed, roundabout route effectiveness of *The Engineer*'s in capturing and distilling information *to learn* from the markets via the debrief. We experienced a reference to this scrapbook, this "commonplace book," with *The Student*.

Then comes using it to capture, distil and digest information to find *conviction* in the markets, an emergence of information at the right time and the right place, and so, eight hundred S&P lots find their way to the market, and stay there.

When *The Engineer* was asked about the "it" moment when he "got" trading and turned profitable, he quickly rejected such a notion of an *Eureka!* bathtub moment. It "all really… emerged, there was no specific moment. All new traders seek this exact thing, but it doesn't exist." A "fractal" slow hunch, then, as pervasive in his individual trades as it is representative of our trader's whole career.

Recall Haywood's observation of how our trader's journaling and debriefing over the years tracked his P&L: slow, agonising, skirting over water for three years, but the "spare parts" were assembling, finally reaching a critical mass to emerge as one career-sized slow hunch.

But how many traders, Haywood and *The Engineer* wonder, give up before this emergence? "The best learning road is slow," concludes David Epstein in *Range*; "it is so deeply counter-intuitive that it fools the learners themselves, both about their own progress and their teacher's skill" (2019: 90). A blasted thing, these financial markets, these "wicked," complex environments!

◆ ◆ ◆

"Then how long does a Chaotic Era last?"

"I already told you. Other than Stable Eras, all other times belong to Chaotic Eras. Each of them takes up the time not occupied by the other…"

"…Civilisation can only develop in the mild climate of Stable Eras. Most of the time, humankind must collectively dehydrate and be stored. When a long Stable Era arrives, so they collectively revive through rehydration. They proceed to build and produce."

Thus went the conversation between the protagonist and another character in Cixin Liu's *The Three-Body Problem* (2015: 108).

This perfectly describes the nature of *The Engineer*'s growth, and of all the traders in the book! The trader is not made in *this* market cycle, but they are made in the next. The trader learns, builds, makes mistakes, iterates and survives while the sun shines, while the markets still provide recurrent opportunities for their trading. *But* only to reap the real rewards in the next cycle when conditions are favourable for his trading once more. That is how to "break through the numbers," as *The Godfather* said, describing *The Warrior*'s growth.

Recall that fifty thousand and five hundred thousand dollars were long-time barriers for *The Engineer*'s P&L. But the ascent to seven figures came in mere moments. "The environment is what kept me there," *The Engineer* said, and it is true—the creep of increasing trading size, the iterative process and the perfected routine. The foundations were cast in the previous market cycle of what made him a six-figure trader, to then use that development to advance his own civilisation, if you will, during the next era most favourable to our trader's edge.

It is then prescient to see the roundabout route in all things, even at this high-career-level view for traders. To build the sails now and catch the wind later. This is to reconcile the deep, unnoticed, productive processes—like debriefing over time with sudden jumps or leaps in the trader's "progress" or his P&L—that he builds off the previous leap. Yet, all too often, a trader notices these dramatic leaps, which are remembered as the "it" moment when it all turned around. And, as Haywood reminds us, it is a dangerous period because the trader often discards the various glacial processes that got them to where they are.

But *The Engineer* shows us that those deep glacial processes are unstoppable once there is enough time to build momentum. "It starts off slow but eventually becomes such a *powerful* force," he said. "That leads to confidence, you see things—you do not second-guess—you execute. You have the confidence to reject meagre trades, as there is no pressure. A cycle of positivity starts."

The Engineer, too, notices this effect with the development of a trader's skills and career in what we will term "cog theory." "I always think about revolutions," *The Engineer* said, referring to the spin of the wheel, or cog, and not the bloody flag-waving kind. "If you can get more revolutions in a skill, you can develop it faster. A value investor will not see a business cycle, a pattern, for six to ten years," he continued. "Whereas if you look at the smallest cog in trading—scalping—there are a lot of incremental cogs as you work your way up through the strategies." The smallest cog, he says, provides you with that fastest feedback to learn from," "and there are a lot of cogs between different timeframes. And that small cog stitches to the bigger one, then into the next. They are all linked in *some* way." So, you understand the revolution of the first cog in how it turns the other, and then the other, he says—"all of a sudden you build a holistic picture while *monetising* it."

To enable this, like *The Engineer*'s seven-figure S&P trade in 'The Engineer: Part I,' you have to forgo the immediate and the small to "build the bullets" for the big. The circuitous route—in all things.

... OF A LONG CAREER

A trader of little experience can quickly learn a singular strategy that works without requiring skill, lateral awareness of markets, context of what they are doing or *why* they are doing it, yet nets money consistently after repeated attempts.

Consider instructing a non-trader to sit in front of a price ladder. "Click here if the NFP number is above four hundred. But click *there* if it is below two." But what you have instead is an algorithm; far better, then, for a computer to do this 'legwork' than a human. This is a wide, contentious topic that we dealt with in 'The Warrior: Part II.' A shallow edge can exist in "kind" environments, where the optimal—*if x, do y*—decision and action is a mere quantifiable exercise and never changes.

And that is why, for example, computers dominate the "kind"– stable, static, calculable—environments, like Chess, and so too the speed at which they trade economic data releases. In other words, this shallow edge works through a single dimension of hyper-specialisation that forgoes any lateral, novel connections and never explores outside the realms of its environment.

It is also a realm which many struggling traders never break out of. They are anchored to a mentality of single, static strategies rather than an open-ended *framework*, to cultivate a process that supports learning that later becomes a tool of conviction, to enable dynamic trading and management, to develop *trade sense* that allows us to thrive in complex, "wicked" shifting environments.

Hence why we have spent time reading about depth, purposeful slowness and the roundabout route; we will not stop here. Because a career in the long run cannot be built on a shallow edge, but only by what we can define as a trader becoming "multi-dimensional."

Traders like *The Engineer, The Hero* and *The Student* can be regarded as the 'authors' of their own trades, where their own preparatory work bears the hallmarks of the product of deep human learning—exclusive, effective and non-replicable. Their ability to think in abstraction—pulling ideas from one domain and integrating them elsewhere—to form connections as the basis of their creativity and reason abductively are firmly the advantages of the human trader, in contrast to their supposed algorithmic "competitors." To reason *inductively* is to form rules after many sample sets, which is the basis of machine learning, and it is often brittle, as the next sample can surprise us by breaking the rules. Instead, the near-exclusive human *abductive* reasoning runs with the best guess after a few sample sets: the reasoning that survives complex, fast-changing "wicked environments." Notwithstanding the distinct human ability to understand cause and effect. That is the basis of all multi-dimensional and *deep* trades—to author your own trade—and that is the pinnacle of our enduring human profession.

And so, *take advantage of it!* It is your moat, your ability to be an act of continual creation, not replication. To avoid copying by other traders and other competitors, to avoid redundancy in a market environment that does not provide bountiful fruit but solicits only scraps even to the most wily, creative, patient, unique traders. The days of the 2012–2015 crucible will come again, and the way to survive those times will require a deep learner—a slow learner who embraces depth and breadth, the irregularities and painful contradictions in a complex, "wicked" environment where the rules become traps, and the best practices become the worst.

The success of *The Engineer*, as he splashes his ink across the page as if signing his authored, distinctive, unmistakable signature trades, is that he embraces the slow emergence of information of high diagnostic value, in keeping with the strengths of the human trader. To embrace time as the facilitator of information. "My core strength is that I can *only* think so many deep thoughts at once," he explains. "And it also takes time for the market to develop, to position itself—at absolute best, there will be three to six trades a week that I can do *really* well. That is where I believe my sweet spot is, to be the biggest I can be."

In other words, he makes the most out of a lower frequency of opportunity for a trader who "worked up" the cogs to piece profiles, structure, flow and market narrative over days to weeks. Because this type of trading seeks higher-quality data but not complete data, and only so much high quality can be amassed in a short period. *Time*, then, is the facilitator of information. And this suits the nature of the abductive thinker, of understanding cause and effect, of running with the best guess.

More conviction, then, and more reason to increase leverage and add size, with lucid expectations. Yet, it is "the quality of data that matters," explains Marko Papic (2021: 31) in the context of geopolitical forecasting, yet it is applicable to our domain too. He reflects on *diagnosticity*, of clues that are useful because they point to a low potential number of causes that solicit an effect. A fever, he says, is of low diagnostic value as it points to a large range of causes. And so, the strategic trader, pieces—layers—the puzzle together not only to reduce variance but to tie together clues of high diagnostic value. A few pieces of high-quality—diagnostic—information are superior to complete information.

The ability to thread the uncertain and certain does not come easy for humans; it is a trade-off, we will concede, of the abductive ability, which is why we emphasised to our readers the need to understand the burdens of a strategy explored with *The Razor*. The balance between certainty and uncertainty varies for different trading strategies; to be multi-dimensional carries with it the void of open-endedness. Many never navigate it successfully. But it is the power of *The Engineer* to mesh creative, diagnostic, forward-thinking trading with iron routine and systematised process. *But not exactly so!* To bend but not break his framework and process, to run with enough information but not too much of it.

And this is the hardest chasm to cross, *The Engineer* says, as our interviews began to address this very notion: a different way to view the expert against the novice, of those stuck and those progressing, those successful and those not, or, rather, those struggling and those struggling while sitting on top of a large trading account.

CHALK AND CHEESE

Why is the game so hard for people in the beginning?
There is so much to learn; there are so many different observation points. And things change in an instant. You think you want to work on something but then not see it for six months—it is *so* complex, always moving and changing. You figure out what you are doing wrong, and then you put that in another environment, and it doesn't

work again! It is just incredibly frustrating. You need to learn to filter it out, to use process and framework to filter noise and signal—that is all you try to do from the beginning. Can you just stick to the signal? A lot of people think they should trade all the time, to learn, but that is like saying they have more signal than an experienced trader, which cannot be true. You should be, instead, more reflective, protecting yourself as you go through repetitions to find the signal. But at the same time, you cannot excuse avoiding trades by declaring you have no "access"—well, how do you know? You have not exposed yourself enough in trading it to declare that! And so, there is this conflict, or tension, between doing too much or too little. Also, remember you have an environment you cannot control. And that is very hard for some people. They can be incredibly successful in many areas of life, but they cannot handle a lack of control over their environment. Perhaps they run a team and manage people, and they like to organise things. With the market, you are always at its mercy, so you have to be open to whatever it throws at you. Some people just struggle with it.

Yes, and our education system makes us constantly seek answers instead of learning how to participate in complexity.
The market, to the rational, does not make any sense. *Why is it doing that? It should go down or should go up!* They do not think of probabilities or think in terms of monetisation, which is most important as a trader, as that is what you are there for. Your only goal is to maximise your wealth over time. It is not today, tomorrow, this week or this year. It is simply—*over time*. When you grasp it, you realise everything you do has to come from sustainable ways to have a foundation. On some level, I always believed this but only put it together when I read *The Dao of Capital*; it is why it resonated with me so much—the roundabout route. It reinforces your work into route, process and systems, framework.

What does a trader with foundations look like to you?
You want to build excellent foundations, so when you put stress on it—to apply size or have a bad run—you are very solid, and you can come back to it and go again. I do not believe you should push trading size too quickly and fast. Otherwise, you will take something that is not very solid, and you might have a good run, but you will ultimately undo it all. Focus on building the core edge so you know exactly what you are doing and looking for. If it is a good or bad run, and you deviate, you know where to come back to. So, you are confident in what you are doing, to build a self-belief when you know the style of your trading, what you look at and what makes sense.

How do you develop great foundations?
To do that, you have to build a track record in the beginning, and you want to give yourself the time; you do not want to blow up in the first few months. Buy time to build understanding and conviction. You will not have enough conviction at the start as you will not know enough. At the same time, you need to trade and try to lean on staying naïve and executing on things that you think make sense to you. Otherwise, you will never build. After you get a year's worth of track record, then you have a blueprint of what you have been doing and what works and what doesn't. Separate those two and look at the really good days and bad days. The behaviours, conditions, all the small pieces. And then start to craft what your edge looks like; then go into it with more depth. *Then*, go and look at the more positive stuff; by default, you will eradicate the negative. I did this in my second year; I broke down the top- and bottom-third trades. I looked at my notes, my debriefing; I understood the trades—I broke down what made sense and did more of it. The rest is just repetitions; do not waste them by not debriefing. It is simple but hard work—after all, this is your business.

THE ENGINEER PART II

◆ ◆ ◆

Foundations, however, can only be productively bored into a specific type of rock, *The Engineer* says, and said rock is what we will term *the good beginner*. And it starts with an important difference—the good beginner must possess an obsessive interest, a deep curiosity, *not* to be confused with passion.

Curiosity, it seems, is a far sturdier and better predictor to survive the years ahead, as experience with new-trader intakes on the AXIA desks has shown us. Disregard the lure of passion, for it is brittle, capricious and instantly vaporised when reality does not meet a certain level of fantasy. Deeper curiosity is amorphous, surprise and revelation are the nature of discovery; a new trader with curiosity who uncovers this domain will only seek it out further.

Put another way, the passionate covet the destination, but the deeply curious revel in the journey, the pursuit on the infinite road of discovery, or, as one might say, the roundabout route. Every dead end, meandering and circuitous path only emboldens the curious and serves to feed the never-ending thirst for discovery, challenge and emergence. The passionate shirk the market's demand for a pound of flesh, avoid its difficulties, procrastinate and quit. The obsessively curious simply ask, *how many pounds do you wish?*

A common mark of the bad beginner, *The Engineer* says, is that "they don't put in the work to understand things better—more deeply—but also to understand things more widely—more 'meta.' To not understand the performance arena, cultivating an edge, understanding themselves and how they learn. They have no conscious realisation of how to tackle it."

Adjacent to this issue is the bad beginner who "constantly seeks answers," as Haywood says. The type, he describes, that treats trading as if it can be "solved" by the consumption or accumulation of a body of knowledge that is covetously kept by secretive, profitable traders—as if it only has to be pried open from their hands, and a continuous stream of questions will achieve that end. The issue, *The Engineer* said, is that type of trader needs to build, to make new things—echoing *The Razor*—to make mistakes and *discover* what makes sense and to continue from there. "Can you trust that all the trader has is a process and routine that is rock-solid? That he can take some money, a computer and then go anywhere and make it?" *The Engineer* asked.

One bad beginner demands their daily fish, yet the other extreme seems to reject any of it. *The Engineer* explains there are those "who come in and you cannot tell them anything. They are interested in markets and making money, but they like the story of being a trader, the *idea* of being one. They have a way of doing things they cannot unlearn. They do not even heed what successful people do and pick them apart, so they never grow. Their strategies might sometimes work, but they never break out."

The first type, our trader says, lacks a framework and work ethic; "the other is consumed by trying to prove themselves right." And so, the commonality among these three bad beginners is that their conception of trading and attitude is invariably born from a twisted or warped sense of passion.

As well-intentioned as they may be, the bad beginner who lacks any self-reflection might be blinded by their newly acquired passion, throwing all they have at it and sustained by the momentum of this newly discovered domain. The second is determined to prove their passion to all—*read determination*—by asking questions, yet in doing so supplanting any real thought or agency. The third does enough to maintain a sense of fantasy, a form of how they perceive trading to be

THE ENGINEER PART II

without going through the pain to be challenged, to learn, evolve and be at risk of losing their passion.

The good beginner has "a high *internal standard* for themselves that they must meet to succeed," *The Engineer* said. "Meeting these standards means different things, but they know they must improve," he continued. "That mentality opens things up, if you are really and truly willing you will put in the work, to read and learn widely—to spend time deep in thought: reflective. And all of this as the bare minimum to survive," our trader said. If the internal standard is not met, he continued, such a person will always change. The good beginner "deals with reality far better. They do not kid themselves—this is not working, or is not good enough. I saw this with *The Veteran* who I sat next to growing up as a trader, and with *The Warrior*."

Haywood agreed, conferring how often *The Warrior* is brutally self-critical, sometimes as if muttering quietly to himself—*are you deluded?* Seldom would he make the same mistake again. "And it is also refusing to be a loser!" *The Engineer* said. "When people push blame around because they're unable to deal with reality, they just sound like a loser. People with an internal standard would not want to associate themselves with that sort of behaviour or mentality. They want to succeed—they want to *win*. To say, *we will find another way*." And so, the difference between the good beginner and the bad, those of obsessive curiosity and those with apparent passion, is like chalk and cheese, as *The Engineer* says.

The life of a trader is a life of antagonism… we never escape it! And for most people, it is too much, our trader agrees, to be constantly battered against one's mistakes so viscerally. "I need to learn by doing but also to protect capital, I need to just watch markets, but I need to learn by being *in* the markets. I need to…," our trader said. The tension between learning and performing! To grow or to cash-flow? To be aggressive yet precise! Convicted but not reckless! And the fine line between the passionate and the curious is just one of the shadows, a shade rendered by this ever-present antagonism.

We shall conclude, then, with the most primordial of *The Engineer*'s character, his intensely high personal standard. He has it from somewhere, Haywood says, whether it came from his upbringing or he was born with it. He attests to our trader's resilience; this is where he grows the most; he wants to be challenged, tested and put on trial. *The Warrior* was once astounded to see *The Engineer* having brushed off a quarter-of-a-million-dollar loss on a Crude Oil trade as he slowly made his way onto the terrace of the London office, beer in hand, to join Friday's barbeque. "Why... is he so happy?" *The Warrior* asked. And our trader always with an unmoving, quiet, still demeanour, a lack of emotion—*composed!*

The Engineer shifted his feet. "I get a lot of pain from trading, so I would not say *un*emotional," he said. "Maybe I just bottle it up more... but I always come back to the fundamental question—do you want this, or not? It's that simple. If I do not want to feel like this, to perform in *this* way, I can stop, quit and do something else. But do I want that? *No*. Well then! I must get better. As hard as it is, it's important to ask that question. When you are on a bad run, and everything feels terrible, when you are tired and frustrated, and you have that reaction, and you do not want to feel like *that*, remember you always have a choice. Don't be bitter—be better. You have to keep the vision of where you want to get to; if indeed that's still the place you want to be, then this is the cost." And so, pay it, as we all must.

THE ENGINEER PART II

PRACTITIONER'S POSTSCRIPT

Explore resources derived from this chapter to further support the practicing trader.

axiafutures.com/
toot

Refer to
The Engineer's
section.

LEARNER'S IMPRESSIONS

Below are some personal impressions that *The Engineer* made on us that we still discuss with other traders.

1. *Weekends are sovereign.* The weekend is special as there is no action. This permits time for reflection without the burden of performance during the week. This is the "boring" part, yet it is where *The Engineer* made his money: eight figures worth. And none of it is standalone; it is all part of the bigger "routine, framework, process" umbrella, an ecosystem. As final as this sounds, it is anything but static. Iteration is the hallmark of the performer. While the debrief enables iteration, it is also fundamental for cultivating trade sense.

2. *In search of lost time.* Slowness is not prized in trading—seemingly. Yet, it has been defining for *The Engineer's* emergence, as it has been for others. From the deliberate deacceleration of the trading day through handwriting thoughts and notes and all the way to the glacial processes that can later become overwhelmingly effective in sustaining a trader's career. Slow-brew traders survive and are

preferred over those who pass like lightning. Inefficiency now is better for later; *that* is how traders emerge—a gradual slow hunch, products of intangible processes, and not an 'it' moment. The trader of the future is a generalist, not a specialist; power to them as they survive the market's sublime and ever-increasing complexity.

3. *Author a trade.* Single, static strategies do not last, because the novice does not understand the *why*—neither are they sustainable, because shallow edge is replaceable. Rather, the slow-brew learner becomes a multi-dimensional performer with an adaptive open-ended framework. This sophistication permits continual learning, as iteration, dynamic trade management and trade sense allow for navigation of the "wicked," complex environment. That is, to engage in the uniquely human abductive reasoning, to string all the disparate pieces together and author a unique trade that is unmistakably theirs. And for their uniqueness, they are rewarded.

What are your impressions? Write them down and converse with this book!

CHAPTER ELEVEN

THE HERO

No way it's going to *bounce!* But it does: 20 ticks—18—14—9—4—*Surely! No. It's coming back! This can't be right—my short...* the Eurostoxx is bid... *No... No... ten ticks offside! And the Eurostoxx is mean... S&P... Spoos... where is it? F–fifty handles up! It can't be... not on this... I don't care, short it too...* ClickClick... *Offside! Two handles—6—14! 20... This can't be.* He is gushing blood, rupturing—negative-fifty thousand—eighty—a hundred thousand... *it can't be... I'm offside on two hundred lots on that too... crap... this cannot—what is going on! Stoxx... Spoos... out, out, out! Just, OUT!*

–$263,241... *I... just got cheated.*

"It's delusional on so many levels," our trader said. And we only just sat down to talk. "Delusion in how you deal with huge losses, and in what you tell yourself." He reflected on *that* episode which took place over a year ago—April 2020. And as the weeks were lived like months, the markets awaited the U.S. unemployment data, the first release to capture the effect of the pandemic lockdown measures.

And the multi-year lows in Eurostoxx looked especially vulnerable—*surely now of all times!* "I was short five hundred Stoxx and onside a decent amount; just waiting for the data, and the figure was double than expected. Nearly seven million jobless," our trader continued. "The Stoxx blipped but then pulled back, and you know the rest. It staged one of the biggest reversals and rallies ever. It was the worst jobless claims release in history, and the S&P and other equity markets ripped higher... I got hit. I just looked at the screen... *I don't know...* I just shrugged my shoulders and left the room." And there is also the delusion of working yourself into a hole, he says, but the real digging only came a week later.

What is this crazy headline? The Crude Oil price ladder blips higher off the screen. *And my S&P! It's coming back to scratch... now offside... what? Sell more! This is some irrelevant Oil crap... there, doubled... sell some crude too... pointless headline.* But then Crude Oil futures bid and bid, it starts to skip entire prices higher... one dollar... two... three dollars a barrel higher! The numbers on the price ladder vanish—it shuts... *Crap, it's white-boxed... let me out!*

...What? I... let me out! He types frantically into his keyboard—*hellp stuk!*——the S&P also continues its bid higher. *Tickticktickticktickticktick*—the Crude Oil ladder auctions higher—three dollars higher—4—6—7... *It's released seven hundred ticks higher?! No... no... come on, man... crap... Holy sh*— Crude Oil bids another two hundred ticks... *please... no... I don't even know my losses—breathe! I can't... So far offside; so, so, so far... My S&P; I've got a hundred lots on and it's bid—offered twos and threes! Oh God... God... how will I get out? What am I doing?*

I am going to lose everything...

What have I done?

"I didn't... I was screaming. I was just screaming. Someone must have thought that I was dying in my room. I was in tears," our trader said. "That was the most frightening moment in my life, and I had many before that. During the space of that Crude Oil white-box—that volatility trading halt—my entire world was flipped upside-down. In that space, this successful, confident and fast-growing trader was reduced to nothing. My entire self-image was crushed; it was crumpled in front of me and dragged through the dirt. Everything changed. I had nothing to lean on. I was *so* scared. I was crippled—*finished."*

◆ ◆ ◆

Within a single week in 2020, our trader lost half a million dollars—a quarter of his trading account at the time—but it was not the absolute numbers that broke him, nor was it the bitterness of poor trading and decision-making. This time it was different; something happened during the white-box. Complete identity obliteration: it was punishment, the white-box lets you out when it's time, and that is unknown, up to the fates, the powers that be, and that cosmic indifference is terrifying. He learnt *fear* that day, and that is a human story.

This once-bulletproof, fearless trader had grown immensely as a paragon of process, routine and structure. We will meet him in this period as he transformed from a three- to eight-hundred-lot trader with a seven-figure trading account to go with it. But over time, his foundations had become rickety, frail; he had gone too far from the very things that made him a trader, a veiled fragility until it was painfully exposed. Perhaps our trader knew it all along, but then the market came calling. And as we know, *the market tests; and chaos they shall receive.* Because, of all the traders to be caught in that white-box, it was exactly—precisely, perfectly—him.

This event horizon destroyed our trader, but it then became his story within the throes of recreation, of resurrection to become *the* trader—*The Hero* of his personal journey. And we will meet him again after this act of rebirth, thankful for his scars and lessons learnt, of growing from loss—of the roundabout route. Our trader experienced this all before the age of twenty-five, the youngest among the pantheon of traders in our book. Growth from loss—*what awaits him in the future?* What terrifying being will emerge from this?

◆ ◆ ◆

There is a certain intensity to *The Hero*, at times his own body barely containing it—head crooked, deep stare, the engorged veins in his neck barely holding on as he processes your conversation—or his great hands frozen in tension, gesticulating, yet as if clutching some heavy object, or enveloping a computer mouse whole. And the pace of his speech! At full throttle, like a car surging down a winding mountain, full of different thoughts and ideas. As if his whole trading career, perhaps much of his life—the accelerator forever stuck to the floor; there is no brake pedal in this car.

It goes on! A true Roman. *The Hero*, too, barges in close to 7 a.m. on the trading floor—hence wooden doors, not glass. You catch his silhouette in the corner of your eye; the door flies open and reveals our trader standing between the door frames—imposing at six foot three, broad-shouldered, a former rugby player. His jawline cut and fashioned with the same intensity; his hairstyles too changed at a pace as fast as his life. But he doesn't speak this time! His wide eyes fixated, beaming at the ground—headphones on at full blast—he stomps to his trading desk. Violence in the air; *intense*.

A presence of this intensity cuts both ways, as with all expedient traits. *The Hero* socially bulldozed over others; curt, direct—*Out of my way, mortals!* But he harbours deep convictions and further down, compassion. He is no philistine. In fact, he was once a favoured candidate to study English Literature at top universities, and it was not unknown for him to ignore your communications, only one day to mysteriously reply with a Keats poem.

But he could not bear to be on a set path in academia or a corporate ladder, to have his energies contained, and his obsessive nature consumed by open-ended environments, the never-ending puzzles that continuously pushed and punished; discomfort as default. It's the only thing to keep him interested! We shy away from uncertainty, he says, yet to be stuck on a path snuffs out *the* spark, the thrill of the chase—*but chase what?*—the evolution of self, Haywood says, and that is what *The Hero* is.

For him, the market is a mirror for the understanding of self, and he hates its reflection as much as he loves it, Haywood continued. He throws himself at it yet has ascended magnificently. But when this intensity becomes untethered, fugitive, let loose, a car with no brake pedal can only stop in so many ways. As it did that week of April 2020. But it is what made him—before *a* trader on the floor and now *The Hero* in this book, and this is the story of how he came to be.

THE BIRTH OF A NAVIGATOR

Our boy trader was adrift! Firm Y's sinking took down accounts like those of *The Razor*, *The Warrior* and *The Engineer*, and threatened to do the same to our trader's nascent career. But he did not go unnoticed. "*The Hero* stood out to me," Haywood recalled; "he was very young but had maturity and had such an intense focus on the price ladder—like the greats of my generation—they all had presence in front of the screens." And so, our promising boy trader was hauled onto the tiny raft that became AXIA in 2016.

His career evolved from understanding deeply to mastering widely. In the beginning, "it was raw, there was no structure to it," *The Hero* said. "I was just fascinated by the price ladder; my trading was very micro." He described a period where he traded exclusively off the ladder, of order flow, forgoing charts altogether. "I think all traders should start at their core fascination; I always thought if I can navigate the ladder, I will always make money," *The Hero* said. "And so, the ladder remains the backbone of my trading. I can always revert back to it." Because the best futures traders, he says, are shrewd navigators of the price ladder.

So began a period of close mentoring from *The Warrior*, an expert in the "micro" of order flow, to develop this deep base while also backing his trading account. This was for good reason; *The Hero's* intensity made him stand out, but it was now directed productively; it was transformed into hours of screentime focus, often recording the same price ladders to rewatch the order flow of his trading and to then relearn and reorientate.

And to our trader, order flow is change over time and prices. "Describe it like a person. What is the mood of the market, what is its health?" he said. Framing it as the changes in "personality," if you will, is how the vast majority of the traders in this book perceive order flow. It is not the "mechanical" study of order flow that has become popularised in recent years, that is, the granular study of volume and volatility at each and every tick, alongside a judicious tracking and analysis of market depth, or birthing entire indicators, spreadsheets and number-crunching out of order flow statistics.

To *The Hero*, order flow is a discretionary process, observed with the powers of the naked eye. But as to the friction between a "mechanical" and a discretionary approach to order flow, "there is a fine balance between the two," *The Hero* says. "You don't want to personify it too much, but by the same breath you don't want to make it cold with no pulse. The broader personification of order flow is what I lean on more. Yet, when I am getting double-crossed, I do use more objective facts that I pull from tools, like a 'footprint' chart." Furthermore, *The Hero* expanded on one of his greatest strengths as a navigator. "You can gain so much feedback from having a relationship with the order flow—how does it make you feel when you interact with it? How *shouldn't* it look, how *shouldn't* it feel? You do not want to be static with the price action, the best traders can make their idea work at that moment in time through successful navigation." *Trade sense!* "Later in your career you need to understand what environments are geared for executing big size and managing it. The volatility and liquidity can change so quickly, which also carries its own risks," he continued.

"But order flow is nothing more than putting yourself in a place to make the best decision; you do not want to think about it too much. If you project too much onto it, you've already lost. Once you have done all your trade preparation, and once the trade happens, you let your intuition take over. My best period of trading is often just knowing when to be involved in the markets or not," he said.

By now, *The Hero* is whipped into a near-proselytising fervour, spirited as the subject becomes deeper, complex, *actually interesting!* Not mere small talk. But then his big gesticulating hands suspend in the air. He pauses; his gaze drifts towards the ceiling as he begins to describe lessons credited in blood. "You only understand this after constant hours of watching the price ladder. I deeply believe in screen time—it is critical. Reading the price ladder is one of the most basic, pure, raw pieces of market information you can find, direct access to the market. You can see it, watch it, learn it—you can *feel* it as well. One way or another, if you are a news trader, technical or hybrid, it is the most important skill to develop as a point-and-click trader."

Constraints are liberating, and in this case, they make for effective learning. By focusing on just a price ladder, the trader can learn key market principles—the nature of order flow, market auction and participant intention, which in turn leads to self-grown insights and discovery of market idiosyncrasies such as "adverse selection," even if these traders never formalise such principles with the same name or label. Understanding a principle allows the novice to arrive at the insight *themselves* rather than learning it by rote or verbatim. Adding anything more at this stage frustrates learning and bewilders the trader with more choices rather than *thinking upstream*, looking at the few key pieces of information from which all else flows.

Yet nearly all novice traders who grow outside the proprietary futures trading environment come to the price ladder last, if at all. Naïve learning allows ill-conceived usage of too many market tools and information; the vast number of choices will overwhelm. The lack of focus on what really matters—the auction and order flow—leaves novice traders in the same place as they started. *The Hero* learned these principles deeply over nearly two years, building whole strategies around them.

But fate would also deliver *The Engineer* to our boy trader, which initiated another close mentor–mentee relationship, and so came the market profile—but really a framework, an overlay—a wider perspective on the markets that serves to "filter the amount of opportunity you interacted with," as *The Hero* said. Because in these early, raw, price-ladder-only days it became difficult to tell the difference between a small and big trade, *The Hero* explained, and so the market profile became a "risk-framing mechanism," to know when to feed his orders in slowly or when to hit them all in; to understand when to hold back, or when the profile structure permits a full-size trade. This overlay, then, became the instigator of consistency which had still been lacking with *The Hero* for over two years.

But while the renumeration had been lacking until 2018, the deep slow-brew process had been happening for years—powerful underground currents, whose beneficial results surface much later. Yet *The Hero* was as committed as ever in the Sisyphean task of the developing trader. And in the next sixteen months, *The Hero* grew his account from flat and into the low seven figures, once trading three lots in the Bund and Eurostoxx futures then three hundred lots, later eight hundred: *intense*.

AUCTION REFORGED

"How fortunate to have sat next to *The Engineer* at the time," our trader paused. "Everything comes down to the right time and place; we clicked so well." Perhaps not so coincidental, with his keen eye for spotting like for like on the trading floor, Haywood often played matchmaker, and now he resolved to put those traders together.

And so, the duo became synonymous with the market profile, reminding us how "archaic" its usage had been at Firm Y. "They used it to collect statistics—the point of control, single prints, value areas—and scalp off those prices. It was fairly retail-minded," *The Hero* recalled. Both traders would also use the profile in their own ways—seemingly novel at the time, yet simple too. Building off *The Engineer's* treatment of the market profile as a "framework," we leave *The Hero's* words below to explain his perspective.

How do you conceptualise the market profile?
It gives me a way of visualising order flow to an extent, to understand it over a longer period of time—over days and weeks. Then how it will evolve into a potential trade idea, and how it should look. Once I started to work closely with *The Engineer*, he gave me a forward-thinking approach on how things may or not start to play out, and then I began to reduce the noise and variance in my trading.

I used to trade raw—very *in* the ladder—constantly involved in the markets. So, the profile gave me a lot of perspective and time to select, to refine my ideas. This is why it is so important to start intensively "micro" and then spin out, which gave the market profile a whole new lease of life. The crux of the market profile is about assessing the health of an auction and understanding what type of price action facilitates this type of trade. How may profile shapes or structures create these conditions? This might sound 'creative' and subjective, but for me, monetising these ideas is all about how it translates into what the price ladder will look like. The introduction of the market profile incrementally made me understand a key principle of my own trading, which is: if I give myself more time to think, I usually have a better chance to make the right decision. This is what makes the market profile so important, in creating trades that suit me.

What do you mean by a "forward-thinking approach"?
The market profile gives you so much *beneficial* hindsight information. For example, to understand how strong or weak a certain area of the market is. Or it allows you to recall how the order flow and price ladder traded in a certain area. Yet it also gives me this forward-thinking information. For example, when the market revisits the area—how should the order flow look? It refined my ability to understand when and where to focus on the price ladder. I get instant feedback from the market, and if it doesn't align with what I want, I can leave it and look at something else. The forward-thinking approach then allows me to ask—how can I build ideas into the future? For example, whenever I have to be involved in sudden volatility events or market repricing headlines, it allows me to be involved quickly and 'effortlessly' as I have done the preparation beforehand. This is not a product of hours of homework in my debriefing; rather, it is a build-up

of a constant assessment of the market profile over time. For instance, I know where the path of least resistance is in the market. Or I understand where the market is skewed towards moving productively in a direction that is beneficial. Lastly, forward-thinking takes the pressure off by making me comfortable with the state of *not knowing*, rather than always trying to 'resolve' markets or to find trades and answers to the market. It allows me to step back from the brutal and immediate flow of the price ladder by adding another layer of understanding. If I am in a trade and feel that I am not fully acclimated to this profile, this auction, I can reset and re-evaluate until the profiles align again.

Would you have more examples to illustrate this?
As much as you are consciously generating trade ideas, the profile is constantly ticking or developing in the background, and it then helps to frame my ideas really well. For example, I expect a certain area of prices to be favourable for *a type* of price action. The shape and positioning of the profile suggest the market can experience a liquidation type of move, let's say. By thinking forward, I can then ask, what would the order flow look like when the move *should* be on? But how this looks on the price ladder changes in each market environment. Now, in this environment [in summer 2021] there should be a lot of inventory on the offer, very heavy; I want persistent reloading on the ladder, net selling, and so on.

I can give you another example—let's say we are in an environment where the Bund and other bonds are extremely bullish, but then we get bearish "black zero" headlines [a reference to Germanys political approach to maintaining budget balance and general fiscal prudence, hugely bearish for German bonds if this changed in a fiscal era pre-Covid]. These are big repricing comments and may invalidate some of these technical levels, but we are going against a strong bullish trend in the profile. *The Engineer* and I would do all this work to map out markets before a position is taken, well in advance. Much of it is subconscious, and you notice the minutiae of order flow over time. So, when a news headline or comment comes out, I already know if it goes against the grain of the market, along the path of least resistance. I have that extra layer of questioning that lets me better validate the trade, but at the same time, I can even short-circuit a whole part of my thinking process and dive into a position, as I know directionally how I want to be positioned.

You can also use this forward-thinking when you are already in a trade. A lot of my thoughts will revolve around this—if this trade were to play out, how would this look in the next fifteen minutes? Or if the market should move from *A to B*, it is likely to print a large TPO structure [letters on the market profile chart] before it breaks again. How much time would it take? Then you translate these to the price ladder and other higher time frame ideas, so you can apply the forward-thinking approach in a variety of ways.

We once discussed how one-dimensional and limited it would be to label you a "technical trader." Why do you have an issue with this term? The market profile just gives me a framework to operate within, it just so happens this framework uses profiles. *The Engineer* and I just happen to like associating what profiles mean to us with raw information. We feed so much into the market profile—fundamentals, news events and so forth. It can work both ways. As much as I do not like the word, if we have prepared our "technicals" we can then ask if there are any volatility events, such as news headlines, and economic data releases, that line up with them.

Other times, we are seeking the path of least resistance. For instance, let us say in a given market, the path is clearly lower, and this week, there are a lot of risk events. Then, we can ask what is really needed in terms of risk event severity to change our "technical" thinking. In the end, the market profile gives me a structure when I can tie it all together with order flow. Therefore, market profile is just a language I choose to speak. It makes sense to me. You can get lost reading news articles and opinion pieces. That information has a time and a place, but I am interested in how I can fit that with the profile so the information is more concentrated and meaningful to me.

This is why market profiles give you much more than an approach of just "picking levels," as novice traders often do. Instead, it allows you to frame the whole world while also slowing everything down, and it helps to deal with contradictory external inputs and influences. This is why I recommend such a framework through the profile to anyone who feels lost. Remember it is all about *simple ideas executed well*. I feel this is very different from most people's ideas of what a "technical trader" looks like.

How else do the market profiles permit a different perspective on the markets?

You eventually start to see how the personality of different markets is reflected in the profiles. For example, once Bund turns into non-traditional, unhealthy-looking profiles—stodgy, near-square-looking—that is an indication that I want to divert attention away from that market. Until I start seeing traditional normal distribution profiles, I will not be interested as the participants in that market are not aligned well with how I trade. At the moment [in summer 2021], we are finally starting to see varying kinds of profiles, shapes and distributions in the Bund. It indicates that there is some kind of participant in the market, like a barometer of the health of the market. As I've said, it portrays order flow on a large scale. The never-ending pursuit of trading is trying to figure out what is working *now* and knowing when it stops working. [*Meta-game!*—*The Godfather.*] There is no one solution to it, as you are constantly retuning and recalibrating. This is part of my questioning—is my way of thinking aligned with the market?

Other markets "open up" their profiles when volatility increases, and you start to notice a more natural-looking profile and auctioning process. The Eurostoxx can make you pull your hair out, but when it gets volatile, it can be one of the best markets to trade with a market profile. This reflects that the participation has shifted or changed. Before I really grew as a trader, I did not trade anything other than the Bund and Eurostoxx. All of a sudden, my transition and ability to jump between markets became one of my biggest strengths. [*Adjacent possible!*—*The Student.*] This overlay, or framework born from the market profile, allowed me to navigate between different markets, as I saw the same things that made sense to me through the profile.

Also, it allows me to know when to be careful of certain markets or avoid some completely. For example, Copper futures were a contentious choice from a profile perspective during the U.S.–China trade war during the Trump era. Even when Bitcoin futures were first launched, I looked at its profiles and instantly knew that it did not facilitate my kind of trading—perhaps due to liquidity or other factors; I just knew the profile did not look right. This is not the same information you can see just from candlesticks, other charts or anywhere else.

Are there any new things you are discovering about the market profile?
Yes—understanding time as a mechanism, as a validator or invalidator of ideas. I still don't fully grasp this crucial concept now. I've been debriefing this a lot recently through a trade I took in the S&P. Time was so important in this particular trade, as there was not enough of it spent in facilitating this trade. It is easy to get caught up in price,

volume and other metrics. This is why *The Engineer*'s approach is so important to me: understanding how the profile should look to eventually create the trade. At what point does it flip from too little time to *enough* time spent to become favourable? At which point does it become so favourable that you *have* to trade it? Again, this is why a forward-thinking approach is critical for using a market profile. All my best trades are multi-day, multi-week structures accumulated over time. When I evaluate a bad run or trade, I often did not give myself enough time to understand, or there was more information I could have waited for to put myself in a better position to make the right decision.

Can you further explain the concept of how the market "should not" look?
I am now in a place where if I am trading at best, I am always thinking of how the market *should not* look. Starting with a negative is important as we are always seeking out ways to confirm our own biases. As much as I wish to be formless and without bias, you will always form them, even unconsciously, and it is impossible to avoid it with this kind of job.

Therefore, starting with a negative helps to build confidence and frame your thoughts. For example, during a central bank meeting day, you might have reasons to believe that this is *not* how the market should look to promote a hawkish move. Or you might realise a certain market is not set up the way you like it to be. In the days leading up to a central bank meeting, *The Engineer* and I ask, what is the market primed for, and what is it not primed for? Especially, for example, when you keep track of expectations and sentiment building up to the event when you may notice the overt hawkish conversations between research pieces and social media. Other times, this prepares you for the eventuality that the trade is not as "easy" as you may think; it could be a crowded trade idea already. It is just having the discipline to constantly question, question and question again.

Lastly, what are your reflections about increasing your trading size from a handful to hundreds of lots?

I think most people don't assign the quality of their idea versus the size risk they should put on. For whatever reason, I was always innately ready to put on size. As long as the quality of my idea matches the level of my conviction and if I check in with my conviction levels, my trading size should reflect that. If I have so much conviction, why am I not gearing up to put on more size? If the trade is so prominent or powerful, it is as simple as finding a way to add more.

When you first start trading, you *need* to accumulate ticks and find consistency. Yet, even from day one, I was thinking—which ideas are easiest for me to put size on? It is a very incremental process; I constantly assess my conviction and personal condition relative to my idea. After a while, you find yourself asking for more and more size. I couldn't ask for enough size in 2018 and 2019. The more conviction I got in the quality of my ideas, the more I asked for. This is not to say I was constantly throwing around huge size; rather, it was very sustained and incremental. I had such a belief in my process and understanding myself, and the conviction relative to my idea. If you do not understand this concept, then you should not increase size.

TACTICS AND STRATEGY: A SPECTRUM

Our trader's evolution from trading frequently and "micro" on the price ladder to further afield permits a straightforward way to introduce a mental model—a rough proposal, if you will, to understand the traders in this book but also to provide *context* for the novice trader on how their skills and future development rest against the wider backdrop.

THE HERO

Consider *The Razor* as the purest tactical trader, and *The Engineer* as the most strategic trader. Therefore, both sit at opposite ends of the spectrum. The rest of the traders featured in this book sit somewhere in between, and often, their own career development moved them along the spectrum as they adapted to new markets and novel situations, like *The Student*. The definitions of tactics and strategy are contentious, as they are often blurred in their use in sports, business, politics, warfare and so on. Yet we will stick to the domain we briefly introduced earlier—chess.

There is a general view—but know that it is fiercely debated—that beginner to intermediate chess is mainly tactical chess. These tactics exploit weaknesses of the opponents' positions through a handful of moves, usually through an attack to gain material. Complete focus on tactics at this level of the game is possible because such opportunities, or the opponent's structural weaknesses, are prevalent enough to lead to the endgame.

Yet, these tactical opportunities are increasingly harder to find against stronger players as they shore up weaknesses; they only exist due to an overt blunder or mistake. To progress at this stage, therefore, understanding *strategy* becomes a necessity—let us just define it broadly, for now, as possessing a long-term plan or looking at the bigger picture. We can—*contentiously!*—use what is regarded as "positional" chess to examine what strategy is to a trader. Positional chess involves understanding simultaneously broad and deep concepts of piece mobility, placing them in various ways that often confer advantages by shaping the board over the long run, and negating opportunities and weaknesses for the opponent to exploit. Chess legend Bobby Fischer put it best: "tactics flow from a superior position." In other words, the strategy seeks to *create* tactical opportunities where there were none before.

What about trading? For tactical traders, we can regard them as the best at exploiting small-scale or "micro" price opportunities, in which the market *provides* these opportunities for different reasons. The fast and nimble trading of news-headline-driven momentum, or capitalisation of awkward order flow created by large market orders and participation, exemplifies this. Specific *tactics* and fast execution can be enough to trade these events. This mirrors *The Hero*'s early development, a native of the price ladder and of hyper-focus on the "micro"; he too traded in this tactical manner. Master tacticians can seek to dominate in their own niche, like *The Razor* with his single-tick trades, or *The Warrior* with his news trading. One can imagine both traders could be thrown "blind" into a volatile market day with no context and still be profitable. Yet, the market must still provide these tactical opportunities, whereas strategic traders *create* their own tactical opportunities.

The Engineer and the ultimate development of *The Hero* exemplify this evolution of the strategic trader. To use their own vernacular, understanding the "technical landscape" through piecing together various bits of information from the market profile, order flow, macro-development and more allows them to prepare for an opportunity which would go unnoticed until it is too late. This became

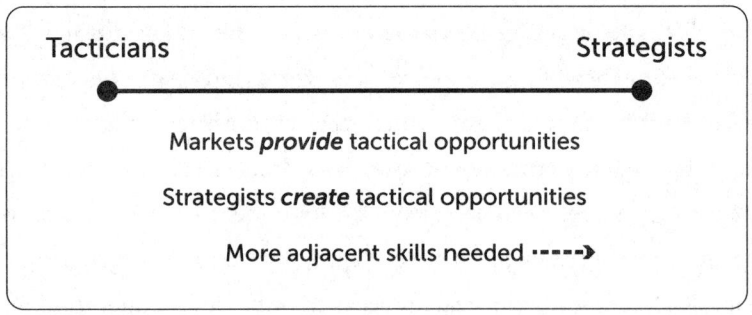

Figure 11.1 Tactician to strategist spectrum.

starkly evident when *The Engineer* and *The Hero* would experience a wildly profitable trading day when other tactical traders would have barely traded in the same "quiet" market conditions.

To visualise this rough mental model, we can draw a horizontal axis, a spectrum of the most niche tacticians against the broadest horizon-looking strategists (Figure 11.1).

And importantly, all the traders in this book started in a *tactical* manner for good reason. This provided the shortest "revolutions," as *The Engineer* explained, the shortest feedback-learning loop, and the fastest way to consistently gain ticks from the market. Or it can be said in reverse: none of these traders started as *strategic* traders with no experience or understanding of the "micro," that is, of tactics. Because in the correct environment, tactics can be sufficient; yet by definition, strategy cannot be implemented without tactics, and it is strikingly obvious to those who try in vain. Likely, new traders who first tried a strategic approach with no foundational tactical skills, the "micro," were ultimately not successful proprietary traders and are just not present on this spectrum.

Much time was devoted to discussing this observation with *The Hero*, who also echoed how traders must understand the "micro" first—the price ladder and order flow—to piece together tactical trades and understanding. From there, a trader can later evolve into a strategist once his adjacent skills develop, once he pushes the boundaries of their "adjacent possible," as we explored with *The Student*.

For example, once a new trader gains an intimate understanding of the market auction, order flow and price ladder, transferring this to the market profile should be a relatively 'quick' process; the same then can be said for other skills or usage of market tools like the 'footprint' charts. Suddenly, a trader can evolve from understanding one thing well to quickly collecting and assimilating adjacent skills to grow into a strategist. "That is where it all changes, that tactical trading is also where you develop your biggest plays, which feels somewhat like a paradox," *The Hero* said. "This is why I was able to increase trading size so quickly—because I had such an ability as a tactician in my early days. I could put on these big plays because I also know when to go from a single clip trade to maximum size or cut it instantly if need be."

In fact, part of the routine that both Haywood and *The Hero* heavily credit towards our trader's development was regularly recording his debriefing of trades over 2017–2019. In an archive which is now called "Journey of 3 to 300 Lots," a mountain of videos slowly reveals the period of his incredible growth over *those* eighteen months. But it is also insightful; 2017 was the evident "micro" focus on the price ladder—the tactical years. By 2018, a strategic trader started to emerge, crossing the spectrum, as he implemented the market profile, but really a whole framework, to reduce his engagement with the market. By 2019, his skill and trading size had noticeably matured. The videos reveal how a strategic trader is built out of his tactical skills. *The Hero* regards it as a career necessity for most traders. That is, to be on either extreme of the spectrum is nearly insurmountably difficult for most.

"Those who can stay there, like *The Warrior*, are a very special, unique breed of people. To become a phenomenal tactician out of a mediocre one is very hard," *The Hero* said. "You can be stuck as a mediocre tactician for a very long time. Yet it is not the end of the road, you just need to leverage your skills in a more strategic manner. If you can't be like *The Warrior* or *The Razor*, you will need to broaden out to a strategic perspective. It will take pressure off struggling traders, as it filters down through their interaction with the market." And so, *The Hero* unearthed a truism that is prevalent in other domains—a sound strategist can overcome average tactical ability.

To our readers who are struggling, consider the tactical–strategic spectrum as a diagnostic tool. Are you trading too strategically with no sound "micro" price ladder skills, or do you lack understanding of order flow, the market auction and its mechanics? Perhaps as *The Hero* said, you need to add a strategic layer to reduce variance and your interaction with the market. Simple awareness of these issues can be enough to stimulate traders into action, and you are now halfway there.

LOSING MY REFLECTION

The intense, near-unbelievable growth of eighteen months between 2017 and 2019 was, as they say, an overnight success years in the making. In these years *The Hero* was exemplary in routine and process. His strongest edge is not of order flow trading or strategic use of the market profile—as nuanced as they are—but, as Haywood says, it was his powers of debriefing, learning and, most of all, reflection that made our trader.

And this was as unassuming in creating success for our trader as it invited disaster once lost. Reflection is simply "conscious effort away from the trading desk, devoted to thinking about *what* you are doing," *The Hero* said. "You consciously need to check in with yourself. I do this formally through writing or even verbal expression of what is going on. How you do it is irrelevant; it just needs to be done. I didn't realise how much information I could get out of previous decisions I'd made until I spent hours reflecting on this.

"Even if some other traders on the floor may not specifically debrief," *The Hero* continued, "they certainly have a conscious moment of reflecting on what they are doing. Just having *that* moment. It is so hard to tell a new trader this. When they come in, they want to learn technicals and fundamentals, and they want to size up. It is hard to deal with something more intangible."

But *that* week of April 2020 was actually not the most dramatic low point in his journey; it was merely the end of the beginning, and then a soul-crushing grind began. Throughout the rest of 2020 our trader withered away the remaining one and a half million dollars to just over a hundred thousand. And *The Hero* addressed it bluntly: "I ran away from it because the questions were hard to answer."

And the market mirror began to reflect something terrifying. "The most important part of my growth was having a balanced lifestyle. I saw this very slowly start to slip away; I even asked—am I going to rein this in? I did not have the discipline to do so," *The Hero* continued. "I disregarded so much the all-important need for *reflection*. Out of all of the things going wrong, losing this is what hurt me the most. I discarded what *The Engineer* stood for—the process, methods, and routine." By 2019, uncharacteristically, he started to party. Soon, pastimes became addictions; partying, alcohol and other forms of escapism became part of his life.

And a car with no brakes! Just like trading, *The Hero* plunged straight into these worlds. He says its details are best left unwritten, but they can be summarised as *traumatic*. It was a period of great shame, our trader says, especially as he had always been alert to the stereotype of a trader's fast success and fast life, and felt it was one best avoided. But this self-immolation continued, and not only did his trading account suffer, but so too did his personal relationships, health and sanity. "The drinking became numbing, and no one saw that behind the scenes, I kept it hidden. I was living fast, and I didn't understand that I was merely, only *just*, maintaining a certain level of performance in my trading. I was getting all the wrong feedback from the market. I was going through a bad period, and I thought the next trade would fix it, and it often did,"

The Hero said. "I was trying to fix what is going on in the immediate term via future decisions, to provide solutions via trades rather than reflecting and checking in with the market," he continued. "And, in retrospect, that was one of my biggest skills: knowing when I was out of touch with the markets. You never want to be too far away. Like a fighter, you want to be within touching distance of making weight—you don't want to be overweight. If I feel like I am getting away with some trades and starting to trade too loosely, I will say I need to have a reset, to go back and ask *what* am I doing."

And that, he said, became the impossible question to answer as he was now wholly absorbed into his midnight double life. Perversely so, the market now transformed another key strength of *The Hero* into gasoline for his self-immolation. As always, the market will seek to flip strengths into weaknesses. "Before, even if I was on a 'bad run,' I would still increase my trading size a little bit. I understood where I was relative to the market, and if I keep asking myself the right questions, I know I will put on a good trade at some point," he explained.

"But then in 2020 I was never so far out of touch with the market, in such volatile conditions *with* such size to trade—it was the perfect storm," he continued. "Every single factor you could have thrown into this cocktail of destruction… it all came at once, instantly, after a period in which I had been doing well. My office routine, debriefing and periods of reflection had all gone out of the window. The markets moved so fast I had no time to think of what had just happened—my biggest edge had evaporated."

The Hero paused, frustrated, as he had been gesticulating and discussing his views on order flow, profiles and the nature of trading with such fervour, but now the room turned into something of a confession box, cathartic. "You will be driven to the point of having such a monumental disaster; you have no choice *but* to understand you are at a turning point in your entire existence. What are you going to do? I put myself through so much pain enduring it, but I did not ask why I was doing it. As my account ground down, my behaviour got worse and worse," *The Hero* said. "I had no accountability; I was alienating others." "Do you have an addiction issue with pain?" Haywood asked. "I have an addiction with everything," replied *The Hero*.

PROFITS (UN)FOLLOW PROCESS

An opportune moment, then, to examine the "non-linearity of performance," as Haywood calls it, an important phenomenon to understand in all high-performance pursuits. Haywood has observed the powers of this intangible process over the past two decades. It is adjacent to the nature of the slow-brew effect, as we discussed in 'The Engineer: Part II,' but the non-linearity of performance addresses the frustrating lag between a trader's P&L and their development, learning and experiences. Even at a fast learning speed *that damned P&L curve does not budge!*

We interchange learning as the process of debriefing, routine and reflection. As Figure 11.2 illustrates, the P&L curve will catch up and dramatically surpass the speed at which a trader becomes a proficient learner, the exponential inflexion point that often leads to "emergence," as *The Engineer* says, of the trader and as *The Hero* did in the span of eighteen months.

But! The lag effect also works in reverse. The catch-up of the P&L curve creates a slingshot-like effect. It can run on its own legs, sustained by the momentum of strong improvement and growth of the learning curve. The P&L curve will begin to overpay the trader after years of underpaying, which creates a dangerous situation—

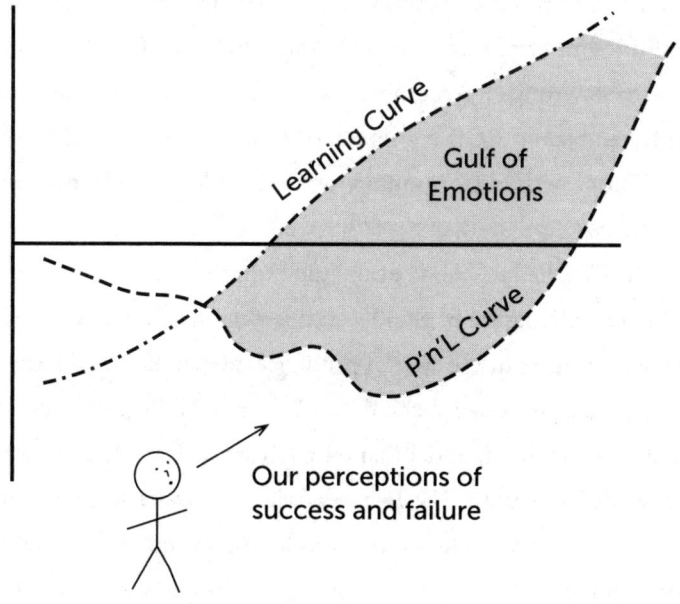

Figure 11.2 A trader experiencing the non-linearity of performance.

creating a feeling that the trader does not have to keep up their adaptation, their iterations, to refine their process, to push along their learning curve. Instead, maintaining the status quo feels sufficient for outsized returns, creating a dangerous confirmation that their current state is *enough*.

And so, the trader relaxes his processes and learning *but* still enjoys better returns than ever. The learning curve has now plateaued, perhaps regressing, and it is a matter of time before the spread will close—violently. Insidiously still, as in *The Hero*'s story, the erosion of his learning, processes and routine was incremental; the cracks were not exposed as deep fissures until the last moment. So, the lag effect now, covertly, works in reverse, nefariously confirming the trader of his invincibility.

Haywood fills in the details of this particular effect upon *The Hero*. "In 2019—his breakthrough year—and into 2020, *The Hero* could not put a foot wrong. I remember him coming into the office late at midday and some ECB commentary came out. He bought the high in the Bund with eight hundred lots and made over a hundred thousand on that."

The Hero had reached "peak bullet," in the parlance of Haywood, the bulletproof nature of a trader in this stage when he gets away with so much for little in the way of prudence, preparation and hard work. Trading maximum size at the drop of a hat, with little preparation on a relatively inconsequential market move, was certainly not *The Hero*. "I discussed this with *The Engineer*, who was more forgiving of *The Hero* after witnessing the same episode. He would say, 'It's fine; he is young and learning his way.' Rather, I had so many more sample sets that it was *not* fine. The inertia would catch up. *The Hero* was a product of his process and routine. The wheels fell off in spring 2020 because the process stopped eight months before."

An important warning sign at the time, *The Hero* said, was his reaction to losses. "I used to have big swings as my account was growing, but back then, I framed the swings as something to learn from," he said. "Yet when I had lost the two hundred and fifty thousand on Eurostoxx, over the initial jobless data, my first reaction was feeling like I got cheated. I turned off my computer and just sat on the couch, with no debriefing or reflection at all." Some traders might do away with their learning framework, routine and process altogether, Haywood observed, as they are riding on the high of past successes. Confidence turns into hubris, a discerning mind replaced by delusion; perhaps an underdog's *earned* good fortune degrades into cheap dumb luck. And, as apt for *The Hero* as it is for us—the human story—"You don't know how important it is until you lose it," our trader concluded.

THE HERO

RESURRECTION

"*The lessons!* He's going to need to work, and it will be brutal." Such were the conversations between Haywood, Kyriacou and *The Engineer* at the time. "If he is going to come out of this, he is going to be so much wiser about himself and the game," Haywood continued. "Through 2021, we witnessed his resurrection, not only of process and trading but of life itself. How *The Hero* sees his place in the world, his happiness; he has used trading nearly as his therapist in his own, indefinable way." After committing to sobriety and a return to prudence, balance, routine and structure in March 2021, *The Hero* staged a comeback that validated the one critical trait Haywood and Kyriacou look for in all traders: *grit!*

There are three parts to *The Hero* that are important to discuss: weekly reflection, a process refresh and a particular weekend process that is unique to him. They are vital to supporting his growth, and, as our trader said, their importance was magnified by their absence, which was keenly felt.

The *weekly reflection* is now, to our trader, a misnomer, as reflection should be top of mind, a constant practice and not an exercise scheduled for the weekend. This is soul-searching for the trader in terms of where they are relative to the markets, to their processes, and if things in their life have come in-between. Prudent, effective *reflection* is an act of consistency, and it is fundamental in everything from career direction to understanding risk management in the very next trade. Often, *The Hero* understood that a recent bout of losses were "good" losses to take—from market variance—and it was, therefore, wise to hold or even increase size on the next trade, an insight that came from effective reflection.

A *process refresh* is particular to our trader and is indeed scheduled for each financial quarter, or if *The Hero* believes he is no longer in fighting mode, too removed from the markets. These are scheduled, overt and systematic breakdowns—like a debrief—of his trades and decision-making. *The Hero* is particular about understanding his behaviour at various stages of account drawdown, or a period of consistent intense profitability, or too much volatility in his returns. The results and conclusion become a pamphlet, important reminders and hints—often printed and stuck to the wall to keep on hand during the next emotional test. This is a broad manifesto directed at himself and not a series of generic rules.

Our trader's *weekend debrief* focuses on a particular area to improve. For example, in 2019, he compiled a "tilt" tracker—poker parlance for a loss of control over prudent decision-making due to "negative" emotions for reasons specific to that trader. *The Hero* was trying to find his. At other times, the weekend debrief will be skewed towards improving different market profile patterns and trades.

These provide a small window into the vast support structure *The Hero* learnt from *The Engineer* and made his own. Often, our trader re-emphasised his trust in this foundation, a belief that while the markets have their own caprices, the trader must control what he can, that is, his processes and ability to reflect.

But these now fractured foundations were abruptly shone back into *The Hero*'s eyes during the fateful Crude Oil futures white-box, and he had to consciously face his foundations being ripped out from under him. "I had nothing to lean on, I was *so* scared, I was crippled—finished."

By early 2022—the time of our final interview—our trader had successfully rebuilt his account and was now pushing new frontiers. The demons of the past were now exorcised, and wounds healed. "Yet, I am so grateful for what happened in 2020, for having this experience; it was ultimately a period of enormous growth," *The Hero* said.

"Whenever I now have some drawdown, it doesn't make me run for the hills. This is a part of what it means to be a trader; I've been there, done that, and *felt it*. This time I acknowledge it instead. If you come in here and tell me that trading is sitting in an elegant office wearing a nice suit, and you just click and pull money out of the markets, well, that's bollocks. It's not how it works," he continues. "Instead, you must be completely in tune with getting the feedback from the market. That is how you make your money. It is how you manage yourself relative to the feedback you are constantly getting. Always remember how intangible it is, and how easy it is to lose sight of it."

PRACTITIONER'S POSTSCRIPT

Explore resources derived from this chapter to further support the practicing trader.

axiafutures.com/
toot

Refer to
The Hero's
section.

LEARNER'S IMPRESSIONS

Below are some personal impressions that *The Hero* made on us that we still discuss with other traders.

1. *Constraints teach.* Singular focus on the price ladder—abstaining charts—permits intuitive self-learning. Modern digital tools do away with 'analogue' friction and provide many options, as do the conveniences of charts, indicators and screens. But they prove a

poisoned chalice for beginners who must learn effectively by overcoming constraints creatively. This focused, effective learning about the market's principles enabled *The Hero* to transfer these skills adjacently, effectively and quickly onto the market profile and other tools.

2. *Tactics, then strategy.* Our trader's path, from the tactical "micro" trader to the strategic use of the profile, is seemingly the most straightforward. But all the traders in this book evolved in this way; even if in a meandering, roundabout way, they were all smart navigators of the price ladder *first*. Often many new traders attempt the reverse with no street-fighting tactics and experience to execute and implement a strategy effectively or realistically. Lastly, strategy, as a means of isolating instances of reduced variance, becomes necessary if the trader cannot overcome a tactical 'skill ceiling,' which will be the case for most traders.

3. *Once you lose it...* Routine, process and a solid framework were foundational to *The Hero* as much as they led to his destruction once lost. The non-linearity of performance helps traders as much as it hurts them—the lag in P&L can create confusing feedback from the market, nearly always reinforcing the worst ideas at the worst time. Yet this is not limited to forgoing routine, process and framework at your career heights. Other practices unique to a trader, tactics which created them, can also be what break them if done away with altogether. This can also be leaving a trading floor and its "extended mind." What made you in the first place? Keep it; improve it!

What are your impressions? Write them down and converse with this book!

CHAPTER TWELVE

THE VOYAGER

Do not ask a trader where they are, but how they got there. What, then, of this upcoming trader? He is a freshly minted seven-figure trader with secure finances, the owner of various properties and assets and a husband and father of two.

And, like *The Godfather* and *The Student*, he takes care of the latter but is focused on the former and capable of multi-six-figure trading days with highly consistent returns in the past five years. But he also enjoys an active social and sporting life, all while he has been establishing a new life in a new country. He has achieved maximum results without *becoming* a maximalist, that is, trading as a detriment to health and family or anything else that is often regarded as a necessary sacrifice.

Our trader was joyful and relaxed, seemingly… serene… as we interviewed him at the Wrocław trading floor in Poland, *The Razor's* "House of Trading." As a passionate tennis player, the sport's minutiae became tangled with trading discussions. Haywood and our trader casually recounted and reviewed large trades and large numbers as if discussing mere afterthoughts… *Eh, you know, this and that, some lots there, I sold some more there; anyway—did you practise your serve?* And our trader seemed untouched by cynicism, like *The Student*—that sort of exhaustion, a wound merely scabbed over by pithy sarcasm and dismissiveness.

But that is *shocking!* His nearly decade-long, tortuous route to becoming a trader is almost tragic considering how close he was to "success." Instead, he endured years of the market's testing of his faith and conviction; he had all the reasons to bare his scars! Instead, discussions with our trader felt like he processed a long, cathartic experience, one of understanding, of being on a long voyage and lost at sea for years, desperate to find land, often shipwrecked. And, in retrospect, a long odyssey, a homecoming to find success in the place he had first started. Therefore, his alias, *The Voyager*.

Our trader is also a story of stalled potential, who had what he needed yet suffered from the effects of insidious, hidden and long-term processes that we have covered in the book so far. That is, a question of strategic career direction and positioning, of the market forces and processes that create the illusion of what *seems* to be the right thing to do but is instead a perfect trap in these complex, opaque, forever-adaptive markets. As one might say, a wise approach is to turn one's weaknesses into strengths, but so, too, these wily old markets turn strengths into weaknesses.

That is the story of *The Voyager*'s first decade, and he is only just getting started. Yet *getting there* is of immense value, an opportunity, and a gift for us to tie together, appreciate and reflect upon the concepts we have investigated in the preceding chapters. If we have flown the conceptual aeroplane throughout the book, then this chapter will serve as a landing strip before we make our end and turn to *The Sphinx*.

THE POWER OF ENVIRONMENT

We can roughly mark out four phases in *The Voyager's* career. The first begins at Firm Y, which was composed of about fifty traders with a strong lineage of skills, knowledge and expertise that provided seeds of inspiration and were absorbed by many of the traders in this book, who grew up there. The extended mind was strong, with different strategies and approaches but all within the domain of outright futures trading, which helped reveal previously hidden dots, which the individual trader could connect in their own way. In other words, more "spare parts" were being accumulated; the trader's *adjacent possible* was widening, and the edge of their known world was being pushed further out. This goes a long way to describing a highly valuable trading floor as much as it describes the slow brew of a highly valuable trader.

But when *The Voyager* moved away from Firm Y and onto a new trading floor, he moved because of *success*, not failure! By early 2011, his consistent successes saw his P&L and account grow. But then a lure—the second phase—as *The Voyager* moved away from Firm Y and onto a new trading floor. He moved because this new firm offered an overwhelmingly better profit split for *The Voyager*, an ostensibly difficult deal to turn down, but in so doing, he also gave up a highly valuable trading floor early in his career. This new firm, which offered a better profit split, was comprised of only a handful of non-profitable traders, with the exception of two, one of whom was *The Voyager* himself.

But where would he now find random, novel connections to develop his *adjacent possible*? Where would he find new experts if he, by default, was one of the "best" at this new firm? "This is a pattern I see with a lot of young traders, when they get their first taste of money," Haywood said, "A new confidence hits them, and they suddenly think—*I know how to do this!* But they know how to do it in *this* environment. These traders are at their most vulnerable if they do not keep up the process of learning, routine and structure. They forget how they learnt in the first place—through the environment, interaction and exchange of ideas. You are a product of the environment. Kyriacou and I can recount many stories of young traders who left to trade by themselves perhaps, and no one hears from them again," he said. Then, once this fledging trading floor ran its course, *The Voyager* relocated to another in Madrid in 2012.

"In the beginning, it was going well for me in Madrid—I only had one down-month in a year, making somewhere between a few thousand euros to over ten thousand each month," our trader said. "But then the market changed in 2013, the volatility dried up and my strategy stopped working... my biggest regret was to have left Firm Y so early. If I stayed, I would have picked up ideas from other traders at the time. I really needed external help in those hard moments, and instead, I was stuck elsewhere, alone and by myself." So, these two prop firms in *The Voyager's* second phase of his career can be evaluated in the same way—the lack of an extended mind, with nothing to develop our trader's adjacent possible.

In Madrid, "there were around fifteen people, but no one was trading futures except one who traded spreads but was struggling. Others traded U.S. equities, some cash fixed income... the atmosphere was great, but they were not too serious; no one was really making any money," *The Voyager* recalled. And so began a long four-year slog of regression and a lack of income, all built off a structure of a now outdated meta-game as this new non-volatile, grindy market required new skills, inputs and expertise, but none could be found.

By joining this environment in Spain, there were no further serendipitous interactions with other outright futures traders. It is all about the little things lost, the little nodes of information that all traders benefit from on a collaborative and competent floor. *That* is what will allow traders to quickly adapt to new environments to change or learn new strategies altogether. Had *The Voyager* not been successful so soon, he might have stayed at Firm Y far longer, enough to learn from a high-value trading floor and adapt to the new market environment.

Then, in 2017, *The Voyager* visited Wrocław and *The Razor*, who had long become the dominant expert in his niche of fast-acting single-tick trades. It was completely different trading, but it all made sense—notwithstanding a deep well of expertise *The Voyager* could plug into. "It was a revelation. It was where it all started. The four days I spent visiting the floor were crucial," our trader said. "I saw the potential of the floor and the strategies the traders were using. After testing it, I was convinced! *That's it! I'm moving to Poland!* I had faith."

And the all-important faith goes further. While a trader is a product of the environment, it is not limited to the trading floor itself. Consider the many careers that were abruptly ended—as Kyriacou and Haywood remind us—by a lack of belief from a trader's family or social circle; there is little to show until there is everything to show, but until then, the credit is paid with *faith*.

One day *The Voyager* sent a long and seemingly cathartic email to his parents while in the depths of his floundering Madrid years. He had finally reached out for help, which he had been pridefully avoiding for so long. So, too, it felt like a confessional letter, but remember that traders live in a removed, temporal space—it is always *half-time!* The years are but days. Besides the confession, *The Voyager*'s dedication and commitment shone through in his words, to still find the grindy years exciting, full of potential and life, a love of the game. "When you think about it, I had already lost so much money, both my savings and trading account. Yet, my parents accepted it and supported me."

But *a* plan was key. And fundamental to a plan is a hard time limit, partly because of the effect of the *trader's resource dilemma*. It is now or never for the shackles to come off, as *The Collector* said. A bit more time to make it work, but this was the last throw. So, he moved to the Wrocław floor, met *The Razor* and prepared—viscerally, fully—ready to do whatever it took to make it work.

And quickly, it came! Learning the principles of *The Razor's* trades and adapting them, *The Voyager* soon became consistent, found traction and greatly increased his trading size in just six months, consolidating between 2017 and 2019. Then came March 2020, which became a key turning point as *The Voyager* traded the global central bank action and *The Razor's* limit-down trade, culminating in a month of over seven figures' P&L.

So began the fourth phase in our trader's career; the P&L buffer and the floor's potent extended mind allowed him to become a unique blend—connecting the dots, or spare parts, in composing and structuring a trade that suited him. It expanded his adjacent possible to adapt these trades into entirely different markets altogether. Whereas the previous trading floors *impeded* his development of the adjacent possible, the Wrocław trading floor had released it, and so too did his potential to *become*, to emerge as the trader.

Note the power of perception; in this case, the dramatic increase in trading size was all the more impressive as *The Voyager* struggled in his early career to trade more than single-digit lot sizes. This is not an uncommon affliction. The very act of seeing other traders apply more size successfully and consistently greatly removed this mental barrier—something *The Voyager* would have never witnessed on his trading floor in Madrid or the one that preceded it. A trading version of Roger Bannister breaking the four-minute mile, Haywood noted. Once Bannister did it, so did many other runners. They no longer held self-limiting beliefs.

Too much time and funds will end a trader's career, as will too little. *The Voyager* experienced this effect multiple times in his career.

First, at Firm Y, where he drew down his account to more than negative-ten thousand pounds. "I was "fired" until I put a plan together and explained how I would turn things around," *The Voyager* said. This was the same ultimatum *The Collector* faced—one last month to turn things around, or it is over. *No Plan B!* It had forced them both to cut the slack and become consistent. And so *The Voyager* quickly did become consistent, unbelievably consistent, experiencing fifty-two profitable or breakeven days with a single, small loss-making day, leading on to a longer run to fund practical living costs for a "young, commitment-free twenty-year-old" with enough funds left over to grow his early trading account.

Instead, consider the alternative effect. *The Voyager* took with him too *much* time and funds to his Madrid trading floor, seemingly the right thing to do! *Strengths into weaknesses.* But this prevented our trader from making substantial change over four years until both his trading account and savings dwindled into dust. Yet he was still dedicated, still held a strict routine and endured long hours, with an eternal confidence that it is possible, that it can be recovered, as an alternative to trading being inconceivable. But this was still not enough to solicit deep, fundamental change.

Then time and money ran out. *No Plan B!* "I had nothing else," our trader recalled. "I realise this was the most important factor: having no other choice. I was very comfortable in Madrid. I loved the city, played a lot of sports, had a good lifestyle and a large group of friends. But I was then ready to leave it all behind," he continued, echoing the same words as *The Godfather* many times in his own career. "I was willing to do whatever it took to make it work."

STRUCTURED AND UNSTRUCTURED: A FRAMEWORK

The "J-curve" account and personal growth *The Voyager* experienced from 2017 also occurred because of shouldering the correct *burdens of a strategy*, ones that fit him. "I saw the potential in *The Razor*'s strategy as it was black and white, binary. I realised I do not manage trades offside [trading against me] well enough. But you do not need to manage these strategies at all; you cannot—the trade is over when it is offside."

And, like *The Razor*, he does not trade news headlines "because that requires that you go offside, and I cannot do that as it is hard to know where you are 'wrong.' I tried for ten years to figure out how to handle a trade offside, but I never did." And so, we see the impact of applying the burdens of a strategy on the wrong shoulders. But witness the performance of the same trader who gets it right, as *The Voyager* dramatically demonstrated in 2017, with a sharp rebound in trading consistency—many days, at worst breakeven, a quick increase in trading size and five-figure-P&L months.

So, it is all the more important for new traders to stick to a thriving floor with a strong extended mind, full of lineage and career experience passed down from one profitable trader generation to the next. Perhaps *The Voyager* would have implicitly discovered the career factors we have been exploring so far much earlier by remaining at Firm Y.

And 'structured' was an intentional choice of words, as we can now combine explanations of 'dynamic versus static' position management that we first explored with *The Adventurer*. Our trader, like *The Razor*, falls firmly on the side of 'all-in, all-out' or static position management. That is, of no discretion when to 'scale in, scale out' like dynamic position management. Most static position traders are also 'structured' in composing a trade, where the details, plan and management of the trade are known beforehand. This is because they seek to reduce variance in trade outcomes by negating certain variables. The opposite, a dynamic trader, is often *unstructured* like *The Adventurer*, with no firm plan, structure and organised method for approaching a specific repertoire of trades. He simply takes *all* the trades, and as examined in his chapter, this reveals his biggest weakness of high variance. In turn, he navigates high variance through dynamic position management—to 'scale in, scale out,' to be suffering minimal losses when offside and to squeeze as much out of a trade that is on or in profit, with as many lots scaled into the trade as possible.

But consider *The Razor*, as the other extreme of a highly structured, static trader. "You need to know everything about the pattern you are trading; all about the entry, exit, money management and size. Anything less than this, and it would be a crime for you to trade." And yet, both traders are highly successful in their respective domains. Their strategies and wider approach fit them perfectly, they bear the burdens they can uniquely sustain which others cannot.

Consider that the "best practices" for a structured, static trader are often antagonistic to an unstructured, dynamic trader. Recall *The Godfather*, who manages his news headline trades with a dynamic approach, allowing him to remain in the market flow for as long as possible, because it can often reverse and trade "the right way" at a moment's notice. Therefore, taking advice and practices from dynamic, unstructured traders is productive—*if* the receiver trades in the same way. Instead, if the same practices are applied to a static, structured trader, the results can be disastrous. Context, as usual, is critical.

Yet, we also observed *The Hero* as he transformed from a tactical, unstructured trader to a strategic one and added *more* structure through an explicit framework centred around the market profile.

Others, like *The Student*, found consistency with strict structure at first, yet he is now pushing his performance boundaries by becoming less structured. And this was the most common route for most of our traders when they began their careers. *The Voyager* found success as a structured, static trader early in his career because he could shoulder the burden of strategy. His trading later suffered for years when he moved away from this. Traction can be found with one approach, yet a trader can evolve with another as their adjacent possible expands.

Importantly, it has been observed in our community that many novices attempt unstructured, dynamic trading to an overwhelming degree. Perhaps, this is due to some romanticising of being in 'the action,' to feel like a boisterous, loud trader or to justify it as "hard work." Or it is because of an inability to be patient—*just sit there and don't touch it!* Certainly, this doesn't apply to traders who are firmly in 'learning mode,' where it is advisable to participate, trade frequently and learn by doing.

But so, too, traders who cross the threshold into "performance mode" must be more lucid in the limitations of their skills or ability to consistently execute dynamic position management at the current stage of their career. Certainly, there are a few who were successful at the beginning of their careers as dynamic and unstructured, like *The Warrior* and *The Adventurer*, but they are in the minority, and we can only chalk this up to intangible reasons—perhaps talent.

Yet, many others found success at the beginning through a more static, structured approach. But the ones who did not change and adapt are not counted as their careers never survived. And for the majority of the traders in this book, they found traction by being able to define themselves and their edge by understanding which trades *not* to take. And that, of course, is the key in transforming from a learner into a performer; they become better defined by the trades they reject.

LEARNING AND PERFORMING REVISITED

"Error-pruning" is the mentality of a trader progressing deeper into performance mode. *The Voyager* emerged as a consistent trader by moving on from learning widely to performing narrowly. Confidence and performance fed each other, enabling impressive growth in trading size and P&L between 2017 and 2020.

But the Madrid trading floor days between 2012 and 2017 reveal the issue of reversing a performer *back* into a learner. Recall that the best practice for learning is antagonistic to performing.

1. The mind as a sponge *versus* the mind as a filter.
2. Trial and error. Expand "competencies" *versus* being restricted to trading only proven "competencies,"
3. Change strategy, method and style frequently. Experimental *versus* no dramatic change; iterant adaptations. Commitment.

And this is especially difficult when a trader was once performing, trading with significant size and living off the profits, especially due to (c); many traders get trapped at the learning and performing crossroads and cannot elicit effective change to be truly experimental and learn from others. They, of course, commit to what they think still works. That is a best practice as a *performer*. Such was the case for *The Godfather* and *The Student*, and they had to forgo being performers *now* to become better performers later; in the middle, they had to revert to becoming learners once more, which came with its own risks and difficulties. The roundabout route, once more.

The Voyager, indeed, was iterating on strategies, but by 2013 they had become outdated due to a redundant meta-game and a new market environment. This, ostensibly, made sense because when a trader is performing, iterations should only be made to current strategies, not wild and experimental changes. Yet *strengths into weaknesses*. Our trader had to become a learner once more. It was hard to see this at the time on a trading floor or community with no critical mass of expertise or extended mind. Remember, we can also assess the quality of a trading floor by seeing how well its traders adapt, how soon they refresh to the new meta-game and what is next.

And the trap becomes more insidious, as even at the worst of the four grindy years, *The Voyager* recalled, "I was still very committed. Never missing a day and working long hours. There wasn't a day I did not want to go into the office." This is an admirable learner's attitude but with the conflated objectives of a performer. Unfortunately, it happens to many traders, who only cease their performer objectives and practices once there is nothing to *perform* on, and their trading account is depleted. Then, there is a choice between leaving the industry or enduring a lucid, committed trip back to the drawing board. To amass new *spare parts*, to re-join the dots in new ways, to learn from peers and experts, to push the *adjacent possible*.

Progress as a performer is measured by error-pruning. That improves consistency, which in turn allows for scaling the business to grow in size as a trader. "Regarding your compulsion to trade, you first need to recognise that the top performers like *The Engineer* and *The Collector* are both very controlled, and you know how ruthless *The Razor* is," Haywood said to our trader. "To reach the top is a removal of these compulsive trades. That will give you room to achieve everything else. You need to become *sick*—physically revolted like *The Warrior* when he commits repeated mistakes, and he therefore rarely does it twice. That is how he got to the top."

That is what *The Voyager* must do as he consciously aims to move from a 'cash-flow' to a 'wealth-building' trader. This is a necessary step as his goals are now aimed at joining the "top five" across all the AXIA trading floors, possible because of the explosive performance of March 2020, subsequently allowing our trader to trade more size and join a different league. The events of March are also an example of being *primed to participate*: to be there at the right time, with the right skills and with an account of the right size. As we explored with *The Engineer*, the trader is made not in this market cycle, or environment, but the next. His trading of central bank action and taking on *The Razor*'s limit-down trade netted a seven-figure-P&L month. His increased trading size to match this became considerably larger, so *The Voyager*, too, can experience six-figure trading days instead of months; now wealth-building, in effect.

But this requires, more than ever, an extreme "performance mode" reductive-like focus! "I became increasingly reckless in the months after March 2020. I even traded a random Crude Oil spread with big size for the first time in my life," *The Voyager* said. "I took all these pointless trades, I only snapped out of it with a big loss, and now my trading has improved dramatically." Interestingly, *The Voyager*'s compulsion to trade can be diagnosed from the process of turning back into a learner and then spending a long time as one of the habits so long formed, that is, to be experimental, to always participate to learn, but as we have seen, these are *bad* practices for a deeply focused performer. This is a common issue, not limited to the trading domain: to adapt and change to seeming antagonistic demands, to be creative but rooted in down-to-earth practicality, to pursue active rest and reflection while working with great focus and long hours, to preserve durable faith while everything *else* says otherwise. Because a trader lives in a state of antagonistic demands, and success necessitates navigation of them. *A life of a trader is a life of contradiction!*

CAST-OFF

So, what comes after? There is a clear delineation in our trader's career, as he evolved from high-salary-like P&L to business-owner-like wealth-building. But this juncture is another antagonistic, trap-ridden path. *Let me enjoy some of my success!* "This can now become a simple story of success killing hunger," Haywood said. "Some traders struggle to remain focused and motivated after their best ever years. This is another time a trader is most vulnerable in their career. With top performers, conversations often revert back to, *what is the meaning of all this? Of my life?*"

Perhaps *The Voyager*'s ability to keep the grindy test of faith of his meandering years was rooted in purpose, objectives and suffering. Some traders seek the struggle and suffering of *becoming* a trader if they are (un)fortunate that their modern life lacks it. And as we have explored, the markets turn strengths into weaknesses through creeping, glacial and often invisible processes. If 'success'—as fleeting and fickle it can be—has upended struggle and suffering, what, then, for a trader who sought meaning from them? The answer is open-ended: "I do not want to regret later in life not having pushed at this stage," says *The Voyager*. And power to those who remember where they have come from and how they *became*. That will tell them where they can go next.

PRACTITIONER'S POSTSCRIPT

Explore resources derived from this chapter to further support the practicing trader.

axiafutures.com/
toot

Refer to *The Voyager's* section.

LEARNER'S IMPRESSIONS

Below are some personal impressions that *The Voyager* made on us that we still discuss with other traders.

1. *The greatest opportunity cost.* Forgoing a spirited, imaginative and professional trading environment for cost-saving or convenience's sake can be fatal. *The Voyager* is likely one of the few who survived it. But he also demonstrated the quick resuscitation of his career once this mistake was undone. Learn to properly assess the value of your environment—if there is one at all—through the framework of the extended mind, and anything else that develops your ability to learn and push the meta-game. If valued highly, it will often exceed the marginal renumeration of moving elsewhere.

2. *Fit you like a suit.* Might you be better off trading static-structured like *The Voyager* rather than dynamic–unstructured? Align your trading with the burdens you can tolerate. Can you be in the markets for long? Or not at all? Can you be sufficiently patient not to click? Or place yourself in a dynamic, fast-trading environment where impatience is a virtue? The right decisions are working with what you've got. Push the adjacent possible later. A powerful change can occur quickly like it did for our trader.

3. *Primed to participate.* As it happened, our trader was in good stead to take advantage of March 2020—the "once in a lifetime" trade that, in fact, happens rather frequently. All traders of any type can participate for outsized gains. This perhaps resurrects a junior graduate trader. A growing trader joins an altogether different league in the *next* cycle while they build the bullets in this one. But sometimes it can all happen in one month, or one day. Had

The Voyager remained isolated, without confidence and without growing his trading size and account, March 2020 would have yielded little in practice. You can't eat percentage gains, only hard cash.

What are your impressions? Write them down and converse with this book!

CHAPTER THIRTEEN

THE SPHINX

You find him on the terrace, with orange-brown leaves strewn across the floor; some glide down from the branches that hang above.

The trading floor roars! Traders are dug in; markets fickle, headlines fire all morning, but these damned Bunds don't care! *The Warrior* tormented as he smashes immovable bids all day; *The Godfather* scoffing, frustrated at these devious bonds. They are belligerent, in a red haze of fatigue, yelling, stomping.

Do something; give in!

Good God, man; Wake UP!

His tall figure cranes over the glass railing, his bony arm stuffed in the pocket of his baggy jeans; long fingers envelop a cigarette pack... he lights one and takes a draw, then gazes at the red brick wall across the terrace... long lazy draws continue... puffs of smoke... "Hmmm."

"En ginete reee!" *The Warrior* pleads; hounded, wounded.

The markets are devouring everyone—

The Hero twists and squirms.

The Collector shouts and curses in disbelief.

The desks are smashed, pounded with fists; the floor rumbles, an orchestra of anger, despair and uproar escape through the window.

A long draw... a puff... He clears his throat and continues his gaze, still hunched over the railings... a long draw... behind him, the window blares out the cries, the agony of the traders—a puff... wisps of smoke float above his head... a long draw—"*En ginete reee!*" You hear the banging this far out, only now louder... a puff... a long draw... He stubs out the cigarette and flicks it to the ashbin. His scrawny, lanky, hunched figure turns and glides across the terrace, up the stairs and back to his trading desk. Not slow nor fast, but on his own time.

◆ ◆ ◆

Our trader flashes a wide grin. He is now playful—like a cat toying with a mouse—as we ask questions. Instead, even the most basic queries elicit a reply of two or more questions of his own: *return to sender!* This verbal sparring is like a three-dimensional chessboard as we try to pin our trader down with a tangible answer. But he is also easy-going, jovial, self-deprecating, the type to play aloof in an attempt to mask a fierce intelligence and deep perceptiveness—*Eh... but do I really want to try?* Cue a shoulder shrug. So, direct questions are deflected with sarcasm, as if waiting for the *real* question, the correct question as an answer to the riddle, to unlock the mysteries—to be worthy. *Hence!* An apt alias, The Sphinx—let us pass!

Oh, pass, will you? Very well! To then reveal no mystery at all. *The Sphinx*, amused by what your questions implied, your desire to give form to something that does not exist, to handcuff thin air—there is no secret; there is only what you think you want. And in that very gulf, in that vacuum, rests an entire career.

This feigned aloofness carries its own special charm, a unique blend of detachment, *but* it is earned. First, through the gauntlet of time—*The Sphinx* has been through and seen it all, failing and failing again. It took roughly four years before our trader withdrew slivers from his account, with gyrating fortunes—once fired as a trader and hired as an analyst. He came back, but only to find some consistency by his sixth year and to lose it twofold all again. It was only after a grindy *decade* that our trader found consistency, and stability. His P&L curve now looks like it is making up for lost time, but he certainly does not act as if set on a frantic pace. And soon after, he has become a seven-figure trader, from strength to strength in the previous few years. "No one seems to take losses as well as *The Sphinx* does; it's like water off a duck's back," Haywood said. *Certainly so!* He spent ten years doing just that.

This meandering, longest-of-the-slow-brew journey produced a different perspective on the markets, a refreshingly distinctive take. From the outsider's perspective, *The Sphinx* is the prototypical news trader: highly informed, quick to act, he draws upon a bottomless reserve of well-timed one-liners. A trader of "market themes and flow," he conceded.

Yet, categorising him in this way is futile, for this trader eschews form and structure in his craft, a pervasive theme one will notice throughout his wider philosophy. At his essence, *The Sphinx* simply aims to remove layers of abstraction between himself and the "market truth," that of order flow. For him, executing as close as possible with the market is akin to flawless trading. The market price action and order flow dictate what is the truth; in other words, the market is always right, even when it is wrong. And nothing else matters, not your rules, your charts, your opinions, your deep research; who cares about your prep?

The beauty of *The Sphinx* is a direct reminder to challenge, be sceptical and be uncomfortable with anything too neat, as the world is not.

Like *The Engineer* and most other traders, *The Sphinx* emerged. That is, all the pieces coalesced over a decade. There was no *Eureka!* moment. Between 2007 and 2017, our trader was thrice resurrected. From deep account drawdowns to some profitability, only to then lose it all during Firm Y's infamous meltdown, which sealed the fate of the first sustainable period of his career. His trading experiences ran the gamut, holding positions that ranged from nineteen months on a single short Copper futures trade to split-second fast-and-fierce clicking on news and data releases. From currency pair positions held for months over central bank posturing, all the way to playing hot potato with currency and bond futures during live central bank meetings. And to then repeat all the above again—in a shorter three-year window—except the next account destruction was self-inflicted, built on a house of cards, he says. But the subsequent resurrection was self-sustained, and our trader finally... became. *Ah! Meat on the bone. Sphinx! After all of this, tell us:*

"What advice or help would you have given yourself, over a decade ago, if you could, to have improved your learning curve, to hurry yourself up?"

"I couldn't have said anything," our trader replied. "I would still have to go through everything again."

Did he just describe it? Everything! Our job, craft, sport? The Journey? Case closed, on the very first interview for this book!

"Maybe because of the way I pursued trading, it took such a long time because I needed to acquire huge amounts of knowledge and information in order to finally start progressing," he said. "If there *is* a shortcut, where you can start making money with a lot less information, you would develop into a different type of trader. But it just so happens that to be *formless* within the market and its structure, I needed to learn and understand so much before I was able to be... *me*."

As if *The Sphinx*'s observation and his worldview we are about to explore had enough of a faint magnetic pull to make our desert compass ding, only we were not always looking at it—because you cannot. This book, too, like *The Sphinx*, had to emerge. Because to know the path ahead is to follow what has been trodden; to know the solution ahead prejudices creativity. How can a book about traders *becoming...* emerging... be developed in any other way? *What could we have said to ourselves to have completed this book sooner?* We defer to our trader's answer. *Nothing.* We would have to go through it all again, meanderings and all.

But his faint pull had always been there, and now we receive his magnetic north loud and clear. A common language to understand the depths of his simple mastery. Formlessness, emergence; the market truth, complexity. It is all here, and has been from the start, ever since the book's very first chapter.

COMPLEXITY REDUX

To understand how a bicycle works, you can simply separate the parts. It might be *complicated*, perhaps, but the bicycle can be reduced to its component parts. Put it back together, and you have exactly what you started with—a bicycle. A cause and effect, and specifically a *linear* cause and effect: '1 + 1 = 2' will hold true. Even disassembled, we can predict how the bicycle will work once we put it back together. We will *not* be surprised.

But financial markets are not two wheels, pedals, a frame and a metal chain. The markets are closer to a rainforest, closer to a weather system, or an ant colony (see Mitchell, 2011: 1–13). Break their components down, study them, put them back together and the output or result is very often something different entirely. We cannot predict the output reliably, and we *will* be surprised. That is because the interaction of 'the parts' is *non-linear*; '1 + 1 = 3' will happen, and happens often. The interaction of the environment's parts produces outsized reactions which are not tethered to the linear progression of *time*. At least, as we perceive time in a linear, no-going-back kind of way.

And so, we have identified some features of an entirely different environment! That is, a *complex* but not *complicated* environment. *Ah!* Another old friend we visited in *The Warrior*'s chapters. John H. Holland (2014: 5–6) identifies "several kinds of telltale behaviour" of a complex system:

- *self-organisation* into patterns, as occurs with flocks of birds or schools of fish
- *chaotic behaviour*, where small changes in initial conditions ('the flapping of a butterfly's wings in Argentina') produce later changes ('a hurricane in the Caribbean')
- *'fat-tailed' behaviour*, where rare events, e.g., mass extinctions and market crashes, occur much more often than would be predicted by a normal (bell-curve) distribution
- *adaptive interaction*, where interacting agents, e.g., markets or the Prisoner's Dilemma, would modify their strategies in diverse ways as experience accumulates

And lastly, he writes: "*emergent behaviour* is an essential requirement for calling a system 'complex.'"

So is the *complex* behaviour of rainforests, social human interaction, traffic and much more described. Then what description could be more fitting of the behaviour of "the markets?" *If it quacks like a duck...*

This chaotic behaviour, this sensitivity to initial conditions, is why you cannot easily reassemble the component parts of a complex system and reliably anticipate the same outcome each time. Chaos is a feature of a complex environment. Should you repackage it with minuscule differences, entirely tolerable for a bicycle or a racing car, then the iterative outcome of a complex environment becomes dramatically different, chaotically so.

That is because, in a complex environment, the "sum of the parts is greater than the whole"; *something extra* comes off the top—it emerges. New behaviours or properties emerge. Consider Holland's example of water molecules. A single water molecule is not wet, yet aggregate enough water molecules together, and, at a certain point, 'wetness' as a property emerges (Holland, 2014: 4). Or consider how consciousness does not exist within each individual neuron in the brain but emerges from an aggregate of neurons working together.

In other words, "the aggregate exhibits properties *not* attained by summation," writes Holland (2014: 4). Again, this is the non-linear outcome of putting together the component parts in a complex system. And non-linearity, coupled with sensitivity to starting conditions (chaotic behaviour), alongside unpredictable *emergent* behaviour and patterns, is mostly responsible for 'fat-tailed' nature in complex environments. These are the—*surprise!*—sample-set-of-one, blind-siding instances we investigated with *The Warrior*. And that is surprising to an inductivist, sample-set-thinking, rule-creating market operator. Because the foundations of that approach are linearity and reductionism.

Lastly, any practitioner of the markets and casual observer will agree with the market's ability to 'self-organise' without central control or leadership. This is as much a feature and tenet of free-market economics as it is of an individual tradeable market. This is the case, at least, in highly liquid, transparent market exchanges with high levels of participation. Other esoteric or low-liquidity environments where market-making is done over the counter, held at a lunch or dinner, are a different game. Lastly, but importantly, we can casually observe how the market spontaneously produces patterns like that of a school of fish or a flock of birds.

But what about emergence? It is rooted in "adaptive interaction" between agents: the traders themselves! The market's participants change, so you change—and thereby the participants change again. This feature of the market is where we will be investing our time, going deep to prepare newfound appreciation for *The Sphinx* and his message. Because "emergence" as a feature is not only necessary to define an environment as complex but, as we said in the Introduction, it is the tagline for why you must approach the markets differently from how you might initially think to approach them. Because it is highly likely you think, act and have been educated reductively (Mitchell, 2011: ix–x)—"Break it down for me." To even know *how* to approach the markets differently to most other endeavours; we need to know *why*. And that is rooted in the market's ability to self-organise and express adaptive behaviour. This will be vital to understand *The Sphinx*, and to lucidly bring forth the nature of the very domain we might have only been feeling around the edges of.

As we venture forth, remember the following that we discussed in the Introduction: the simpler the rules that govern a system, the more complex the behaviour that emerges. And that has deep implications for how you approach your trading.

Strap in.

THE SPHINX

IT IS *I*, THE MARKET!

As traders, we intuit and observe how the markets price in expectations. Participants, in turn, buy and sell in anticipation of other participants basing their actions within the very same market that is *about* to price in expectations. In doing so, the cumulative participant activity self-fulfils, and the markets start to price it in!

And round and round in this *expectations–pricing–buying–selling–expectations* loop we go. A loop... what a very "strange loop"... *Ah!* Not a coincidental choice of words. We borrow it from Douglas Hofstadter's works: "Despite one's sense of departing ever further from one's origin, one winds up, to one's shock, exactly where one had started out" (2007: 102).

Hofstadter writes in *Gödel, Escher, Bach: An Eternal Golden Braid* (1999: 10) that a strange loop exists in a "tangled hierarchy," where there is no highest or lowest level, or obvious starting and end point within a system. Spend enough time moving through these levels and suddenly you find yourself right back where you started. For example, you get into the elevator on the fifth floor to reach the eleventh; you feel the slight heaviness in your legs as the elevator accelerates upwards, but all of a sudden, the doors open on the ground floor!

There is no obvious beginning or end, no 'levels' or hierarchical structure that can be discerned, such as the linear, chronological 'hierarchy' of the beginning, middle and end of a story. The beginning is 'the start' and impacts the middle, which neatly affects the end. Trapped in this elevator, you experience a surprise return to where you had started. That violates the clear hierarchy that we initially expected.

So, it is the very same for our *expectations–pricing–buying–selling–expectations* loop; at any moment in time when you sit at your trading desk, you could be anywhere within said loop. There is never a clear starting and end point. One day the market is worried, the next it is not; it reacts wildly to a small matter and, at other times, it remains unchanged by what we deem critically important. Is that the end of a move, the end of a theme? Or merely the end of the beginning? Then it goes again, and we find ourselves right back where we started! *Come back for the end of the world on Tuesday...*

Even if a piece of information or theme is "priced," it is only ever temporary—even if temporary might be a decade. Look out far enough, as the poets say, and everything is temporary. "What else is a loop but a way of representing an endless process in a finite way?" Hofstadter writes (1999: 15).

An endless process in a finite way! *Did he just describe it? Everything! Our job, craft, sport? The Journey?* At the very least, the market environment represents an endless process of digesting perpetual, novel information in a human, linear and finite way. Seemingly, in that very core of the market lies a conflict, a contradiction, a paradoxical twist. A "conflict between the finite and infinite," as he puts it (1999: 15).

Because a strange loop is also "self-referential," which has an interesting habit of producing these paradoxical situations, for example, when a statement of language or a system talks to or can look at *itself*: "This statement is false." That is the liar's paradox. Similarly with the children's "opposite day" game, in which everything said is taken as meaning the opposite of what is said: "Today is opposite day." Both of these statements refer to themselves; they are examples of "self-referential statements of language" and are very much a strange loop bottled up in a single sentence. Another example used in *Gödel, Escher, Bach*:

> The following statement is false.
> The preceding statement is true.
>
> (1999: 21)

THE SPHINX

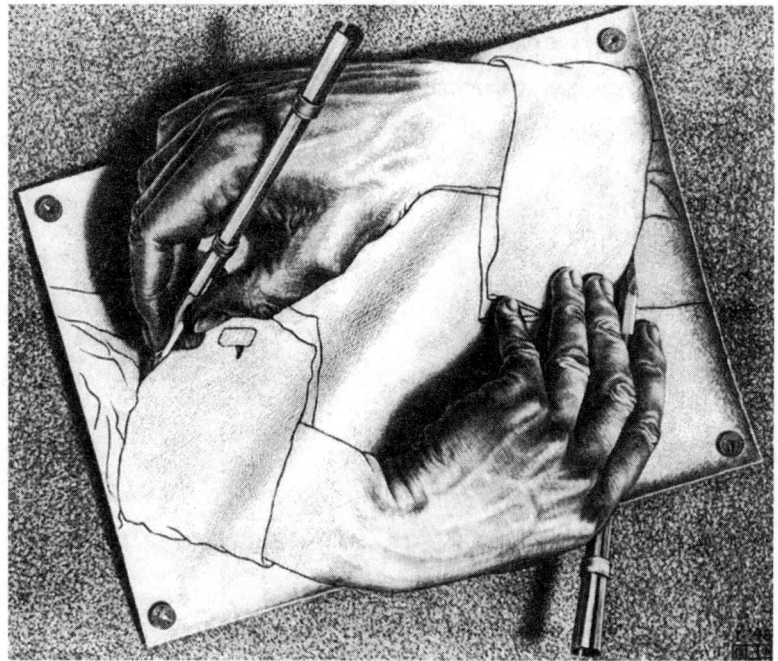

Figure 13.1 M.C. Escher, *Drawing Hands*.

Lo! As Hofstadter writes, each statement "backfires" on the other; the first sentence sends you to the next making you anticipate it is "false," only for the next sentence to *loop* you back to the start, making you anticipate the next sentence must be "true." Or is it the other way around? Up and down the steps we climb or descend? And this strange, two-step loop is said to be self-*referential*. It talks about itself or points at itself.

Hofstadter uses another of Escher's lithographs, *Drawing Hands*, to visualise the same thing (Figure 13.1).

This is a simple but powerful image to summarise the strange *pricing-buying-selling-expectation* loop within "the markets." It goes further. Not only is the market referencing itself—implying self-awareness—but we know this self-referencing behaviour as traders. That is because each market participant is examining the other adaptive interactions between each participant.

Consider Figure 13.2.

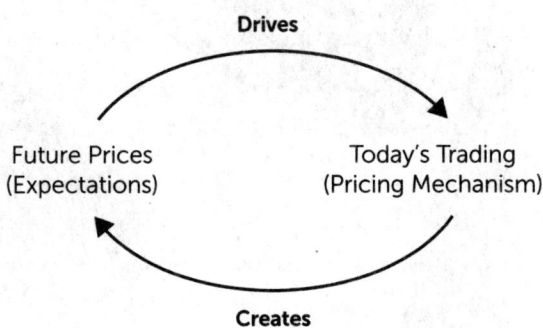

Figure 13.2
Recasting the *pricing-buying-selling expectations* loop.

At a simplified but powerful level, we have this self-referencing behaviour in the markets: our own *Drawing Hands*. "Today's trading" is the product of the only two *immutable* rules of our trading domain, the ability to long or short; to buy or sell. As we said in the Introduction—*Why Think Meta?*— these two rules cannot be simpler nor changed. Change these and you are playing a different game.

But the participant's *decision* to go long or short is driven by "future prices." We buy now because we expect higher prices at some point in the future, whatever the reason. We are short now because we expect this heavy market structure to liquidate in the near future. We go long ten-year treasuries *now* in 2024 because we expect an interest-rate-cutting cycle to begin in the future. We cover our short—by buying it back—to exit our trade defensively because we expect higher prices in the future. Our exit is someone else's trade; our trade is someone else's exit.

So, we are driven by the future. But suddenly, we create that very future because of action *today* driven by our *expectations*. Thereby, we can also equate "future prices" with "expectations," the market expectations. No matter what these expectations are, be they a qualitative summation of the geopolitical risks in the world or a more quantitative expression of where interest rates will be in 2026, the market provides only a single conclusion—price. An answer that always changes.

Likewise, we can equate "today's trading" with the "pricing mechanism" of the market. That is, the actual, *physical* act of buying and selling that moves the market to "price in" information and reach said expectations. The markets can price in information because of the trading it facilitates and only because of the trading that is occurring at this exact moment in time—in the present, seemingly.

If the concept of self-referential markets seems strangely familiar, then you are not wrong! The foundation of George Soros's *The Alchemy of Finance* (1994) and his career is based on the notion of "reflexivity." And Soros takes the descriptions of reflexivity and its implications in interesting directions. More so, Soros credits "Hofstadter's recursive loop" in his book's epilogue. The concepts strongly overlap, nested in one another, joined at the hip. One can say we returned, to our surprise, to exactly where we started!

Soros encapsulates reflexivity as such: "buy and sell decisions are based on expectations about future prices, and future prices, in turn, are contingent on present buy and sell decisions" (1994: 29). Figure 13.2 then takes the core of Soros's reflexivity observation, a market-flavoured tint on Hofstadter's self-referential strange loop. But we will fork it, split it from Soros's reflexivity, for our own purposes and domain.

The latter must be made clear: Soros discussed reflexivity in the context of himself as a speculator and its implications within the market, and economic theory has an inherently long-term view. That is, where real-world fundamentals and economic situations have a material, overriding impact on the markets, a pull like gravity. Because, unlike our domain, there is *time* for the real world to change materially.

But Soros also conceded that meaningful reflexivity does not occur *all* the time. In that context, it might seem that Figure 13.2 is oversimplified as it ignores long-term fundamentals, actual physical and real-world constraints or developments. More so, it ignores that the vast majority of market participation is not here to chase absolute profit; there is hedging activity, commercial interest and more. Other participation is often unwilling—forced liquidations, margin calls and the like.

Yet we are not long-term speculators! And we will go as far as to say that the core of Hofstadter's strange loop, or Soros's reflexivity, is in fact *purer* and occurs much more frequently in our own special niche: our own small pocket of time of intraday futures trading. In our world of "themes and flow," as *The Sphinx* calls it, the vast majority of participants *are* speculators. They are, indeed, playing the same game of absolute profit: zero-sum edition.

That is to say, in our fast-clicking, reactive world of flow, fundamentals do not materially 'exist.' In our hyper-fast minute-by-minute trading, three months in the 'real world' can be three hours in our small kernel of time. Such is the power of volatility. Very little of the real world, however, can change in that period.

But the notion—or perhaps the mirage—of fundamentals *does* exist. We trade *as if* they exist because everyone else acts *as if* they exist, because they know that we, in turn, trade like they do! As Soros says, consider that ideas do not exist in the 'real world' until they are manifested by people taking actions based on those very ideas. That idea or vision of the future has become a reality today.

THE SPHINX

Recall 'risk-off' situations like that in 'A Mexican Stand-Off' within *The Warrior*'s chapter, where a U.S. drone strike killed Iranian General Soleimani in January 2020. There was no immediate, real-world fundamental shift. Yet the markets traded *as if* there was. These flows—the equities offered, bonds, the Yen and Gold bid, Crude Oil bid—were trading because we expected the market to expect these things. It flashed a potential version of the world in the future. And that was a trading opportunity. It is a *feature*, not a bug.

But it all happened so quickly overnight and the following day that it is realistic to assume vast participants, with millions or billions of assets, did nothing. We know this because these moves retraced quickly. The real world did not materially change, there was no full-on war, oil supply disruption and further escalation, and the deep structural positions in the markets did not change meaningfully. The longer-term trends and market structure remained intact. So, the fundamentals do not matter *to us*, but we act like they do. So then, future price expectations drove "today's trading." These flows came into the market because of anticipation of future moves in the market, even if they did not materialise. The pricing mechanism—"today's trading"—did its job very proactively. Or it can be said that we did our job proactively because doing it more proactively than *you* is the objective of the absolute-profit game.

Therefore, we do not trade expectations or "fundamentals," but we do trade expectations of expectations: a derivative. This makes the strange loop, the tangled hierarchy, ever 'purer' and simpler. Hence, it is an even more aggressive, complex environment!

A property of this environment is self-reinforcing—it propels 'sentiment,' which drives the trading flows and creates market themes. Self-organising, reinforcing patterns occur, like momentum moves, trends and bandwagon opinions on social media, that loop back to dominate major newswires and discourse. Or it could be the other way around. Prices, in turn, react to that sentiment and make it 'real.' These themes begin to dominate the markets and the news cycle to such an extent that it feels as if the market cannot focus on anything else. It is the only story in town.

Even when the markets are converging on real structural changes over time, be it large-scale, long-term positioning by large participants or bottom-up changes to economies or various asset class fundamentals, for us as intraday futures traders, in a fast world of "themes and flow," all of this has already 'happened.' These longer-term changes are like echoes that reverberate further away from us but no longer impact us materially. We traded it when the first shouts were heard. Now only the future impacts us materially because the future is only composed of expectations of expectations, and that is what we trade. As *The Warrior* said, "What is next?"

So, the "market themes" of the future are this two-step referential loop in Figure 13.2. Often, there is no real-world material shift—yet—but markets price these in so fast that they no longer surprise the market when they do. "Buy the rumour, sell the fact." That is the game we play, and that is why much of trading is counterintuitive—a hallmark of a complex environment.

The European Central Bank also knows this well; it will release unofficial "ECB sources" with the real goods—potential future policy change—and the market takes it and trades it as if this change already happened... *the future is here!* But nothing has materially changed so far. And when the ECB officially announces that very same policy shift later, the reaction can be muted, or a reversal takes place… buy the rumour; sell the fact. That is, expectations of expectations. Surely there is no better microcosm for double-speak and paradoxical self-reference than central bank communication! *We are not thinking about thinking of raising rates.*

Since we trade expectations on expectations, it does not matter that other market participants think the bank "sources" are hogwash; the activity of others in "today's trading" created "future prices," which in turn drove "today's trading" and materialised this trading action into existence. This is now the "market truth," like it or not.

Then, let us expand the two-step loop into more steps and consider looking at a deeper level of detail of this environment in Figure 13.3. "Today's trading" outcome is essentially generated by "I," the trader, buying and selling based on what "others," the cumulative total of participants, which is the market, will buy and sell today.

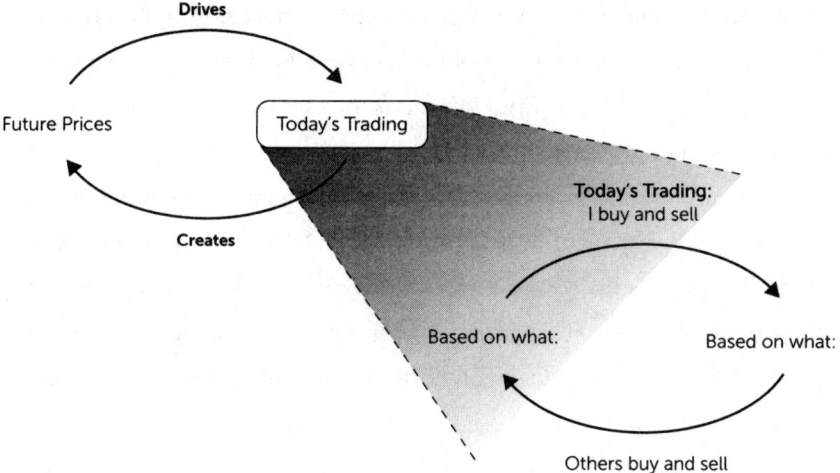

Figure 13.3 A deeper level of detail in 'Today's Trading'.

Importantly! Consider that from your perspective—as a trader—it is always *you* trading on what *others* are buying and selling and the patterns they leave in their wake. And, you rightly might contest: "But I buy and sell based on patterns… charts… and so on. I try not to do what everyone else is doing; I don't think about others!" But, of course, all trading is only possible as a by-product of activity by "others." Whatever your decision framework, you are trading the product of "others," buying and selling, and it is summarised as such. No matter how "right" or "wrong" they are.

This is a crucial point. Our job as intraday futures traders—operators in a self-referential, complex environment—is not to be right on geopolitics or even to correctly forecast any economic, financial or market matters. Sometimes, being "right" can hurt you; calling it "right" will mean the market will make the opposite move, and you'll lose money. To be truly "right" is to do what the market does, even if it is "wrong." Notions like right and wrong are linear; non-linearity demands navigation within expectations of expectations, thus echoes *The Sphinx*. As they say, to hold two competing ideas in one's head is a mark of intelligence. But the mark of successful speculation is to understand both deeply and yet ignore them entirely.

Consider that in Figure 13.3, in "today's trading," each individual trader and participant in the market has an "I," a notion of self that is facing outwardly towards the cumulative market participants as "others." As if a solitary human stands with his arms spread wide and faces the sun. The mass of "others" is something beyond easy comprehension.

And yet, decisions in the market are always made as an "I"—the agent or participant against thousands of faceless entities, traders and participants. It is *I* against the markets. To *me*, everyone else is an "other," and to *them*, I am part of the "other."

Yet those numbers on a screen also see *themselves* as real flesh and blood too, and everyone else as abstract! These "others" also possess a self-adapting thinking loop of trying to outplay you. You learn from them, and they learn from you, learning… *about them*. Returning to where we came from, one could say, the market is composed of countless "I's" buying and selling. All of them are protagonists of their own story.

This is not an arcane point. Take another look at "Today's trading" in Figure 13.3. *I buy and sell based on what others buy and sell, based on what I buy and sell, based on what...* Does this not follow the same circuit as Figure 13.2—"Future prices... drive today's trading... creates future prices"? They do!

Somehow, we have entangled these two loops, now a *strange* loop, because we suddenly return to the start, rendering a "start" or "end"—a hierarchy, in other words—a moot point. They have dissolved. We folded two separate structures into one flat pancake. This is what Hofstadter means by "strangeness": navigation of an environment where a straightforward notion of "left" and "right" cannot reliably guide you. And you will be surprised.

But! A loop inside a loop, in other words, this small kernel of market activity we have identified, can also said to be *recursive* (Hofstadter, 1999: 127). This is to say that one loop is nested within the other: "stories inside stories... movies inside movies, paintings inside paintings... Russian Dolls inside Russian Dolls," Hofstadter explains (1999: 127). And that is where emergence begins.

Recall: the simpler the rules, the greater the complexity. Hofstadter considers breaking out of any "predetermined patterns" as a mark of "intelligence," that seemingly came from nothing, or wholly non-life, to be able to self-modify behaviour (1999: 152). That is the element of "perpetual novelty" that Holland (2014: 10) identified as a feature of a complex environment, of "adaptive interactions" between participants. Fixed inanimate rules, like the number of squares on a chess board, provide structure for agents to operate within, thereby creating a higher level of "intelligence" that emerges from their actions. Attempting to overcome change causes more change. Too abstract? Well, as humans, we are also unaware of our internal workings on most given days. If one were to look at each individual neuron in the brain, one would not be able to tell there is an "emerged" superstructure above this intelligence. Zooming out from each individual neuron, at some point, "I" start to emerge.

We are all these individual "I's," and by our activity, in which we only care about ourselves, of taking the right actions at the right time, we collectively generate *unintentional* patterns, certain reactions that collectively form or allow a higher-level system—the markets—to exist on top of us, which has no real "knowledge" of the countless traders inside it. Yet the market responds as if it were just one "I" rather than faceless thousands. It responds to novel information, prices it in and converges on "expectations" of future events. For the market to be, in fact, *viscerally* reactive like a cat leaping onto a ledge in fright of a perceived risk. In the same way, the market flow is viscerally reactive when it learns of the same perceived risk. An attuned, adapting "intelligence" that, at some level, could be recognised as one of humanity's earliest *unintentional* attempts to create 'life' from non-life, a non-human entity that can tell you what it 'thinks'—prices, the action, order flow—in real time, for example, if a central banker is denying the market's perception of reality, "transitory" repeated in the face of persistent, spiking inflation.

Figure 13.2, then, is the heart of the market's self-reference over the interlocking interaction of countless participants, from which a higher-level, 'intelligent' system emerges. It just so happens that we, as intraday futures traders, are standing close to ground zero. We trade it at its most 'pure.' This small kernel of time is where order flow emerges.

So, the market does not need to know anything about its internal, countless traders to hold a conversation, for example, by telling you where interest rates will be three years out. Perhaps it is intuitive and right that we anthropomorphise the market as if it were alive. Because it is! *The market is speaking… Are you listening?*

And, as the above is all said and done, tell us, trader, how can you reduce the markets to their component 'parts'? Where do the markets really 'start and end'? What is the exact part in the hierarchy where it ceases to be an 'intelligence' and you can identify the pedal, metal frame and bicycle chain?

Consider one final doll within a doll; within each "I," each participant of the market, is the same loop in Figures 13.2 and 13.3: a self-referential mode of thinking and observation. In fact, Hofstadter's thesis is that consciousness itself emerges from a strange loop! Life emerging from non-life. That consciousness emerges based on "an interaction between levels in which the top level reaches back down towards the bottom level and influences it, while at the same time being itself determined by the bottom level," writes Hofstadter (1999: 709), in so doing perfectly describing Soros's reflexivity, and subsequently our forked Figure 13.2! "The self comes into being at the moment it has the power to reflect itself," Hofstadter concludes (1999: 709). It is game on from there. We, the strange loops, the "I's," are looking at seemingly another massive recursive strange loop—the markets. A reflection of us, it certainly is. More so, we are entangled within it, inextricably. The market is "I," and the market is "you."

To that end, what about the future? We saw that future prices drive today's trading. So, I buy and sell, based on what others buy and sell, which is based on what *others* in the future will be doing—what they will be buying and selling. Because that is what the market will be doing; therefore, we can look at Figure 13.4.

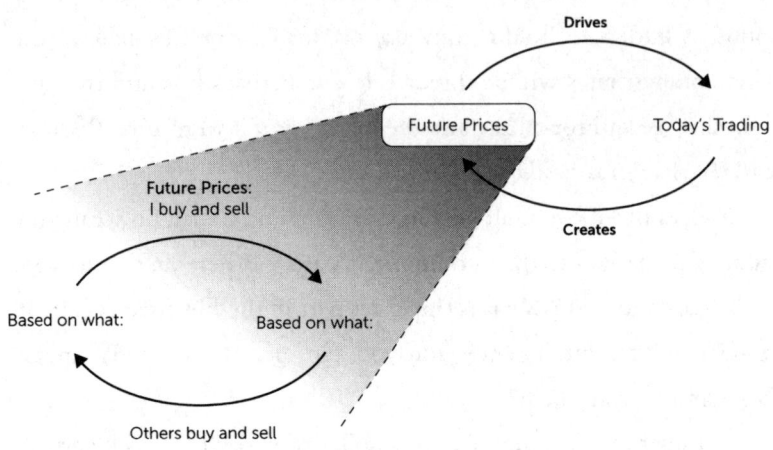

Figure 13.4 A nested situation. Participants impact each other across time.

Surprise! It is the very same Figure 13.3 nested in Figure 13.2! And this… *strangeness*… works. Because both "future prices" and "today's trading" still involve the same pricing mechanism of the market: the physical act of buying and selling that moves the market higher or lower to reach said prices. The "I's" of today are the same "I's" of tomorrow. Our simple two-step rules of buying and selling exist as much today as they do in the future. And because the mechanism is the same, the way the market trades in the future and the present means the participants impact each other *across* time.

If you are trading the "ECB sources" situation, you are taking positions in the market as if it is already a given that the future is *here* now… The future is here? *Yes!* That is the discounting purpose of the market, to "price" the known future *right now*. We trade information as if it has already happened; the "ECB sources" information is discounted, traded *now* and not at next week's press conference. And that becomes a self-fulfilling situation. And so, we arrive at Figure 13.5.

THE SPHINX

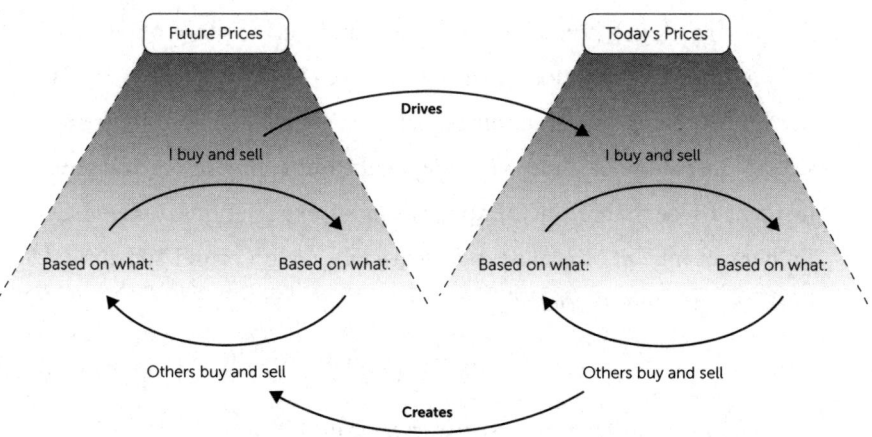

Figure 13.5 A hierarchy collapse! A self-fulfilling super-entangled surprise.

Seemingly, not only have we collapsed this supposed clear hierarchy… we have returned to where we started… we have also collapsed time itself! Into one impossible, confusing *goop—a mess!* Where did we even start? The expectations of future prices, in turn, affect the present—but the future was only created because of today's trading activity! "Despite one's sense of departing ever further from one's origin, one winds up, to one's shock, exactly where one had started out," echoes Hofstadter (2007: 102).

Hence, we are within a "strange loop," and more specifically, we are within this so-called "tangled hierarchy" because it "occurs when what you presume are clean hierarchical levels take you by surprise and fold back in a hierarchy-violating way," Hofstadter continues (1999: 691). There is no further, obvious level of beginning, or end, or any starting point. We are stuck in the paradoxical "conflict between the finite and infinite"—the finite trading day and the infinite future.

And this is why, in our own compressed kernel of time, as intraday futures traders, our strange loop is purer and occurs more often than the longer-term structural situations observed by Soros's reflexivity. At our level, the only material things that exist are *other participants* themselves. They are reality and what they make out reality to be. And you, in turn, affect their reality. Expectations of expectations. Like M.C. Escher's monks in *Ascending and Descending*, we go round and round in the loop: *return to sender!*

... OR IS IT YOU?

That is why the markets can seem hopeless to navigate—they're an impossible object! This makes them, perhaps, even discomforting to look at, like the paradoxical visual impossibilities of Escher. Their otherworldly impossibility becomes too much to handle. And it feels we are not far from this paradoxical world as traders! Look at Escher's *Relativity* lithograph, and you will get a sense of what market navigation feels like. And that is where *The Sphinx* will come in; we will meet him again soon.

But the resolution to the paradox of *Drawing Hands*, to all strange loops, is by "jumping out of the system," as Hofstadter describes it (1999: 37). That is when an agent, actor or participant can pause, remove himself from the environment and observe from the outside. In doing so, he creates a straight, normal hierarchical structure on top of the "tangled hierarchy" of the strange loop.

In other words, to discuss and resolve issues of self-reference in language, a meta-*language* must be created. A language for discussing language. That creates a normal, resolvable level that can exist and be observed from outside a self-referencing strange loop. The artistic left hand drew the artistic right hand, which drew the left, but the "higher level," the meta-artist Escher, simply drew and created those hands. Inside "the system" of *Drawing Hands*, it does indeed seem to be a paradox, but if we jump out of the system, we can witness Escher himself drawing the left and right hands. We now have a clean, obvious hierarchy built on top of the tangled hierarchy, a *meta*-level. A resolution.

Yes! This, indeed, is the *meta-game* we have been discussing throughout the book, especially with *The Godfather*. One could say this whole book deals with trading's meta-game, a ten-man treatise observing the strange loop of the markets, and how they navigate the markets. It would not be a stretch to say that the best traders are those who jump out of it the most reliably, reflect on their behaviour most lucidly, alter it and jump *back in*. This is why Haywood regards the ability of "learning how to learn," and its adjacent meta-principles, as the closest thing traders have to a holy grail. Not an indicator, not a system, nor a secret, for a complex, self-referential environment demands a lucid observer to work outside of it.

Even the terms, for example, "value investors" as opposed to "growth investors," are expressly evident in books and other treatises written about the profession in the late twentieth century—and "relative value," "spread trader," "news-driven trader" or "technical trader." The language we use reflects the higher level we create by having discussions about markets, operating outside of that tangled hierarchy into something more linear and understandable. Nevertheless, this language is precariously *reductive*, as all labels and boxes are.

So, is *Drawing Hands* resolved by acknowledging Escher, its creator? The point is that you would have never seen Escher if you had never left the system in the first place. The *Drawing Hands* world is all you would have ever known.

This, too, is why our *expectations–buying–selling–expectations* market loop appears paradoxical if we are *inside it*, but it never is, for the very reason we are discussing and reading about it right now! We are outside this system to begin with. We, as traders, the agents, the "I's," are observing and acting because of it. The problems for traders occur when we forget this or assume there is nothing to step outside of.

So why has time itself not collapsed with our impossible object of Figure 13.5? That markets are a seeming paradox, but still resolvable. It is possible to navigate them through our trading at certain points in time. We, the participants, "jump out of the system," but also step back inside. The markets do not instantly price in the entire future, because our ability to act on the markets is a linear and finite process. The physical act of buying and selling tethers an abstract, tangled market hierarchy to the real world, as it cannot violate the linear progression of time.

As we now know, we are all "I's," putting on positions and taking them off *across* the next few seconds, minutes, hours, days and so on. Thereby, the market does not magically "instantly" price in information, thereby rendering any edge or profit potential obsolete, as proponents of the efficient market hypothesis argue. It is not a binary light switch; rather, the pricing activity is a process that takes place *across* time. It pokes and prods with higher and lower prices, bound by time, to reach the best evaluation it can to reflect the real-world situation accurately.

Previously, we said that the two simple rules of this game, buying and selling, going long or short, are the only two that can never change. But there is the last—hidden—rule that underpins them both, which must be *time*. We cannot get around it; time limits what can emerge in terms of market strategies, adaptation and behaviour, and it also solves our tangled market hierarchy. This is the "inviolate" level, as Hofstadter describes it (1999: 687), like a chess board, which remains forever static while the approach to the game changes over time. The

THE SPHINX

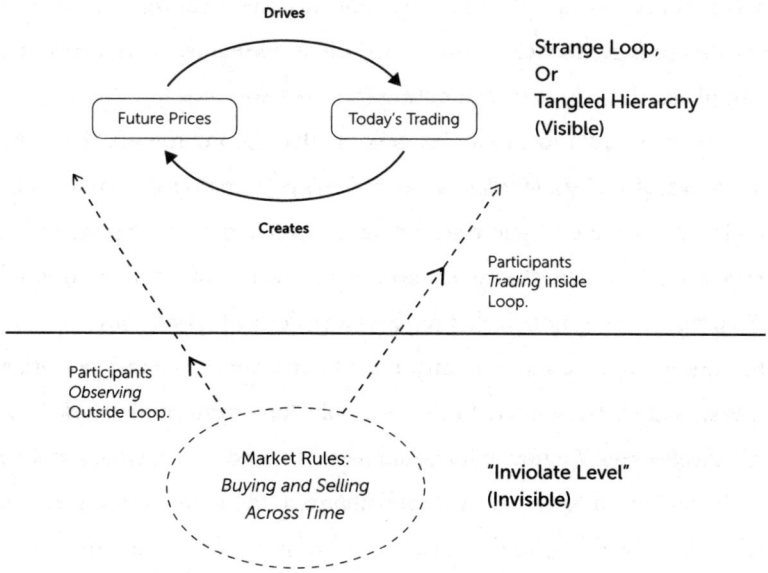

Figure 13.6 "Solving" the market's strange loop.

board, then, *is* the inviolate level. Escher, too, is the inviolate level that solves the tangled hierarchy of *Drawing Hands*. Inspired by Hofstadter's diagrammatic solution of the lithograph (1999: 690), we have made our own (Figure 13.6) adapted from Figure 13.2.

For us, the inviolate level is buying or selling—long or short—*across* the linear progression of time. It is inviolate because these rules operating across time cannot be changed. This gives us a sense of order and structure to our day, a clear and ordinary hierarchy. But on top of this level a strange loop occurs; complexity emerges from simple rules.

Sharp-eyed readers might infer that for the participants to "jump outside the system" and get back in again is different from Escher's drawing of the two hands because, unlike the markets, the hands do not leap from the page and try to strangle their creator. That is true, and that adds further depth and complexity to our domain. That is to say, this strange market loop, in turn, affects us—financially, emotionally, physically—in turn reaffecting the markets.

As we venture forth, we can now say that the full rules of the game *are the acts of buying and selling across the linear progression of time.* And seemingly out of these simple rules we have a self-organising, self-adaptive, responsive, fat-tailed, chaotic environment, which is of our own making! A complex environment that requires a trader to be both observer and practitioner, to have a hand in this environment's very creation. The market speaks, and we must listen, for there is only "one truth of the market," as *The Sphinx* says. We now understand *what* the markets are, which in turn will guide us on *how* to navigate and approach them. And our trader will tell us how he did it, how he became an "I," *emerged...* to become "*me*."

TRUTH

We have arrived upstream. We endured our necessary climb through complexity's meandering canyon to discover the watershed. Here, we find *The Sphinx*, calm as ever, sitting by a dry riverbed and a campfire. He says he is waiting for the rain.

But we perceive him differently this time, from a new dimension, and we realise he is not elusive at all. In fact, he is extremely straightforward, simple… except we were thinking too reductively to notice… *asking reductive questions… wanting complicated answers…*

It is a question of the level of detail. The first introduction and last conclusion of our trader is always, "I want to be formless in a market that has form." And everything flows downstream from there. "The market has a form, a structure, and a way of behaving and will do things according to its own rules. My place within it is to be a formless participant who does not have rules and a rigid structure. There is always a story in the markets and, day by day, things will construct themselves; you have to ask how your trading can fit within that story. Nothing else can come in between," *The Sphinx* continued. And to do that is to trade as close to the "market truth," the answer found in the language it speaks, that is, price, which we experience as order flow. Improvement begins and ends there.

We go further. "Instead of having a narrow view on the market, to then formalise my trading into a set of rules, I always thought to improve my *understanding* of the market instead," *The Sphinx* said. "Therefore, I will be able to interpret and behave in a better way than I did before. That is where my improvement as a trader has come from. Rather than taking failure to heart in my early years, all I could do was come in the next day and improve my understanding. That was it, and that is all I do now," he said. A trader's remuneration, he mentioned, is just a by-product of this process that emerges over time.

"Do that, and your whole story improves. Then you start to understand *your* place in the market, too. And that means seeing the whole picture—the narrative, the structures, how it looks when the moves happen… understanding the order flow because you constantly have to relearn the newest flow in the markets. It is the countless things that go into what makes a market… and then understanding it better and better and better… to the point where I understand where the risk is. But it's never about me trying to improve my 'trading'… to say, 'if I am doing this trade, I should be doing *this* size, and putting in stops exactly here'… I do not approach it that way. If I said my trade execution has *not* improved, that would be false; of course it has. It will improve by itself. If I have the right idea, then I should know how to execute it: managing it, holding it and placing stops and exits. But I never sat there to think how I should improve it. It is always centred around my understanding of the market and how I can be a part of its story," he said. Creating such a structure of rules, categorisation, targets and stops is to think reductively in a complex environment. It is only the market itself that should provide the box, the playing field, and nothing else.

"I just want to capture flow when it comes, ten ticks or a hundred. 'Risk management,' you ask? It is built into how you trade—if the market departs from what you're anticipating, then that is your risk management, isn't it? If I become a 'perfect being' that fully understands everything about the market, then I should always be able to make money... and that doesn't mean 'predicting' it perfectly or never having losing trades. It is just staying ahead and making money over time; the trades themselves are irrelevant." *D'you know what I mean?*

"Because I understand the risks of where the market should and should *not* go, how it should be behaving and how it comes together, I don't want to limit myself... to be sitting there, 'Cut this out, and that, and this,' to try and nail what makes my trading into three or four, or eight different rules or principles. I want to flow and move around with the market, but that requires a very deep understanding of what the markets *are*."

◆ ◆ ◆

The day grew long; dusk was settling. *The Sphinx* pointed at a canoe, and a canoe became. A fire log cracked. There would be no rain tonight, he told us.

"I see you have been discussing complexity in my chapter," *The Sphinx* says as he turns to *you*. "Well, reader, that's it! The issue of being reductive in a complex environment, to reduce something complex into only two or three rough equations, to say *this* is what determines everything, when it could be a whole universe of inputs! To say *that* factor is what made the S&P tip over the edge, and thereby ignore the rest… the other considerations are gone now. No longer in your field of view; your rules prevented you from ever knowing of them," he continues.

"As you read this page right now, consider a contradiction…" *The Sphinx* continues. "For you to break something down to learn it implies you know *what* to break down. But how can you know what to break down if you are yet to learn about it?"

The Sphinx heard echoes from *The Warrior's* chapter, he said, about a certain Angus Fletcher, and he wanted to know more. And we tell him of Fletcher's "curse of method," one of "trying to solve problems efficiently … limiting yourself to answers you predict will work. If you can predict an answer will work, it's not that creative," we said, relaying Fletcher's words. Because "if you can predict the idea in advance it is staying in observed rules and norms," Fletcher continued. (Skillicorn, 2023: 13:50–16:00) In other words, a top-down approach of creating categories *first* assumes the end outcome. And how could a novice, by definition, even assume the end outcome? More so when in a complex—but not complicated—environment, the outcome always changes!

Our trader's eyes flashed with revelation. "That's it! That is why I do not try to debrief in the way by cataloguing what I was doing; I moved on from there." *Why do I not have a journal?* "Maybe I've got too good a memory," you say? Hah!

"Who is to say it is that *one* thing to make someone good? We should not be reductive either about traders. Personally, this is why I specifically do not journal, log, debrief. I do not want to pick *the* two or three most important things that made me decide on a trade. There were likely a vast number of inputs that went into that decision; I need to *allow* myself to learn the vast market universe, to not artificially limit, create rules or blind myself to other inputs. Over time, especially if you are a beginner, you likely will focus on one or two things and ignore countless other important inputs you will never consider... as I say, you need to remove anything between you and the markets."

Our conversation continues with *The Sphinx*, and we discuss how an overeager novice will catalogue and document too much to feel as if they are still in control because the market provides none of it. An observation echoed by *The Student*. We note how it is often the novice trader who is so overt, documented, specific, *reductive*, to quickly identify an edge.

In fact, the more novice and unprofitable they are, the more determined they are to state that it is *this* single factor that provides them with an "edge," and, of course, the P&L to prove it is only ever just out of reach. Or the reductive approach, the trap, to hunt for the *one* thing, to look for the light switch to make them profitable, as opposed to understanding they are a product, an *emergence* of a complex web of processes over time.

Whereas senior, profitable traders will often struggle to *isolate* their edge. They cannot be boxed in like that. Their intangible nature reflects the intangible, complex market. Their open-ended uncertainty permits creativity and adaptation, unlike the rigid guard rails of the rule-bound and reductive trader. Like Fletcher said, providing predictable answers before you test them is devoid of creativity—talented individuals usually display deep uncertainty as to whether something will work. (Skillicorn, 2023: 13:50–16:00)

Recall that with *The Student*, we defined creativity as the ability to connect disparate nodes, information and spare parts. Too-early identification and categorisation—the obsession with databasing everything—precludes the connections from forming in the first place, leading to being cursed by *method*. Our trader, then, is not specifically *anti*-method; his only method is to find himself within the market to do what it does. To be formless in the market that has a form.

THE SPHINX

◆ ◆ ◆

The night had passed, and the chill receded. At dawn, it started to rain. We sat under a canopy with *The Sphinx*. And we asked him what he meant by "allowing" himself to learn.

"Your brain is an extraordinarily sophisticated… 'algorithm'; it takes in multiple inputs, derives a conclusion, decides and then clicks," he said. "Imagine you throw a softball at a three-year-old child—they will want to catch it, but they will be off the mark completely! Their hands will clap instead; the ball will sail over their head or hit them on the forehead. But by seven to nine years old, they will catch it comfortably. Then, in their twenties, they can dive catch a cricket ball flying at them at over one hundred miles an hour."

"*How has that happened?* The brain and the body have learnt how. That child didn't sit there studying physics and mechanics to catch that ball, but in a way, they did learn the required physics and mechanics at the same time! Your brain figures it out by itself. That is *exactly* what trading is. You go from a three-year-old getting hit in the face with a softball to run-dive-catching a cricket ball; your skills emerge, as you also learn sophisticated inputs from the market, and it is about being there to give yourself a chance to do so, to understand the environment yourself, just to observe it," he continued.

"But traders do this badly when they set out to specifically learn what input specifically causes x to happen. They will focus on two or three, but sometimes there could be fifteen inputs! There is no set number, but you decided you will learn only two or three… then you apply that *as a rule*, depriving your brain of learning the other variety of inputs in making an informed decision. These are all shades of the same idea; let me return—I am a strong believer in allowing yourself to absorb *all* information, these inputs," he said. That is, these traders are thinking linearly, reductively. Looking for static processes and clues in an environment that frequently upends them. Last week's clue is today's red herring.

Trading style, you ask? There is no such thing! Reductive questions... "Like trade execution or risk management, it is built into how you trade. I want to be a formless participant; how would I then have a 'trading style'? I only want to do what the market wants to do. You can smash the low, and it trades lower, or you can do the same next time and the market bids higher aggressively. Well? What 'style,' method or technique did I need then? Instead, you need to understand the action and the flow to know when to smash the low with size and stay in the market or scale in. You observe and feel a real heaviness; a strong offer comes into the market. Other times, it can just burst and bid back up before it reoffers. Your 'style' and execution should adapt to your knowledge of the market and its flow—the truth of what it wants to do at that moment in time," he concluded. Trading style, then, is trying to fit a form around the formless *Sphinx*; he can only afford to be shaped by the market; nothing can come in-between.

The rain continued, and the river started to swell. Not long now, *The Sphinx* said, until we could continue downstream. "Over time, you develop the ability to navigate the market in this way," *The Sphinx* said—to navigate this seemingly impossible object. "This is why the biggest improvement in my trading was by removing *myself* from how I feel. If I am a formless participant, I can be the pure product of the tangible and intangible things I have experienced over the years. I *feel* the market will rally. I can only do that if I am not focused on myself. If I come between the market, I am interfering with its version of the 'truth,' and I won't understand what it wants to do. I want my brain so trained on catching that ball, so adapted to navigate the markets, that nothing can come in-between," he concluded.

In other words, he has spent ten decades understanding how the market speaks, and he has learnt to navigate the market's reality, the only truth that matters. Expectations of expectations. In a non-linear complex environment, perpetual novelty demands perpetual observation. But what did *The Sphinx* mean by "removal of oneself"?

DOWNSTREAM DYNAMICS

The rains subsided, but the river was now at full strength. The once-dry riverbed was restored to its former glory. It was now opportune. And we found ourselves in a canoe. *The Sphinx* glided along past us. *Easier than walking*... and we let the current take us further.

What kept you persevering, Sphinx, after a whole decade? "Nothing is for nothing," he began, gliding forward in his canoe. "I could still see great things happening: instinctive, deep trades. Even early on, like in August 2007, trading the Fed's discount rate cut; long in the equities... action in the Bunds. Trading them perfectly with full size. In time, I overcame the fear of *being* in the market through this long-term trading that happened later on. I always felt there was something there... just no remuneration yet; I just had to understand the markets better. The early years are just plugging holes of a massive deficit of deep knowledge, not the development of superficial rules. After that, it is just the aggregation of all the small things, observations... keeping all of that filed away somewhere in your mind to be used at a later date. And updating it."

We continued downriver. "Since 2018, it all came together, as all the noise, the doubts were gone. This was my biggest improvement in how I talk to myself," he continued. *Is that what you meant by removing yourself?*

The Sphinx nods. "It is understanding good and bad-run dynamics. What is a bad run? A hangover in your head, losing today because you lost the day before," he began. "You can't have it both ways—to want good runs only—and trick your brain to ignore the bad. Instead, it's about altering your fundamental belief that this dynamic does not exist, to escape it all together. Forget the positive and you release the negative. To go in with a clear mind, no noise, a goldfish memory from one day to the next."

The Sphinx rested the paddle across his lap. The river would do the rest of the work, he said, and we should allow it to do it too. "Trading is only hard because you believe it to be so," he continued. "If you bring this baggage, this mental overhead with you, you cannot be formless with the market. It makes you want to create rules when there are no rules; these rules sweep the baggage under the rug, to try and trick it out of sight. It makes you ask questions when there are no questions… you do need to *apply* yourself. But that does not mean trading is hard."

The same, our trader said, when traders declare how stressful their profession is. "It is, up to a point! Of when you need money for rent, food… to exist. That is stressful. But after that, there is no stress. You trade, and you move on. These past few years I've traded have been the calmest ever because I have moved beyond that point."

"If you try your best each day and see where the market takes you—why bother having goals and dreams? Just turn up. You must depersonalise. And you have to be *open*, with a real willingness to improve, because many people are truly blocked. They feel they work hard, but there is no willingness to enact change," he said. The *will* to change, our trader continued, cannot be prescribed or described.

"There are planners and plotters… it is easier to be reductive and have comfort in rigid rules—'never sell lows in the Bund'—then it is easier to redo the same mistakes continually, to follow the rules rather truly alter repeat behaviour," *The Sphinx* said. Losses as a form of escapism.

The river takes us further downstream. *If you depersonalise, how do you use emotions in your trading?* "This is the ideal image of *me* as a profitable trader. *The Warrior* might need to get angry. Everyone has ways to peak their performance. But to do this, I believe you don't need to create an environment. I believe it exists in the absence of it.

"Strip it all back, remove the baggage; forget positive and negative dynamics… good runs and bad runs… *just* learn and be with the market," he continued. "You could be loud but use the emotions as you want. Is it because the market is nervy, it doesn't feel right… something is off? That is different. Using emotions in that way to navigate the market is a heightened form of intelligence. There is a difference between using your emotions to gather clues of the complex market rather than anxiety about your positions… because you have specific goals, dreams, and desires… 'I really cannot *afford* for this to go wrong!' These are the emotions of ruin. And that is sub-optimal."

How do I find conviction?

Strong opinions can mimic rules. "When you don't know what you are doing, you start to intellectualise the market… and you cannot afford the risk of having strong opinions on the market, especially if you are new," he continued.

But! Trade conviction is not a strong opinion. "You find conviction in the market in its feedback. Conviction is guided by fact, and the fact is the flow, the action… let the market tell you what the truth is because that is what you are trading." Taking stock of the previous trading days, *The Sphinx* described the disparity of opinion… perception… against the market's truth. A known hawk on the FOMC board was speaking… hawkishly. *No Surprise, no trade!* So some traders claimed, in fact, *The Sphinx* himself was fading the very market reaction… but the market continued and continued, its own reality… the conclusion of this complex environment indeed cared about this 'known,' unsurprising comment. The market spoke. "It *is* relevant," it said, even if its own participants thought the opposite. *That* was the market's truth... fact... so *The Sphinx* reversed his position and followed the market. Whatever you think *will* happen... "You don't know the truth until you see it," our trader continued. "The bears on social media are angry at the Fed of their accommodative policy... fuming, delirious... and when they shifted hawkishly, equities still went up! You cannot risk strong opinions; why must it differ from the market's truth and reality so much?"

◆ ◆ ◆

We had arrived. The river had carried us here, and we disembarked. "All of this is to say, by removing myself and how *I feel*, it allows me instead to feel what the market wants to do. To allow myself, my brain a chance to learn, to take it all in... to present my tangible and intangible experiences to trade only the market truth; that meant the removal of noise, forgetting good- and bad-run dynamics... depersonalise, have no goals or objectives... just be... anything else is interfering with the truth. Then you are behind the curve. I want my experience to flourish with no baggage. To understand the facts, the truth, and be as close as possible with the market..."

We found him on the terrace, with orange-brown leaves strewn across the floor; some glided down from the branches that hung above. The trading floor roared! He was leaning against the railing, cigarette in hand... puffs of smoke. We gazed together at the red brick wall across the terrace as we continued asking *The Sphinx* questions.

"...and that also means to wait for the perfect opportunity. I once heard this metaphor, you know, from Michael Neil... to take the canoe and wait for the rain, to let the dry riverbed fill up," *The Sphinx* said. Why drag the canoe with you, your feet cut up, exhausted, and you barely made it halfway? You won't have it in you to reach the endpoint. Instead, just wait… set up camp… to not force 'conditions' since you can thrive in the absence of them."

"The canoe, the river, markets… they will take me where they want to go. And in turn, I have the flexibility, the formlessness to make the right decisions, to trade the market's universal truth," *The Sphinx* said…

"…and you know what else he said? That applies to his career, too, in the big picture. All the good happened late in his career. It was not heroic overcoming—just coming in the next day and being ready. He lived the life of dragging the canoe, but he learnt to wait for the rain, to take the opportunity when it comes," *we* said to Haywood. A life dedicated to navigating a strange, tangled, complex environment of contradiction, to experience and touch infinity in a finite way.

Haywood beamed with admiration. We discussed more of *The Sphinx* in the taxi. But then the conversation flowed to another trader we were about to visit. "He is reticent…" Haywood began.

Aha… "guarded"… *m-hm…* "shy, private"… *yeah*, Haywood explained in the taxi as it drove towards Wrocław city centre…

PRACTITIONER'S POSTSCRIPT

Explore resources derived from this chapter to further support the practicing trader.

axiafutures.com/
toot

Refer to
The Sphinx's
section.

LEARNER'S IMPRESSIONS

Below are some personal impressions that *The Sphinx* made on us that we still discuss with other traders.

1. *The nature of things.* The markets are complex, like a rainforest, and not complicated, like a car. They generate bouts of patterns, chaotic behaviour and fat-tailed outcomes where participants adapt and readapt in turn; because the rules of this environment are so simple, new behaviour will always emerge. At their core, markets are a seeming contradiction, yet "resolved" through our linear progression of time. And so, navigation of such strange environments—with what we are equipped with—demands an understanding of what it truly is and the limitations of reductionistic, linear thinking. To ask different, accurate questions that fit this environment. Understanding *what* it is brings us closer in *how* to navigate it.

2. *Standing before* The Sphinx. Our trader inverts the usual discourse. *How do I manage risk? What is your trading style? How do I improve? How do I manage myself?* He concedes some answers, but they all revert back to one: understanding the market and its "truth"— whatever it deems that to be. Start from there, and you will answer many of your own questions.

3. *Layers of abstraction.* Thus noted *The Hero* and nearly all traders in this book, including *The Sphinx*. All of them intuit the market's "truth," and they all have different processes to see it and not let themselves put too many things in-between themselves and the market, such as busywork, layers of planning and plotting, building theories upon entire indicators, and charts, and other such ways to see the market, or becoming obsessed with psychology, and ways to deal with mental and historical baggage. To not let themselves *become*.

EPILOGUE

Our explicit suggestions to our readers are always to approach this trading domain by first learning how to learn, that is, meta-learning, the framework, methods and mentality the traders themselves use. Recombine it and push the meta-game further. And that is the most enduring thing of all, as much as it can possibly be.

Instead, too often, we approach it in reverse, trying to understand the most fleeting thing of all—markets—by placing too much weight on the details and desiring permanence. The special secret "tool," your "it" moment of profitability, the one strategy forever, onto an environment that only guarantees change.

But venturing behind the markets, we reach the traders who are something halfway in-between, trying to achieve permanence in a world that tries to disembowel them of it. And those that *thrive* in this gauntlet are sublime—in the awe-inspiring-thunderclouds-of-the-stormy-sea-crashing-upon-the-rocks sense of the word. That is why we cannot replicate them entirely, to copy them and expect to outclass them. To outperform *The Warrior*, one has to become an entirely different, unique, dangerously sublime trader altogether. To trade like *The Razor* is to forever live in his shadow. To risk like *The Engineer* is to misunderstand it all.

So, we return, then, to *process*. That is, to think upstream. We dip our bottles in the river and drink from it, the 'powers' that made these traders. And so, too, will you emerge differently. To become a recreation of the human trader after so many relegated us to the antiques shop, a long answer to the question the taxidermist posed to Haywood in 2015.

To look then at *ourselves*, and as we consider the power of asking for a single tick, the nature of composing a trade, to harness the community's "extended mind," to develop 'soft edge' as serious as a hard trading edge. To understand the advantages of dynamic sizing and the relevance of the static approach while acknowledging the burdens of a strategy and discovering what you can tolerate. To dip into the flow of time by using the lineage of the trading desks; to appreciate opportunity maximisation, the evolution of a cash flow to a wealth-building trader, and the skill of worldbuilding. To ask how to develop your adjacent possible, accumulate more spare parts and know that one must always navigate the crossroads; the antagonism of learning and performing, and to utilise the power of journaling. To know what it means to get it right; discipline and understanding the importance of those around you, family and career end-goal alternatives; reframing success. To understand the place and time of your career and what is appropriate, crossed with the sense of occasion and to know *this* is the time to push and take your pound of flesh. The necessity of developing explicit trading frameworks, developing "trade sense"—a combination of stamina and depth of preparation and precision; to see that iteration is key to quality, and you achieve that all through the debriefing process. To recognise the power of the slow brew and the roundabout route—that slow learning is best learning—and to appreciate the human trading advantage in authoring a multi-dimensional trade as an unassailable edge. To possess humility in understanding the dangerously necessary act of *No Plan B!* and purge redundancies, break it all and rebuild. Because originality means to break best practices. To then one day move to a

EPILOGUE

state of reductive mastery—to become unique, to emerge as *the* trader. *A Trader of Our Time*.

In the Preface we considered that we cannot "see" life but only its after-effects, which ripple outwards, to hear its echoes but not understand the source. At least, to never *agree* on the source. But so too, through the meandering exposition of this book, we can consider that one cannot directly "see" the markets—to understand, explain them to another—but we can rather mostly achieve this by looking at its traders instead. And each of our ten traders reveals different aspects; the amorphous market takes shape through them. And so, their shape, their aspect is their *story*. We recast the aspects of our traders as such.

The Razor—Denial
The Collector—Finality
The Adventurer—Perception
The Warrior—Belief
The Student—Observance
The Godfather—Reinvention
The Engineer—Emergence
The Hero—Loss
The Voyager—Environment
The Sphinx—Wonder

We reveal a particular aspect of the market through a trader because that was our focus at a moment in time. But that does not imply the aspect of perception does not apply to each and every one of them—or to you. *Can you believe like The Warrior, abstain like The Razor, emerge like The Engineer?* This is why their aliases are a bonus. You can melt their identities and their stories, which are now charged with meaning. *Denial* means a whole new thing after we learn about *The Razor*'s story. So, you ingest this capsule; it is lodged within you and at the next inflexion point in your life, it could change your behaviour and alter your course of action. So, change has been elicited. This book, as technology, has worked!

So, how does a trader find purpose beyond "success"? The toughest question is posed to those fewest in number. What is the meaning of it all? Consider that to render chaos into the mortal is how an artist becomes; to *explain* what these strange markets are through your very trading activity is how you ascend this domain. Thereby you become unique and emerge from the masses. An "individual" who reveals an aspect of the market through the power of their trading. How you render markets into our mortal plane through your unique trading *is* your artistry—to represent change, contradiction, antagonism and life—and, dare we say, to render a very human experience. Could it be anything else?

And because we bare ourselves to the markets so frequently, to navigate the upside-down financial world means we are simultaneously also chained to a rock and suffer for it too. Performance has a cost, and that is the price of admittance to a company of a *very* select few, as it is in all endeavours. But the price of staying and thriving is not a cost but a burden—to know that success is always fleeting for a trader, but that failure is permanent.

As the trader navigates the market's contradictions, they create a story, reflecting the truisms of the "real world" onto our strange market—a mirror world. And if we learn through a trader's story, then we have elicited change—in others and ourselves. The trader, through their artistry, has harnessed the infinity of the market—a product of its antagonism—into something tangible and human. And *that* has

EPILOGUE

meaning; your ascension as a trader is a rediscovery of meaning. Make it yours. Trade it anew.

But as it always has been in art, we go our own way, warts and all. Because this strange mirror world is what creates meaning *for us*. We understand ourselves through it, as much as we love and hate it—thus speak *The Warrior* and *The Hero*, but so too echo all traders in this book.

This is a landscape of infinite stories, a story of *you*—and stories of us. All of the excesses, the bad, the failures! But so, too, stories of overcoming, improvement, resurrection. Where one sees trading as the pinnacle frivolity of modern life, the excesses of capitalism, the dangers of greed—we see the frontiersmen, the daring, the poets, the gladiators, the conquerors. This is their medium, *our medium*. Permanence is permanent recreation; to be timeless is to be recreated forever. That is what it means to be, and remain, a *Trader of Our Time*.

AXIA FUTURES

Want To Train With Us?

"Seize every big moment; make the most out of it— achieve something great."
The Warrior

We are looking for talent. It is always found in the unexpected. Join our mission to recreate *the* trader.

Find Out More About:

o Career Pathways
o Flagship Career Programme
o Bespoke Training & Mentoring

axiafutures.com/path

All Experience Levels Desired. Curiosity Required.

ACKNOWLEDGEMENTS

No trader is an island, and neither are these authors. We are grateful to all.

First, we thank each of these ten traders for their generosity in time, information, and their candid nature. You are the bones of this book and have set the stage for the next generation. Special thanks to both *The Warrior* and *The Razor* for their exceptional contributions. There have also been various readers at each stage of development—we thank you all.

My (Bogdan) personal and deep thanks to my wife, Adina, whose endless talents also extended to great editorial suggestions, countless improvements, with the sheer guts to advocate for the hard, but right thing. She has been my trusted reader and inexhaustible cheerleader well before the first word hit the page. I also deeply thank my family, alongside the many people that have supported me along the way.

And, from one co-author to another—Alex, we finally got there! I am grateful for this incredible and unique opportunity. Thank you for your patience, trust and support to give enough time for this book to emerge.

My (Alex) personal thanks to this band of brothers. To all the traders at AXIA—we have spent more time together than my own family.

ACKNOWLEDGEMENTS

We went through the pains and losses. Of understanding what it means to be a trader. We would not be here otherwise. The journey continues.

My gratitude to Roger Carlsson and Mario Kyriacou for believing in a new generation, of taking the risk to break away from dogma and to back innovation and experimentation. My thanks to both Richard Bailey, and Eric Jousse, who have been with me on this long journey, and have excelled in training and advancing new and veteran talent. I trust them to take traders to the next generation. My gratitude and thanks to Stephanos Mavrommatis who is the pillar of Axia Futures upon which it all runs.

Special thanks to Angus Fletcher, who has shaped many of my ideas and leader on modes of training, creativity and training protocols that have helped to innovate in developing traders.

Immense gratitude and thanks to the two strong women in my life—my mother and my wife, Elizabeth—for their unending support, and who contributed to the slow genesis of this book.

Our thanks to the Whitefox team, especially Sarah Rouse and Chris Wold, for their project management. Further thanks to Peter Salmon, Dan Shutt and Setanta O'Mahoney for their excellent work as editors.

BIBLIOGRAPHY

Ahrens, S., *How to Take Smart Notes: One Simple Technique to Boost Writing, Learning, and Thinking – for Students, Academics, and Nonfiction Book Writers* (CreateSpace Independent Publishing Platform, 2017)

Caro, Robert A., *Working* (New York, London: Vintage, 2021)

Csikszentmihalyi, Mihaly, *Flow: The Classic Work on How to Achieve Happiness* (London: Rider, 2002)

Dalton, James F., Eric T. Jones and Robert B. Dalton, *Mind Over Markets: Power Trading with Market Generated Information* (Hoboken, NJ: John Wiley & Sons, Inc., 2013)

Epstein, David, *Range: How Generalists Triumph in A Specialised World* (London: Pan Books, 2019)

Fletcher, Angus, *Creative Thinking: A Field Guide to Building Your Strategic Core* (self-published, 2021a)

Fletcher, Angus, *Wonderworks: Literary Invention and the Science of Stories* (London/New York: Swift Press, 2021b)

Fletcher, Angus, "Why Computers Will Never Read (or Write) Literature: A Logical Proof and a Narrative," *Narrative*, Vol. 29, No. 1, 2021c, DOI: 10.1353/nar.2021.0000

Geis, Darlene (ed.), *M.C. Esher, Twenty-Nine Master Prints* (New York: Abrams, 1983)

Hofstadter, Douglas R., *Gödel, Escher, Bach: An Eternal Golden Braid* (New York: Basic Books, 1999)

Hofstadter, Douglas R., *I Am a Strange Loop* (New York: Basic Books, 2007)

Holland, John H., *Complexity: A Very Short Introduction* (Oxford: Oxford University Press, 2014)

Johnson, Steven, *Where Good Ideas Come From: The Seven Patterns of Innovation* (New York/London: Allen Lane, 2010)

Larson, Eric J., *The Myth of Artificial Intelligence: Why Computers Can't Think the Way We Do* (Cambridge, MA: The Belknap Press of Harvard University Press, 2021)

Liu, Cixin and K. Liu (trans.), *The Three-Body Problem* (London: Head of Zeus, 2015)

Mitchell, Melanie, *Complexity: A Guided Tour* (New York: Oxford University Press, 2011)

Papic, Marko, *Geopolitical Alpha: An Investment Framework for Predicting the Future* (Hoboken, NJ: John Wiley & Sons, Inc., 2021)

Paul, Annie Murphey, *The Extended Mind: The Power of Thinking Outside the Brain* (New York: Houghton Mifflin Harcourt, 2021)

Skillicorn, Nick, "Angus Fletcher – Improving Creativity through Narrative and Movement," *Idea to Value* podcast, S07E162:, 16 Aug. 2023, www.ideatovalue.libsyn.com/podcast-s7e162-angus-fletcher-improving-creativity-through-narrative-and-movement (accessed 18 Sep. 2024).

Snowden, David J. and Mary E. Boone, "A Leader's Framework For Decision Making," *Harvard Business Review*, November 2007, www.hbr.org/2007/11/a-leaders-framework-for-decision-making (accessed 3 June 2024)

Soros, George, *The Alchemy of Finance* (Hoboken, NJ: John Wiley & Sons, Inc., 1994)

Spitznagel, Mark, *The Dao of Capital: Austrian Investing in a Distorted World* (Hoboken, NJ: John Wiley & Sons, Inc., 2013)

Theil, Peter and Blake Masters, *Zero to One: Notes on Startups, or How to Build the Future* (London: Virgin Books, 2014)

Tarkovsky, Andrey, and Kitty Hunter-Blair (trans.), *Sculpting in Time: The Great Russian Filmmaker Discusses His Art* (Austin: University of Texas Press, 1986)

INDEX

adaptive behaviour, 31, 426
"adjacent possible", 231, 234–5, 237, 239, 263, 266–7, 295, 386, 391, 405–6, 408, 412, 414, 417, 460
Adventurer, The, 41, 123–48, 242, 299, 307, 410–12
  dynamic sizing, 130–7, 148
  financial security, 145–6
  and Firm Y, 127, 129, 143, 339
  lifestyle, 123–7
  Market Path Diagram, 136
  P&L, 142
  Perception, 461
  and perception shifts, 128–9, 143, 147–8
  and skiing, 127–9, 140–1
  and talent, 137–8
  and *The Warrior*, 137–8
Ahrens, Sönke, 251
artificial intelligence (AI), 200–2, 213–14, 219, 227

AXIA, 18, 27, 67, 72, 76, 80, 82, 110, 129, 176, 195, 275, 321, 330, 358, 367, 377, 415
  AXIA–FCT partnership, 79, 344
  Axia Futures, 51, 56
  The Collector joins, 115–16
  failed traders, 326, 355
  and families, 263–4
  The Godfather joins, 286, 288, 293
  good and bad beginners
  Risk Room, 46–8, 228
  The Student joins, 237–8, 246, 248
  trading floor, 35–57
  training room, 50–1

Bailey, Richard, 51, 113, 115, 174, 339
Bank of England, 280, 300n, 301–3
Bank of Japan, 220

INDEX

Bannister, Roger, 408
beginners, good and bad, 367–9
Bitcoin, 386
Bobl, 236, 237, 273, 278, 282–3, 285, 288
Boone, Mary E., 202n
Brexit, 52–3, 79, 81, 156, 209, 289
BTP, 119, 232, 289, 291
"build days", 21
Bund, 55–6
   The Adventurer and, 142
   Bund–Bobl–Schatz butterfly spread, 282, 288
   The Collector and, 105, 107, 116, 119
   The Engineer and, 319, 322–3, 341–3
   The Godfather and, 274–6, 282, 285, 288, 293, 302–3
   The Hero and, 381, 383, 385–6, 398
   price ladder, 42
   The Sphinx and, 419, 453–4
   The Student and, 232, 237, 250
   The Warrior and, 149, 168, 175–6, 182, 189, 204–5, 207, 209–10
Buxl, 301–3, 305

Cable, 53, 293, 301–3
Carlsson, Roger, 51–2, 93
Caro, Robert, 348
central banks, 26, 45, 68, 101, 103, 117, 149, 151, 156, 183, 206n, 222–3, 258–9, 276, 178, 187, 314, 316, 324, 327, 352–3, 387, 408, 415, 422, 438
   see also European Central Bank
"champion's fallacy", 126, 180
chess, 30, 201, 356, 361, 389, 420, 437, 444
Chicago Mercantile Exchange, 18, 59
Chicago Purchasing Managers' Index, 106
Cixin Liu, 359
Collector, The, 19, 40, 50, 100–22, 127, 135–6, 143, 183–4, 221, 236, 239, 270, 273, 408, 414, 419
   agency, 117, 120–1
   and *The Engineer*, 116, 340
   final warning, 105–6
   Finality, 461
   and Firm Y, 101, 105, 113, 115, 127, 174, 339–40, 409
   health, 116, 119–20
   learning from environment, 104, 109–18
   joins AXIA, 115–16
   P&L, 115, 120, 122
   and *The Razor*, 105–6, 108–9, 114, 120
   and *The Sphinx*, 105, 115
   and *The Warrior*, 112, 115–16
copper futures, 386, 422
counter-intuitive thinking, 32, 35, 119, 147, 359

INDEX

Covid-19 pandemic, 22, 58, 81, 150, 156, 183, 188–9, 191, 212, 256, 327, 383
creative destruction, 39
crude oil, 18, 43, 107, 123, 132, 161, 163–8, 170, 178, 188, 232, 258, 370, 374, 400, 433
 and Russia–Ukraine war, 204, 206–10
cryptocurrencies, 65
Csikszentmihalyi, Mihaly, 261

"daily risk", 21, 348
Dalton, James F., 312–13
DAX, 107, 110, 153, 206–7, 210, 288
Draghi, Mario, 36, 319

efficient market hypothesis (EMH), 23
endowment funds, 178
Engineer, The, 16, 40, 51, 130, 140, 160, 190, 310–72, 414–15, 422, 459
 and boredom, 339
 and "closed loops", 348, 350
 and *The Collector*, 116, 340
 Emergence, 461
 and Firm Y, 311, 317, 339–40, 343–4, 352, 377
 and *The Godfather*, 270, 339, 356
 handwriting, 251, 348
 and *The Hero*, 314, 316, 335, 348–9, 354, 356, 362, 380–1, 384, 387, 390–1, 393, 396, 398, 400
 laconic character, 310–11
 P&L, 328, 331, 334, 344, 353, 358–60
 and psychology, 350–1
 and *The Razor*, 321, 326, 339–40, 344, 364, 368
 and "reciting the idea", 332–3
 and static analysis, 346–7
 and *The Student*, 247, 250–2, 258, 260, 351–2, 358, 362
 and "technical landscape", 320–1
 and TPOs, 316–17
 and trade sense, 326–7
 training talk, 345–6
 and *The Veteran*, 340–2, 369
 and *The Warrior*, 321, 340, 369–70, 344
 weekend debriefing, 354–5, 371
Epstein, David, 356–7, 359
Escher, M. C., 429, 442–3, 445
Eurex Exchange, 18, 43, 53
Euribor, 232, 274, 288
European Central Bank (ECB), 38, 119, 168, 190, 204, 222, 259, 269, 319, 352, 398, 434, 440
 long-term refinancing operation (LTRO), 236

INDEX

European Central Bank (ECB) *cont.*
"vigilance", 278, 280–2, 294, 296
European Debt Crisis, 49, 101, 112, 181, 182–3, 196
European Union, 289
Eurostoxx, 55–6, 149, 153, 206–7, 238, 343, 373–4, 381, 386, 398
Eurozone, 43, 220, 289
"extended mind", 109, 111, 115–16, 122, 221, 236–7, 239, 273, 276–7, 283, 402, 405–6, 408, 410, 414, 417, 460

FCT Europe, 81, 51, 79, 344
Federal Open Market Committee (FOMC), 46, 144, 190, 222, 224, 293, 326–8, 455
Federal Reserve, 39, 58, 185–6, 223, 327, 453, 456
The Warrior and, 149–51, 156–7
Financial Crisis, 23, 49, 51, 58, 101–2, 107, 149, 182, 272
Firm Y, 27, 51–2, 238
and *The Adventurer*, 127, 129, 143, 339
and *The Collector*, 101, 105, 113, 115, 127, 174, 339–40, 409
and *The Engineer*, 311, 317, 339–40, 343–4, 352, 377
and *The Hero*, 377, 381
and *The Razor*, 77–8, 80, 127, 174, 339–40, 344, 377
and *The Sphinx*, 174, 339, 422

and *The Voyager*, 339, 405–7, 409–10
and *The Warrior*, 157, 174, 192, 195, 339–40, 344, 377
Fletcher, Angus, 14, 202n, 213–14, 225, 449–50
flow states, 261–3, 285
fractal markets, 313, 358
FTSE, 103, 288
Fukushima nuclear disaster, 285

Gilts, 103, 282, 288, 300–5
Godfather, The, 40, 47, 50, 103, 108, 268–309, 325, 386, 403, 419, 443
and Bund–Bobl–Schatz butterfly spread, 282, 288
elastic approach, 298–300
and *The Engineer*, 270, 339, 356
and interest rates, 278–81
joins AXIA, 286, 288, 293
North London boy, 270–1, 290–1
P&L, 276, 279, 285, 292, 295, 299, 302, 308
and *The Razor*, 283–4
Reinvention, 461
and *The Student*, 237, 264–5, 273, 286, 307
and *The Sphinx*, 270
trading the fly, 282–4
two fathers, 284
and *The Voyager*, 409, 411, 413

INDEX

and *The Warrior*, 164, 169, 172, 270, 287–9, 295–7, 299–300, 303–4, 359
gold, 18, 45, 88, 107, 116, 161, 164–6, 168, 170, 206, 210, 301, 433
Greek debt crisis, 238, 343

handwriting, 251, 348
Haywood, Alex, 25–8, 40, 46, 52, 54, 102, 190, 198, 228, 460
   and *The Adventurer*, 124, 126, 128, 130–1, 138, 144–5
   and *The Collector*, 104, 109, 111
   and "effort zone", 330, 335
   and *The Engineer*, 312, 320, 323, 328, 330–5, 339, 344, 353, 355, 357–60, 370
   and "error pruning", 120
   and flow states, 261
   and *The Godfather*, 275, 278, 293, 297
   and *The Hero*, 377, 392–3, 398–9
   and "interoception", 138
   and journaling, 255, 353, 358
   and "learning how to learn", 443
   and *The Razor*, 60–2, 64, 73, 77, 85, 89, 93, 95–6
   and R&D, 351
   and "reciting the idea", 332–3
   and "roundabout route", 357
   and "sense of occasion", 326
   and *The Sphinx*, 421, 457
   and *The Student*, 228–9, 246–51, 255, 257, 260–1
   and *The Voyager*, 405–8, 414, 416
   and *The Warrior*, 150, 154–5, 157, 159–60, 175, 182, 196
Hero, The, 19, 24, 35, 40, 47, 51, 230, 373–402, 411, 419, 458, 463
   and *The Collector*, 116–18
   debriefing, 393–6, 400
   and *The Engineer*, 314, 316, 335, 348–9, 354, 356, 362, 380–1, 384, 387, 390–1, 393, 396, 398, 400
   and Firm Y, 377, 381
   handwriting, 251, 348
   intensity, 376, 378, 381
   Loss, 461
   non-linear performance, 396–7
   P&L, 396, 402
   personality, 160
   process refresh, 399–400
   and *The Student*, 233, 243, 251–2, 258, 348, 362, 386, 389, 391
   tactical trading, 388–93
   and *The Warrior*, 378, 390, 392
high-frequency trading, 18, 25–6, 30
Hofstadter, Douglas R., 31n, 427–9, 431–2, 439, 441–2, 444–5

INDEX

Holland, John H., 31n, 424–5

illiquidity, 43, 53, 60, 83, 286
imitation, learning through, 109–11
inflation, 45, 206, 222, 278, 301, 342, 346, 438
Intercontinental Exchange (ICE), 300n
interest rates, 46, 178, 185, 190, 206n, 216, 219–22, 269, 327, 430–1, 434, 439
  negative, 43
  zero, 26, 101, 156, 222, 283, 301
  The Godfather and, 278–81

jiu-jitsu, 160, 270, 305
Johnson, Steven, 231, 234–5, 352, 357–8
journaling, 74, 229, 241, 243, 249, 251–2, 254–5, 257, 259–60, 266–7, 349, 352–4, 357–8, 460
Jousse, Eric, 51, 248

"kind environments", 356
Kyriacou, Mario, 46–7, 51–2, 54, 56
  and *The Adventurer*, 124, 143
  and *The Godfather*, 286–7, 290, 295, 305
  and *The Hero*, 399
  and *The Razor*, 60–1, 79, 93, 95
  and *The Student*, 246

and *The Voyager*, 406–7
and *The Warrior*, 195

Larson, Erik J., 201n, 202
Lefèvre, Edwin, 13–14
liar's paradox, 428
"limit-down" trades, 59, 77, 81, 83, 85, 94, 97–8, 144, 408, 415
liquidity, 43–4, 93, 132, 196, 205, 379, 386, 426
  see also illiquidity
literature, and computers, 213–14
Livermore, Jessie, 13
London Inter-Bank Offered Rate (LIBOR), 279
London International Financial Futures and Options Exchange (LIFFE), 269, 272

market auction theory, 312–13, 315
market correlations, 150, 155, 176–7, 181, 206, 222, 254
market profile, 40–1, 51
  The Collector and, 115
  The Engineer and, 312–14, 316–17, 319–20, 322, 324–5, 336, 340–2, 354
  The Godfather and, 282, 295
  The Hero and, 380–7, 390–3, 400, 402
  The Student and, 230, 246, 253–4, 257–8, 266
  The Voyager and, 411

INDEX

Masters, Blake, 71
meta-game, 32, 50–1, 103, 227, 232, 386, 406, 413–14, 417, 443, 459
   The Godfather and, 291–3, 296, 299, 308
morality, 22–3

NASDAQ, 189, 329
natural gas, 18, 233
Neil, Michael, 456
"netting", 53–6
New York Mercantile Exchange, 43
news trading, 40, 49, 87, 155, 159, 211, 251, 271, 443

"open trade", 53–4, 56
OPEX, 329
order flow, 44–5, 50
   The Adventurer and, 135
   "bear flattening", 45
   "breakout" pattern, 69–70
   The Collector and, 100, 107, 118
   The Engineer and, 313–14, 316, 320–1, 324, 326, 329, 331, 336, 349
   The Hero and, 378–85, 390–1, 393, 395
   and price ladders, 44–5
   The Razor and, 58, 68–70, 72–3, 75
   "risk-on" and "risk-off" flow, 45

The Sphinx and, 421, 438, 447
The Student and, 230, 254
The Warrior and, 155–6, 159–60, 167, 175, 177–8, 189, 192, 212
outright trading, 103, 232–3, 238–9, 246, 249, 257, 406
   The Godfather and, 273–5, 282, 286–7, 291, 293–5, 304

Papic, Marko, 363
Parkinson's Law, 107
Parmalat, 65–6, 70
Pascal's wager, 48
Paul, Annie Murphy, 109, 111, 117
pension funds, 38, 178, 301
Peso, 288
Pfizer Covid-19 vaccine, 188–9, 212, 256
pit trading, 14, 44, 49, 272
Powell, Jerome, 46, 223
price ladders, 41–5, 50
   The Adventurer and, 127, 134
   The Collector and, 107, 118
   "depth of market", 42
   The Engineer and, 311, 313–14, 320–1, 331, 341, 348, 355, 361
   The Godfather and, 275, 280
   The Hero and, 374, 377–80, 382–4, 388, 390–3, 401–2
   The Razor and, 62, 69–70, 72, 75, 82–3, 85, 94–5

price ladders *cont.*
   The Student and, 230, 238, 246, 253, 257–8
   The Warrior and, 150, 155, 162, 164–5, 168, 175, 181–2, 189, 194, 207, 225
pricing-buying-selling-expectations loop, 429–30
Prisoner's Dilemma, 424
profit and loss (P&L), 17, 107n, 241
   The Adventurer, 142
   The Collector, 115, 120, 122
   The Engineer, 328, 331, 334, 344, 353, 358–60
   The Godfather, 276, 279, 285, 292, 295, 299, 302, 308
   The Hero, 396, 402
   The Razor, 63, 84, 98
   The Sphinx, 421, 450
   The Student, 229, 232, 242, 244, 246, 249–51, 254, 259–60, 263
   The Voyager, 405, 408, 410, 413, 415–16
   The Warrior, 151, 153–7, 166, 168–71, 180, 187, 189–90, 193, 205, 208, 225
prop traders, 39, 67, 101, 116, 299
Purchasing Managers' Index (PMI), 118
Putin, Vladimir, 204, 206, 208, 210–11

quantitative easing (QE), 39, 101, 222, 313, 319, 341

Razor, The, 40–1, 58–99, 130, 135–6, 143–4, 159–60, 315, 392, 403, 459
   Caribbean holiday, 81–2
   and The Collector, 105–6, 108–9, 114, 120
   consistency, 63–5, 67, 68, 72, 76, 79–80, 87–8, 91, 97–8
   and contamination, 70, 72–6, 109
   Denial, 461
   and The Engineer, 321, 326, 339–40, 344, 364, 368
   and Firm Y, 77–8, 80, 127, 174, 339–40, 344, 377
   and The Godfather, 283–4
   "limit-down" trades, 59, 77, 81, 83, 85, 94, 97–8, 408, 415
   P&L, 63, 84, 98
   patience, 64, 75, 78, 89–90, 98, 339
   recapitalisation and move to Poland, 77–80
   risk aversion, 64, 67, 71, 75, 85, 87
   tactical trading, 389–90
   training in England, 66–7
   variance aversion, 64, 85, 87
   and The Voyager, 407–8, 410–11, 414–15
   vulnerability, 96–7

and *The Warrior*, 188, 190, 227, 238, 321
reasoning
  abductive, 202, 213–14, 216, 218, 362–4, 372
  inductive, 201, 202n, 227, 362
risk management, 39, 137, 159, 176, 185, 214, 244, 399, 448, 452
Rouble, 205, 207
Russia–Ukraine war, 156, 203–12, 223, 259

S&P, 107n
  The Adventurer and, 125
  The Collector and, 112
  The Engineer and, 327–9, 331–2, 334, 337, 346–8, 358, 361
  flash crash, 286
  The Godfather and, 103, 286, 288, 293, 302–3
  The Hero and, 373–4, 386
  The Razor and, 58–9, 81–4, 94–5
  The Sphinx and, 449
  The Warrior and, 149, 152–3, 156, 162–5, 167, 170, 175–6, 189, 204–5, 207–10
Schatz, 43, 103, 232, 237, 269, 274, 280, 282–3, 288
"scratch trades", 64
Sharpe ratios, 21
"slow hunch", 358–9, 372
Snowden, David J., 202n

"soft edge", 120, 122, 460
Soleimani assassination and Iranian retaliation, 22, 156, 161–70, 296, 433
  see also Warrior, The, 'Mexican Standoff'
Soros, George, 431–2, 439, 442
Sortino ratios, 21
"spare parts", 231, 236–9, 241, 244, 248, 263, 267, 298, 352–3, 357, 359, 405, 408, 414, 450, 460
Sphinx, The, 16, 40, 50, 123, 404, 419–58
  and *The Collector*, 105, 115
  and complexity, 423–6, 448–50
  and Firm Y, 174, 339
  and *The Godfather*, 270
  P&L, 421, 450
  and "themes and flow", 421, 432, 434
  and "today's trading", 433, 435–7, 439–41
  and *The Warrior*, 164, 168–9, 172, 220–1, 270, 424–5, 433–4, 449, 455
  Wonder, 461
Spitznagel, Mark, *The Dao of Capital*, 358, 365
sport, 16, 19–20, 24, 36, 65, 102–3, 144, 192, 198, 350, 389, 403, 409, 422, 428
  The Adventurer and skiing, 127–9, 140–1

INDEX

spread trading, 49, 134, 443
  The Godfather and, 273, 276–7, 279, 285–7, 292–3, 295–6, 300
  The Student and, 232–4, 239–45, 249, 253, 266
Steidlmayer, J. Peter, 313
Student, The, 40, 228–67, 450
  all-seasons trader, 230, 246, 257
  benchmark trade, 258–60
  and The Engineer, 247, 250–2, 258, 260, 351–2, 358, 362
  family, 263–5
  flow state, 261–3
  and The Godfather, 237, 264–5, 273, 286, 307
  handwriting, 251, 348
  and The Hero, 233, 243, 251–2, 258, 348, 362, 386, 389, 391
  joins AXIA, 237–8, 246, 248
  journaling, 229, 241, 243, 249, 251–5, 257, 259–60, 266–7, 352
  Observance, 461
  P&L, 229, 232, 242, 244, 246, 249–51, 254, 259–60, 263
  self-awareness, 249–50, 252, 256, 267
  spread trader, 232–4
  transition from spread dealing, 239–45
  underperformance, 256
  and The Voyager, 403–4, 412–13

  and The Warrior, 233–4, 247, 258, 260
Sullivan, Jake, 205
survivorship bias, 23

Tarkovsky, Andrey, 14, 16
technical trading, 40, 49, 443
  The Collector and, 115–17
  The Engineer and, 312, 315–16, 320, 324, 336, 350
  The Hero and, 379, 383–5, 390, 394
  The Student and, 229–30, 246, 248–51, 253, 257–9, 261–3, 266
TED spread, 231, 233–4, 236–8, 273–7, 279, 281, 287–8, 296
Thiel, Peter, 71
time decay, 86–7
TPOs (time, price and opportunity), 316–17, 342, 344, 384
"trade sense", 326–7, 329–33, 335–6, 346, 355, 362, 371–2, 379, 460
trader's resource dilemma, 108, 122, 408
trading strategies and principles
  "adjacent possible", 231, 234–5, 237, 239, 263, 266–7, 295, 386, 391, 405–6, 408, 412, 414, 417, 460
  adverse selection, 131–3, 380
  "bond vigilante", 301

482

INDEX

cash-flow, 179–81, 196, 198, 295, 369, 414
champion's fallacy, 126, 180
"classical trading", 115, 117–18
dynamic sizing, 130–7, 148, 460
"error pruning", 120, 241, 251, 413–14
"fading", 130, 455
four types of participation, 313–14
fundamental principles, 63–4
"hitting the bid", 30, 43
and "interoception", 138
"learning architecture", 345
"lifting the offer", 43
open strategy, 282–3, 298
opportunity maximisation, 182–6, 460
"picking levels", 385
pressing the initiative, 182, 186–8
protective barriers, 83–5
queuing strategy, 282–3, 285
"reciting the idea", 332–3
"scalping", 167, 175–7, 179, 190, 196, 283, 314, 341–2, 360, 381
"sitting on the bid", 319
"slippage", 76
"thinking with experts", 109–11, 114
"thinking with peers", 111–12, 114

wealth-building, 179–80, 198, 295, 414
"transactive memory", 117, 122
Treasuries, US market
   Five-Year, 47
   Ten-Year, 132
   Thirty-Year, 18
Trichet, Jean-Claude, 278
Trump, Donald, 81, 156, 167, 169–70, 188, 209, 288, 386
Truss, Liz, 300

UK Mini-Budget crisis, 300
unemployment data, 373–4
US–China trade war, 156, 183, 190, 212, 386
US Non-Farm Payroll data, 276, 353, 363

value investors, 31, 314, 360, 443
variance (definition), 134–5
Veteran, The, 340–2
Voyager, The, 403–18
   Environment, 461
   and Firm Y, 339, 405–7, 409–10
   and *The Godfather*, 409, 411, 413
   "J-curve" account, 410
   and Madrid, 406–9, 413
   P&L, 405, 408, 410, 413, 415–16
   and *The Razor*, 407–8, 410–11, 414–15
   and *The Student*, 403–4, 412–13
   and *The Warrior*, 412, 414

Waitzkin, Josh, 160
Warrior, The, 16, 24, 27, 40, 47, 50–2, 54, 56, 123, 130, 140, 149–227, 229, 238, 419, 459, 463
and *The Adventurer*, 137–8
and adverse selection, 133
Belief, 461
and *The Collector*, 112, 115–16
consistency, 156–7, 164, 171, 179–81, 196, 198
down-days, 193–4
"dying at the desk", 159
education, 173–4
and *The Engineer*, 321, 340, 369–70, 344
and Federal Reserve rate cut, 149–51, 156–7
and Firm Y, 157, 174, 192, 195, 339–40, 344, 377
and *The Godfather*, 164, 169, 172, 270, 287–9, 295–7, 299–300, 303–4, 359
and *The Hero*, 378, 390, 392
impatience, 191–2
and market correlations, 176–7
'Mexican Standoff', 161–72, 183, 185, 188, 190, 205, 213, 218–19, 296, 433–4
opportunity maximisation, 182–6
P&L, 151, 153–7, 166, 168–71, 180, 187, 189–90, 193, 205, 208, 225
personality, 157–60, 198
pressing the initiative, 186–8
proximity to office, 184–5
and remote trading, 195
and "scalping", 176–7
and *The Razor*, 188, 190, 227, 238, 321
and Russia–Ukraine war, 203–12
and *The Sphinx*, 164, 168–9, 172, 220–1, 270, 424–5, 433–4, 449, 455
and *The Student*, 233–4, 247, 258, 260
and trading as sport, 192–3, 198
and *The Voyager*, 412, 414
worldbuilding, 215–21, 224–5, 227
West Texas Intermediate (WTI), 18, 43, 178, 204, 207, 232, 258
white-box, 55–6, 286, 374–5, 400
Wrocław, 40–1, 50, 58, 61–3, 76, 80, 129, 139, 144, 146, 403, 407–8, 457

Yen, 18, 45, 220, 288, 433

Zelensky, Volodymyr, 210–11